Avid® Editing

Avid® Editing: A Guide for Beginning and Intermediate Users

THIRD EDITION

by Sam Kauffmann

ELSEVIER

Amsterdam • Boston • Heidelberg • London
New York • Oxford • Paris • San Diego
San Francisco • Singapore • Sydney • Tokyo
An imprint of Elsevier

Focal Press

Acquisitions Editor: Elinor Actipis
Project Manager: Dawnmarie Simpson
Developmental Editor: Becky Golden-Harrell
Assistant Editor: Robin Weston
Marketing Manager: Christine Degon Veroulis
Cover Design: Alisa Andreola

Focal Press is an imprint of Elsevier
30 Corporate Drive, Suite 400, Burlington, MA 01803, USA
Linacre House, Jordan Hill, Oxford OX2 8DP, UK

∞ Recognizing the importance of preserving what has been written, Elsevier prints its books on acid-free paper whenever possible.

Library of Congress Cataloging-in-Publication Data
Kauffmann, Sam.
  Avid editing : a guide for beginning and intermediate users / Sam Kauffmann.—3rd ed.
    p. cm.
  Includes index.
  ISBN-13: 978-0-240-80816-1 (pbk. : alk. paper)
  ISBN-10: 0-240-80816-9 (pbk. : alk. paper) 1. Video tapes—Editing—Data processing. 2. Motion pictures—Editing—Data processing. 3. Avid Xpress. 4. Media composer. I. Title.
  TR899.K38 2006
  778.5'2350285—dc22

                                                                                    2005030330

British Library Cataloguing-in-Publication Data
A catalogue record for this book is available from the British Library.

ISBN 13: 978-0-240-80816-1
ISBN 10: 0-240-80816-9

For information on all Focal Press publications
visit our website at www.books.elsevier.com

05 06 07 08 09 10   10 9 8 7 6 5 4 3 2 1

Printed in the United States of America

Working together to grow
libraries in developing countries

www.elsevier.com | www.bookaid.org | www.sabre.org

ELSEVIER   BOOK AID International   Sabre Foundation

For Katie, Allie, and Derek

"Our deepest fear is not that we are inadequate.
Our deepest fear is that we are powerful beyond measure."

—Nelson Mandela

Table of Contents

Introduction

A lot has changed since I wrote the first edition of this book during the summer and fall of 1999. High-definition television (HDTV) seemed a long way off, and video cameras and film cameras had very little in common. Now some high-school students are shooting high definition, and video cameras can produce images that imitate the look of film. In addition to teaching you Avid editing skills, this third edition aims to help you navigate the confusing world of high definition and to make 24p digital filmmaking a reality.

When the first edition of this book was published, the Avid was the best-known nonlinear editing (NLE) system in the world. In many ways, it was just about the only game in town. Apple's Final Cut® was just a speck on the NLE horizon. Since then, Avid has maintained its position as the leader in the film and television industry, but Final Cut has become a popular choice among students and independent film and video makers. Since the second edition of this book came out in 2003, Apple has benefited from the incredible popularity of the iPod, which has helped drive sales of the Macintosh line of computers and introduced even more people to iMovie® and Final Cut. Many of these people are the next generation of editors.

Avid doesn't intend to be your grandfather's NLE, so it has created the most complete set of professional features and made them standard on all versions of Avid software, from Xpress DV to the Symphony Nitris. Unlike Final Cut and Adobe's Premiere®, the Avid works on Macs as well as PCs and as such is the only global NLE system. Outside of North America, you'd be hard pressed to even find a Mac computer.

The Avid continues to be the dominant player in the film and television industry. It is used on 85% of all feature films and 95% of all prime-time television shows. The Avid's standard-definition and high-definition lineup is used by the Big Four networks in the United States and most of the networks overseas. A few features films have been cut on Final Cut, but the vast majority of theatrically released films are cut on the Avid. Steven Soderbergh (*Traffic*, *Ocean's Twelve*) edited one feature on Final Cut and has sworn never to do it again, so frustrating was his experience.

While it's true that lots of people cut on Final Cut systems, more often than not they're working on their own editing systems and don't do a lot of hiring. Most commercial editing houses and post-production companies use the Avid. When my students graduate, they get paying jobs simply because they know how to cut on an Avid system.

This book covers all of the Avid's editing systems but concentrates on the Avid Xpress family: Xpress DV, Xpress Pro, and Xpress Pro HD. It's my belief that the majority of beginners will start their Avid experience on an Xpress system, and this book's primary audience is the beginner. But, because all Avids share the same interface, you can learn to cut on the Xpress DV or Pro, then get a job on a Media Composer Adrenaline and not need much time to get up to speed.

Think of this as a textbook, workbook, and user manual all rolled into one. It's written so you can read it at home, studying a chapter's contents, or while sitting in front of an Avid, following the book's step-by-step instructions.

Suggested assignments at the end of most chapters are there to encourage you to practice the techniques and skills explained in that particular chapter. Each chapter builds on the ideas presented in the previous chapter, so it's a good idea to practice one set of skills before moving on to the next.

I believe you will learn to use the Avid more quickly if you start by editing a short narrative scene rather than a short documentary project. With a script for the scene in front of you, you know where you are going and you can concentrate on how to get there. To get you started, I've enclosed a short scene for you to edit, entitled "Wanna Trade." It's on the DVD-ROM that comes with this book. Step-by-step instructions are provided in Chapter 1 to guide you through the editing process. A two-page script for the scene is included as well.

Ideally, your professor, instructor, or teacher will mount the scene onto the Avid so you can begin editing after the first or second class. If you will be mounting the DVD-ROM yourself, there are instructions for doing so at the end of the book. If your instructor has material she or he is more comfortable with, then by all means use that material for the first assignment.

My goal is to get you editing as quickly as possible. The capturing process is an important part of this book, but I've postponed it until Chapter 6. Once you've cut a scene, you'll find the intricacies of capturing much more understandable.

There is a great deal of new material in this edition. Chapters 15 and 16 are especially important additions because they address the latest changes in digital filmmaking. Chapter 15 explains how to create and edit projects using 24p technology and the ins and outs of 16:9 editing. Chapter 16 is devoted to HD and HDV.

The DVD-ROM that comes with the book contains a second scene for Xpress Pro users. Whereas "Wanna Trade" is a relatively easy scene to get you started while reading the first chapter, "Gaffer's Delight" is more complicated and was shot in the 16:9 aspect ratio. This scene was covered by many different camera angles and involved several takes, making it a good candidate for the Avid's Script Integration features, explained in Chapter 17. The script for "Gaffer's Delight" is included on the DVD-ROM so you can bring the script into your Avid and then, following the instructions provided, attach clips to the action and dialog.

Although Xpress DV users don't have Script Integration or the ability to edit 24p formats, they can edit 16:9 projects, so the DVD contains 16:9 clips intended to give Xpress DV users a chance to practice 16:9 editing.

Because Avid systems come on Windows and Macintosh platforms, I've used both Macintosh and Windows screens to guide you through the instructions. Mac and Windows screens are almost identical. The main difference between cutting on a Mac and cutting on a Windows is the shortcut keys you'll use. On the Macintosh you'll often use the Command key (). If you are using Windows, you'll use the Control (Ctrl) key instead. Windows users will also use the Alt key instead of the Macintosh Option key. That's it. That's about the only difference between the Mac and Windows versions.

Avid is continually adding new features to the software, so you should always work with the latest version. A quick trip to www.avid.com will get you a free download of the most recent update. Obviously, no one book can hope to explain all of the Avid's features or keep up with changes. I won't show you every technique found in the Avid's many manuals, but I'll show you all the ones you need to know. The Avid's interface is the most stable in the industry, and this edition should last you for many years.

I have many people to thank for their assistance, none more so than the many students I've had the pleasure to teach during the past decade. There are too many to name, but all of them taught me as much as I taught them. Special thanks go to Matt Feury and Michael Phillips, of Avid, for their many suggestions along the way. Special thanks also to Christopher Bowen; William Buccalo, Ph.D.; and Howard A. Phillips for their careful reading of the manuscript and many excellent suggestions. Christopher Bowen, who works at Avid and teaches Cinematography at Boston University, even tested the DVD on a variety of Avid systems for me.

My colleagues at Boston University have given me advice and encouragement throughout my teaching career. Jamie Companeschi, Jose Ponce, and Jim Baab all offered invaluable technical assistance and helped my students over difficulties whenever I wasn't there. Jamie, Jose, and DP Bob Demers shot one of the scenes on the enclosed DVD. I also wish to thank Charles Merzbacher, Bill Lawson, Mary Jane Doherty, Bob Arnold, Geoff Poister, Ray Carney, John Augliera, and Dean John Schulz.

Thanks to Joanna Jefferson, Mary Choi, Brad Kimbrough, Loren Miller, and my siblings, Margaret, Louise, and Bruce Kauffmann, who were my first friends and teachers.

Special thanks to Kate Shanaphy and Tim Eberle, who are Kate and Tim in "Wanna Trade." And thanks to Josh Wingate and Rachel Neuman, who play Peter and Michele in "Gaffer's Delight."

This book could not have been written without Kate Cress, who gave invaluable support and advice every step of the way.

Getting Started

THE EDITOR'S JOB

What does an editor do? Some say an editor's job is to simply take out the slow parts. Others say it's to follow the wishes of the director and to string together the best takes. Ask an editor what the job entails, and he or she will say it's to breathe life into a film or video or to find and expose its heart and soul. Ask that same editor at the end of a long and difficult project, and you'll probably hear, "It's to make everyone else look good." All are true, and yet none comes close to capturing the critical role the editor plays in any production. I think a great editor is like a great chef. Someone may hand the editor the ingredients and even the recipe, but the editor puts those ingredients together in a way that fires the viewer's imagination, stokes the thought process, and stirs the passions.

There are thousands of tasks involved in editing a film or video, and thousands of decisions must be made along the way. And all of them are important. Which take is best? Is the lighting and composition better in this shot or that? Is the pacing of these shots too fast? Will cutting out the character's entrance make the scene more or less confusing?

Although the editor's primary job remains the same, the manner in which an editor works was transformed during the 1990s by the development of computer-based nonlinear editing systems (NLEs). The Avid was one of the earliest NLEs, and it is perhaps the best known system in the world.

Today, the transformation from analog editing machines to computer-based editing systems is practically complete. Only a tiny percentage of films and videos are still edited on analog machines. Compared with analog devices, computer-based systems make the editor's job much easier and faster, yet these systems can also make an editor's job harder and take a lot longer to complete. It may seem like a paradox, but it's true.

Editing on a computer is much easier and faster than on an analog machine because nearly every task is executed with a single keystroke or the push of a button. Want to splice a shot into your project? Click one button and it's done. Want to make a shot two seconds longer? Click and drag a roller and it's done. Want a freeze frame? A few clicks of the mouse and it's just the way you want it. Yet, there is a price for all this speed. The Avid and the other popular computer-based systems are much more difficult to master than analog film or a video system. Today, when you buy an Avid, it comes with nearly 1500 pages of documentation. And, because the Avid comes with so many sophisticated tools, the editor is supposed to do things that were once handled by scores of other people. In the past, someone else designed and shot the titles, there was a team of sound and music editors, and a highly trained group of talented individuals created all the special effects. Now a single editor is often the entire post-production team!

Today's NLE editors are expected to be computer savvy while possessing video engineering skills. Often, an editor must set up, connect, and troubleshoot an incredible array of video decks, operating systems, audio drivers, and FireWire cards. So, while it's true that a computer can make an editor's job easier and faster, it can also make the job more difficult and take longer.

An editor's job *has* gotten more difficult and complex, but the rewards and satisfaction are greater as well. You, the Avid editor, have far more creative control over the project than at any time in the history of editing. You may have more to do, but you don't need much help getting the job done, and you can make sure everything looks and sounds just the way you want it.

AVID'S ROOTS

Many of the people who designed the first digital editing systems were filmmakers who found themselves doing a lot of videotape editing—and they didn't particularly like it. Still, there were things about video editing that they liked better than film editing. So, they used the emerging power of personal computers to fashion a hybrid system that borrowed the best from both worlds.

Film and Video—The Old Way

The main advantage film editing always had over video editing was that it was nonlinear. You could remove a shot in the middle of the film and put it at the beginning, or *vice versa*. It took time to do all that unsplicing and splicing of polyester tape, but you could make changes at any time to any part of your film. Videotape editing was always more automated and faster. You pushed buttons on a machine to set editing points, and the machine made the edits. But, video-tape editing was linear—you couldn't switch shots around as you could with film. You recorded the shots you wanted from your camera tape onto a new tape, one shot at a time. If, midway through editing, you decided you wanted to change the order of shots, you had to start over again. When the Avid was designed in the early 1990s, the idea was to combine the speed of video editing with the flexibility of film editing.

AVID'S DIGITAL APPROACH

The Avid simply takes videotape (or film that has been transferred to videotape) and captures the images and sounds in digital form so that you, the editor, can access the material almost instantly. Because all your pictures and sound are 0's and 1's, they are truly at your fingertips. There is no need to wind and rewind through 20-minute videotapes to find a shot, or to wind and rewind through 36-minute lab reels of film. If you're at the end of a 10-minute scene and you want to return to the beginning of that scene, simply push a button and you're there. You don't like what you did four cuts ago? Hit undo and it's undone.

Figure 1.1   Students at Makerere University in Kampala, Uganda, using Xpress Pro.

The Many Parts of Your System

Avid's Media Composer and Symphony systems are sold as turnkey systems; when you buy them from a certified Avid reseller, you get the hardware, the software, and all the peripheral devices needed to run them. You turn the key and the Avid starts working. One of the reasons the Xpress family (Xpress DV, Xpress Pro, and Xpress Pro HD) costs so much less than a Media Composer is that the Xpress family is primarily a software system. You buy the software from an Avid reseller and then you purchase the computer and peripherals and put the system together yourself. Because some people believe the job of configuring and connecting a computer system is a bit too daunting, a number of companies have sprung up to do the job for you, and they charge you extra for the service. In effect, you buy a turnkey Xpress system from them. What's nice about the turnkey approach is that you know whom to turn to if problems arise. On the other hand, you can save money by putting a system together yourself. If you are computer savvy on your platform of choice, or have a good friend who is, then putting together your own system won't be a stretch.

The Computer and CPU: Of the three main players in the NLE sweepstakes—Final Cut, Adobe Premier, and Avid—only Avid is cross-platform, meaning it runs on both Macs and PCs. The central processing unit (CPU) is the chip that does the actual computing, and Macs and PCs use different kinds of chips. Whichever platform you choose, your computer must have a fast chip or processor—dual processors are even better—with substantial random access memory (RAM). Even Xpress DV recommends 1.5 GB of system memory. If you are buying the computer yourself, get the fastest processors you can afford. The Avid website maintains a list of supported computers that are approved for the Xpress family. Go to www.avid.com/products/xpressFamily/index.asp to find the system you're interested in and check out the recommended specifications. All Macs and PCs have internal hard drives. On a Windows computer, it's the C: drive, and on a Mac it's the Macintosh HD (hard drive). The Avid software comes on several CD-ROMs and is mounted onto your internal hard drive or C: drive, just like a spreadsheet or word-processing program. The process is almost automatic. You just load the CD and follow a few screen prompts and everything's loaded within minutes.

Figure 1.2 Xpress DV on a laptop computer.

Capture Boards: The Xpress family uses an IEEE 1394 capture board, called FireWire or iLink, to bring in both video and audio. It's specifically designed for DV (digital video) tapes. All Macs and most PCs are sold with IEEE 1394 cards already installed. If your PC doesn't have one, it's not hard to install. I bought a PYRO digital video card for under $70 and put it into one of the computer's PCI slots. If you will be working in high-definition (HD) formats, you will need two PCI IEEE 1394 (FireWire) cards in your computer chassis, each on a separate bus, in order to capture and output some HD formats directly over FireWire. We will discuss HD and HDV in Chapter 16.

Media Drives: In the past, all media drives were external to the computer, but today many computers have large internal drives that store media efficiently. Make sure you have 60 GB or more. Drives run at different revolutions per minute; you should make sure that the drive you store your media on runs at 7200 rpms. PC users should make sure they create a *partition* so the C: drive holds the Xpress software and a separate partition holds their media. But, even if your computer comes with 80 GB or more of storage, it's often a good idea to store your project and media on an external FireWire drive. That way you can carry your media to another Avid if your computer goes down or is needed elsewhere.

How large should your external storage device be? Here, size does matter. You can store about 12 hours of Mini-DV footage on a 160-GB drive. Many people start with 160GB and go up from there.

Computer monitor   CPU   External FireWire Drive

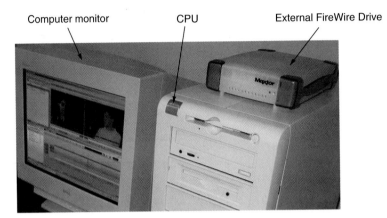

Figure 1.3 Xpress system on a PC with an external FireWire media drive.

The Dongle: The Avid comes with a special key on a chain, called a *dongle*. You attach it to the CPU by inserting it into one of the USB ports in the back of the computer. Without the dongle, you can't turn on the Avid software. The dongle prevents software piracy and enables certain functions, or extras, you may have purchased.

Monitors: It used to be that the Media Composer was designed to work with two computer monitors and the Xpress was designed for one. Now it's your choice. Some people switch back and forth. When they are on the road, they use a portable computer with its single monitor, and when they are back home or at the office, they hook up a second monitor.

Speakers: Sound is a critical part of any film or video, and having good external speakers is of utmost importance. The turnkey systems come with speakers. If you are putting your own system together, don't try to save money here. Plan on spending about $100 for a speaker system.

The Client Monitor: A television monitor (not a computer monitor) is helpful no matter which system you cut with. With DV-based systems, a client monitor may seem less critical, because you can't alter the image coming into the system, but you can change it inside the Xpress, and knowing how the signal will look on a television screen once you have put it back out to tape is important. The television monitor has long been called a "client monitor" because it's the one the client is supposed to look at when the editor hits Play. Look for a client monitor that can handle both 4:3 and 16:9 formats.

Figure 1.4 An Xpress Pro on a laptop with a client monitor.

UPS: When you spend thousands of dollars on a computer, you should consider buying an electrical back-up device called a UPS (uninterruptible power supply). Because your work is important and because you can't run a computer without electricity, common sense suggests that you plug the CPU, the computer monitor, and the media drives into this back-up system, which provides a stable electrical current and will keep everything running in case of a power failure. The idea is not that you keep editing, but rather that you use the back-up power to save your work and then shut down your system. If you do not get a UPS, at least get a surge protector.

Input Devices: Xpress DV is designed specifically for capturing DV tapes. Xpress DV users will probably start out using their cameras to capture tapes into their Avid. After awhile, the need for a DV deck will become increasingly apparent. The Avid website maintains a list of supported DV devices that work well with the Xpress DV. Go to the page that lists Xpress DV specifications: www.avid.com/products/xpressdv/specs.shtml. If the page moved (as they often do), search Avid's website (www.avid.com). I really like the Sony DSR-11 deck, which can handle NTSC and PAL tapes.

The Xpress Pro and HD are designed to bring in all sorts of tapes, not just mini-DV or DVCAM. You could connect a DV 50 deck to Xpress Pro, and HD and HDV decks into the Xpress Pro HD. Avid sells Mojo (Figure 1.5), a combination accelerator and connection device, that lets you bring into the Xpress Pro and

Pro HD a variety of standard definition signals besides DV, including S-Video, composite, and component. This means you can easily hook up and capture signals from a DVD player, CD player, VHS deck, and even a Beta SP deck. The advantage of using Mojo is that it can capture the video signal at a resolution higher than DV. And, just as these devices will help you bring sound and picture into the Avid, you will also use them to output the work you have created.

Figure 1.5 Mojo.

Transcoders: Even without Mojo, you can bring in just about every kind of videotape into the Xpress DV and Pro if you attach a transcoder—otherwise known as a media converter. These units convert all sorts of tapes to IEEE 1394 DV. For instance, if you plug your Beta SP or VHS deck into the transcoder, it converts it to a DV signal and sends it, via a FireWire cable, to the media drive. Whatever the source tape once was, it's now a DV signal. Many DV decks can also serve as transcoders. I use my DSR-11 to bring in different format tapes.

A Word about Timecode

All NLE systems, Avid included, are based on the videotape tracking system called *timecode*. As sound and pictures are recorded onto the videotape by means of a camera or deck, unique numbers, the timecode, are placed onto the video-tape as well. There are approximately 30 frames of video per second, and each frame has its own timecode number. Whereas film numbers are based on the length of the film, timecode is measured in time. The first frame on the video-tape is designated as 00 hours : 00 minutes : 00 seconds : 00 frames, or 00:00:00:00. The next frame is 00:00:00:01. Since video is based on 30 frames per second, after 00:00:00:29 the next frame would be 00:00:01:00. Because each frame has its own unique address—its timecode—it's easy to keep track of them. Computers are good at numbers, so it is through timecode that the Avid keeps track of your pictures and sound.

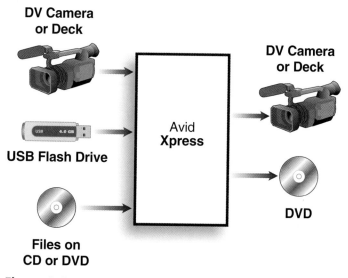

Figure 1.6 Avid connections.

Avid Editing Workflow

Because the Avid is different than a film or videotape editing machine, the way you organize your work is also somewhat different. We will examine your high-definition (HD) workflow in Chapter 15.

Gather Tapes and Files: First, gather together all the picture and sound elements that form the source material for your project. These may include:

- *Videotapes*—DVCAM or Mini-DV
- *Film*—Currently, there is no way to input film directly into the Avid; film is first transferred to videotape (which we will discuss at length in Chapter 19)
- *Audio*—CDs
- *Picture and audio files*—Computer graphics, animation, pictures, and audio files on a flash drive, CD, or DVD

Create a New Project: When you start up the Avid software, it asks you to tell it which project to open. You might share an Avid with other students or other editors, all working on different projects. If you're beginning a new project, you would click the New Project button, name the project, and begin work on your new project.

Capture: The Avid will open up the *Project window* for your new project. You now begin to capture all your source material onto your computer's media drives. As soon as you capture something, the Avid creates two things: a *media file*, which is the digital version of your picture or sound, and a *master clip*, which is a virtual copy of the media file (I'll often say *clip* for short). Media files are stored on media drives. One media file is created for each track of video and audio. If you have video and stereo sound, the Avid will create three media files for that digital material. You don't edit or work with media files; you work with the clips. Think of the clip as a shot. You can edit the shot, duplicate the shot, or flip the shot, and all these actions affect the clip, while the media file (the captured picture or sound) is safe on the media drive.

Create Bins: When you digitize or record your source material, you organize it into *bins*. You might have a bin for all the shots from tape number one and a second bin for all the shots from tape number two. Bins are like folders on your home or office computer, but for people used to editing films "bin" is a familiar name for a place to store material being editing. The Avid recognizes that you might be starting an ambitious project involving the creation of many bins, each holding up to 100 clips, and provides sophisticated search-and-find tools to help you locate just the shot you are looking for. The steps listed above are all about getting organized before you begin editing. If you are about to edit a feature film or an hour-long documentary, you will appreciate how important the organizational steps are. Now that you have organized the material, it's time to edit.

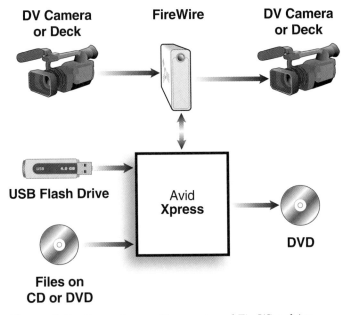

Figure 1.7 Connections with an external FireWire drive.

Edit: When you open up a master clip (think of an entire shot from head to tail) and select a part of it to be included in your project, you are making your first cut. The Avid calls any material that is cut together a *sequence*. You create a sequence by editing together clips. In traditional film editing, the editor starts by putting together an *assembly*, which includes all the clips that might appear in the final film, spliced together in the right order. You could call your first sequence an "assembly sequence." Once you have assembled the material, the next stage is to create a *rough cut*, in which the clips are placed in the right order and trimmed to approximately the right length. You might call this a "rough cut sequence." Because the material is digital, sequences are easily duplicated. You might create a sequence on Tuesday, duplicate it on Wednesday morning, and start making changes to it. At any time, you can open up the Tuesday version for comparison. As you get to the end of your editing, you are working on what is normally called a *fine cut*. Shots are trimmed to give each scene the right pace and timing.

Add Titles and Effects: Once you have edited your sequence, you can easily add titles and effects to it. The Avid has tools for creating multilayered effects and titles. Titles can be created and added to a sequence in minutes. Most effects take only a few seconds to create. When all the titles and visual effects have been added, you have reached the stage called *picture lock*. No more changes are made to any of the picture tracks.

Do Sound Work: Once you have reached picture lock, it's time to add the many sound effects and music cues that will make for a rich and powerful sound track. The Avid can monitor between 8 and 24 tracks, and by using built-in tools you can make intricate sound adjustments to any and all tracks.

Output Your Project: Finally, the end of the Avid workflow takes place when the final edited sequence is sent out into the world. There are many output options, such as:

- Record the finished sequence onto videotape.
- Create a DVD.
- Create an Edit Decision List (EDL) for an online videotape editing session.
- Create a film Cut List so a negative cutter can conform the original camera film to the Avid sequence.
- Turn your sequence into streaming files for posting on the Web.

With that overview behind us, let's turn on the computer, launch the software, and explore the workspace the Avid provides us. Your system may be set up in a slightly different manner than what is described here, but all systems are fairly similar.

TURNING ON YOUR AVID

I am assuming that you have already mounted the "Wanna Trade" project found on the DVD that comes with this book or that your instructor has done it for you. If not, this would be a good time. If you have another project mounted and want to work on that instead, excellent. If there are no projects mounted and you are under a tight deadline and have to edit a project immediately, please turn to Chapter 6 for instructions on how to capture. Please return here once you've captured your tapes.

The process for starting your system is pretty much the same, whether you're on a Mac or are using Windows. When the software is first loaded onto the system, a shortcut/alias is usually created and left on the desktop so that, once everything is turned on, you simply click on the shortcut/alias icon to launch your Avid software (Figure 1.8).

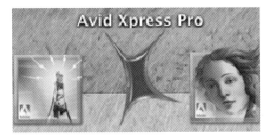

Figure 1.8 An alias located in the dock on a Mac. Click it to launch.

To launch your Avid:

1. Turn on the power to all the devices that make up your system *except* the computer. That means the speakers, the external media drives, the deck or camera, and the client monitor. Wait a few seconds for everything to spin up.
2. Press the Power key or button that turns on the CPU. Wait for the system to mount.
3. If there is a log-on process, type in your user name and password.
4. Click on the shortcut or alias for the Avid Xpress or Media Composer application.
5. When the Avid Project window appears, click on the project you have been assigned. If Private is chosen, click on Shared. If it has been mounted, click on "Wanna Trade." (See Figure 1.9.)
6. Click OK. The project will open, showing you the Avid interface.

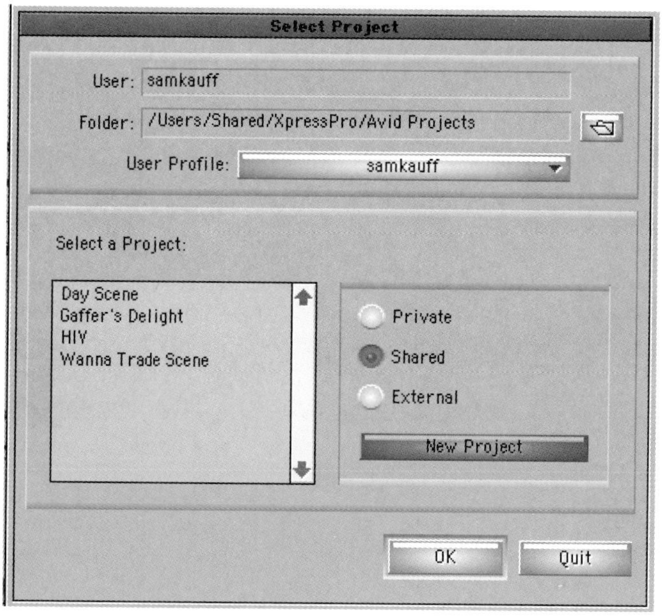

Figure 1.9 Project window.

THE AVID INTERFACE ON YOUR COMPUTER

Toolset Menu

Before we begin editing, let's make sure we are all using the same editing interface. The Xpress models have two editing modes, Basic and Source/Record. Go to the menu bar at the top of your computer screen and pull down the Toolset menu. I want you to select the Source/Record Editing mode, as shown in Figure 1.10. It's probably already set that way, but if not let's all start off on the same foot. Just drag your mouse down the menu list and select it.

Figure 1.10 The Toolset menu.

The Xpress family is designed to work with just one computer monitor, which contains the Project window, containing all your bins; the Composer window, containing the Source and Record monitors; and the Timeline. You select clips in the bins and place them in the Source Monitor, on the left, which holds the clips that will be edited into the project. The Record Monitor, on the right, shows the edited sequence. The Timeline presents a visual representation of the clips in the sequence.

An open bin
containing clips

Source and Record Monitors

The Project window
contains all the bins.

Timeline

Figure 1.11   Avid Xpress interface.

Project Window

The Project window is like a home page. It lists all the bins, and it must be open for you to work on that project, so don't close the Project window until you are ready to quit for the day.

Open Bin icon ──────▶

Unopened Bin ──────▶
icon

Figure 1.12

Bins

You place the digitized material (clips) into bins to help organize the material. You can name the bins anything you want. Common bin names are Tape 001 and Tape 002, Dailies Day One, Assembly, Sound Effects, or Music. Whatever makes it easiest for *you* to organize your material is the best system. If you double-click on the bin icon labeled Dailies Day One, the bin will open and you'll see it contains master clips and columns (Figure 1.13). This one shows columns for the clip name and the starting timecode.

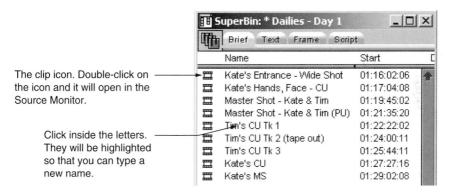

The clip icon. Double-click on the icon and it will open in the Source Monitor.

Click inside the letters. They will be highlighted so that you can type a new name.

Figure 1.13   An open bin.

Clips

The clips in the bin are the footage and sound—the shots from your source tape. The clip icon is on the far left. Next to it you see the name that I gave the clip, followed by important information about each clip. Clips don't take up hard drive space. Instead, each one is connected to the media file it represents. The media file is the actual digital picture and sound, and it resides on the media, or external, hard drive. The clip contains all the timecode information (such as start and end timecode) about the media file.

Bin Views

You can look at the clips in the bin in several different ways:

- Brief View shows a minimum amount of information in column form.
- Text View looks like Brief View but can show many more columns of information.
- Frame View shows a picture of a frame from a clip.
- Script View is like Frame View, but there is space for you to write comments.

You can change your view simply by clicking the tab at the top of the bin.

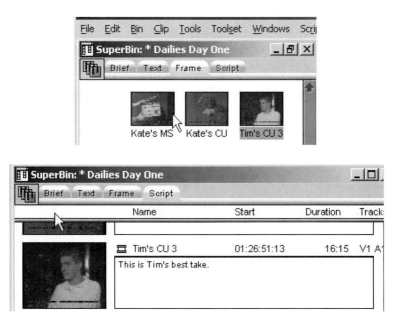

SuperBin

In this mode, all your bins can open in the same window, with only one showing at a time. This saves screen space and keeps the screen from getting cluttered. Instead of double-clicking a bin icon in the Project window, you simply click once and it opens in the SuperBin. If you want to open another bin, instead of double-clicking it, you click once on that bin's icon and it replaces the bin already there.

Source Monitor

When you double-click on a clip, it appears in the Source Monitor. This is where you determine what will be edited into your project. Beneath the Source Monitor is a position bar with a position indicator, and beneath that is a toolbar with buttons (Figure 1.14). The toolbar contains buttons that carry out commands. Click a button with the mouse, and that command is executed. From left to right, you'll see a button for creating a Motion Effect and buttons for moving backward and forward one frame at a time. You also have a button to place an IN edit mark, the Play button, and a button to place an OUT edit mark. There's also a button to place both an IN and an OUT mark and a button that allows you to remove your IN and OUT marks.

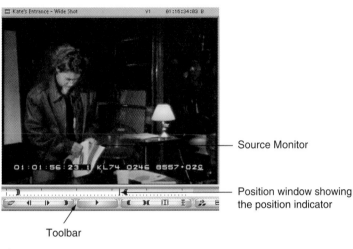

Source Monitor

Position window showing the position indicator

Toolbar

Figure 1.14   Source Monitor.

Record Monitor

The Record Monitor shows you what is in your sequence; it shows what you have created by editing clips together. Just like the Source Monitor, it has a position window, position indicator, and toolbar. Figure 1.15 shows the Source Monitor and Record Monitor together.

Source Monitor   Record Monitor

Figure 1.15   Source Monitor and Record Monitor.

Timeline

The Timeline (Figure 1.16) shows a graphic representation of the shots in your sequence, in track form: V1, A1, A2, A3, A4. The Timeline has Source and Record track selectors, Scale and Scroll bars, and a blue position indicator.

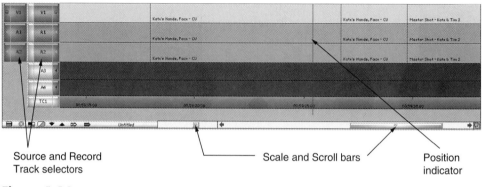

Source and Record
Track selectors

Scale and Scroll bars

Position
indicator

Figure 1.16

Commands

You will instruct the Avid to do what you want through commands. Some of the commands are offered as buttons below the monitors, and some are hidden inside Fast menu buttons (often called *hamburgers* because of the resemblance). Click and hold the Fast menu and a palette appears. You can click and drag any palette and it will tear off, so you can place palettes anywhere you like. Once the palette has been torn off, a click on the palette's close button will send it back inside the Fast menu. Many commands are also offered as keys on the keyboard.

When you click on a Fast menu button,
a palette of command buttons appears.

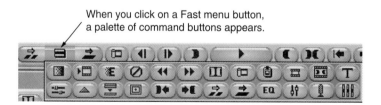

The Keyboard

The keyboard is an important part of Avid editing. Many of the most important editing commands can be executed by simply typing a key on the keyboard. The default or standard keyboard for Xpress can be seen in Figure 1.17.

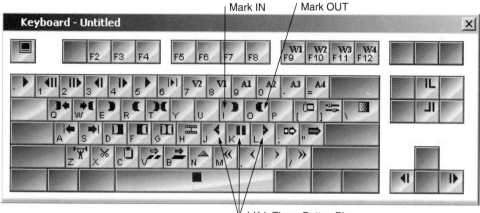

Figure 1.17 Keyboard commands.

When you buy a Media Composer system, you normally get a special keyboard with the Avid command keys inscribed directly on the keys. Xpress users don't get special keyboards, but Avid supplies stickers that you can apply yourself. Because all of these keyboard command keys are mappable, meaning you can change them to suit your own preferences, I recommend that you wait until you read Chapter 3 before you apply any stickers. For now, use these diagrams to show you where the command keys are located. Third-party suppliers sell keyboards that have all the keys properly marked. Google search "Avid keyboards," and you'll find a number of companies to choose from.

Three-Button Play

An extremely important keyboard combination involves the three letters on the keyboard J–K–L. Press the L key to play your clip or sequence forward; the K key is like a pause key; and the J key will play the clip or sequence in reverse. By placing three fingers of your left hand (with the middle finger on the K key) on those three letters, you have a wonderful controller. Many people call this the *three-button play*. I urge you to get into the habit of keeping three fingers of your left hand (or right hand, if you are left-handed) on these keys at all times.

You can use these keys to play the sequence at different speeds. If you press the L key twice, it will play the clip or sequence at twice the sound speed. Press the key again, and it will run at three times the sound speed. Press it again and you are running at 150 frames per second, or five times the sound speed. Once more will bring you to 240 frames per second. Pressing the J key works the same way, but backward. If you hold down the K key while pressing either J or L, the Avid will creep in slow motion, backward or forward.

The Spacebar

The spacebar has always acted like a large Stop button. If you are playing a clip or a sequence, hit the spacebar and you'll stop playing. The spacebar is also a Play button. Just tap the spacebar and the clip or sequence will play. Tap it again and it will stop.

The I and O Keys

Like J–K–L keys, the I and O keys on the keyboard are particularly handy. When you press the I key you are marking an IN, telling the Avid where the start of your clip will be. When you press the O key, you are marking an OUT, telling the Avid where the end of the clip will be. Notice that these two keys are right above the J–K–L keys. Lift your middle finger off the K key and mark an IN. Lift your index finger off the L key and mark an OUT.

Other Important Commands

Examine the list of some of the most important commands and their symbols shown in Figure 1.18. Most are available on the keyboard, as buttons on the computer screen, or in a Fast menu. Two of the most important commands are Undo and Redo. To undo an action, simply hold down the Command key (Mac) or Ctrl key (Windows) and press the letter Z. To Redo a previous action, hold down the Command key (Mac) or Ctrl key (Windows) and press the letter R:

- Undo—Command–Z (Mac) or Ctrl–Z (Windows)
- Redo—Command–R (Mac) or Ctrl–R (Windows)—

You can go back and undo or redo up to 32 previous actions. Memorize the keyboard keys listed here and you'll have the Avid down in no time. Really, these are about the only keys I want you to memorize. I want you to know, for instance, that whenever you want to remove both the IN and OUT marks, you'll press the G key.

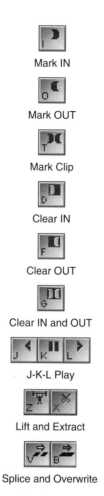

Mark IN

Mark OUT

Mark Clip

Clear IN

Clear OUT

Clear IN and OUT

J-K-L Play

Lift and Extract

Splice and Overwrite

Figure 1.18 Commands.

Active Window

As you can see, there are a number of windows and monitors on the Avid screen: the Timeline, the Source Monitor, the Record Monitor, and the Project window. If you want to work within a particular window, you need to make it active. Many beginning Avid users get confused when they press a command button and nothing happens, or the command gets executed in the wrong place. If you want to work in the Source Monitor, click on it first. The same is true of the Timeline or a bin window.

CAPTURING

The step of bringing in material from a videotape used to be called *digitizing*, then *recording*, and now it's *capturing*. This process can be among the most complicated and frustrating parts of your Avid experience. That's the reason why I have provided a DVD containing scenes for you to edit—so you can practice editing without having to capture anything.

PRACTICE

There are many more commands and menus to discuss, and we'll get to all of them, but for now, let's practice what we have done so far by starting an editing session. True, you haven't been shown how to use many of Avid's most powerful tools, but you have the basic tools to put together a rough cut of a scene. Just follow the instructions provided in the next section. They will guide you through your first edits and get you started. If you are cutting a different scene and not "Wanna Trade," simply substitute your clip names for the clip names I provide in the instructions.

Before you make any edits, look at the script for the scene you'll be cutting to get an idea of action and dialog. If you are cutting "Wanna Trade," you'll find the script on pages 29 and 30. Most of the action has been shot from several camera angles. Each actor has a master shot and a close-up (CU). Some of the action has more than one take. Your job is to make the scene come to life and to choose among the best parts. Examine the performances and also determine which angle works best for that section of the scene.

STARTING AN EDITING SESSION

The screen in Figure 1.19 shows the Xpress as it would look during an editing session. The Project window is in the lower left. The Dailies Day One bin is open in Frame view and shows the clips that make up the "Wanna Trade" scene. One clip, a close-up of Kate, has been opened in the Source Monitor. Several shots have been spliced into the Timeline, creating a sequence. The Record Monitor is on the right-hand side and shows what is in the Timeline. We're looking at a close-up of Tim, because the blue line position indicator in the Timeline is parked on that clip.

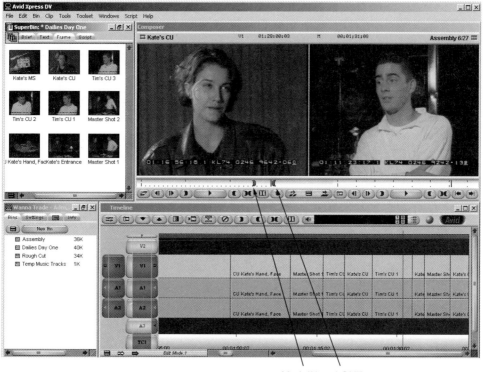

Mark IN and OUT

Figure 1.19

We'll start by loading clips into the Source Monitor. The Source Monitor is like a holding tank. Every time you double-click on a clip icon, it appears in the Source Monitor. The Source Monitor has a menu that shows all the clips you have loaded into it. Click on the name of the clip in the upper left of the Source Monitor to see that menu and a list of all the clips that are held there. Drag down and release to choose another clip from the list; that choice replaces the one currently in view.

Click and drag here
to see the list of clips
in the Source
Monitor.

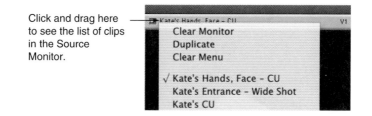

Making Your First Cut

Follow these step-by-step instructions that will guide you through your first editing session:

1. In the Project window for "Wanna Trade," you'll see two bins: Dailies Day One and Assembly. Click once on the Dailies Day One bin icon. It should open in the SuperBin. If you double-click on the bin icon, it will open, but it won't go into the SuperBin. To get it to go into the SuperBin, you'll now have to double-click on the empty bin icon in the Project window (it's grayed to show that it has already been opened).
2. Click once on the Assembly bin icon. It will appear in the SuperBin, replacing the Dailies Day One bin. In the Project window, click once more on the Dailies Day One bin icon. It will spring into view, replacing the Assembly bin.
3. In the Dailies Day One bin, you'll see a number of clips. You are probably in Frame View. Click on the tabs at the top of the bin to switch views. Switch to Brief View. Switch to Text View. Try Script View.
4. In the Dailies Day One bin, double-click on the Clip icon for *Kate's Entrance—Wide Shot*. The clip appears in the Source Monitor. You can also place clips in the Source Monitor by dragging clips from the bin and then dropping them onto the Source Monitor.
5. You can play the clip by selecting the Play button under the Source Monitor, but I suggest you get into the habit of using the J–K–L keys on the keyboard and practice playing the clips using those keys and your left hand. Hit J or L several times to go fast reverse or fast forward. Hold pause (K) while holding J or L to go backward or forward in slow motion.
6. To move quickly through the clip, drag the blue position bar inside the position bar window in the Source Monitor.
7. Once you are familiar with the clip in the Source Monitor, choose your cut points. Mark an IN somewhere after the slate and mark an OUT after Kate is through searching for the papers on the desk. Use either the I and O keys or the Mark IN and Mark OUT command buttons in the Source Monitor, as shown in Figure 1.20.

Mark IN and OUT

Figure 1.20

To make your first edit, click the Splice button.

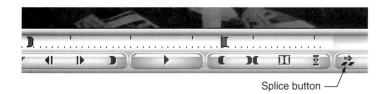

Splice button —

A dialog box may appear, asking you where you would like the "Untitled Sequence" to go. Select the Assembly bin and click OK. Presto! You have just created an "Untitled Sequence" and the Timeline will show you that the picture and tracks are spliced in your sequence.

In the Assembly bin, click on the "Untitled Sequence" letters (not the sequence icon) so you can type a name, such as Assembly #1.

Practice navigating the Timeline by playing the shot at various speeds using J–K–L or by dragging the blue position indicator.

Adding Shots to Your Sequence

1. You are ready to cut in the next shot. The clip you want next shows a close-up of Kate's hands searching the papers on the desk. The shot then tilts up to a close-up of Kate's face. Go to the Dailies Day One bin and double click on the *Kate's Hands, Face—CU.*
2. Play through the clip so you know what your choices are.
3. Click anywhere on the Timeline. Navigate along the Timeline, looking for a spot to cut this shot of her hands into the wide shot of her searching the desk.
4. Place your IN in the Timeline where you want to cut to the close-up. Do this by placing the blue position indicator at the correct spot in the Timeline and click on that spot. Now press the "I" key on the keyboard or click the Mark IN tag command button on the Record Monitor. This puts a mark IN tag on the Timeline.
5. Click anywhere on the Source Monitor to make it active, find a point in the *Kate's Hands, Face—CU* clip where you think the cut will work, and mark an IN. Go to the very end of the clip and mark an OUT.
6. IMPORTANT: It takes three marks to make an edit, and you now have three—an IN and an OUT in the Source Monitor and an IN in the Timeline, on the TC1 track. Count to make sure you have three.
7. Now, you have two choices. You can select the Splice button, or you can select the Overwrite button. The Splice button inserts material into the sequence at the IN mark and pushes everything after that point to the right. The sequence gets longer. The Overwrite button replaces (writes over) what is already in the sequence with new material. In this exercise, I want you to press the Overwrite button.

Splice and Overwrite

8. First, check the Timeline's track selection buttons to make sure the source and record tracks for V1 and A1 and A2 are selected (colored in). Click on them if they are not. Now, press the Overwrite button. The extraneous part of *Kate's Entrance* has been replaced with the insert of her hands at the IN point you selected. Now play the entire sequence

to see if you like the way it works. If you don't like it, hit Command/Ctrl–Z (undo) to undo your last action; your overwrite is gone. Choose new edit points by clearing the IN or OUT in the Source Monitor or the IN in the Timeline and setting new marks.

9. When you cut an assembly together, you are normally overwriting—placing a new shot over the tail of the last shot in the Timeline.

10. Now try cutting in a close-up of Kate's face. Drag or play along the Timeline until you find a new point for your IN. Place the IN using the I key on the keyboard or the Mark IN command in the Record Monitor. Then return to the *Kate's Hands, Face—CU* clip. To make sure it's the active window, click anywhere on the Source Monitor. Now, choose your IN and OUT points. You have three marks. Hit the Overwrite button. You should now have three shots in your Timeline.

11. If you want to cut extraneous pictures and sound out of the Timeline (say, the end of a shot is too long), mark an IN and then an OUT in the Timeline, as shown in Figure 1.21. Make sure all of your tracks are selected (highlighted). Now, hit the Extract key (X on keyboard). Undo (Command/Ctrl–Z) if there is a problem, and try again after correcting it.

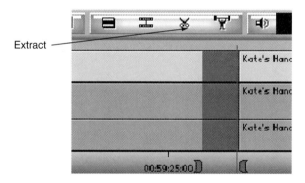

Figure 1.21

There are two takes of the Master Shot; one covers the entire scene, and the other is a pick-up. There are several takes of Tim's close-up. Kate has a close-up and a medium shot. Look at the performances, examine the choices, and continue cutting together the sequence. Leave your shots a bit long, and we will trim them up later.

ENDING AN EDITING SESSION

1. To close your project, click anywhere inside the Project window. That's the window that contains all the bins. Hit Command/Ctrl–S to save all of your changes. Press Command–Q (Mac) or Ctrl–Q (Windows) to quit the program, or choose Exit from the File Menu or Quit from the Xpress menu.

2. *Mac users:* When you return to the main computer screen, go to the Apple Menu and choose Shut Down. *Windows users:* When you return to the main computer screen, go to the Start Menu and choose Shut Down. In the dialog box, click OK.

3. When the computer shuts down, turn off the power to the deck or camera, the speakers, and the television monitor, and turn off the power to the external media drives.

Well done.

Script for "Wanna Trade"

The two-page, lined script for the scene "Wanna Trade" can be found on pages 29 and 30.

1   1A

1 INT. PHOTOGRAPHER'S STUDIO - NIGHT

A door slowly opens. Light pours into a darkened room. A
figure, in silhouette, enters cautiously. After a few steps
the figure is illuminated by moonlight coming from a high
window. KATE WINSLOW, attractive, in her mid-twenties, is
wearing jeans and a leather jacket. She turns on a desk lamp
and then crosses the studio in order to switch on a floor
1B lamp. She steps in front of a desk covered with papers and
begins rifling through it. Suddenly, TIM HARPER steps from
the shadows. He is a fashion photographer and looks the part:
handsome, sleek and self-satisfied.

    1C Master 1D Tim 1E Kate 1F Kate

      KATE
Geez, you scared me.

      TIM
What are you doing here?

      KATE
I was in the neighborhood and I
thought I'd drop off the jacket.

      TIM
Bull. You're looking for a small
stack of perfume-scented letters.
Aren't you, Kate?

      KATE
Yeah, maybe I am.

      TIM
You figured, he doesn't need them
anymore. I dumped the jerk . . .

      KATE
Tim, we've been through that a
million times . . .

      TIM
So why not break into his studio
and steal those juicy,
embarrassing, and I-can't-believe-I-
ever-wrote-them love letters

      KATE
Where are they?

Tim looks down at the desk and starts shuffling papers.

      TIM
I guess they're not here.

            (CONTINUED)

1 CONTINUED:

1C 1D Tim   1E Kate

      KATE
     (outraged)
Those are my letters.

      TIM
No, Kate. You sent them to me.
They're mine now, and I can do
whatever I want with them.

      KATE
Bastard.

Tim is pleased with himself. Kate turns and heads for the
door. Tim grabs her arm and spins her around.

      TIM
Hey!

      KATE
What?

      TIM
That's my jacket. Give it here.

      KATE
No, Tim. You gave me this jacket.
Remember? And I can do whatever I
want with it.

      TIM
Jerk.

Kate holds open the jacket, displaying it like a model.

      KATE
Wanna trade?

Tim considers the offer. He dismisses her with a wave.

      TIM
Not a chance.

Kate turns and exits.

           FADE TO BLACK.

2

Basic Editing

EDITING RULES

Unfortunately, or fortunately, depending on your perspective, there are no editing rules. That is not to say there isn't an aesthetic at work, or that any ordering of shots is "correct." If that were the case, a trained monkey would be as good an editor as Thelma Schoonmaker, who edited *Raging Bull* and *Goodfellas* and won an Oscar for *Aviator*.

So what makes an editor good? When you're editing a sequence involving a number of different shots, many skills and talents come into play. First of all you must be able to choose from among the choices given to you. To make the right choices you must understand the script and not just the storyline but also the subjects' or characters' needs. If you don't know what motivates a character or subject, you can't really determine which shot or which take will work best. You also must judge performance, composition, screen direction, blocking, camera movement, lighting, and sound, for all those elements can help draw in your audience. The ability to judge the material is critical whatever the nature of the program you are editing, be it documentary, narrative, commercial, or experimental.

Once you have picked, from among the choices, the material that will work best, you must cut it to the right length and attach it to the right shot. And, once you think you have done that, the most important skill of all comes into play. To be a good editor you must be a good watcher. It sounds simple, but it's not. Good editors can stop being editors and quickly transform themselves into good viewers. You have to be able to erase from your mind all your worries, hunger pangs, sore muscles, random thoughts, and anything else that could impede your concentration. And then you must really, really watch! And, as you watch, you are asking yourself one question: Does it work? Hopefully, you'll know the answer to that question by the end of this book.

STARTING YOUR SECOND EDITING SESSION

Follow the instructions provided in the first chapter to start up your Avid. When the software launches, you'll see the Select Project window, like the one shown in Figure 2.1.

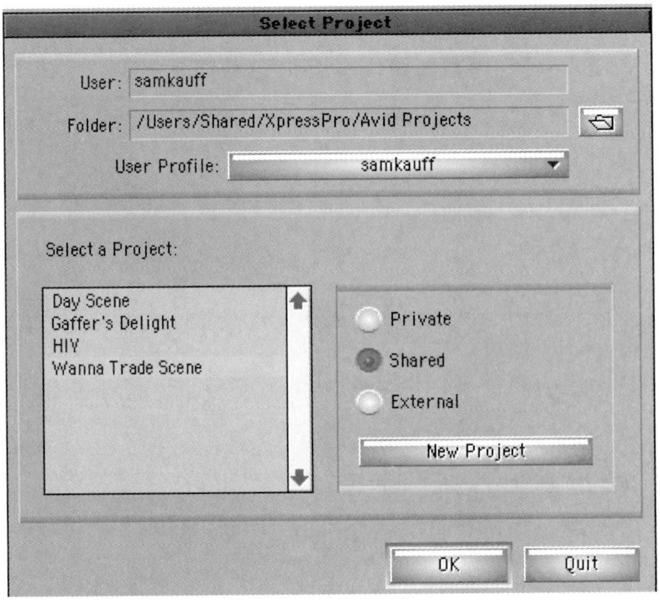

Figure 2.1   Select Project window.

If you're working on "Wanna Trade," just click on it so it's highlighted and press OK. If your instructor has loaded a different project for you, click on it and press OK. When you reach the Project window, open the Dailies Day One bin and the Assembly bin. Find your sequence, which you created during your first editing session. You probably named it something like Assembly 1. There are two ways to get a sequence into the Record Monitor (the monitor on the far right). You can click on it and drag it to the Record Monitor, or you can double-click the sequence icon. It will load in the Timeline, and you are ready to continue.

BASIC EDITING SKILLS

Let's review what we learned at the end of the first chapter. Start by opening the bin containing your clips. SuperBin users will single-click on the bin icon, while those not using SuperBin Mode will double-click. Now, double-click on a clip to load it into the Source Monitor.

Marking Clips

Splice and Overwrite enable you to put your shots together in the order in which you want them to appear. They help you build your sequence. They may be the most important commands at your disposal, but to use them you must first select the material you want to splice or overwrite into your sequence. You select this material by placing an IN where you want to start and an OUT where you want to end the shot. Click anywhere on the Source Monitor to make it active. Use the J–K–L keys to play through the clip, or click and drag the position indicator in the monitor's window. Once you are familiar with your clip, choose your cut points. Mark an IN and mark an OUT. You have just determined what will be spliced or overwritten into the sequence. You can clear your marks by clicking the Clear IN and OUT button.

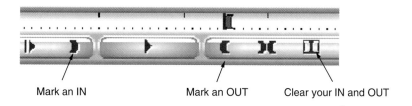

Mark an IN   Mark an OUT   Clear your IN and OUT

Instead of using the buttons under the Source Monitor, use the Mark IN and OUT command keys on the keyboard to set your marks. They are the I and O keys. It may be slower at first, but I think you'll find it faster in the long run.

Now you must determine where that material will go. Click anywhere on the Timeline to make it active. Play through the sequence. Using the keyboard, place an IN mark.

Remember, it takes three marks to make an edit, and you now have three—an IN and an OUT in the Source Monitor and an IN in the Timeline. Count to make sure you have three.

Now, you have two choices. You can select the Splice button or you can select the Overwrite button.

Splice and Overwrite

Splice and Overwrite

The Splice button inserts material into the sequence at the IN mark and pushes everything after that point downstream. The sequence gets longer. The Overwrite button replaces (writes over) what is already in the sequence with new material. Let's say your third shot, Kate's CU, is a bit too long. You can use overwrite to trim the end of the shot while putting in the fourth shot. In Figure 2.2, the tail of Kate's CU is a bit long. I place an IN mark in the Timeline where I want the fourth shot to go. Overwrite will place Tim's CU right at the IN mark and get rid of the tail of Kate's CU.

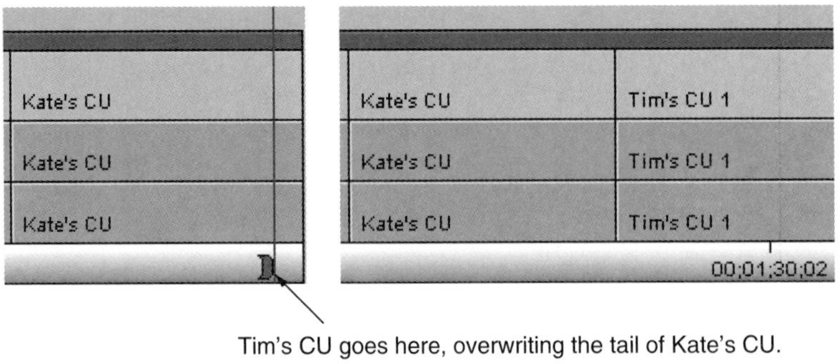

Tim's CU goes here, overwriting the tail of Kate's CU.

Figure 2.2

SOURCE MONITOR MENU

Double-clicking on a clip icon loads that clip into the Source Monitor. If you want to put more than one clip at a time into the Source Monitor, just Shift–click and drag a group of clips to the Source Monitor screen. Once the clips have been loaded into the Source Monitor, they are available in the Source Monitor menu. Just press and hold the cursor on the clip name at the top of the Source Monitor screen. When the list comes down, drag and release on the clip you want to open in the Source Monitor. Figure 2.3 shows that three clips have been loaded into the Source Monitor. The check mark shows which one appears in the monitor.

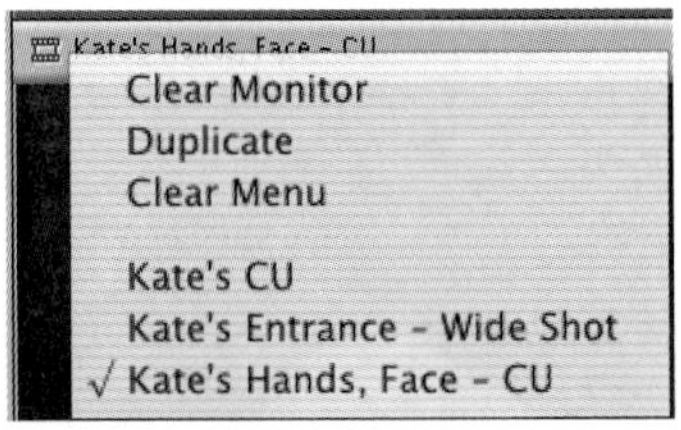

Kate's Hands, Face - CU
Clear Monitor
Duplicate
Clear Menu
Kate's CU
Kate's Entrance - Wide Shot
√ Kate's Hands, Face - CU

Figure 2.3

The menu lists the clips in alphabetical order. One neat trick to remember is that if you hold down the Option (Mac) or Alt (Windows) key and then drag down the menu, you'll see the clips listed in the order you last used them.

THE TIMELINE

As mentioned in Chapter 1, the Timeline is a graphic representation of the shots in your sequence. It is one of Avid's most intuitive and user friendly features.

Selecting and Deselecting Tracks

The Track Selector panels are on the left of the Timeline. When you have a clip in the Source Monitor, the Source Track Selector panel appears next to the Record Track Selector panel.

Before making any edits, always check to see which tracks are selected before splicing and overwriting. In Figure 2.4, if we were to try to splice the material in the Source Monitor into the sequence, the sound coming in on tracks A1 and A2 will not get spliced in. Why not? Because the Record Track buttons for A1 and A2 are *deselected*. To select the record tracks for A1 and A2, simply click on the track buttons.

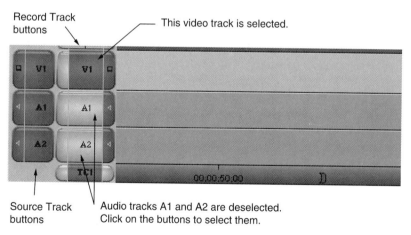

Figure 2.4

If the record tracks are selected but the Source Track buttons aren't, the source material won't get spliced or overwritten into the sequence either. Check your tracks before splicing or overwriting.

Navigating the Timeline

It's easy to move around the Timeline: Use the J–K–L keys, use the mouse to drag the blue position indicator, or press any number of keyboard buttons that will move you to various frames or edit points. Two keys are particularly helpful:

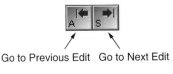

Go to Previous Edit   Go to Next Edit

Figure 2.5

Select the track whose cut points you wish to navigate. Press these buttons, and you will jump to the cut points on the Timeline. If there is nothing on a track, such as V2, pressing these keys will take you not to the next cut point but to the head or tail of the entire sequence. Deselect any tracks that are empty, and only select the tracks whose cut points you want to see. To deselect a track, click on the Record Track button, as shown in Figure 2.4.

Home and End

Click anywhere in the Timeline to activate it and then press the Home key, which you'll find on the keyboard. You'll jump to the beginning of the sequence. Hit the End key, just below it, and you'll jump to the end of the sequence. If the Source Monitor is active, Home and End work there as well. Laptop users will need to press and hold the function (fn) key in order for the Home and End keys to work.

Snapping to Cut Points

More often than not, you will use the mouse to get where you want to go, either by clicking in the Timeline or by using the mouse to drag the Position Indicator. Often when editing, you'll want to get to the end of a shot to mark an OUT or go to the head of a shot to mark an IN. But, getting the position indicator to quickly land exactly on the beginning of a shot isn't all that easy. If the position indicator in the Timeline isn't parked on the first frame, and you started splicing, you'll have little orphan frames hanging around. To quickly jump to the head of a clip in the Timeline, press the Command key (Mac) or the Ctrl key (Windows) and click the cursor near the transition you want to snap to. Try it.

To quickly snap to the tail of a clip, press the Option–Command (Mac) or Ctrl–Alt (Windows) keys and click near the transition you want.

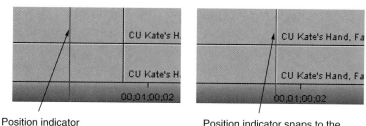

Position indicator

Position indicator snaps to the transition or cut point.

Figure 2.6 Snapping to transitions.

Position Indicator

The position indicator snaps to the transition or cut point.

- *Hold the Command (Ctrl) key* and click near the transition you want—you'll snap to the head, or first frame of a shot.
- *Hold Option and Command (Ctrl–Alt) keys* and click near the transition you want—you'll snap to the tail, or last frame of a shot.

Practice this technique until it's automatic.

The Timeline Fast Menu

The Timeline has a Fast menu, and it contains a number of options that allow you to change the Timeline's appearance and the view you have of your sequence. Just click and hold on the Fast menu button, and the Fast menu opens.

Click on the Timeline Fast menu to open...

Figure 2.7 The Timeline Fast menu.

One of Timeline's options is the ability to choose the color of your tracks in the Timeline. To change the default color, select the track(s) you want to change and then choose Track Color from the Timeline Fast menu by holding and dragging the mouse to a color you would like to see. Release the mouse, and your track(s) will reflect your selection. Normally, I keep stereo tracks that go together the same color. I'll have one color for V2, another for V1, a third for my sync tracks, a fourth for my music tracks, and so on.

Scaling and Scrolling the Timeline

There are times when you want to see the Timeline of the entire sequence, and there are times you want to view just the section you are currently editing. Obviously, if you have a show that is an hour long, involving a thousand cuts, showing the entire Timeline isn't useful because all you'll see is black lines. For editing purposes, you'll want to look at a specific edit point, or five or six shots. The ability to zoom in and out is obviously important. And, once you've zoomed in, you may want to scroll ahead or back to another section of the sequence.

Scale slider and Scroll slider

There are two bars along the bottom of the timeline. The bar on the left contains the *Scale bar*. Drag the small slider to the right, and you're zooming in to look at just a few cuts—or even just a few frames. Try it and see. Drag it to the left, and the Timeline compresses so you're looking at a much larger percentage of the sequence.

The rectangle on the right is called the *Scroll bar*, which has its own slider. You won't actually see it until you drag the Scale slider to the right. Then it appears because there are clips hidden from view. When you drag the Scroll bar to the right, it shows you a different section of the Timeline. When you drag the Scroll bar slider you are determining which section of the project is displayed in the Timeline.

You can also use the keyboard's page up and page down arrows to zoom in (up arrow) and zoom out (down arrow). It's very fast.

The Timeline Fast menu gives you additional ways of controlling your view. You can either select one of the bottom six items listed in the Timeline Fast menu (see Figure 2.7) or learn the keystrokes. The Zoom In and Zoom Back are the only ones that aren't self-explanatory. When you select Zoom In—Command+M (Mac) or Ctrl+M (Windows)—the cursor changes. Now click and drag across an area of the Timeline with the cursor. Let go, and that's the section displayed in the Timeline. Press Command+J (Mac) or Ctrl+J (Windows) and you'll restore your original view.

Finally there's the Focus button (Figure 2.8). Click once, and you zoom in. Click once more, and you zoom out. Practice changing your Timeline views using all the choices.

Fast menu Focus button

Figure 2.8 Focus button.

Enlarge or Reduce Tracks

You can make the tracks in the Timeline larger or smaller. This is handy when you're working with more than four tracks. With six tracks, it's difficult to fit them all in the Timeline unless you make them smaller. To change the size of all your tracks, press:

- Command–L (Mac), Ctrl–L (Windows) to enlarge
- Command–K (Mac), Ctrl–K (Windows) to reduce

It doesn't matter if tracks are selected or not—all change size.

If you want to change the size of just one track, you can do so by carefully placing the mouse cursor at the bottom line of a track button. The pointer changes shape and becomes a *resize track cursor*. In Figure 2.9 it is between A1 and A2. Drag this cursor down, and A1 track gets larger. Drag it up, and the track gets smaller.

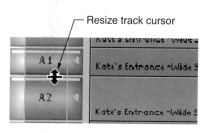

Resize track cursor

Figure 2.9

Track Monitor Icons

These curved buttons hold tiny monitor icons (Figure 2.10). The audio monitor icon looks like a tiny speaker, and the video monitor icon looks like a tiny screen. They show which tracks will be seen and heard. If the button on a track is empty, you won't see or hear anything. The exception is when you have more than one video track. If the top video track has the monitor icon, then all the video tracks beneath it will also be monitored.

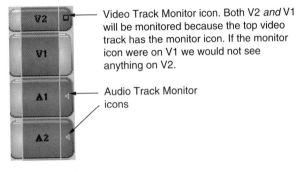

Video Track Monitor icon. Both V2 *and* V1 will be monitored because the top video track has the monitor icon. If the monitor icon were on V1 we would not see anything on V2.

Audio Track Monitor icons

Figure 2.10

Click on the box, and the monitor icon indicator disappears. You won't hear (or see) that track. Click again, and the indicator reappears and you'll hear (or see) the track.

Marking Clips in the Timeline

One of the most useful buttons at your disposal is the Mark Clip button. Often you will be working on your sequence and see that you want to get rid of a shot. One way to do this is to work in the Timeline and place an IN mark at the head of the clip and an OUT mark at the tail of the clip. But, there's a much simpler way to do this:

1. Put the position indicator in the clip you want to mark (make sure all of the active tracks are selected).
2. Press the Mark Clip button.

The Mark Clip command can be found on the T key on the keyboard or on the row of commands above the Timeline.

Figure 2.11 The Mark Clip button.

You'll see an IN mark at the head and an OUT at the tail of the clip. The entire clip is highlighted. Note that if you have tracks that are empty of clips and they are selected, Mark Clip will mark the entire sequence. Deselect all empty tracks first!

Now we're ready to master two important commands: Lift and Extract. But, before practicing these commands on your sequence, let's *duplicate* it first, so if we get too excited by all our lifting and extracting and totally mess it up, we won't care because the original is still in the bin.

DUPLICATING A SEQUENCE

The ability to save versions of your work is critically important. Let's say you have a brilliant idea and edit furiously. Then suddenly you see it doesn't work at all, and the whole Timeline is a disaster. If that happens, you want to be able to revert to your previous version. So, get in the habit of making a duplicate of your sequence before trying that brilliant idea, and always create a duplicate sequence at the end of every editing session so you start fresh the next day. That way you can keep track of your changes and go back to an earlier version if need be. Here's how:

1. Go to the Assembly bin and find the sequence you've been working on.
2. Select it (click on the sequence icon and it will be selected) so it is highlighted.
3. Go to the Edit menu and choose Duplicate or type Command–D (Mac) or Ctrl–D (Windows). You have created an identical copy of your sequence. The suffix ".copy.01." is added to it so you can differentiate between the two versions.
4. Get rid of the suffix ".copy.01" and replace it with today's date or a new name so you can tell your versions apart.
5. Double-click on the new sequence icon. Now you have a new version to work with.

LIFT AND EXTRACT

Now let's start exploring Lift and Extract, two commands that are important in helping us understand Avid editing. Because they are so important, you'll find them right on the keyboard; they are the letters Z (Lift) and X (Extract).

Lift and Extract

Let's go to the third shot in the Timeline. In my sequence, it's Master Shot 1. For this exercise, we'll be using the Mark Clip button to select the clip for lifting and extracting. Place the position indicator anywhere in the clip and then press the Mark Clip button.

Now press the Lift button. The clip is gone and black *filler* is in its place (Figure 2.12). Notice that when you lift, the length of your sequence does not change. The Timeline is the same length.

Figure 2.12 The Master Shot has been lifted from the sequence.

Press Command–Z (Mac) or Ctrl–Z (Windows) to undo the Lift.

Now use the Mark Clip button to mark the Master Shot again. This time, hit the *Extract* button. Hey! The clip's gone and the Timeline has shrunk (Figure

2.13). This one can fool you sometimes because it happens so fast you don't see it, and you wonder if you actually did anything.

Figure 2.13 The Master Shot has been extracted from the sequence.

If you want the Master Shot back, press Command–Z (Mac) or Ctrl–Z (Windows) to undo the Extract.

Now try lifting clips and extracting clips with the video track (V1) deselected. You'll see that the Lift button will take away the sound, leaving the picture and black filler where the sound used to be. In this example, I have selected the audio tracks but not the video track, and then I hit the Lift button. The picture remains, but the sound has been replaced by black filler.

Lift works without a problem, but watch out for the Extract button! By extracting the audio and leaving the video clip in place, you shift all the audio that comes after this clip! Let's examine how Extract differs from Lift in this situation.

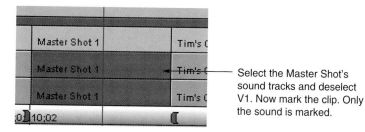

Select the Master Shot's sound tracks and deselect V1. Now mark the clip. Only the sound is marked.

As we've seen, if you *lift* the Master Shot's audio, the audio is removed and replaced by filler. The audio downstream of this point isn't "pulled up" to fill in the space left by the missing audio because there's something there—the black filler. But when you *extract*, there is no filler. The audio rushes in to fill in the gap. Notice how Tim's audio moves into the gap caused when the Master Shot's audio is extracted, throwing everything out of sync.

This is not something you want to do. Because you extracted 184 frames of audio, while leaving the video in place, the audio becomes 184 frames out of sync everywhere after the extraction.

Fortunately the Timeline shows you when you are out of sync and by how much. Plus and minus signs indicate the direction of the sync problem. The frame count indicates the extent of the sync problem.

Be careful when you use Extract. It's a great tool, but only when all tracks are selected. Be prepared to use Undo to fix problems with Extract.

Trim Shots Using Extract

A common way to quickly trim the head or tail of a shot is to use Extract. Let's say the head of a shot that you cut into the sequence seems too long. Find the point where you want to cut it. Mark an OUT. Snap to the head of the clip (Command/Ctrl and drag the position indicator) and mark an IN. Hit Extract, and the shot is trimmed to the desired length.

IT TAKES THREE MARKS TO MAKE AN EDIT

This is a rather simple statement of fact, yet, when you really understand it, it makes profound sense. Whenever you make a splice or overwrite, you need to make three marks. There are only four possible choices. Look at the choices in the chart below. So far, we have concentrated on the first choice. In the Source Monitor, you mark the material you want to edit into the sequence with an IN and an OUT, and then you mark an IN in the Timeline where you want it to go. You've got three marks.

Source Monitor	Record/Timeline Mark
1. Mark IN and OUT	IN
2. Mark IN	IN and OUT
3. Mark OUT	IN and OUT
4. Mark IN and OUT	OUT

Let's look at the other three choices. They are most often used with the *Overwrite button*, whereas choice 1 is used most frequently with the *Splice button*.

Choice 2 is useful whenever you want to replace a shot (or audio) that you've already cut into your Timeline with a better shot. Let's say you've cut a shot of a smiling baby into your sequence. When you play the sequence you see that it would make more sense to use the shot of a crying baby. You like the length of the shot, but not the content. So you simply mark the clip (use the Mark Clip button) in the Timeline and then find the clip of the crying baby in the bin. Play through the crying baby shot in the Source Monitor and mark an IN where you want the shot to begin. Now hit Overwrite. Now the shot of the smiling baby is replaced by the crying baby. The length of the sequence doesn't change. You've simply replaced one shot with another.

Choice 3 is just like choice 2 except it marks the clip in the Source Monitor from the OUT rather than the IN. Think about it. You mark your clip in the Timeline that you want to replace. Then you find the shot you want to put in its place. Perhaps the end of the shot of the crying baby is what makes it special. So you use an OUT mark rather than an IN mark. You've got your three marks, and now you hit Overwrite. The shot of the smiling baby is replaced by the crying baby. The length of the sequence doesn't change. You've simply replaced one shot with another.

When I drove a truck for a living, I was told that 99 percent of all trucking accidents occur when backing up. That's the reason why you'll seldom use choice 4. With this choice, the material is backed into the Timeline and can end up erasing material you want to keep; however, this choice is handy whenever you're laying in music, as we'll see in Chapter 8.

Like a Mantra

It takes three marks to make an edit. Think about this simple sentence. Examine the choices. Imagine different situations where you would use each of them. Try them out. See what I mean? Profound.

USING THE CLIPBOARD

The Clipboard is one of the Avid's most useful tools. You can mark a section in the Timeline, with an IN and OUT, and then place it into the Clipboard by pressing Lift or Extract or the Clipboard icon.

Unlike Lift or Extract, which removes the material from the Timeline, when you press the Clipboard icon the material stays in the sequence and a copy of it, including all the audio and video tracks that you've selected, is saved to the Clipboard. This way you can take something you've done and place an exact copy of it elsewhere. You could even place it in another sequence.

To get material that you placed in the Clipboard, go to the Tools menu and select Clipboard Monitor (Figure 2.14). A Pop-Up Monitor opens. Mark the material you want to cut into the sequence with an IN and an OUT, and then mark an IN in the Timeline. Now you can splice or overwrite the clipboard contents into the Timeline.

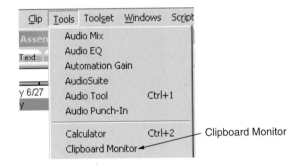

Figure 2.14

The Clipboard holds whatever you have stored there only until you press Lift or Extract or the Clipboard icon again. Then, whatever was there is gone—replaced by the new material.

UNDO/REDO LIST

As we noted, you can Undo and Redo your actions simply by pressing Command–Z (Mac) or Ctrl–Z (Windows). If you press the Undo command four times in a row, you can undo your four previous actions. There is an easier way to do this. Go to the Edit menu at the top of your computer screen and pull down the Edit menu. Drag down and then hold open the Undo/Redo List, like the one shown in Figure 2.15. You'll see a list of your actions. If you've been working for a long stretch, you may have up to 32 actions in the list. Find the one you want to Undo or Redo and select it from the list. Just remember that all previous actions—those actions above it on the list—will also be undone. Who said you can never go back in time?

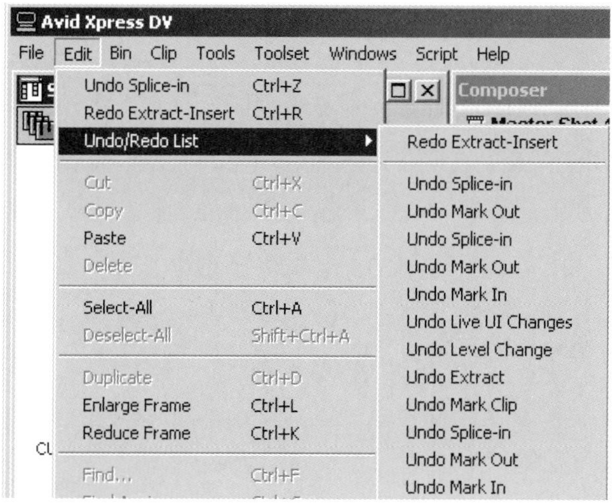

Figure 2.15

SUGGESTED ASSIGNMENTS

1. Duplicate your sequence. Change the name of the duplicate version to "Rough Cut" and add today's date.
2. Continue to work on the new version of your sequence until you have a rough cut of the entire scene.
3. Practice using all the commands discussed in this chapter.

3

The Project Window

The Project window, as you recall from the first chapter, is like the home page of your project. To get you editing on the Avid as quickly as possible, we skipped some important information about the bins in the Project window; that information now needs our attention.

CREATING A BIN

Often, you will want to organize different kinds of material, and the simplest way to do that is to create a new bin for each category. For instance, in addition to your video footage, you might have voice-over narration, music, and titles. As you edit your footage, you might have a bin for your assembly sequences, one for your rough-cut sequences, and, as your work progresses, one for your fine-cut sequences.

Figure 3.1

Let's try creating a new bin and putting something in it.

1. In the Project window, click on the New Bin button, and a new bin will open (Figure 3.1). It will be titled "Wanna Trade bin." The bin is named for the project. You'll want to give it a more helpful name, and the Avid knows this. Notice that the name is highlighted.

2. Simply type the name you want, such as "Rough Cut."
3. Now double-click the Assembly bin and click on the duplicate of your sequence in the Assembly bin which you made while working on Chapter 2. Drag it into the Rough Cut bin.
4. You now want to change the name of the sequence from "Assembly" to "Rough Cut" and the date—"Rough Cut v. 9/25." Just select it and type.

Remember, to duplicate a sequence, simply select it in the bin so it's highlighted, and then press Command–D (Mac) or Ctrl–D (Windows) or select Duplicate in the Edit menu.

ALL ABOUT BINS

The bin is like your project's library and card catalog all rolled into one. We'll spend much of this chapter learning about bins because that's where everything begins.

Bin Views

Remember that there are four ways to view material in the bin. Brief View, Text View, Frame View, and Script View. If you're working on a single monitor, where screen real estate is at a premium, Brief View is helpful because it takes up the least space. Brief View provides you with just five columns of information: the name of the clip, the starting timecode, the duration of the clip in seconds, the clip's video and audio tracks, and whether the clip is online (meaning there is digital media on a media drive).

In Text View, there are something like 30 columns to choose from, such as scene, take, camera roll, and videotape; it's particularly useful when you want to organize and search through a lot of clips. Frame View is most useful when you're working on a documentary involving lots of different visuals clips. I hardly ever use Script View.

Selecting Clips

As with any Windows or Macintosh software, you can easily select more than one clip at a time by shift-clicking or lassoing. Command–A (Mac) or Ctrl–A (Windows) is particularly helpful because it selects all the clips in two quick keystrokes.

Working in SuperBin Mode

SuperBin takes a bit of getting used to, but it's a great feature if you are on a laptop or only have a single screen to work with. It gives you an easy way to keep your bins from taking over your editing space. For the Xpress user, SuperBin is active and available as soon as you launch your software. In other systems, you may have to make SuperBin the default mode. We'll learn to do that at the end of this chapter.

Let's look at what happens when I double-click the bin I recently created to hold my rough cuts. It opens in Brief View, just to the right of the project window (Figure 3.1). On a system using two computer monitors, you've got plenty of room to move the bin around and place it wherever you choose. But, if you have just one computer monitor, it can get in the way.

When you *single-click* a bin's icon in the Project window, it opens the bin into a special holding place—or SuperBin. You know right away when you're in SuperBin Mode because the bin says SuperBin, and there's an icon showing bins stacked on top of one another (Figure 3.2). Because the default view in SuperBin Mode is Frame View, that's what you'll get.

Figure 3.2 SuperBin.

Try opening the Dailies Day One bin into the SuperBin. Just single-click on the bin icon, and it opens in the SuperBin. If you want to see the Rough Cut bin, single-click on its icon in the Project window. It doesn't matter if the bin is open or closed. Single-click on any bin in the Project window and it opens in the SuperBin.

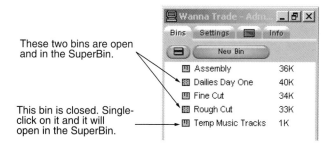

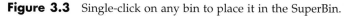

Figure 3.3 Single-click on any bin to place it in the SuperBin.

If you want to open the bin on its own, outside of the SuperBin, that's easy—just *double-click* on the bin icon in the Project window. To put it back into the SuperBin, double-click again.

To review:

1. Single-click to place a bin in the SuperBin.
2. Double-click to open a bin on its own.
3. Double-click to move a bin on its own back into the SuperBin.

Changing the Default View

Frame View seems to be the default view whenever you place a bin in the SuperBin. That's fine if you're working on a documentary, but I find Brief View to be more helpful when I'm working with a narrative project. Let's change the default view. Click anywhere on the SuperBin to make it active. Switch to Brief View by clicking on the Brief tab. Drag the resize box to line the SuperBin up against the Source Monitor. Now, go to the Toolset menu and choose Save Current. From now on, you'll be in Brief View (Figure 3.4).

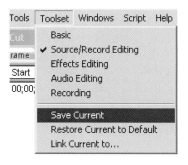

Figure 3.4

Bin Headings

We're living in the information age. Billions of facts are available to us through the Internet. It makes sense, therefore, to have all the facts about your clips available as well. Single-click Dailies Day One to open it in the SuperBin area. Go to Text View, and drag the resize box or scroll along the bin box to see more of the columns. At the top of the bin you'll see columns listed such as Name, Tracks, Mark In, Mark Out. There are about 30 column headings available to you, each providing specific information about each one of your clips. You'll notice that not all the columns are displayed. To see all the choices, go to the bottom of the bin and you'll see a Fast menu (looks a bit like a hamburger). Hold it, and the

Bin menu appears. (This is the same Bin menu found at the top of the computer screen.) One of the choices is *Headings*. Select it, and you will get a dialog box like the one in Figure 3.5.

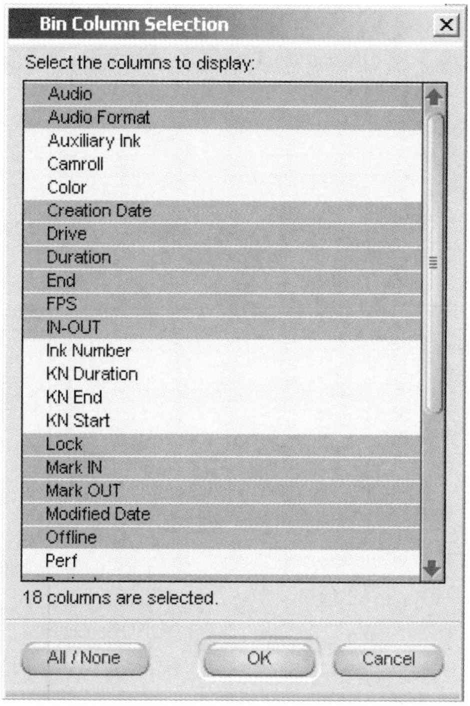

Bin Column Selection

Select the columns to display:

Audio
Audio Format
Auxiliary Ink
Camroll
Color
Creation Date
Drive
Duration
End
FPS
IN-OUT
Ink Number
KN Duration
KN End
KN Start
Lock
Mark IN
Mark OUT
Modified Date
Offline
Perf

18 columns are selected.

All / None   OK   Cancel

Figure 3.5

You can select or deselect headings by clicking on them. Some headings are more useful than others, and you'll want different headings at different stages of editing. Having all the headings on display is more confusing than helpful. Select those you find useful and deselect those representing information you don't need. Here are my choices for the early stages of editing:

Duration	It's helpful to know the length of a clip.
Start	The clip's starting timecode locates it on the source tape.
End	This is the clip's ending timecode.
Audio SR	This is the sample rate of the clip's audio.
Creation Date	This is the date and time the clip was captured.
Offline	This is helpful whenever you've erased media files.

Other column headings, like the ones on the next page, will be more helpful later on, when we talk about film projects or video projects that were shot to look like film:

Scene	Scene number, as found in the shooting script
Take	Take number
FPS	Frame per second rate
Pullin	Frame in a film project or a project shot at 23.976 fps

To return to your bin, click OK.

Moving Columns

Now that you have the columns you want, you can arrange them in any order. Simply click on the column heading (the entire column is highlighted), drag the column to a new location, and release the mouse. I wouldn't change the position of the Name column, because that's the most useful column and should be flush left, next to the icon. But, you might want to set up your columns like this: Name, Start, End, Duration, Tracks, Video. You can delete a column by selecting it and hitting Delete. It's still available under Headings. You can jump from column to column and row to row with Tab, Shift–Tab, Return, and Shift–Return. In the Bin menu is an Align Columns command that will organize the columns if they are unevenly spaced.

Sorting

Another really useful command is *Sort*. When you select a column and then choose Sort from the Bin menu, the Avid will arrange the column's contents in either alphabetical or numerical order. You can also use the keyboard to sort. Press Command–E (Mac) or Ctrl–E (Windows).

Let's say you want to look at the clips in your bin in the order in which they were shot on the source tape. Listing them alphabetically by name won't give you that information, but listing them by starting timecode will. Click on the Start column and choose Sort from the Bin menu, or use Command–E (Ctrl–E). The clips in the bin now appear listed according to the starting timecode. To switch back to listing the clips by name, simply click on the Name column and choose Sort from the Bin menu, or use Command–E (Ctrl–E).

There are times when you may want to invert the order in which items appear. To sort in descending order, hold down the Option key (Mac) or Alt key (Windows) key and then press Command–E (Mac) or Ctrl–E (Windows).

Frame View

Sometimes it's easier to edit material if you are looking at the choices as pictures rather than as columns of words and numbers. Frame View shows the clips in picture view.

Figure 3.6

Click on Frame at the top of the bin, and all the clips will become frames from the clip.

- You can enlarge the frames by selecting Enlarge Frame from the Edit menu or pressing Command–L (Mac) or Crtl–L (Windows). (Think of enLarge.)
- You can reduce the size of the frames by selecting Reduce Frame from the Edit menu or using Command–K (Mac) or Crtl–K (Windows).
- Repeat these commands, and the frames will keep getting bigger or smaller.

You can't enlarge or reduce just one frame, as the command affects all the frames in the bin, but you can change the frame of the clip you are looking at.

Look at Figure 3.6. "Kate's MS" shows a slate with an open clapstick. The sticks don't give us much visual information about the clip. By selecting the frame (just click on it) and using the J–K–L keys, you can play the clip. Whatever frame you stop on becomes *the reference frame*—the frame you'll see from now on. You can also drag the clips all around the bin, putting them in any order. If things get messy, go to the Bin menu and choose Align to Grid.

Another useful Bin menu item is Fill Window. When you select it, the frames are positioned nicely in the bin window.

STARTING A NEW SEQUENCE

Often you want to start over again—to try something new or different. The Avid makes it easy to do this. Go to the Clip menu (top of your screen). You'll see that the first choice is New Sequence. Select it, and you'll have a new, untitled sequence. If you have a number of bins open, a dialog box will appear asking you which bin you'd like the new sequence to go to. Choose one, such as the Rough Cut bin.

| Pro | File | Edit | Bin | Clip | Special | Tools | Toolset | Wind |

New Sequence ⇧⌘N
New Video Track ⌘Y
New Audio Track ⌘U
New Meta Track
New Title...

Now, go into the bin and give a name to "Untitled Sequence."

DRAG AND DROP EDITING

Drag and Drop is an amazingly quick way to put together an Assembly or Rough Cut. First, create a New Sequence, as outlined above. Go to the Source Monitor and mark an IN and an OUT in any clip. Now, click and hold the cursor anywhere inside the monitor window. Now drag the clip to the Timeline and drop it (let go of the mouse button). Open a new clip, mark IN and OUT points, and click and drag it to the end of the Timeline. It gets spliced onto the tail of the last clip you just placed in the Timeline. You'll notice that, as you drag the clip from the Source Monitor, the cursor changes appearance and becomes a hand (as shown in Figure 3.7).

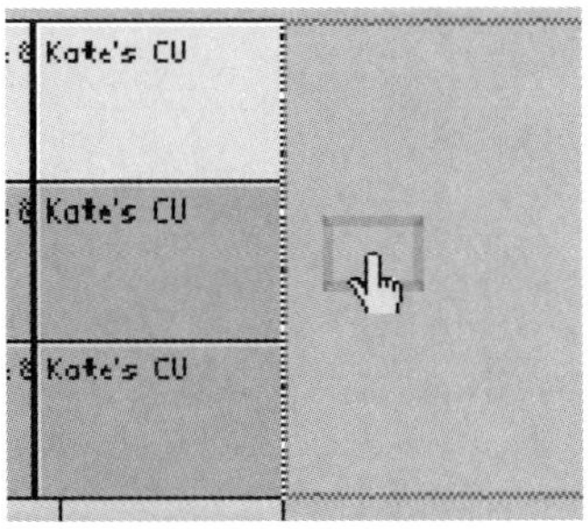

Figure 3.7

You don't have to drag to the end of the sequence. You can actually drop the clip on any transition point in the Timeline and when you let go the clip is spliced right there.

Practice this technique. It's amazingly fast. Just mark the clip in the Source Monitor, then click and drag to the Timeline.

SUBCLIPS

You may have clips that are overly long. Perhaps when you captured a tape, you kept several different shots together in one long master clip. For example, you might have a single clip that includes a wide shot of a man climbing a ladder, a close-up of his face, and a shot of a crowd of people watching him. You realize that it would make editing easier if each shot were separated from the others. You can do this by making subclips. It's easy.

To create a subclip:

1. Double-click on the clip to place it the Source Monitor.
2. Play the clip and mark the IN point and then mark an OUT point.
3. Mac users—Press and hold the Option key and then click and drag the picture from the Source Monitor to the bin in which you want to store the subclip. Windows users—Simply click and drag the picture from the Source Monitor to the bin in which you want to store the subclip.
4. Drop it in the bin.

Notice a couple of things. When you click and drag the clip in the Source Monitor to the bin, the mouse pointer turns into a hand. Once the subclip is in the bin, you'll see that the subclip has the same name as the clip it came from but with the addition of *Sub.n*, where *n* is the number of times that the master has been subdivided. Also notice that in Text View the subclip icon is like a mini-clip icon (Figure 3.8).

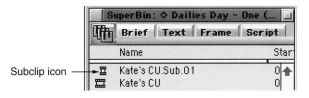

Subclip icon

Figure 3.8

During editing, subclips behave like clips.

DELETING SEQUENCES AND CLIPS

You can delete just about anything you've created. You do this by working in the bin. Say you wanted to delete a sequence. Just click on the sequence icon and press the Delete key on the keyboard. Because you don't want to accidentally delete something important, the Avid will immediately bring up a dialog box—kind of an "Are you sure?" prompt just like the one in Figure 3.9. The dialog box provides a list of things you can delete. If you have selected a sequence, the sequence button is checked. Click OK.

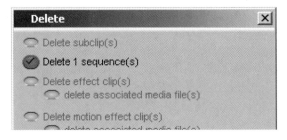

Figure 3.9   Deleting a sequence.

You'll probably delete a lot of sequences in the course of your work. Let's face it—not everything is worth saving. But, think twice before you delete a master clip. Remember that a master clip is "the" shot. It's your footage or sound. It has two parts: the master clip itself, which contains all the timecode information, and the media file, which is the captured material on the hard drive.

Figure 3.10   Deleting a master clip.

If you have selected a master clip for deleting, the buttons will not be checked. You have to click inside the button to check off your choice. You can delete either the master clip or the media file(s), or both. This is an important decision! Let's look at why we might want to delete any part of a master clip.

Let's say you select a clip in one of your bins and press the Delete key. Figure 3.10 shows the dialog box that appears. Here are your choices:

1.   If you want to get rid of the shot because it's worthless, you will never use it, and you want to permanently remove it, then check *both* boxes: *Delete master clip(s)*, and *delete associated media file(s)*. The clip and its

media file are deleted. Yes, the footage still exists on your source tape, but the Avid doesn't know anything about it.

2. If you are running out of storage space and you need to make room for other material, delete the associated media file but not the master clip itself. In this case, click *only* the box *delete associated media file(s)*. The actual footage gets erased from the media drives but all the information about the clip, including editing choices about the shot, remain with the Avid. If you used the shot in a sequence, all that information is still there. Whenever you look for that clip you will find it in the bin, but a "Media Offline" tag will appear in Frame View. To get your clip back, you'll need to recapture it. The neat thing about the Avid is that once you recapture that clip, not only is it restored in the bin but it will also reappear everywhere that it has been cut into a sequence.

3. The third choice isn't a choice at all. You'd almost *never* want to check the *Delete the master clip* by itself. If you did, you would be using up space on your hard drive to store material you can't use because the Avid can't find it.

GETTING FOLDERS

If you're editing a large project involving scores of tapes, you may find the need to store bins in folders so the Project window isn't an unruly mess. On the left-hand side of the Project window you'll see the Bin Fast menu. Pull it down, and you'll see a list of commands. Just select New Folder from the Fast menu, and when it appears in the Project window, name it and drag into it the various bins you want it to hold (Figure 3.11).

Bin Fast menu

Creates a folder to store bins

Figure 3.11

We've examined the Bin and the Bin menu in considerable detail because it's at the heart of nearly everything you do with your clips. The other important part of the Project window has to do with Settings.

SETTINGS: HAVE IT YOUR WAY

The folks from Tewksbury, Massachusetts (Avid's Headquarters), have created an editing system that you can configure and rearrange in so many different ways that it's mind-boggling. Some critics say there are too many choices and too many ways of doing the same thing and that all those choices have turned what was supposed to be an intuitive and fun-to-use editing machine into anything but. I can understand where the critics are coming from. This is mature software, in computer life cycles, and it has gone through many changes. While the Avid has gained lots of features along the way, it hasn't lost many, and, as any kid knows, if you keep adding blocks to your tower, it can grow out of control.

Because this book is primarily for beginning users, I'm only showing you what I think you need to know in order to create outstanding films or videos. If I included every trick or feature, you could be overwhelmed. The Settings window is one area where you can easily feel swamped. Still, setting the Avid up to suit your editing style is one of Avid's best features.

Let's examine a few of the ways the Avid can be set up. We'll explore this in greater detail later in the book, but for now, we'll just get our feet wet.

Figure 3.12

User Profile

If you go to the top of the Project window and click on the Settings button (Figure 3.12), the Settings window appears.

In the Project window there is a pull-down menu listing all the different users (Figure 3.13) on the computer. You'll probably see your name at the top of the list. Up until now, you've been using the default settings. As you begin to select your own settings, under your name, those settings will stay with you every time you open the project under your name. You can even create several different user profiles. You might, for example, want the Avid to have a certain look for client screenings that is different from the look it has when you're engaged in heavy-duty editing. Any changes to the way the Avid is set up will be saved under Client Screenings.

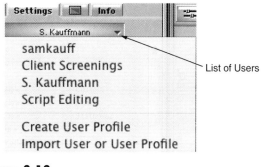

List of Users

Figure 3.13

To create a new user profile, simply choose Create User Profile, type a name, and click OK. Now go to the pull-down menu whenever you want to select a different profile.

Kinds of Settings

On the left of the Settings window you'll see a Fast menu, which lists the setting options: Active Settings, All Settings, and Base Settings. For now, select All Settings.

Beneath the Settings window you'll see the main scroll list. If you want to see more of the list, drag the size box or scroll down the long list of settings.

Almost every feature on the Avid can be altered to suit your preference. The scroll list shows you the Avid features you can change. To make changes, double-click on the setting whose parameters you want to change, and a dialog box with a number of choices or options will open. Simply type in the changes, or check a box and click OK.

We are not going to go through each item on this scroll window, because we don't need them all yet. We'll get to other settings later in the book. As you become more familiar with your Avid, I recommend that you go through all the items. By then you'll be able to make informed choices. For now, let's open up some of the items that are the most useful at this stage in the learning process.

Double-click on the bin name to see the options.

Figure 3.14

Bin Settings

When you double-click on "Bin" in the Settings list, the dialog box shown in Figure 3.15 opens. These choices provide you with options for backing up and saving your work.

Your work is important, and any bugs or glitches that suddenly crash the system and wipe away your morning's work could be upsetting. To avoid such a calamity, the Avid has an Auto-Save feature. You determine at what time interval the Auto-Save kicks in. As you can see, 15 minutes is the default setting. I prefer 10 minutes, so I type in 10. There is also a feature called Inactivity period;

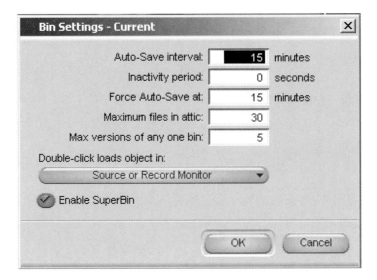

Figure 3.15

the Avid will wait before it saves if you are really editing like crazy. Genius should not be interrupted. Change it to 10 seconds, and it will wait until you've paused in your work for 10 seconds before beginning the auto-save. But, what happens if you never pause that long? That's where Force Auto-Save comes in. It will interrupt you to force a save no matter what you are doing.

You can always save manually. Remember, Command–S (Mac) or Ctrl–S (Windows).

The *attic* is appropriately named. It's a place on the computer's internal drive where the old versions of your bins are stored. The Avid sends your work to the attic whenever you, or it, executes a save. The attic stores a certain number of files, and when that number is reached, the attic begins discarding the oldest in favor of the newest. That's what the last two choices are about. We'll go into more detail about the attic later.

The pull-down menu item "Double-click loads object in," gives you the choice of loading clips and sequences directly into the Source or Record Monitor (default) or opening them as Pop-Up Monitors. Make sure "Source or Record Monitor" is selected.

Here is where the "Enable SuperBin" choice can be found. If you're working with a single computer monitor, then you'll probably want to check this button. If you have two monitors, then you might want to deselect this. Remember, you can always come back and change the setting.

Interface

Double-click on the Appearance Setting, and a dialog box, like the one in Figure 3.16, opens. One setting I like to select is the "Automatically Launch Last Project at Startup." This saves time if you're working on only one project and you don't want to be bothered having to pick from the choices when you launch the Avid software. Click on the button to make it happen.

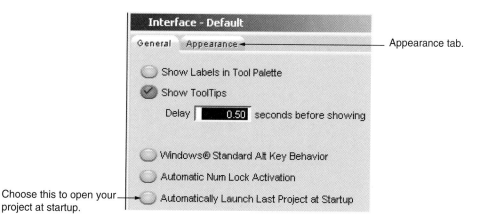

Figure 3.16

If you're not happy with the way your computer screen looks, click on the appearance tab and you'll see that you can change every aspect of the Avid's interface, from the shape of the buttons to the color of the bins.

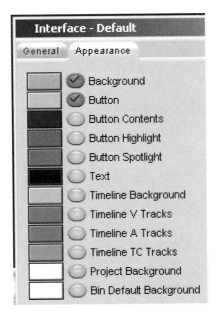

Figure 3.17

You can go wild with all these settings. Personally, I don't want too many bright colors staring me in the face late at night or early in the morning, but have it your way. You can always go back and change them again.

Keyboard Settings

All Avid keyboards are mappable. You can change every single key. Not only can you place any of a hundred different commands on any key, but you can also place items found in any of the pull-down menus onto keyboard keys.

   Let's make some changes. First, though, we're going to make a duplicate of the Default settings and then make changes to the duplicate rather than the Default:

1. Click on the Keyboard Setting so it's highlighted.
2. Press Command–D (Mac) or Ctrl–D (Windows).

3. Click on the space just to the right of the name and in the box type "Default" in one and "Mine" in the other.

Figure 3.18

4. Now, double-click on "Keyboard" (Mine) to open it. A picture of the keyboard opens. Now go to the Tools menu and select the Command Palette (Figure 3.19).

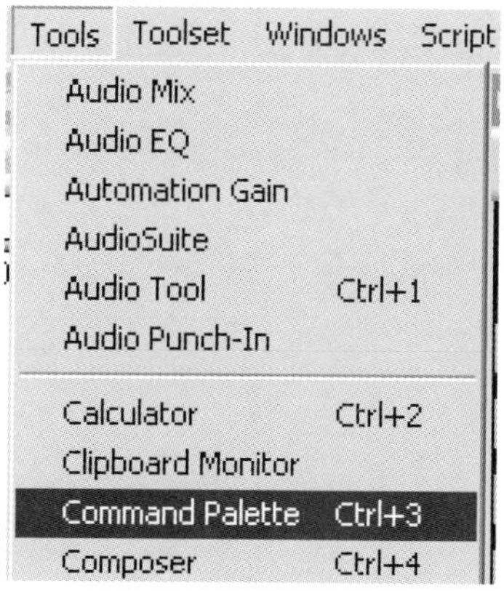

Figure 3.19

You'll see that all the command buttons have been organized according to their function and are accessible by clicking on one of tabs. In Figure 3.20, I have opened the Other Command Palette by simply clicking on the Other tab. Explore the different tabs. At the end of this chapter, as a handy reference, I have included a screen capture for all ten tabs found on the Xpress Pro. The Xpress DV has fewer tabs.

Row of tabs

Figure 3.20

What I'm about to propose may seem heretical, but instead of adding commands to the keyboard, the first thing I'm going to ask you to do is to remove commands from the keyboard. I'm a firm believer in J–K–L play. I want you to place three fingers of your left hand on the keyboard and use those keys to play, as well as to mark IN and OUT with the I and O keys. Well, it sometimes happens that your fingers land on the wrong keys. Two keys just to the right of the J–K–L keys can be particularly troublesome. These are the Segment Mode keys, and although we'll use them a lot later on, for now they can cause problems if you press them by accident.

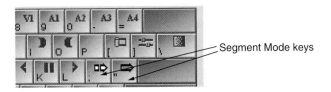

Segment Mode keys

So, to prevent an accident, we're going to remove them. Go to the Other tab in the Command Palette and look for the blank button.

Blank

To replace a keyboard key, make sure the radio button next to "Button to Button" Reassignment is red (Figure 3.20). Now simply drag the blank button on top of the yellow arrow key and release—it's gone. Now repeat this process and put the blank button on top of the Red arrow key, so the result looks like Figure 3.21.

The Segment Mode keys are gone.

Figure 3.21

The changes won't take effect until you close the Keyboard window. See? That was easy. Let's try another.

Go to the "More" tab. Drag the top Add Locator button (it's red) to the F5 key. You won't need this yet, but we'll use it in Chapter 13.

Resist making any more changes just yet. Let's wait until you're more familiar with all the commands and can decide which ones you use most frequently.

By the way, the Command Palette works like a giant Fast menu. You can open it from the Tools menu, click on a tab, and then click on the Active Palette radio button. Now press any command, and it is executed.

Let's go back to the Project window. Notice the Keyboard Setting "Mine" has the checkmark. If at any time you want to go back to the Default keyboard, just click the mouse in the area just left of the name.

Click here to activate a setting.

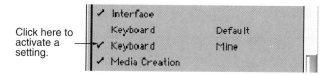

Changing Command Buttons

The Avid lets you change any of the command buttons on the computer monitor. The process is basically the same as changing the keyboard commands. You go to the Command Palette in the Tools menu, and then you drag commands to the buttons you want to change or replace. Look at the buttons on the tool bar beneath the Record Monitor.

I propose we make just one change now (and as many as you want later). We're going to replace the Mark Clip button that is on the Record Monitor tool bar and put in its place a command called Match Frame. The Mark Clip button is already on the keyboard (the T key) and on the Timeline, so we don't need this one as well. Open the Command Palette and go to the Other tab. Look for Match Frame. Drag it on top of the Mark Clip button (Figure 3.22).

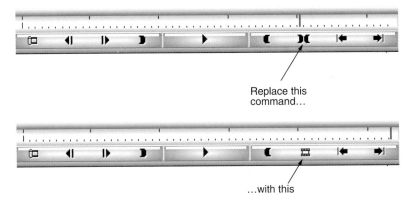

Replace this command…

…with this

Figure 3.22

We'll learn about the Match Frame command in Chapter 9, but, trust me, it's a useful key to have in front of you.

Wait until you're further along in this book before you map more command buttons. By then you'll have a better idea of which commands you like on the keyboard, which ones you like on the tool bars, and which ones you'd rather click with the mouse.

SUGGESTED ASSIGNMENTS

1. Create a new bin. Name it.
2. Duplicate your sequence. Change the name of the duplicate version to today's date.
3. Place this version of your sequence in the new bin.
4. Examine your clips in Frame View, Brief View, Text View, and Script View.
5. Delete the duplicated version of the sequence you just made.
6. Open the Headings list and change your headings.
7. In Text View, move the columns around.
8. Sort the columns using various headings.
9. Reverse the selections.
10. Open a clip and make a subclip of a portion of it.
11. Open the Settings window. Scroll through the list and examine various settings.
12. Duplicate the Keyboard Setting and name it.
13. Use the blank button to remove the Segment Mode keys.

COMMAND PALETTE COMMANDS

4

Trimming

Whenever I'm teaching a class on editing, one of the questions students often ask me is, "How do you know how long to hold a shot?" The first time I was asked that question I gave the worst possible answer. I said, "I don't know. (beat) You just know."

I've given the question a bit more thought since then. Sometimes it's obvious how long to hold a shot. If the shot is of a specific action, you've got to hold the shot until the action is finished. For example, if someone is putting a cake into an oven, you don't want to cut before the cake is safely on the cooking rack. But everyone knows that. The ones that are tricky involve the length of a cutaway, or the how long to hold on a person who is talking, or how long to hold a static shot or a reaction shot. My students know there is no one answer, just as they know there are no rules. What they are really asking is: How do you learn timing?

The answer is to learn to really *watch*. You make the cut the way you think it should be, and then you watch it. And you watch it again, and you pay attention to the timing. Is the cut too fast? Too slow? Confusing? Does it increase the energy of the scene or drag it down? You try adding and shortening the shot, until it's just right.

This is where digital editing machines, and especially the Avid, are light years ahead of analog systems. The Avid has a special feature called *Trim Mode*. In Trim Mode you can quickly and easily lengthen or shorten the shots in your sequence. This is the tool that has made the Avid famous, and it's the main reason an Avid will make you a better editor. Not only is it easier to shorten or lengthen shots, but you can also make those changes while you are watching! Remember, the key to being a good editor is having the ability to really watch. In Trim Mode, you can cut and watch at the same time. Sounds incredible, and it is.

TRIM MODE

Most of your editing with the Avid takes place in the Timeline, and that's particularly true of Trim Mode. Trim Mode takes place at the transitions. Some editors call them *edit points*. On the Timeline, these are the lines that show where one shot ends and the next shot begins.

GETTING INTO TRIM MODE

To enter Trim Mode, click the cursor near the cut point, or transition, you want to work on and then click the Trim Mode key on the keyboard. Because it is so useful, the Trim Mode command is also located on the Timeline toolbar.

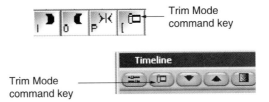

Figure 4.1   The Trim Mode command.

To help explain what happens when trimming, editors talk about the A-side and B-side of the transition. The A-side is the outgoing shot, and the B-side is the incoming shot. Because we have a sequence involving two actors, we will place Kate's CU on the A-side and Tim's CU on the B-side so you'll be sure of what you're looking at in Figures 4.2 and 4.3.

When you press the Trim Mode command, two things happen. First, the Composer monitor changes to a split screen, and you see a different set of tools appear in the tool bar. You see the last frame of the A-side (Kate's CU) and the first frame of the B-side (Tim's CU). Second, you will see colored rollers appear on either side of the cut point in the Timeline. You are seeing the Trim Mode display.

Lassoing the Transition

There's a faster way to enter Trim Mode: Click the mouse pointer in the gray area above the tracks and to the left of the transition you want to work on. Drag down, left to right, encircling the transition, including all the tracks, and let go (Figure 4.4). You are instantly in Trim Mode. Lassoing the transition is the fastest method, because you don't need to select the tracks. It's the method you should practice most often.

A-side. This is the last frame of this segment, often called the Tail.
B-side. This is the first frame of this segment, often called the Head.
Composer

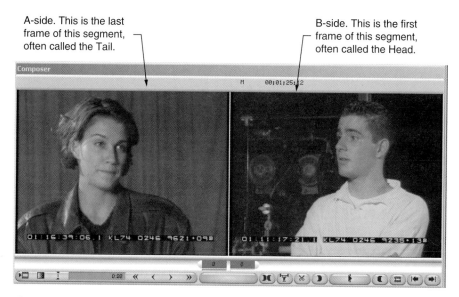

Figure 4.2 Trim Mode display.

Kate's CU
Tim's CU 1
Kate's CU
Tim's CU 1
20;02
00;01;30;02

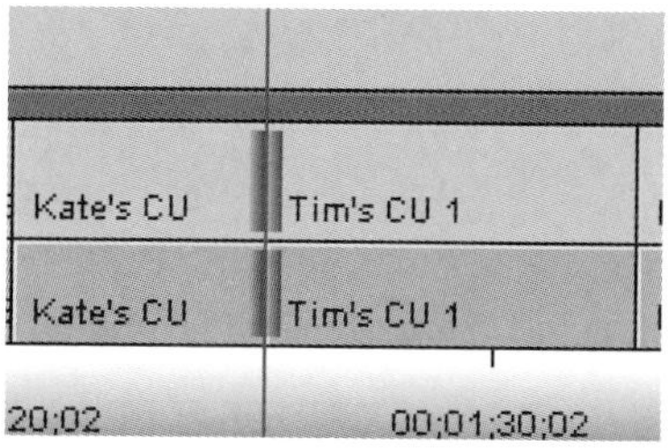

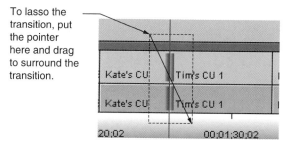

Figure 4.3 Rollers appear on either side of the transition point for all selected tracks.

To lasso the transition, put the pointer here and drag to surround the transition.
Kate's CU
Tim's CU 1
Kate's CU
Tim's CU 1
20;02
00;01;30;02

Figure 4.4

You can put the cursor above and to the right of the transition and lasso right to left. Left-handed editors may prefer this.

Be careful that you don't lasso an entire clip. If you do, you'll enter Segment Mode (see Chapter 9) and the entire clip will be highlighted. The Avid behaves quite differently in Segment Mode. If you inadvertently enter Segment Mode, click on whichever Segment button is highlighted at the bottom of the Timeline (Figure 4.5). You'll be back in Edit Mode. Now, try lassoing just the transition.

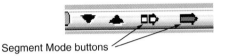

Segment Mode buttons

Figure 4.5

Now that you know how to get into Trim Mode, you need to be able to get out of Trim Mode.

LEAVING TRIM MODE

Any one of these methods will take you out of Trim Mode:

- Press either one of the step-one-frame buttons (the left and right arrow keys).

- Press the Trim Mode button again.
- Click the mouse in the timecode track (TC1) at the bottom of the Timeline.

Click anywhere in the Timecode track, and you will leave Trim Mode. The position indicator will jump to the spot you clicked.

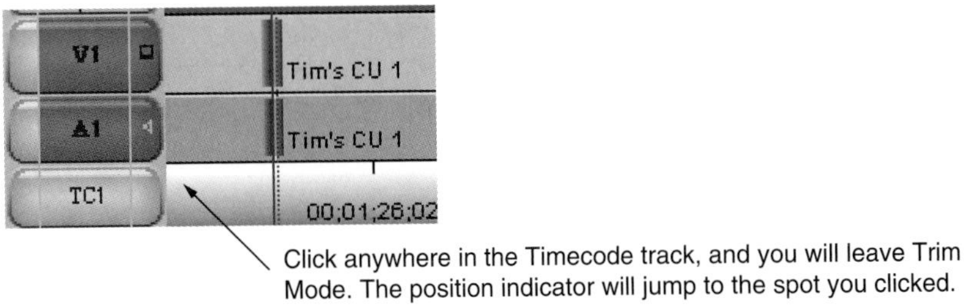

I prefer to click on the timecode track to get out of Trim Mode. I usually click to the left of the transition. That way the position indicator jumps to the spot where I clicked, and I'm ready to watch the transition I just trimmed.

There are two kinds of Trims: Dual-Roller Trim and Single-Roller Trim.

DUAL-ROLLER TRIM MODE

Dual-Roller Trim is the default Trim Mode. When you press the Trim button or lasso a transition, you go into this mode. In Dual-Roller Trim Mode:

- The overall length of your sequence remains the same.
- You can lengthen the A-side while shortening the B-side.
- You can shorten the A-side while lengthening the B-side.

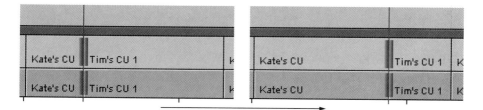

As you can see from the two screen captures, Kate's CU has been lengthened, while Tim's CU has been trimmed. If Kate's CU was lengthened by 40 frames, Tim's CU would be shortened by 40 frames.

Trim Frame Keys: If you look at Figure 4.6, you'll see a number of Trim Frame keys. The <, > keys are single-frame trim keys. They will trim the shot by one frame. The ≪, ≫ keys will trim the shot by ten frames.

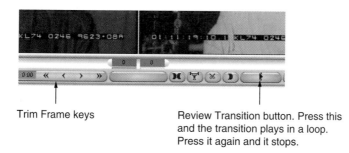

Trim Frame keys

Review Transition button. Press this and the transition plays in a loop. Press it again and it stops.

Figure 4.6 Trim Frame keys.

Let's look at a specific cut and see what happens as we Dual-Roller Trim. Here Kate is finishing her dialog, and Tim is beginning to say his dialog.

Kate's CU	Tim's CU 1
Kate's CU	Tim's CU 1

- If you press the > key once, you are adding one frame to the tail of Kate's CU and taking one frame off the head of Tim's CU.
- If you press the > key five times, you will add five frames to the tail of Kate's CU and take five frames off the head of Tim's CU.
- If you click the < key, you will trim Kate's CU by one frame and lengthen Tim's CU by one frame.
- The ≪, ≫ keys add or trim in increments of ten frames.
- The boxes above the trim keys keep track of the frames you have moved.

Review Transition Button: After you have trimmed in either direction, press the Play Loop button (Figure 4.6), and you'll see how the scene looks with the new transition points. This button will review the scene as you just cut it, in a continuous playback loop. Press the button again, and you'll stop the loop and return to the Trim Mode display.

Trim by Dragging: You don't need to click on the trim keys at all. Once you are in Trim Mode, you can simply click on the rollers at the transition point and drag the rollers to the left or right. Try it. It's not as precise as clicking the Trim keys, but it really gives you a sense of how the rollers work. If you drag the rollers so far that you reach the end of the shot, you'll hear a beep and see a small red marker in the frame to indicate that you can't roll any further because there are no more frames to extend.

SINGLE-ROLLER TRIM MODE

This is the Trim Mode that you will use most often, but because Dual-Roller Trim is the default mode we started there. To sum up Single-Roller Trim Mode and compare it to Dual-Roller Trim Mode:

- The overall length of your sequence *will* change.
- You can lengthen or shorten the A-side.
- You can lengthen or shorten the B-side.

Let's work with Single-Roller Trim Mode.

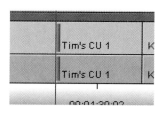

Figure 4.7

As you can see in Figure 4.7, when you enter Single-Roller Trim Mode, there is only one roller, and it falls on one side of the transition point. Here we are working on the B-side, the head of Tim's CU.

Getting into Single-Roller Trim Mode: You enter Single-Roller Trim Mode the same way you enter Dual-Roller Trim Mode:

1. Click the Trim button or lasso the transition, and you are now in Dual-Roller Trim Mode.
2. Place your mouse in the Trim Mode display and click on the A-side picture (left). The rollers move to the A-side in the Timeline.
3. Place your mouse in the Trim Mode display and click on the B-side picture (right). The rollers move to the B-side in the Timeline.

We clicked on Tim's picture in the Trim Mode display (Figure 4.8), and the rollers jumped to his side of the transition.

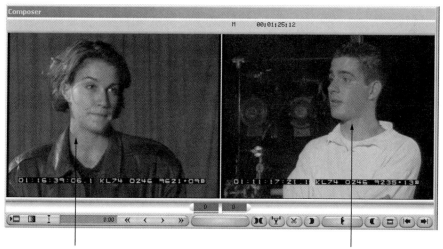

Click anywhere in here to enter Single-Roller Trim on the A-side.

Click anywhere in here to enter Single-Roller Trim on the B-side.

Figure 4.8

Now, if we drag the roller to the left, we will be making Tim's shot longer. If we drag the roller to the right, we will be making Tim's shot shorter.

In Figure 4.9 you can see that we have lengthened Tim's shot by moving the rollers to the left. We moved Tim's rollers by clicking on one of his rollers and dragging it to the left, or we could have clicked on the Trim Frame keys (≪, <).

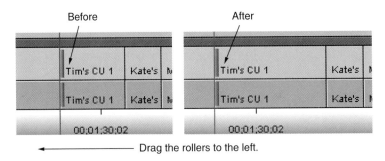

Figure 4.9

Now, let's examine the Trim Frame keys while looking at Figure 4.9:

- The ≪ and < keys will make Tim's shot longer.
- The > and ≫ keys will make Tim's shot shorter.

It took me a while to figure out how the Trim Frame keys worked with single-roller trims. Remember, when you're in Single-Roller Trim Mode, all the Trim Frame keys affect just one side—in this case, the B-side (Tim's).

If we now click on Kate's picture in the Trim Mode display, the rollers will jump to the A-side. All the Trim Frame keys now affect Kate's shot.

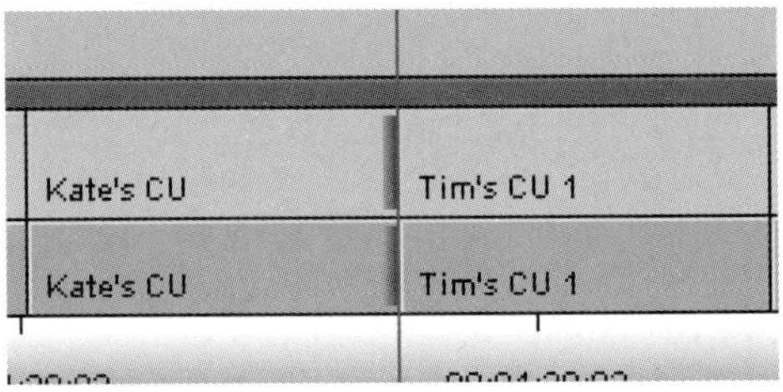

Figure 4.10

Look at the Trim Frame keys as you look at Figure 4.10:

- The ≪ and < keys will make Kate's shot shorter.
- The > and ≫ keys will make Kate's shot longer.

Examine Figures 4.9 and 4.10 closely and review the explanations that go with them. You must understand the relationship between the direction the rollers travel and the effect that has on a shot's length before you go any further.

TRIM PRACTICE

Let's look at a specific cut and see what happens as we Single-Roller Trim. In Figure 4.10, Kate is finishing her dialog and Tim is beginning to say his dialog. Let's say you are working on the part of the scene where Kate asks Tim for her letters.

> KATE:
> Where are they?
> TIM:
> I guess they're not here.

Imagine that when you spliced it in, you cut Kate too soon—she doesn't quite get her last word out before you cut to Tim. The tail of her shot needs to be lengthened by about 12 frames. In Single-Roller Trim Mode, it's easy.

To get into Trim Mode:

1. Go to the transition.
2. Lasso the transition point, including all of the audio track, *or* press the Trim Mode key.
3. Click the cursor on Kate's image—the rollers jump to the left of the transition.
4. Click *once* on the trim-by-ten-frames key (≫), and you'll be adding ten frames to the end of Kate's shot.
5. Press the Review Transition button. Now, watching the cut, you see that Kate finishes her line, but it needs a bit more.
6. Press the Review Transition button to get it to stop. Click *twice* on the trim-by-one-frame key (>) to add two frames to her segment.
7. Press the Review Transition button. Now, watching the cut, you see it's perfect. You have added 12 frames.
8. Press the Review Transition button to get it to stop.

To get out of Trim Mode do one of the following:

- Click the mouse in the timecode track (TC1) at the bottom of the Timeline.
- Press the Trim Mode button again.
- Press either one of the step-one-frame buttons.

UNDO IN TRIM MODE

You can undo and redo work in Trim Mode. For instance, if you click the > key and you want to get back to zero, just press Command–Z (Mac) or Ctrl–Z (Windows). If you made several trims, keep pressing Undo until you're back where you started.

FRAME COUNTERS

The frame counters in the Trim Mode Display show you how many frames you have added or subtracted to the segment. If you press the trim keys that point left (≪, <), the numbers will be minus. If you press the trim keys pointing right (>, ≫), they will be positive numbers.

Press these keys and the numbers are negative.

Press these keys and the numbers are positive.

MORE PRACTICE

Before you learned how to use Trim Mode, you used splice and overwrite to lay down the shots, leaving them long to begin with. If you wanted to shorten a shot, you marked an IN and an OUT in the Timeline and used Extract to shorten the shot. If you wanted to lengthen the shot, you spliced in more. Now that you have Trim Mode at your disposal, the way you edit changes significantly. If you see that a shot in the Timeline is too short or too long, it's easy to trim it to just the right length.

Let's say you are playing your sequence, and you see that the tail of Kate's shot is much too long. When you spliced it in, you marked it at the wrong point, and you've got her standing around when you want to see Tim. You need to shorten the shot.

Action	Result
Go to the transition and lasso it.	You're in Trim Mode.
Click on Kate's picture in the Trim Display.	You're in Single-Roller Trim Mode.
Click the ≪ Trim key.	You've shortened Kate's shot by ten frames.
Click on the Review Transition button.	The new cut point plays in a loop.

As you watch it, you see that trimming ten frames wasn't quite enough.

Action	Result
Click on the Review Transition button.	The looping stops.
Click on the < button three times.	You've trimmed three more frames (13 total).
Click on the Review Transition button.	The new cut point plays in a loop.

When you watch it, you see the new transition point works. Now you want to get out of Trim Mode.

Action	Result
Click on the Review Transition button.	The looping stops.
Click in the timecode track.	You're out of Trim Mode.

Changing from Single-Roller to Dual-Roller Trim Mode

If you're in Single-Roller Trim Mode and you want to be in Dual-Roller Trim Mode, simply move the mouse to the Trim Mode display and click on the line *between* the outgoing and incoming frames. You don't have to click exactly on the line. A bit on either side will work.

Adding and Removing Rollers

Once in Trim Mode, you sometimes want to add a roller or remove a roller so you're working with some tracks and not others. If you get into Trim Mode and notice that one or more of your tracks don't have rollers, it's probably because the Track Selector box wasn't selected. To add rollers to that track, simply click on the track selector. Deselecting A1 will remove a roller on that track as well.

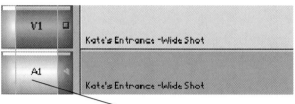

Click here to add a roller to A1

Another quick way to add or delete rollers is to hold down the Shift key while clicking on the transition point you want to change (Figure 4.11).

- Shift-click on a roller to remove it.
- Shift-click on a transition to add a roller.

Shift-click on this spot to add a roller.

Figure 4.11

ADVANCED TRIM MODE TECHNIQUES

Assuming that you are comfortable with trimming as explained in this chapter, and you want to work even faster and with more precision, let's look at a couple of advanced techniques.

Trimming While Watching

We have talked about the important role that watching plays in every phase of editing. There's a very simple technique that involves trimming a cut while watching it. Instead of using the trim keys in the Trim Mode display, you will be using the trim keys that are on the keyboard. Examine Figure 4.12. As you can see the keys on the keyboard are identical to the trim keys in the Trim Mode Display. What you're going to do is press Review Transition button, and as the transition point loops around you will press the trim keys on the keyboard with your fingers, while keeping your eyes on the screen. Watch and trim, watch and trim, until the shot works.

Figure 4.12

Let's try it.

1. Get into Trim Mode.
2. Choose a side that you want to work on, either the A-side or the B-side.
3. Press the Review Transition button.
4. While the transition is looping, hit the keyboard trim frame keys (≪, <, >, or ≫).

When you're just starting this exercise, you'll want to hit the trim-by-ten-frames keys (≫ or ≪) so you can see a big change. What happens is that the Avid makes the trim and then shows you what the new transition point looks like. You can keep hitting the trim keys until the cut looks right. You can go in either direction, depending on what works. Go ahead and try this.

For example, let's say you are trying to fix the head of Tim's shot to give him just the right amount of pause before he speaks (Figure 4.13).

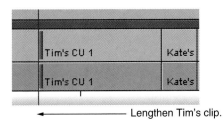

Figure 4.13

Say you press the Review Transition button and then click the ≪ key, lengthening his shot by ten frames. As the loop plays, you see it needs even more, so you press the ≪ key again. Now you like the length of the shot. When you press the Review Transition button to stop the loop, you'll still be in Trim Mode.

Look at the frame counter under Tim's frame in the Trim Mode display. It will display 20. You added a total of 20 frames to the head of Tim's shot. But notice that it is –20 (minus 20). Why? Whenever you go left the numbers are negative, even though you added to Tim's shot.

How many frames you add and remove doesn't really matter. What matters is that the shot is now working. And it's working because you trimmed and watched, trimmed and watched, trimmed and watched—until you got it right.

Trim One Side, Then the Other

It often happens that after you've finished cutting one side, it becomes apparent that the other side needs to be trimmed. Without leaving Trim Mode, simply click on the other frame in the Trim Mode display and the rollers will jump to the other side. Now press the Review Transition button and use the Trim Frame buttons to trim the other side.

If you want to shorten the tail of Kate's CU, you would press the ≪ or < button. Let's say the transition point was way too long to begin with. Kate finishes her line, and then she just stands there. Click the ≪ key three times, and you've trimmed 30 frames (a second) off Kate. You see that's too much. Click the ≫ once, and now you've put ten frames back on. You've now shortened her shot by 20 frames. You can fine-tune the cut by using the trim-by-one-frame keys (< and >) until the cut looks right. Say you decide to add two more frames (press > twice). Now you have shortened Kate's shot by 18 frames.

Figure 4.14

Now, without ever having left Trim Mode, you've worked on both sides of the transition, and the frame counters will show you what you've done. They would look like this:

Why? Because you trimmed Kate's side by 18 frames and you added to Tim's side by 20. They both are negative numbers because in both cases we dragged to the *left*—left to shorten Kate, and left to extend Tim.

Trim Settings

In Chapter 3 we learned about Settings. Both the Xpress and Media Composers give you the ability to shorten or lengthen the amount of time the loop takes whenever you press the Review Transition button. Go to the Settings window and double-click on Trim. A dialog box appears (see Figure 14.15).

The default length is 2 seconds of preroll (the A-side) and 2 seconds of postroll (the B-side), with no pause at the end of the loop (intermission). You can change this to whatever length works best for you. I like 2 seconds when I'm trimming picture and sound, but if I'm working on sound I like to hear the changes I've made with the Trim keys more quickly. So then I change the settings to 1 second for both preroll and postroll. I don't like an intermission, or pause, but if you'd like a second to gather your wits then type in 1 second and see if you like the pause.

Figure 4.15

Dragging to a Mark

Earlier we discussed dragging the rollers to extend or shorten a shot. By simply clicking on the rollers, you can drag them left or right. It's less precise than using the Trim Frame keys. However, if you combine dragging with placing an IN mark or an OUT mark, then dragging can be very efficient. Use this technique when you know where you want to go with the trim.

Before you go into Trim Mode, play your sequence. If you find a shot that needs trimming (or lengthening), you place an IN mark if it's to the left of the transition and an OUT mark if it's to the right of a transition. Now, enter Trim Mode. Hold down the Command key (Mac) or Ctrl key (Windows), and click and drag the roller to the mark. The Avid stops precisely on the mark.

In this case, I have quickly trimmed the head of this segment. This technique works with either Single-Roller or Dual-Roller Trim Mode.

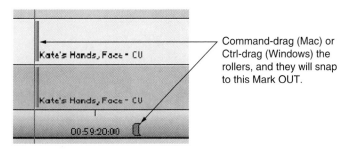

Figure 4.16

Picture and Sound Overlaps

Just about everyone knows what a straight cut looks like. When the picture and sound end at the same point, you have a straight cut. When you splice in the next shot, it too is a straight cut. So far, we've worked with straight cuts, but it often happens that the best place to cut the picture isn't necessarily the best place to cut the sound. When a picture and its sound are cut at different points, you have an overlap. Some editors call these overlaps *L-cuts*.

Let's say you have spliced two shots together, and you love the way the dialog flows from one person to the next. But you're not really happy with the picture cut point. You decide to create an overlap or L-cut. This is where Dual-Roller Trim Mode excels.

Let's say we have Kate finishing her line and Tim about to say his line. You decide to remove 30 frames of Kate's picture and replace it with 30 frames of Tim's picture. The sound stays where it is.

1. Enter Trim Mode by lassoing just the video track at the cut point. You are now in Trim Mode with the dual rollers on V1 but not on the sound track.
2. If you do get rollers on the sound track(s), remove them by clicking on the track selector box. They're removed.
3. Drag the rollers 30 frames to the left or press the trim-by-ten-frames key (≪) three times.
4. Press the Review Transition button to see how it works.

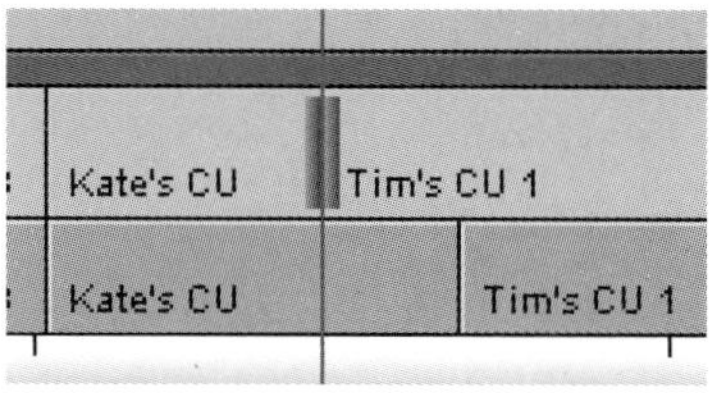

Figure 4.17

When the overlap is made, you have Kate talking, then before she finishes talking we see Tim listening to her words, and then Tim talks. Tim's picture has overlapped Kate's sound.

Here's another example: Say you have a three-shot sequence. First you have a shot of a woman sitting at her desk, telling a man she must leave to catch a plane. Then you have a medium shot of the woman putting papers in her brief-case. Then you cut to a shot of the woman walking through a busy airport. When you edited them, you used straight cuts. The pictures are cut perfectly, but you realize that the sequence of shots would have more power if we heard the sound of the airport come in over the shot of her packing up her briefcase.

How? Simple. What you'll want to do is to get into Dual-Roller Trim Mode, deselect the video track so the rollers are only on the sound track(s). Then drag the dual rollers on the sound track to the left. You'll be replacing some of her office sounds with the sound of the busy airport.

When the audience first hears the airport noises breaking into the shot of her in her quiet office, they may be momentarily confused, but that confusion creates a bit of suspense, which is quickly resolved when the picture of her walking through the airport comes onto the screen. Sound overlaps like this are used quite often to set up the next scene. How much should you overlap the sound? Try about 3 seconds of overlap, and then trim from there.

Removing an Overlap

After working on a transition and creating an overlap, you might decide that in fact a straight cut would work better. A quick way to turn an overlap back into a straight cut is to Command–drag (Mac) or Ctrl–drag (Windows).

1. Get into Trim Mode.
2. Select the track that has been overlapped and deselect the track that is already a straight cut.
3. Hold down the Command key (Mac) or Ctrl key (Windows) while you drag toward the straight cut. The trim will snap to the transition point.

A word of caution: You always want to create overlaps using Dual-Roller Trim. Because you are working with one track and not the other, Dual-Roller Trim Mode keeps everything in sync. If you use Single-Roller Trim and trim one track and not the other track, you will immediately go out of sync.

Creating overlaps is Dual-Roller Trim's main purpose. Use Single-Roller Trim for adjusting the length of your shots.

SYNC PROBLEMS IN SINGLE-ROLLER TRIM MODE

This is a good time to examine what happens when you use Single-Roller Trim Mode on one track and not on the other(s). In Figure 4.18, I went into Single-Roller Trim Mode, but by mistake only the video track was selected. The trim action affected only the picture. Without thinking, I trimmed anyway and dragged the roller to the left, thus I lengthened Tim's picture by ten frames. Because the audio was not trimmed, the clip went out of sync.

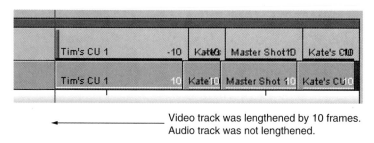

Video track was lengthened by 10 frames.
Audio track was not lengthened.

Figure 4.18

Tim's audio is ten frames shorter than his video. As you can see, anything downstream of this transition point will also be out of sync by ten frames. Kate's CU wasn't trimmed, but because Tim's is out of sync, her clip is thrown out as well. Remember, in order to keep the picture and sound in sync, you must cut the picture *and* sound at the same time. When you add picture, you must add sound.

To get back in sync, we must either trim ten frames off of Tim's picture, or add ten frames to Tim's audio. Let's add ten frames to Tim's audio.

When you're out of sync, you need to go into Single-Roller Trim Mode to fix the problem. Now, we need to click on the A1 track and deselect the V1 track. The single-roller will jump to trim Tim's audio. Remember, we want to lengthen his audio by ten frames. We can use one of several methods:

- We can hit the ≪ frame key once.
- We can drag the roller to the left and watch the frame counter until −10 appears.

ENTER TRIM MODE ON SELECTED TRACKS

It often happens that you want to enter Trim Mode on an audio track. Perhaps you want to create an L-cut (sound overlap) by trimming the audio track instead of the video track, but you can't lasso just the audio track without lassoing the video track as well. Yes, you can click on the Track Selector buttons to deselect the tracks where you don't want rollers, or you can Shift-click on the specific rollers you don't want, but all that's time consuming. There is an easy way to do this.

Hold down the Option key (Mac) or Alt key (Windows) and then lasso just the track(s) you want, and it works beautifully. Examine Figure 4.19. Here I'm lassoing not the video and audio tracks, but just the audio track. This won't work unless I *first* hold down the Option key (Mac) or Alt key (Windows). Press Option or Alt and *then* lasso the transition from the middle of the track above.

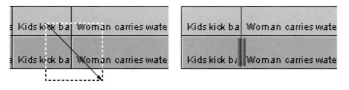

Figure 4.19

Now I can create a sound overlap by dragging the rollers either way. I stay in sync because I'm in Dual-Roller Trim Mode. Practice this. We'll use it often when working with multiple audio tracks, or when we have several video tracks in the Timeline.

J–K–L TRIMMING

Avid has an advanced Trim Mode that Final Cut and other editing software have copied, called J–K–L Trimming. I don't want you to get overwhelmed with information, so we'll wait until Chapter 9 to explain it—once you've mastered all these techniques.

TRIM MODE REVIEW

We've spent a lot of time discussing Trim Mode, devoting an entire chapter to its many advantages and features. Let's review some of the hows and whys of Trim Mode.

Getting into Trim Mode

- Lasso the transition.
- Click the cursor near the transition and press the Trim Mode key.

Getting out of Trim Mode

- Press the Trim Mode button again (Xpress).
- Press either one of the step-one-frame buttons.
- Click the mouse in the timecode track (TC1) at the bottom of the Timeline.

Switching Trim Modes

- To go from Dual-Roller Trim Mode to Single-Roller Trim Mode, click either the A-side or the B-side frame in the Trim Mode display.

- To go from Single-Roller Trim Mode to Dual-Roller Trim Mode, click the frame line between the A-side and B-side frames.

Add Rollers and Delete Rollers

- In Trim Mode, Shift-click on the transition side where you want to add a roller.
- If there is a roller you want to remove, Shift-click on it and it will be removed.

Drag the Rollers

- Click and drag the rollers left or right.
- Command–drag (Mac) or Ctrl–drag (Windows) to IN or OUT marks.
- Command–drag (Mac) or Ctrl–drag (Windows) to transition points.

Trim While Watching

1. In Trim Mode, press the Review Transition key to have the transition go into a loop.
2. Use the keyboard Trim Frame keys (≪, <, >, and ≫) to trim as you watch.

SUGGESTED ASSIGNMENTS

Although Trim Mode is a fantastic feature, it isn't always intuitive. Study this chapter and then practice, using all of the many techniques discussed.

1. Make a duplicate of your sequence and give it today's date.
2. Practice getting in and out of Trim Mode.
3. Practice Dual-Roller and Single-Roller trims, trimming and lengthening the A-side and the B-side and creating picture and sound overlaps.
4. Practice dragging the rollers.
5. Practice trimming while you watch, using the Trim Frame keys.
6. Practice adding and deleting rollers.
7. Using Trim Mode, create a fine cut, with sound overlaps where appropriate, of "Wanna Trade," or whatever assignment you have been editing to date.

5

A Few Editing Tips

You've been working on "Wanna Trade" for a while now and it's time to get some feedback. That means bringing in friends, classmates, and relatives—whoever you think can help you improve your scene by telling you how he or she honestly feels about your work. If you edited a different scene for your first project, it doesn't matter, because we'll be exploring the whole process of screening your work. But, before you subject yourself to all that honesty, let's go over a few editing pointers. These may seem obvious, but they have helped my students over some bumps, so perhaps they'll help you, too.

WHEN TO CUT

Everyone agrees that a cut brings energy to any film or video. By changing the angle of view or cutting to a new location, you are participating in the essence of filmmaking. Without editing, movies are no more than recorded plays. If you go to a theater to see a play, you buy your ticket and take your seat, and everything happens from that one vantage point—your seat. No matter what the action—a swordfight, a kiss, a verbal argument—you see it from the same distance and angle.

But what if you could change seats? If you could move to any seat in the theater to better see what is going on? You might go to the front row to see the kiss, and you might move up to the balcony to see the sweep of the swordfight, but if the lead actor gets stabbed and falls you might race back to the front row to hear his dying words and see the expression on his face.

As the editor, it's your job to give the audience the best seat in the house. Whatever the action, you pick the shot that gives the audience the best vantage point to see and hear what is going on. Establishing shot, long shot, medium shot, close-up, over-the-shoulder shot, reaction shot, master shot—these all describe what the camera is seeing. Don't worry about the names or following some half-baked rule about cutting from one to the other. Instead, look at the choices and decide where the audience would want to be in order to view that action, and once you've picked the best seat then cut to the next shot as soon as you feel the audience wants to change to a better seat.

CONTINUITY AND EYE TRACE

Most narrative films are shot using one camera. With all the lights, technicians, and sound equipment on a set or location, a second camera is useless because it would film the crew and equipment. So, instead of shooting with multiple cameras, the camera is moved, the crew and equipment are placed out of frame, and the action is repeated. The problem with this method is that there are often continuity problems. The actor holds the cup in his left hand in the long shot, but the cup is in his right hand in the medium shot. You want to cut from one shot to the other but that cup is making it hard. Perhaps the problem isn't as blatant as a cup in the wrong hand. More often it's the position of an arm, or the position of someone's head that changes on the cut. But, no matter what the problem, how do you, the editor, make such a cut when it's so blatantly awkward?

There are a couple of tricks. The easiest is to go to a cutaway; the audience forgets the continuity problem and you're home free. Unfortunately, this almost never works because that's not what the audience wants to see. That cutaway is not the best seat in the house. A better choice is to find movement and cut on it. Make the cut when the actor sits down or gestures with her arm. Then you'll be cutting on the action, rather than before or after the action. This will hide, or at least obscure, the continuity problem.

Eye trace is another important concept. The bigger the screen, the more our eyes are attracted to different parts of the screen. Where do we look when we watch a film?

- We look at the eyes and mouth of the person talking.
- We look at the part of the frame where there is movement and not where things remain still.
- We look at bright areas before dark ones.

Pay attention to where your eye goes as you watch a shot. Ask yourself, "What am I looking at when I cut to the next shot?" Examine your eye trace. If your eye is on the far right of the frame, and then when you cut there's not much there to look at, your eyes search the frame to find something of interest. Your eyes move around the frame to find a face, or movement, or brightness. If your eyes have to search the frame after you cut, that's not a smooth cut. Use this to your advantage. There are two approaches:

1. Cut so the viewer's eye moves the least. This makes the cut appear smooth and hides the continuity problem.
2. Hide the continuity problem by directing the audience's eyes to look at the part of the frame that is away from the problem.

SCREEN DIRECTION

Often good directors and their editors use screen direction to help tell a story. In Oliver Stone's Oscar-winning film *Platoon*, edited by Claire Simpson, there is a climatic scene in which Willem Defoe's character is murdered by Tom Berenger's character. This cold-blooded killing is wonderfully telegraphed by the screen direction of the two characters. Defoe is running from the left of the screen to the right (left to right) to battle Viet Cong soldiers, and for a while Berenger moves from screen left to right, as if he too is going to battle the enemy. But, suddenly he turns and begins moving from the right of the screen to the left (right to left), toward Defoe, setting up the final confrontation. Unfortunately, most directors and editors get hopelessly lost when dealing with screen direction, and the result is a lot of confusion for the audience.

Look at Figure 5.1 to get a better understanding of screen direction. In Figure 5.1a, Kate is on the left-hand side of the frame looking to the right. Another way to say this is that she is looking from screen left to screen right (left to right, or L–R). And in Figure 5.1b, Tim is looking screen right to left, or R–L.

Figure 5.1   (a) Screen L–R; (b) screen R–L.

Make sure you understand what I mean when I say someone is looking L–R (Kate) and R–L (Tim).

Now, the way Kate and Tim are looking makes sense. They are talking to each other and facing each other. The screen direction is correct. But, often, when new editors cut shots taken from various angles, they end up making it look as though one of the characters has turned around and is looking in the same direction as the person he or she is talking to. Examine Figures 5.2a and 5.2b. Kate is looking L–R and so is Tim. This is wrong and confuses the audience.

Figure 5.2   (a) Screen L–R; (b) screen L–R.

I realize this is an easy one. Everyone can see it's wrong, so let's examine a different scene that has more choices and examine what happens.

Figure 5.3   (a) Michele, L–R; (b) Peter, R–L.

In Figure 5.3a we have Michele looking left to right (L–R) and talking to Peter (Figure 5.3b), who is looking right to left (R–L). This is correct. They are looking at each other as they speak. But now, let's see what happens when Michele has to leave the room. She turns to exit toward screen right, as we see in Figure 5.4. Now, when we cut to Peter, watching her leave, we have a screen direction problem. We are cutting from Michele, looking from left to right, to Peter, who is also looking left to right. It's more subtle than Figures 5.2a and 5.2b but confusing just the same. Believe me, it looks even worse on screen.

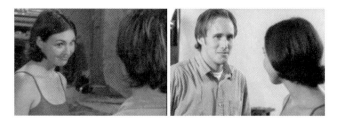

Figure 5.4   (a) and (b) Both Michele and Peter are looking left to right (L–R).

This sort of cut is also called *crossing the line* or *breaking the 180-degree rule*, but that's the language of camera operators and directors. For editors, it's called a problem, and our job is to fix it.

Don't cut Michele here. Using skills we mastered in Chapter 4, get into Trim Mode and jump the rollers onto the A-side (click on Michele) and extend her so she walks further to the right, cutting her just before she crosses in front of Peter—you are adding frames to the A-side. Now place the rollers on the B-side (click on Peter), and trim frames, cutting her until she is just about to walk in front of Peter. After trimming frames, we start this shot just as she crosses in front of him. Now the screen direction problem is much less noticeable. Remember to cut on motion whenever possible.

Examine Figures 5.1 to 5.4. Understand that nearly every shot involving people has screen direction. The person is either walking left to right or looking left to right (or walking right to left or looking right to left). Obviously, two people walking toward each other must have the opposite screen direction. When you cut from different angles and takes, make sure your actors don't suddenly share the same screen direction, as happened in Figure 5.4.

PACING

Pacing is crucial to effective editing, yet it is perhaps the most difficult skill to write about or to teach. But here goes. Let's start with a conversation between two people. The content of their conversation, together with the actor's delivery, determines the pacing. A talk between friends or an amiable exchange between people, where each person is listening to the other, would be slower paced and involve more pauses. Instead of cutting as soon as one person stops, you might want to let the dialog breathe by putting in pauses before each person talks; we can see them thinking or reacting, rather than delivering lines. An argument where two people aren't really listening to each other would be faster paced. You would have more cuts with few if any pauses between lines. At times, one person might cut in before the other person finishes.

Reaction shots and L-cuts are important components of any conversation. You don't want to always stay on Kate until she finishes her lines, and then cut to Tim, while he says all his lines—always on camera. It is often better to start that way, so the audience learns who is talking and gets a handle on their voices, but once the audience gets it you can depart from the talking-head approach and spice things up with reaction shots.

If Tim says something hurtful or ironic or funny, we want to see how Kate responds. True, the length of the cutaway depends in part on the reaction, but you would tend to want the reaction to be a bit longer during a normal conversation than during an argument or fight. You use the length and frequency of reaction shots to speed up or slow down the pace.

L-cuts (overlaps) are also useful. Instead of staying on the person who is talking, we use Dual-Roller Trim to change the video cut point. For example, you have a close-up of Kate talking, but instead of waiting to cut until after she stops you drag the rollers on V1 to the left (Figure 5.5), so Tim's face is seen while we hear Kate finish talking, and then Tim talks. An L-cut is like a reaction shot in that we watch Tim as he digests what Kate is saying, and then Tim responds.

Drag rollers left to make L-cut

Figure 5.5

Be careful that you don't overdo L-cuts, because they often make the scene go by too quickly. The brief pauses that you create by straight cutting from one person to the next—the moment when an actor waits to talk or thinks before speaking—those pauses often get lost when L-cutting. My students complain that their scenes sometimes behave like runaway trains—they go faster than they intended. The culprit is always the same—they've used too many L-cuts.

STORY STRUCTURE—BEGINNING, MIDDLE, AND END

Students often get confused when they hear screenwriters talk about three acts. What's in the first act? How long should it be? Why not six acts? It's not rocket science. *Every* story has three acts, including our lives. Everything has a beginning, a middle, and an end. And every film should, too—be it a narrative or documentary. Editors often lose sight of this as they grapple with hours of footage and thousands of choices, but whether you're working on an hour-long documentary with twelve sections or a feature film with forty scenes, everything should fit into the beginning, middle, or end. If it doesn't, you can probably cut it out. Go ahead, throw *Memento* or *Pulp Fiction* at me in rebuttal, but both started with a beginning, a middle, and an end—the writers simply scrambled them after the story was written.

Obviously, the intended length of the project determines how much goes into each section. And, speaking of length, too often filmmakers crafting their first projects think that longer is better. Yet festival judges, film curators, and busy agents greatly prefer short and tight. Fight to get your projects as short as possible. Be ruthless in cutting away nonessential material. Be willing to cut out every shot that doesn't carry its weight.

DOCUMENTARY ISSUES

Editing a documentary often means working with talking-head interviews or voice-over narration. With talking-head interviews, you often cut away from the subject's head to more interesting visual material. In television speak, that visual material is called *B-roll*. The subject talks about the stress of flying a helicopter, and then you cut to a shot of a helicopter making a dangerous maneuver.

If you have a lot of talking-head interviews, I suggest you get the producer to transcribe the audio so you have a written copy of everything the subjects say. It's so much faster to read through hours of interviews than it is to watch it all over and over again. I often photocopy the transcript and then do a paper edit so I can connect good material. I then watch the footage and see if the material is as interesting on tape as it was on paper. If it is, I cut the interview into the Timeline onto V1 and A1. Usually, I start with the talking-head on camera, put in a lower-third title identifying the person, and then go to visuals that amplify what she or he is talking about (Figure 5.6).

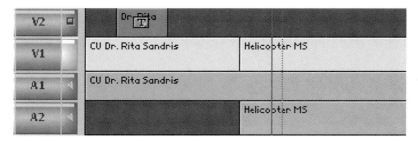

Figure 5.6

I overwrite the visual onto V1, replacing the talking head, and if the visual has natural sound, like a helicopter, I put that sound onto A2. We'll learn in Chapter 8 how to lower the volume of the helicopter so it does not detract from the subject's voice on A1.

Because I'm cutting to a visual—the helicopter—I can edit the subject's audio on A1 (as she is no longer on camera) and extract pauses, coughs, ums, and even extraneous parts. If the subject is saying something interesting or it has emotional content, I like to see the person saying it on camera. If it's strong on camera, I don't replace it with B-roll. With voice-over narration, you don't have a talking-head so it is all B-roll.

The problem many editors have is in choosing the B-roll material. Too often the visual they choose is identical to the narration. The narrator says, "It was a cloudy day" (we see clouds in the sky). "The wind blew the leaves along the ground" (we see leaves blow across the ground). This is called *Mickey-Mousing* (long story). You're repeating the information twice. Try to find footage that amplifies the narration so the audience gleans more information, rather than showing exactly what the narration describes. But, be careful you don't undercut the narration. If the narrator says, "We owe it to our children to give them a cleaner, less polluted world," don't show smokestacks billowing out pollution. That undercuts your narration. A shot of kids swimming in a mountain lake would work better.

SCREENING A WORK IN PROGRESS

Now we're ready to show our work. We've got a good cut, but we need some honest feedback. Most editors place a high value on screening their work while still editing it. Call it a rough cut or a fine cut screening—whatever name you give to it—it's a screening of your work in progress. You have spent a lot of time and energy cutting the material; you've given it your very best, but usually you have been working in a vacuum. What you're looking for now are fresh eyes and ears. You want an audience (it can be one or two people or a classroom full of fellow students) to tell you what's working and what isn't. Nothing teaches you more about your work than screening it in front of an audience. Sometimes screenings are painful, sometimes they are exhilarating, and always they are useful.

Being Your Own Projectionist

Before your audience arrives, get the screening room ready. Even if it's just a computer screen and two speakers, make sure everything is just right. Are the speakers on? Are they set at the right level? Are the sightlines good, or will someone have an obstructed view? What about the ambient light? Can you pull a shade to make it darker? If you close a window, will the traffic noise diminish?

You're going to have a lot of these screenings in your career, and you will need to wear a new hat—that of a professional projectionist. I've screened my films all over the world, and I've learned many painful lessons, the most important being that, if you want it to go smoothly, then you have to get deeply involved. You have to arrive at the theater early and do a sound check so the sound level is right. You have to check out the lighting to make sure the screen is uniformly bright. Sometimes, if the film is projected, you even have to correct the focus. Believe me, it's worth it. If you don't do it, it may work out fine 8 times out of 10, but chances are there will be that one screening when the sound is too low or the focus is soft and you'll kick yourself for not checking it out ahead of time.

Grilling Your Audience

Whenever possible, I like to start off small, with an audience of just a few people. I like to split my attention between the audience and the screen. Usually if something isn't working, I know it by feeling the attention (or lack of attention) the audience is giving to a particular section. After you've screened the footage, start your inquiry as wide as possible and then work toward the specific. Take notes! If the audience members aren't all that forthcoming, ask them questions. How did it work? Were you confused about what was going on? What emotion did it evoke? If it's a narrative piece, you might ask about the actors' performances. Which actor did they like best? Because you're working on a digital machine, you can quickly go to any section to review it. If your project is over ten minutes long, there's probably a lot to talk about in terms of structure, pacing, character development, and dramatic tension. With a scene as short as "Wanna Trade," you can probably move on to an analysis of specific editing problems. At this stage, you're trying to find places where your audience tripped over things that didn't work. If you're lucky, the audience will give you feedback that's right on the money:

Audience member: When Tim searches the desk, pretending to look for the letters, I didn't like the cut from the master shot to Tim's close-up.
You: Why not?
Audience member: I couldn't see what he was doing.

That's specific. Or someone might say that she thought a cut seemed awkward or an actor remained on the screen for too long before you cut to the next shot. More times than not, especially if your audience knows nothing about video or filmmaking, they won't tell you what tripped them because they honestly don't know. In those instances, you have to play detective to figure out what's going wrong. It's not easy, but it can be rewarding. I've often found that, when people who don't know much about editing say something doesn't work, the problem isn't always where they think it is; it's usually before that. If they can't tell you what is bothering them, but they feel a bit confused, I suggest you slow down the beginning. Make sure the audience is grounded at the start. Once they know who's doing what, then you can speed things up.

Whatever you do, don't argue with your audience. You might be the expert on the project you're cutting, but they're the experts on their feelings about it. If they criticize your work and point out shortcomings, it's human nature to be defensive. I've never met anyone who *liked* being criticized. But, if you argue with them, you're missing the point of the screening, which is to learn what is working and what isn't. You don't have to take any of their suggestions. If you think they're way off base, so be it. Toss out your notes and find another audience.

Sometimes you leave a screening embarrassed. The suggestions were so good you feel embarrassed that you didn't see the problems yourself. Other times you feel grateful because you identified a problem, know how to fix it, and can't wait to get back to work. Then there are the times when you realize there are lots of problems and it's depressing to think how far you have to go. Those are the days when, if possible, you take the afternoon off and go for a long walk. Once in a while, people will pat you on the back, shake your hand, and tell you it's brilliant, but unless you get raves from everyone you'll probably head back to work, fix the problems, and try to schedule another screening with another group with fresh eyes and ears.

Developing Thick Skin

This test screening process should be repeated at least three times for a short and twice as often for a feature. Yes, it can be painful, but it's much better to endure the pain now, when you can fix the problems, then later on, when it's out in the world and getting rejected by festivals or excoriated by the press. These sessions can be invaluable, if you take the criticism to heart. They can be a waste of time if you ignore what your teachers, friends, and loved ones have to say. Develop a thick skin now; learn to learn from these screenings. Soon, you'll get the applause you've earned and a chance to raise high your share of gilded trophies.

SUGGESTED ASSIGNMENTS

1. Hold a screening of your edited scene, taking notes of the various suggestions.
2. Duplicate the sequence.
3. Make changes to the new version of the sequence.
4. Compare your old version to the one that is based on the feedback you received.

6

Capturing

Now that we've finished cutting "Wanna Trade," it's time to move on to new material. It is my suggestion that you now work on documentary footage or even a public service announcement (PSA). Many of the techniques we will introduce in the next few chapters work nicely with visual footage and narration. A script-based, dramatic scene with sync dialog, like "Wanna Trade," is great for introducing you to the Avid basics, but as we move on to more complex tools, documentary or visual material is best for showing off these features.

STARTING A NEW PROJECT

When you double click on the Xpress icon, you are launching the Avid software. Soon the Avid brings up a dialog box that asks you to let the Avid know which project you will be editing (Figure 6.1). The left-hand column lists all the projects that are currently in postproduction on this machine.

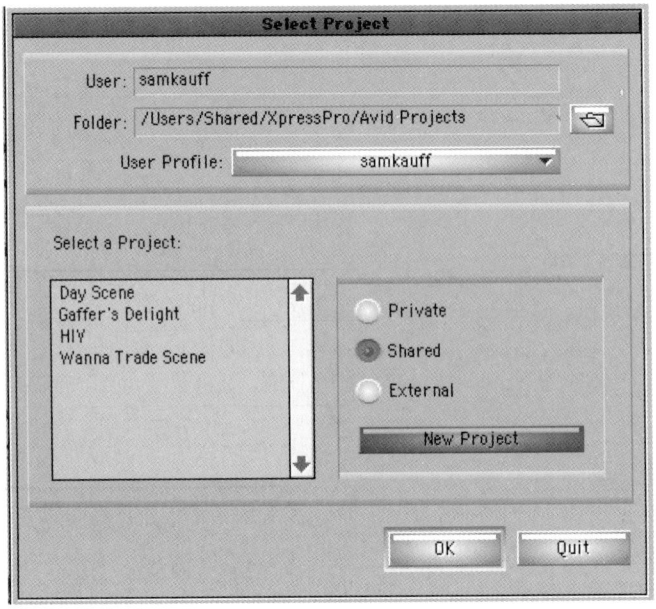

Figure 6.1   Select a Project dialog box.

If you are going to start a new project, one that the Avid has never dealt with before, you must first decide if you want to restrict access to your project (Private) or if you want others to be able to work on it. Shared and External permit anyone who has access to the computer to open it. Select External if all the information about the project will be stored on an external drive or shared storage.

After you've made that decision, press the New Project button. A dialog box appears. First, give a name to your project by typing it into the Project Name box. The name is often the title or working title of the video or film. Next go to the Format pull-down menu (Figure 6.2) and choose from the list of formats the one that is correct for you. Xpress DV users will have fewer choices than Xpress Pro or Pro HD users. Let's first look at the choices appropriate for standard definition projects—not high-definition (HD) projects. If you're starting a project that was shot in high definition, or HDV, please go to Chapter 16 and then return here.

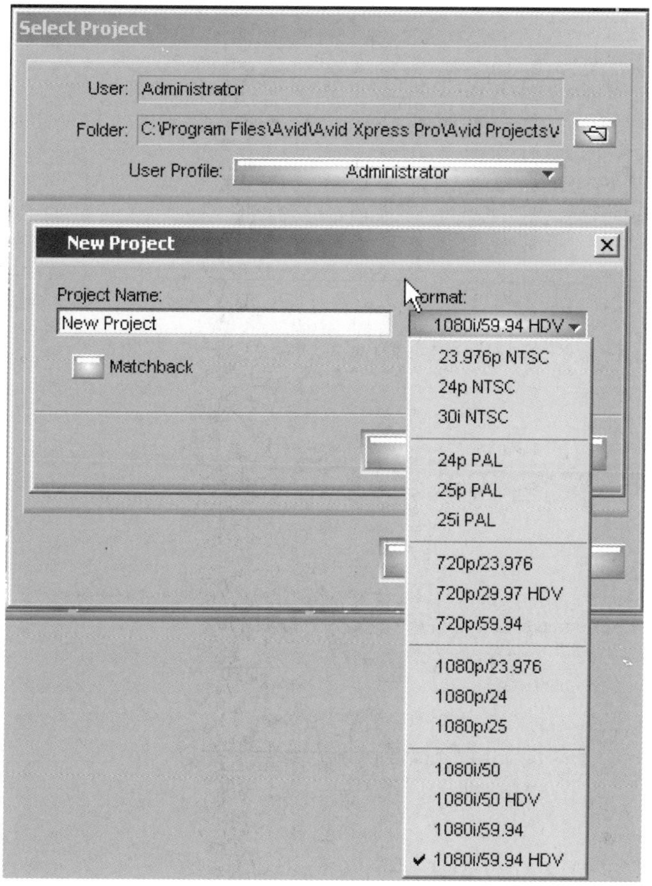

Figure 6.2 Project Format choices.

- 23.976p NTSC: You would select 23.976p NTSC if you shot with a Canon XL2, Panasonic DVX100, or Panasonic DVX900 for a North American audience and chose 23.976 as your frame rate. We explore this option in Chapter 15.
- 24p NTSC: You would select 24p NTSC if you are editing a film project that was captured on a Media Composer. We explore this option in Chapter 19.
- 30i NTSC: If you shot for North American audiences using a mini-DV or DVCAM camera, Beta SP camera, or DigiBeta camera, then 30i NTSC is more than likely the choice you want.

If you are shooting outside of North America, PAL (Phase Alternating Line) is the standard you are most likely using. It is the television system common in Europe, Africa, and many other parts of the world. If you are using just about any mini-DV or DVCAM PAL camera, select 25i PAL. We will examine 25p PAL and 24p PAL in Chapter 15.

The other choices in the format pull-down menu (shown in Figure 6.2), which come below the NTSC and PAL ones just described, are all HD and HDV choices, which we will examine in detail in Chapter 16. Don't worry, you'll be an expert on all of them by the end of the book.

To repeat, your most likely choice is 30i NTSC if you're in North America and 25i PAL if you're in Europe or English-speaking countries of Africa and Asia.

Once all the boxes are selected, click OK. You are returned to the Select a Project window, where you will select the newly created project and click OK. Now, the Avid brings you to the Project window for that project. From now on, this new project will appear in the Select a Project window.

STANDARD-DEFINITION TAPE FORMATS—ANALOG AND DIGITAL

The standard-definition videotape world is divided into two parts: analog videotape and digital videotape (DV). In the analog world, Hi-8 and S-VHS are popular formats. VHS is still in use, and there are millions of VHS decks in homes throughout the world. Betacam SP is a high-quality analog format that had a long reign as the industry standard, but the world is rapidly moving away from analog to digital tape. There are several professional digital videotape formats; I won't list them all, just several of the more popular ones:

- Digital Betacam
- DVCPRO50
- DV, including mini-DV
- DVCAM
- DVCPRO

The growth of the DV format is fairly astounding. Introduced in 1995, it has taken the production world by storm. Although it was originally seen as a "pro-sumer" format, professionals quickly adopted it for use in demanding situations and discovered that it could handle everyday tasks as well. Now even the most sophisticated cameras are using the DV format—some for recording high-definition signals.

COMPRESSION AND SUBSAMPLING

When people think of DV, they generally think of mini-DV, DVCAM, and DVCPRO cameras and tape. The question often asked is how does all that gorgeous image quality fit onto a tiny mini-DV tape? The answer is that the picture information is *compressed* and *subsampled*. The camera compresses the image to produce a data rate that is 25 megabits per second, which is why it is often referred to as DV25. This translates into a compression ratio of 5:1. If 1:1 represents no compression, then 5:1 is a good deal of compression. When the camera compresses the video signal, it keeps a certain percentage of the signal and throws away the rest. Obviously, the more signal you throw away, the worse the image looks, but the smaller the data rate. The reason the image looks so good is that the compression algorithm that DV uses is so intelligent—it tosses out mostly redundant information.

The other way in which the data stream is reduced is subsampling. The components that make up a video signal are brightness, also called *luminance*, and the color signal, also called *chrominance*. The color signal can be subdivided. In most systems, it is divided into two parts: red minus the luminance signal and blue minus the luminance signal. The system is described in the following way:

- Y stands for luminance.
- R–Y stands for red minus luminance.
- B–Y stands for blue minus luminance.

If you're wondering what happened to the green signal in the RGB color system, it's imbedded in the luminance signal—it's part of the Y. Huh? I know—don't even ask.

Now let's say that four samples of each would represent the highest quality signal. So, if we have four samples of Y and four samples of R–Y and four samples of B–Y, then we would have a 4:4:4 subsampling ratio.

A DV tape could never handle 4:4:4 subsampling. That would be way too much information. Digital Betacam, a very high-end format, uses 4:2:2 subsampling. For every four samples of luminance, you sample two of R–Y and two of B–Y. Standard DV can't even handle that, though. It uses 4:1:1 subsampling.

The Avid does not compress the image when you capture it. All the compressing and subsampling are done inside the camera. The Avid brings it in as 0's and 1's—just as pristine as it is on the tape.

A few years ago Panasonic came out with a format that is like DV, only better. It's called DV50. It has a data rate of 50 megabits per second and uses 4:2:2 subsampling. Xpress Pro users can capture and edit DV50 tapes as easily as any DV25 tape.

CAPTURE SYSTEMS AND TECHNIQUES

The Avid Xpress DV is designed for DVCAM and mini-DV tapes. You'll be using an IEEE 1394 capture board (FireWire/iLink) and capturing your DV tapes digitally. To bring other kinds of tapes into your Xpress DV, you can purchase a *transcoder*, also called a *media converter*, which converts other formats to DV. Many DV decks can act as transcoders. With the right cables, you could bring in an analog tape such as VHS or Beta SP through your DV deck. Keep in mind that whatever format you bring in through a transcoder will have the same resolution, or image quality, as DV25 (25 megabits, 4:1:1). Xpress Pro and Xpress Pro HD can accept a range of digital tapes and keep them at the tape's native resolution. If you have an Avid Mojo device, you can bring in a range of analog tapes as well, including Beta SP (see pages 124–127).

CONNECTING YOUR EQUIPMENT

In order to capture the picture and sound, you need to run cables from your tape deck to your Avid video and audio capture boards. In a school setting, the cables have probably been connected for you and all you need to do is turn on the power to the deck, boot the Avid, and insert your tape. In case you're on your own, though, let's take a minute to examine the cables going from your deck to your computer's CPU.

With the Xpress DV, you need concern yourself with only one cable—the FireWire cable. This cable will control the deck, or camera, and carry both the digital picture and sound. The same cable is used later on to send the digital signal out of the Avid to your camera or deck for putting your finished project onto tape. You plug one end of the FireWire cable into the FireWire connection on the back of your computer and the other end into the video deck or camera.

FireWire cables are either 6-pin (larger) or 4-pin (smaller). Computers take the 6-pin connection and cameras and decks usually take the 4-pin connection. Most cameras and decks are sold with a FireWire cable that is 4-pin on one end and 6-pin on the other (like the cable on the right in Figure 6.3). The 4-pin end goes into the camera or deck and the 6-pin end goes into the computer.

Figure 6.3   FireWire cables.

To edit with an external FireWire drive, you need two cables: a cable with 6-pin connectors on both ends (6 × 6), and a cable with a 6-pin connector on one end and a 4-pin connector on the other (6 × 4). Plug the 6 × 6 cable into the computer's FireWire port and the other end into the external drive. Now, grab your 6 × 4 pin. Plug the 6-pin end into the external drive and the 4-pin end into the camera or deck, as shown in Figure 6.4. If you are using a deck, make sure the deck is set to DV and not S-Video or Video.

6x6 pin FireWire cable to computer

6x4 pin FireWire cable to deck

Figure 6.4

Configuring a Deck or Camera

If you just mounted your Avid software onto your computer or downloaded a new version, chances are your Avid has not been set up to recognize a deck or camera. When you try to capture, you'll get a message saying "NO DECK," even though you have a deck or camera attached. First you must add a channel or "handshake" so Avid sees your camera or deck.

1. Click on the Settings tab in the Project window.
2. Double-click on Deck Configuration (Figure 6.5).

Settings tab

Deck Configuration

Figure 6.5

3. When the window opens, click on Add Channel (Figure 6.6).
4. Make sure Firewire and OHCI are selected, as shown in Figure 6.6. Click OK.
5. Now click on the Add Deck button.

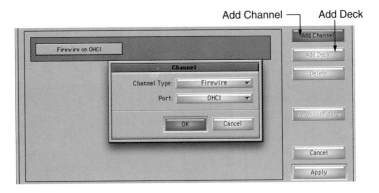

Add Channel — Add Deck

Figure 6.6

6. Choose your camera or deck from the list of devices (Figure 6.7).

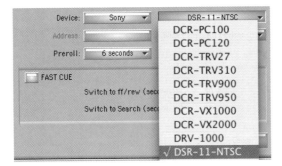

Figure 6.7

7. Now click OK to make that camera or deck the one that appears in the Deck Configuration window, as shown in Figure 6.8. I selected a Sony DSR-11-NTSC.

8. Click Apply.

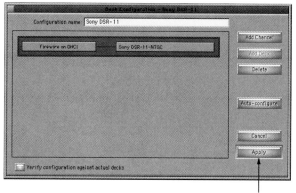

Click Apply

Figure 6.8

9. The window will close. Now enter the name of the deck in the Settings window.

Type here to name

If you don't see your deck or camera in step 7, choose one that is from the same manufacturer and a similar model. Now you have a FireWire channel and a deck (or camera) properly configured. Make sure the checkmark is next to the Deck Configuration you created. You can now click on the Bins tab in the Project window to view your bins.

Image Resolution

In some ways, Xpress DV editors have an easier time starting a new project because they don't have to deal with the issue of image resolution. They will edit the material at the same image resolution at which it was shot: DV 25. Xpress Pro editors must decide whether to bring the video signal in at the highest resolution (most beautiful image quality) or at some resolution that sacrifices image quality. Years ago, when 20 gigabytes (GB) of storage cost thousands of dollars, editors often captured their source tapes at a lower resolution to save space and then, after editing, recaptured just the shots in the final sequence at the highest resolution. Because FireWire drives are so cheap, compared to the past, the decision is often based on what you intend to do with the project. If you're going to the Web, it might make sense to start off with smaller files, so you'd choose 15:1s; otherwise, you'll always want to be at the highest resolution.

The Xpress Pro offers three resolutions (more if you are using Mojo):

- DV 25 411 OMF—The standard setting for DV tapes; no compression
- DV 50 OMF—For use with a DV 50 camera or deck; no compression
- 15:1s OMF—Lots of compression; one field of video is tossed out

When you capture at 15:1s, the Avid *compresses* the video signal. It keeps a certain percentage of the signal and throws away the rest. Because each frame of video is made up of two fields, one way to save storage space is to capture only one field. You would think 15:1s would look terrible, but it actually looks quite good, considering.

Look at the chart below to see how many gigabytes you'll need to store your tapes if you select DV 25:

30 minutes	60 minutes	2 hours	6 hours	12 hours
6 GB	12 GB	24 GB	72 GB	144 GB

If you capture at 15:1s instead of DV 25, 60 minutes of tape will take up only 3 GB on your drive—one-quarter as much as DV 25. DV 50 requires twice the storage capacity as DV 25, so 60 minutes of tape would take up 24 GB.

AUDIO

Before we begin to capture our video we need to remember that we also recorded sound on our tapes, and the decisions we make about our sound are as important as those we make about our picture. Sound takes up a fraction of the storage space required by video, so you don't have to worry about running out of media drive space whenever you capture sound.

File Formats

The latest versions of the Avid's software handle four different types of audio files: WAVE, AIFF-C, SD2, and MXF. Sound Designer II (SD2) is a sound format for Mac computers, and WAVE is a Windows-based format. MXF is a new fileexchange format primarily used with high-definition signals. The Audio Interchange File Format (AIFF-C) works well with Mac and PC computers. This is the audio file format you should choose in the Audio Project Settings window whenever you begin a new project because it makes it easy to move your audio files to another application or system.

1. Go to Settings in the Project window and double-click on Audio Project.
2. In the dialog box that appears, open the Audio File Format menu and select OMF (AIFF-C).

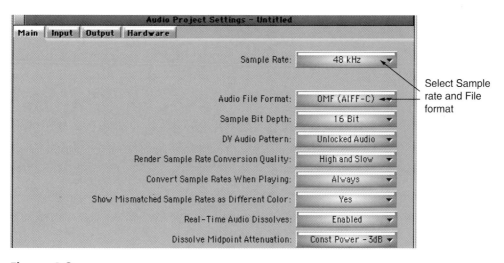

Figure 6.9

Audio Sampling

When analog audio is captured, the signal is sampled and then converted to digital information. *Sampling* means that not all of the sound is converted, but a representative sample of it is. The more samples that are taken, the better the fidelity, or faithfulness to the original analog signal. Compact discs use 44.1 as their sample rate. The trend today is for higher quality—such as 48kHz—and that's the setting I recommend you choose.

With digital tapes, the sample rate is determined by the camera. Many digital cameras let you choose the sample rate before you shoot, so set it on the highest rate available. Don't assume it is set on the sample rate you want. If you don't see 48kHz, look for 16-bit audio and set your camera on that, not 12 bit.

In the Avid's Audio Project Settings window (Figure 6.9), you can select the sample rate for your project or tape. If you're bringing in an analog tape using Mojo or a transcoder, then use 48kHz as your setting.

The Avid has the ability to change the sample rate of the audio. For instance, when you bring in music or sound effects from a CD which are at 44.1 kHz, Avid will ask you if you want too convert them to 48 kHz, and you will simply say yes.

NAMING YOUR TAPES

After you have gathered together your source tapes and decided on an appropriate resolution, you should come up with a system for naming the tapes. In a way, you might want to consider your system of naming tapes even before you start shooting, so the name you give the tape in the field is the same name you give it when capturing. One of the worst mistakes you can make when capturing is to give two tapes the same name. Your naming system need not be complicated. Whenever you begin a new project simply call the first tape 001. The second tape is 002. Because the Avid knows which project you are working on, you don't have to include the project name with the tape. So you do not have to type Wanna Trade 001. Just 001. Keep it simple.

ORGANIZING YOUR BINS

Before you begin the actual capture process, you must decide into which bin your newly captured material will go. On film projects, many editors prefer to organize their bins according to what was shot on a given day. All the tapes from the first day of shooting would go into a bin called *Dailies, Day 1*. On a video project, it makes sense to have a bin for each camera tape; thus, Tape 001 would go into a bin called *Tape 001*.

THE CAPTURE TOOL

Start by clicking the New Bin button at the top of the Project window and a new bin will be created. Click on the name the Avid gave it (the name you gave the project), and type Tape 001. Remember, before you open the Capture Tool, open the bin you want the material to go to and close any other bins that may be open.

Open the Capture Tool by going to the Toolset menu and choosing Capture. Examine the Capture Tool's user interface (Figure 6.10). Parts of it look exactly like a video deck. Other parts are logical renditions of the actions they perform. The buttons on the deck control are self-explanatory. You have buttons for fast rewind, fast forward, stop, pause, play, step one frame backward, and step one frame forward and a slider that acts like a shuttle control. There's even an eject button. There are little triangles for opening and closing sections of the Tool. Your J–K–L keys work with the Record Tool's deck controls to play, pause, and play at faster than standard speed.

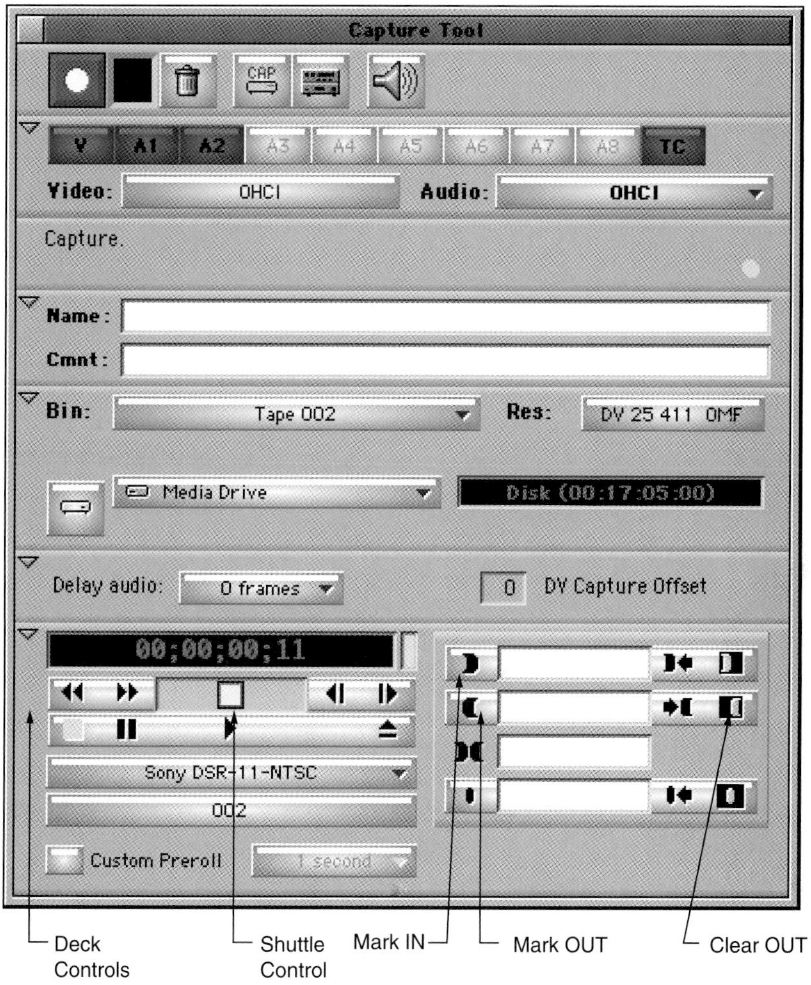

Figure 6.10 Capture Tool.

LOG OR CAPTURE

The Capture Tool has two modes of operation, one for logging the shots and one for capturing them. When you *log* your tape, you are choosing the shots you want to capture, marking IN and OUT points but not capturing them. Many editors log each tape first and then capture those clips they selected. Why? Basically it's better to divide your tasks. Concentrate first on selecting the shots to be captured, and then later on perform the capturing task. In some cases, you may find it is better not to log but to capture each shot on the tape as you come to it. Say you're in a hurry and just want a couple of clips from a tape. In this case, it may be faster and easier just to capture those few clips.

Configuring the Capture Tool

1. *Select the tracks.* As you can see in Figure 6.11, the video track is selected (V), and the audio tracks A1 and A2 have also been selected. Make sure the TC (timecode) track is selected as well.

Figure 6.11

2. *Select the target bin.* If there are several bins open, the Avid might select the wrong bin.
3. *Select the resolution.* With Xpress DV, your only choice is DV 25. Xpress Pro users go to the resolution pull-down menu and pick from the choices.
4. *Select a target drive.* Your instructor may have assigned you a drive. If not, you'll want to use the drive that has the most space. Go to the drive window (Figure 6.12) and drag down to select the assigned drive or the drive with the most space. That drive is always the one in bold letters.

Figure 6.12   Drive window.

Make sure you don't capture any media onto your System (C:) drive (Windows).

5. *Select Log Mode or Capture Mode* (Figures 6.13 and 6.14). Press the Log/Record selector button to switch from Record Mode to the Log Mode, and *vice versa*. When you press the button, the tool will switch to Log Mode. Notice that the pencil icon shows that you are in Log Mode.

Capture Mode icon

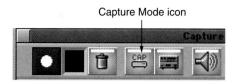

Figure 6.13 Capture Mode.

Log Mode icon

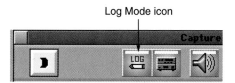

Figure 6.14 Log Mode.

6. *Select the type of Video signal.* If it is from a DV camera or deck, choose OHCI.
7. *Select the type of Audio signal.* If it is from a DV camera or deck, choose OHCI; if it is from a microphone, choose either Internal Microphone or Line in.
8. *Insert your first tape into the camera or deck.* A prompt will appear, asking you either to select the tape's name, if a name has already been entered, or to give the tape a new name. Because we haven't named any tapes, you will click on the New button and then type the name 001. Once you have typed the name, you'd think you could click OK, but you can't.

After typing, you have to click on the tape's icon to highlight the tape name before you can click OK (see Figure 6.15).

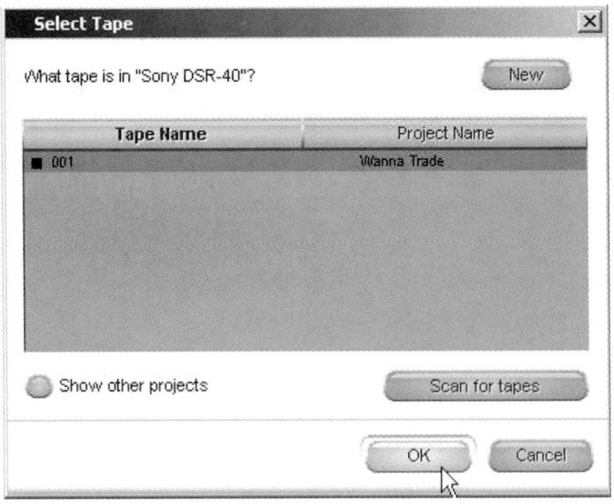

Figure 6.15

Now, you should have control of the tape through the deck controls on the Capture Tool. Hit the play button on the Capture Tool, and the tape plays. Hit the rewind button, and it rewinds. Notice how the tape's timecode appears in the Timecode window, just above the deck controls. You can use the J–K–L keys, as well. You can even shuttle the tape at faster than normal speeds by pressing J and L several times.

If the Avid Says "NO DECK"

If for some reason your Avid doesn't recognize that a deck or camera is attached, go to the pull-down menu just below the play button and select Check Decks (Figure 6.16). That should force the Avid to recognize the camera or deck you are using. If that doesn't work, and you've checked to make sure everything is properly connected and gone through the checklist of items provided above, try quitting your Avid application and then launching your software again.

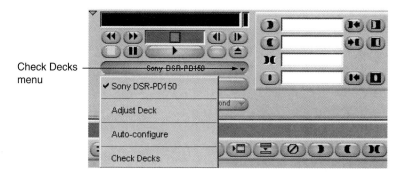

Check Decks
menu

Figure 6.16

What Should Happen

If everything is working correctly, when you press the Play button, you should see the tapes play in the Record Monitor. The sound should come out of the speakers inside the computer or the speakers attached to the computer. If you are using a client monitor, the picture (and sound) coming from the client monitor will not always play in sync with the picture and sound coming from the computer's Record Monitor. Don't be alarmed. The client monitor is hooked up to the video deck, *not* to the Avid, and it takes time for the Avid to buffer the signal. You'll see that, once you have captured the clip into a bin, the sound and picture will play together in sync in the Source and Record monitors. If you're having a problem, remember to select the V1 and/or A1 and A2 tracks on the Capture Tool. If they are not selected, you won't see or hear anything!

THE CAPTURING PROCESS

Because we are capturing digital tapes, we can't adjust the video or audio levels. We're simply transferring 0's and 1's. Later in the chapter, we'll explain how to bring in analog material and how to set audio levels. There are three ways to capture your material: Logging, Capturing, and Capturing On-the-Fly. We'll examine all three.

Logging

In this method, you log the clips first and then capture them after they have been logged. To get into Log Mode, click the Log/Capture toggle. The pencil icon appears in place of the Capture icon (Figure 6.17).

Figure 6.17

1. Play the tape using the deck controls. When you come to the first clip you want, go to the beginning and mark an IN. Notice that the time-code of the exact spot you chose is displayed in the window next to the IN marker (Figure 6.18).
2. Now play the tape until you come to the end of the clip you want. Mark an OUT. The timecode for that spot is displayed, as well as the duration of the clip, listed in the IN to OUT window.
3. Pause the deck. Hit the Pause button or K key on the keyboard.

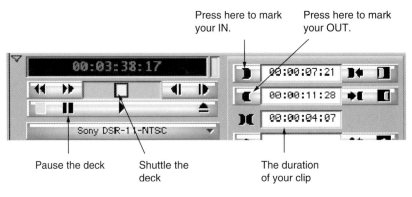

Figure 6.18

4. Enter a clip name. Use names that best describe the shot. If the shot is of a man on a ladder, name the clip Man on Ladder. You can add comments as well.

5. Now press the Pencil icon. The shot is logged in the bin.

Click to log
clip in bin

6. Repeat the steps above to log all your shots.

Batch Capturing Your Logged Clips

Once you have logged all the clips on the tape, you're ready to *Batch Capture*. Do not log another tape until you have captured all the clips on this tape.

1. Select all the clips in the bin. Hit Command–A (Mac) or Ctrl–A (Windows) to select all the clips or lasso the clips, Shift–click all the clips, or go to the Edit menu and choose Select All.
2. Go to the Bin menu and select Batch Capture.
3. A dialog box will appear. Because you have no media, it doesn't matter whether or not you check the button "Offline media only," but later on you'll want this box selected, so get in the habit of checking it. Then click OK.

Batch Record   ✕

✓ Offline media only

4 clip(s) selected

The Avid will rewind the tape to the first clip, find the IN point, roll back a few seconds for preroll, and then begin capturing. It will stop when it reaches your OUT point. After capturing the first clip, it will go to the IN of the second clip on the tape and capture it. You can watch the bin and see the progress the Avid is making as it captures each clip. Or you can go have lunch.

Capturing

If you only have a couple of clips from a tape or if you're in a hurry, this method will work best for you. With this method, you mark the clip and then capture it before going to the next clip. To get into the Capture Mode, click the Log/Capture Mode button. The CAP icon replaces the pencil icon.

Figure 6.19

Now:

1. Play the tape using the deck control, and mark an IN.
2. Play the tape using the deck control, and mark an OUT.
3. Hit the large Capture Button; the box next to it will flash red.
4. Name the clip in the bin.
5. Repeat the steps above to capture all shots.

You can abort the capturing process by clicking on the Trash icon, next to the flashing red box.

To save time, you can actually type the clip's name without waiting for the capture to end. Just start typing as soon as the red button flashes. When the clip has been recorded, the name you typed will appear in the bin. Press the Tab key to enter comments.

Capturing On-the-Fly

When you use this method, you don't bother using the Mark IN or Mark OUT controls. You simply capture various portions of the tape as you play it. To get into the Capture Mode, click the Log/Capture toggle. You'll know you are in Capture Mode when the CAP icon replaces the pencil icon (see Figure 6.19).

Play the tape using the deck control, and press the large Capture button as you approach the material you want (the IN). The red button will flash to show you that it is recording material.

1. When you reach the end of the segment of the tape you want (the OUT), press the Capture button again.
2. Repeat the steps above to record all the material on the tape.

You can abort the capture process while it is in progress by hitting the Trash icon.

If you use the Capture-on-the-Fly method with material that has timecode, the Avid will provide IN and OUT points determined by the point on the tape where you pressed the Capture button to start or stop the capture process. I often use this Capture-on-the-Fly method whenever my IN point is too close to a timecode break. The Avid often needs five seconds of preroll to Batch Capture a clip. If there isn't five seconds, the Avid chokes when trying to preroll. So I play the tape, wait until the Avid is across the timecode break, and then press the Capture button.

SETTING AUDIO LEVELS

When you capture digital video through a deck or camera, you can't change the level of the audio because it's digital—just 0's and 1's—and you don't need to read this section. But, when you bring in *analog* audio through a transcoder or via Mojo, you can change the signal strength (volume) by adjusting the output of the source deck or tape player. You don't want to capture the audio at a level that is so low that it's barely audible or so high that it overmodulates and breaks up. To help you bring in the audio at the right levels, the Avid provides you with the Audio Tool. Simply press the speaker icon at the top of the Capture Tool, and the Audio Tool appears.

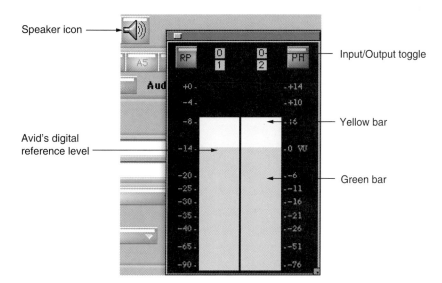

Figure 6.20 Audio Tool.

The tracks should be set to I for input. If they are set to O for output, as shown in Figure 6.20, just click on the Input/Output toggle, and they will change to I.

Setting audio levels on the Avid is similar to setting levels on a tape recorder. The Avid has a Peak Level Meter, which uses colored bars instead of a needle to show signal strength and includes both a digital scale (left) and an analog VU scale, measuring in decibels. As the tape plays, watch the levels.

Play your tape. If the tape has *color bars* and a *tone* (1000 Hz) at the head of the tape, you should use that tone to set your levels. Using a 1000-Hz tone, adjust the output of your source deck to Avid's reference level. On the one I am using, it's −14 dB (other Avid's may be set at −20 dB). The reference level is the digital decibel signal that's equal to 0 dB on the analog (right-hand) side. That's where the 1000-Hz tone should fall. If there is no tone, play the tape until you come to a sound that best represents what was recorded in the field, and use that as a reference.

As you can see from Figure 6.20, I let loud sounds go above −14. The solid green bar turns yellow as it passes −14. That's correct because loud sounds should be loud. Quieter sounds fall between −40 and −25. Average sounds fall around −14. Never let your sounds hit +0 on the digital scale (+14 on the analog scale). They will break up and sound awful.

CAPTURING MATERIAL WITHOUT TIMECODE

Without timecode, the Avid can't control the deck, and it can't remember IN and OUT marks if no timecode exists. That doesn't mean the Avid can't capture the tape; it just means that the material will not have timecode associated with it. For example, the Avid can't control a Nagra 4.2 tape recorder or a VHS or 8-mm deck, but you can still bring that material into the Avid.

Let's say you have audio that was recorded on a Nagra analog tape recorder or a VHS deck. You connect the camera or tape recorder to the DV deck using standard RCA cables: yellow cable for the composite video signal, red and white for audio signals.

Now, bring up the Capture Tool. Because the Avid can't control the camera or deck, you need to configure the tool a bit differently.

Deck Control button

Figure 6.21

Press the Deck Control button, and you'll notice that a "you can't do that" line appears across the picture of the deck. Once in this mode, the Capture Tool changes appearance. Your deck controls disappear. To name the tape, look down at the Tape Name? button at the bottom of the Capture Tool. It's probably flashing. Click on it, and the Tape Name dialog box appears. Give the tape a name.

Click here to name the tape.

Because you are not bringing in timecode, the TC track is missing from the Capture Tool, but make sure the correct video and audio tracks are selected.

Your only choice is to record on-the-fly. You can't mark IN or OUT points. Instead, play the tape, using the camera's (or deck's) controls. When you reach a section you want, hit the Capture button and begin the recording process. When you reach the end, hit the button again. Now, go in the bin and name the clip. Keep doing this until you've captured all the material you want.

Once the material is captured, it behaves just like any other captured material. In fact, the Avid will provide fake timecode as it records the material. Don't be fooled, though; the numbers have no relation to your video or audio.

OTHER USEFUL SETTINGS

In Chapter 3, we discussed settings. I suppose I should have talked about several useful settings that pertain to capturing at the beginning of this chapter, rather than at the end, but I really didn't want to overwhelm you with information. When I first learned how to use the Avid I found this whole business a bit confusing, and so I'm sensitive to the quantity of information involved, but perhaps you're a quicker learner than I am. Let's look at some useful settings. Remember, in the Project window, click on Settings and then double-click on the name of the setting you want to change. Here are some recommendations.

- *Audio*—Select "All Tracks Centered." Dialog and narration should be centered. Music should be left and right. If you are bringing in the spoken word, this is the setting you want. If you're bringing in music, change it back to "Alternating L/R."
- *Media Creation*—Under the Capture tab, select your media drive and then select "Apply to All." This way, all your master clips, titles, and motion effects will go to your media drive.

- *Video Display Settings*—If you want to see your video image in a client monitor, first close all open bins. Now open Video Display. Check the box "Enable Confidence View."
- *Capture*—In Figure 6.22 I've shown you my choices for capturing under the General tab.

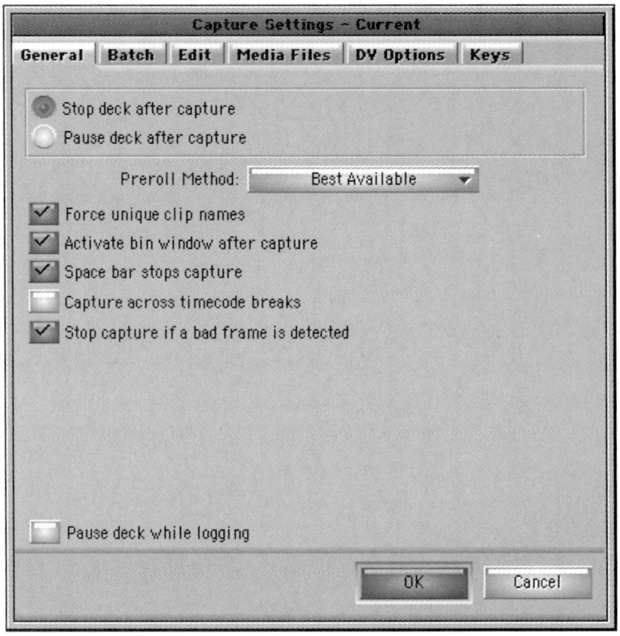

Figure 6.22

The last one, "Pause deck while logging," is deselected because I don't like having the deck pause while I'm logging. When I log, I like to mark an IN. Then I play the tape and as I approach the end of the shot I keep clicking on the OUT button—many times. The OUT point will keep changing as the shot plays and I keep clicking. Then, even if I set the last OUT just past the shot, there's no need to rewind and mark an exact OUT, because my last click was close enough. With "Pause deck while logging" selected, I can't do that. As soon I press the first OUT mark, the deck pauses. It drives me crazy.

MOJO (NOT AVAILABLE ON XPRESS DV)

If you're using an Xpress Pro or Xpress Pro HD, you can hook up a Mojo Digital Nonlinear Accelerator (DNA) and use it to bring in signals from a variety of decks and cameras. Just connect the DV, S-Video, or Composite video cable from your deck to the Mojo and then run a 6-pin × 6-pin FireWire cable from Mojo to your computer. According to Avid, Mojo takes all these different signals and changes them into Avid-specific data. When you have finished editing your project, you use Mojo to send this data back out to a deck, a DVD, or the Web.

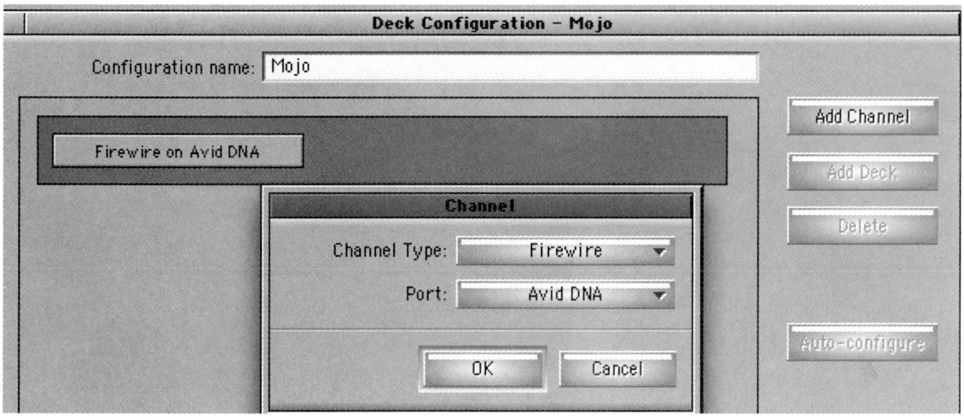

Figure 6.23

Mojo is fairly easy to set up. Plug in the power cable, connect the video and audio cables from the deck to Mojo, and then connect the FireWire cable to your computer. The first time you use it, you'll have to press a button to allow the software to shake hands—all automatic—then reboot and you're done.

The first time you go to capture, you may find that the Capture Tool says "NO DECK." This is because you're not going from a camera or deck to the Avid—you're going through Mojo DNA—so you need to set up a new Deck Configuration, like we did earlier in this chapter. For a quick review, turn to the "Configuring a Deck or Camera" section. Now do the following:

1. Go to Settings.
2. In the Fast menu, select All Settings.
3. Click once on Deck Configuration and duplicate it (Command [Ctrl]–D).
4. Name this new Deck Setting "Mojo."
5. Double-click this setting to open it.
6. Click on Add Channel. The Avid will sense you are connected through Mojo and supply "Firewire on Avid DNA" (see Figure 6.23).
7. Click OK and then select Add Deck and choose the one you are using.
8. Click OK and then Apply.
9. Make sure the checkmark is next to the Mojo Deck Configuration and not the one you set up earlier.

Now the Avid Capture Tool will recognize your deck.

Power

RCA audio
plugs-In

Composite
video-In

S-Video-In

DV In and Out

FireWire

Figure 6.24 Mojo

Most of the time you'll use standard RCA plugs (yellow, red and white) to connect your analog equipment to the Mojo, or, better yet, S-Video for the video and RCA plugs (red and white) for the audio, as I have in Figure 6.24. When using a DV camera or deck, you'll need a 4-pin to 4-pin FireWire cable (4 × 4). When you're sending your work out, the top plugs on Mojo are the ones for output.

You can purchase a special cable from Avid which lets you bring in high-quality *component* video—like the signal from a Beta SP deck. To bring in Beta SP tapes you connect a Betacam deck to Mojo. Although Mojo doesn't have component inputs, there's a special Avid cable, which you can purchase from Avid for about $75, that does the trick. Connect the cable to the three BNC connectors on the back of the Beta deck and connect it to Mojo's S-Video input and Composite video input (yellow connection). To bring in the Beta SP's audio, you'll need 2 XLR (male)-to-RCA connectors. The one caveat is that the Mojo wants −10-dB line levels, and most decks with XLR connectors put out a hotter signal: +4 dB. If the deck has a switch for −10, use it; otherwise, you'll need to go to Radio Shack and get a level converter.

When Mojo is connected to your computer, you're no longer limited to capturing DV tapes. Now, under the Video pull-down menu you'll suddenly see four choices: Composite, SVideo, Component, and DV (Figure 6.25). You need to tell the Capture Tool which signal you are bringing in.

- If you're using the yellow RCA plug, it's Composite.
- If you're using an S-Video cable, it's SVideo.
- If you're using the special Avid cable, it's Component.
- If you're using a 4-pin FireWire, it's DV.

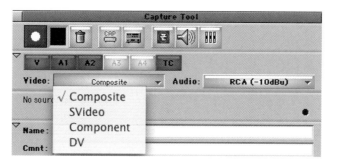

Figure 6.25

Mojo Resolutions

With Mojo, you don't capture everything at DV 25. Now you have a new resolution—1:1. Avid recommends that if you have Mojo DNA, you bring *everything* in at this 1:1 image resolution; it's not just for Beta SP tapes captured with the special component cable. So, if you bring in DV 25, composite, or component video, select 1:1 in the resolution pull-down menu. If you have a project with footage coming from a variety of formats, Mojo is a good choice because you can capture them all at 1:1.

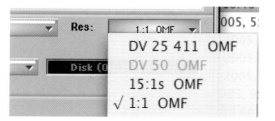

If you disconnect Mojo from your computer and you have 1:1 video, you will see a "Wrong Format" warning; you should always have your Mojo connected when editing 1:1 material.

SUGGESTED ASSIGNMENTS

1. Create a new project, create a new bin, and then open the Capture Tool.
2. Name your source tape.
3. Record five clips from the tape by marking IN and OUT points and then capture them. Name the clips in the bin.
4. Log five clips into the bin. Now, Batch Capture the clips into the bin.
5. Capture five clips on the fly. Name the clips in the bin.

7

Menus

In this chapter, we're going to take a look at the various menus and menu commands the Avid provides, including those at the top of the computer screen and those found on the monitor screens. We'll discuss each command, point out the ones you'll use most often, and explain when you will find them most useful.

Pull-down menus are at the heart of the Macintosh and Windows interface. On the Avid, a lot of choices and commands are located on the menus. Sometimes an item is grayed out, meaning it isn't available. You'll need to select something or do something for that item to come into play.

Different Avid systems have different pull-down menus. Menus change as Avid software is upgraded. Xpress DV has fewer menu functions than Xpress Pro. Given all the different Avid systems and software upgrades, there is really no way to keep up with all the changes in a guidebook like this one.

Even so, I believe it's useful to examine the many menu commands in some detail. All Avids share about 90% of the same commands, and they tell us a great deal about how the Avid functions. By going over each command, you can learn a lot about the work you'll soon be able to do. Some commands are geared for advanced users, and we won't go much beyond the brief description provided here. Others are so important to our daily use of the Avid that we will review them often and in greater detail in later chapters.

Because the book you're reading is probably yours—you paid for it and own it—I suggest you use a highlighter pen and highlight a command the first time you use it. That way, the ones you use will be highlighted, and the ones you don't use won't get in your way. When you want to look up a command, you'll quickly look at the ones you use, and your eyes can skip over those you don't. Over time, you'll use most of them, but it might be interesting to see how many you never use.

As you will see, some of the commands have keyboard equivalents. Either drag down the menu and select an item, or memorize the keyboard equivalent and type it instead. On a Macintosh, the main keyboard modifier is the Command key (⌘), whereas Windows PCs use the Control key (Ctrl).

For the most part, the Xpress family shares the same menu items (which are similar to the Media Composer family). I have included menus from the Xpress Pro, and I'll explain which ones are not included on Xpress DV.

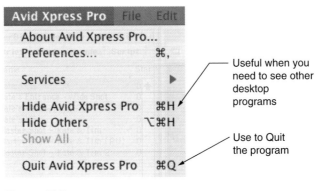

Figure 7.1

Figure 7.1 is a Mac-only menu, and we'll use only two of the items from this menu. The first is Hide Avid Xpress Pro, which we'll use whenever we want to hide the Xpress on the Mac. This menu item acts a lot like Minimize on a Windows PC, and we'll use it whenever we need to view the desktop. We will also use the command Quit Avid Xpress Pro whenever we want to exit the Avid program.

FILE MENU

If you've used just about any software on a Windows or Mac computer, you're already familiar with most of the File commands shown in Figure 7.2. Open, Close, Save, Print—they're all standard. The rest are very Avid specific.

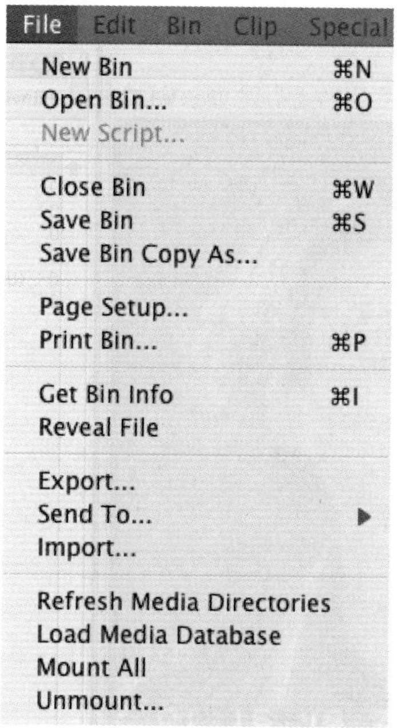

Figure 7.2 File menu.

New Bin. Creates a new bin. In the past, we clicked on the New Bin button on the Project window. Avid gives you many ways to do the same thing.

Open Bin. In fact, this is more than it seems. If a bin is selected and you choose this, the bin opens, but usually you'll probably just double-click on the bin to open it. This command does more than just open a bin. When you select this menu command, you're presented with a dialog box. That dialog box taps into all the bins on all the projects on the Avid. Let's say you want to take a clip of music from another project and use it in this project. Select Open Bin and then navigate through the computer's hierarchical menus until you find the bin you want. Open it and you can open a music clip from another project and put it into your current project.

New Script. This command works with the Script Integration feature, which we will discuss at length in Chapter 17.

Close Bin. This command closes the active bin; however, we usually click on the Close box in the corner of the bin itself.

Save Bin. This saves any bin that is selected. The Avid has an auto-save function that automatically saves your work, but if you want to make sure you save what you just did then type Command–S (Mac) or Ctrl–S (Windows) or select this menu item.

Save a Copy As. This saves a copy of the open bin.

Page Setup. If you have a printer hooked up to your computer, you can print out a lot of different items and information. This command opens a dialog box so you can determine the page setup.

Print Bin. This opens a dialog box that lets you choose what you would like to print on your printer—an active bin, a frame of a clip, or the Timeline.

Get Bin Info. This tells you the name and the start timecode for the clip you have selected and information about the number and length of clips in your bin. To tell you the truth, I rarely use this because it also places items in the Console, and I try to avoid the Console, which is designed for Avid programmers.

Reveal File. If you select a master clip, you can use this command to go to the computer's Finder level to locate the media file associated with that master clip. It is handy for keeping track of your media and locating items that you may want to delete or move.

Export. Because Avid deals with digital information (1's and 0's), almost any digital file can be brought in or sent out. The Avid allows you to bring in and send out many kinds of files—picture files, animation files, and audio files. When you export, you send out digital information you have created in the Avid. Perhaps you want to get a close-up of one of your actors for a flyer you're creating. You could export a frame from your Timeline as a TIFF file and bring it into a program such as Adobe Illustrator®.

Send To. This is like Export, only it deals with sending sequences or media files to specific programs. This menu item (Figure 7.3) opens to reveal the following choices:

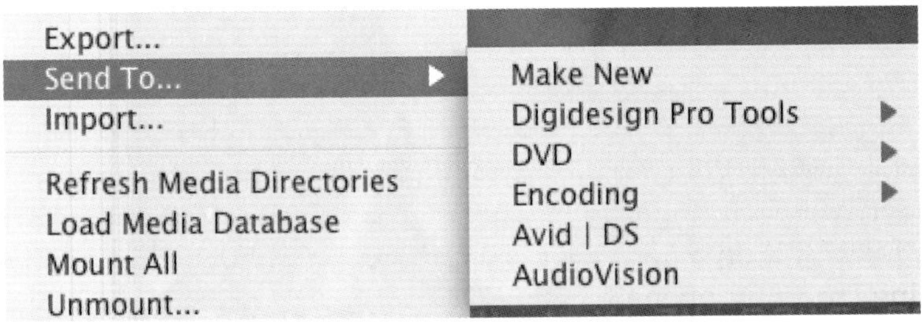

Figure 7.3

Make New. This choice lets you design your own Export settings, so that when you want to export, all your settings are saved and ready to go.

Digidesign Pro Tools. Pro Tools® is the top audio mixing software in the world, used throughout the entertainment industry. We'll explore how to send sequences to Pro Tools in Chapter 14.

DVD. This menu item creates a QuickTime Reference movie of your sequence for use by DVD software. We'll discuss this further in Chapter 18.

Encoding. This item will send your sequence to encoding software mounted on your computer such as Sorenson Squeeze. Encoding software compresses the media so it can be converted to a DVD.

Avid | DS. This is Avid's most sophisticated turnkey system, and this menu item is for sending your sequence for polishing and finishing on an Avid | DS.

AudioVision. Like Pro Tools, AudioVision® is an audio editing system that locks digital video in sync with audio for audio sweetening. This menu item helps you send your sequence to AudioVision.

Import. Import is the flip side of Export. You use Export to send files you created in the Avid to other computers. You use Import to bring all sorts of files into your Avid. You could import digital photographs, digital audio, animation you created in After Effects®, or titles you created in Photoshop®. The list of importable files is quite extensive. We'll spend some time learning how to export and import in Chapter 14.

Refresh Media Directories. If you remove a media drive from the Avid or delete a lot of media files, you will want to let your Avid figure out what is still available. You do this by refreshing the media directories.

Load Media Database. The media database is like a card catalog that keeps track of what's being put on and taken off the external drives. The Avid doesn't keep the entire database in memory all the time. After certain actions, some of your sequences might be offline—the images or sounds don't play, and you'll see that the media is listed as "Media Offline." When you load the Media Database, the Avid may find the missing offline material.

Mount All. This command mounts, or makes active and available, all the media drives attached to your Avid.

Unmount. This opens a dialog box that allows you to select drives or disks for ejection or unmounting.

Exit. Like Quit on a Mac, Exit is the Windows command that closes everything currently opened, including bins and monitors, and quits the Avid application software. You are returned to the computer desktop.

EDIT MENU

The Edit menu contains some commands that are quite similar to those found on other common software types, so, again, much of this will be familiar to you. Cut, Copy, Paste, Undo, Redo, and Duplicate are commands I'm sure you have used before. They behave a bit differently here, but probably as you would expect.

Undo Mark Out. You are no doubt already a devoted user of this command. The Avid gives you 32 levels of Undo. You can go back and change actions that you took up to 32 actions ago.

Redo Lift. Redo replaces the action that you undid. It is just as handy as Undo.

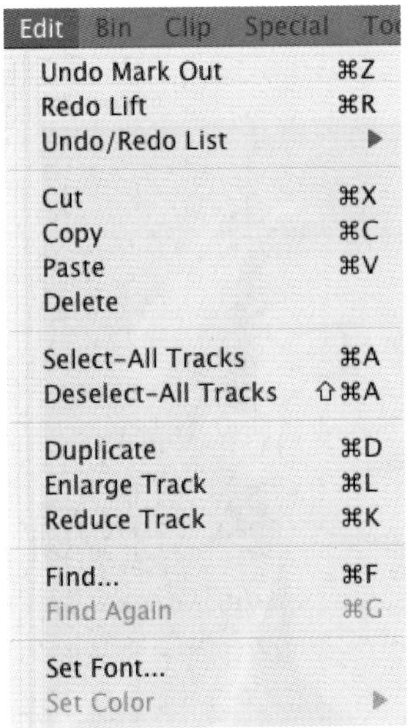

Figure 7.4 Edit menu.

Undo/Redo List. This list outlines your last 32 actions (either Undo or Redo). Instead of working through all of them, one at a time, to reach the one you want, with this list you can search the list and then select the action you want to change. Remember that all previous actions—those actions above the one action on the list—will also be changed.

Cut. If you select material in the Timeline by using an IN mark and an OUT mark and then choose Cut, the selected material is removed and immediately goes into the Clipboard. Cut works just like Extract.

Copy. If you select something by using an IN mark and an OUT mark and then choose Copy, the selected material is copied to the Clipboard, where it is stored until you paste it in somewhere. This is a great way to get audio from one area of the sequence, copy it to the Clipboard Monitor, and then put it somewhere else.

Paste. This command places whatever is in the Clipboard at the blue position indicator, or at an IN mark in the Timeline.

Delete. This works just like the Delete key. It opens a dialog box for deleting clips from a bin or tracks from the Timeline.

Select–All Tracks. This is a terrific way to quickly select all of the things you're working on. You can select all the clips in a bin or select all the tracks in the Timeline.

Duplicate. We already practiced this in Chapter 2. There will be many times when you want to duplicate sequences. Just select the sequence you want to copy, and hit Command–D (Mac) or Ctrl–D (Windows). Rename the copy, and you can make changes to the new version while holding onto the previous version.

Enlarge Track. This enlarges tracks in the Timeline. It also enlarges frames when you're working in the bin in Frame View.

Reduce Track. This reduces frames in Frame View or reduces tracks in the Timeline. You'll use this frequently.

Find. This is just like Find in most word-processing programs, but it is used to find clips in the Timeline or text you've attached to a locator. It's great if you have a Timeline with hundreds of clips.

Find Again. This command repeats the previous Find command.

Set Font. You can customize the way things look on the screen, including the font used in bins and certain windows. This is useful if your eyesight is such that you find it difficult to read the bin information.

Set Color. Like Set Font, this command is for those who want to make their bins and Composer window look different.

BIN MENU

Now we arrive at the pull-down menus that are not like those found on most word-processing programs. The Bin menu is made up of commands that act on things you'll find in a bin. It seems obvious, but sometimes we overlook the obvious. Often you need to have a bin open and selected in order for these commands to be available.

Batch Capture. This opens a dialog box that leads you through the process of capturing selected clips. Normally you use this command after you have *logged* a number of clips. When you log a clip, you have set the IN and OUT timecode for the clips but you haven't captured them. By invoking Batch Capture, you can go to lunch while the Avid digitizes each of the selected clips.

Batch Import. Some projects contain a great many imported files, such as graphic and animation files. Batch Import makes it easy to make changes to files on another computer or with different software and then bring those changed files back into the Avid.

Figure 7.5 Bin menu.

Decompose. This command takes your sequence and breaks it into all the individual clips that make up the sequence. Let's say you captured 1000 master clips when you captured your tapes, and to save space you captured all those clips at a low resolution, like 15:1s. And, let's say your final sequence is made up of only 50 clips. After decomposing your final sequence, you have those 50 clips in a bin and you simply recapture just those 50 at a higher resolution, like DV 25 or 1:1. Decompose is a handy command and one we'll examine in Chapter 18.

Consolidate/Transcode. *Consolidate* lets you send media files to the drive of your choice, which means you can better organize your media files. It also helps you get rid of material that you digitized but no longer need, enabling you to reclaim a large amount of space on your hard drives. When you consolidate a sequence, you are telling the Avid to keep all the media from the clips that went into the sequence and to throw out all the media from the clips that didn't get edited into the sequence. You don't want to consolidate until you've made a very fine cut. *Transcode* is an advanced feature not found on Xpress DV. You use transcode when you want to convert a sequence or clip from one format to another. You could use Transcode to convert a high-definition sequence to a standard-definition one. We'll do this in Chapter 16.

DV Scene Extraction. Whenever you stop and start a DV camera, a marker is put down on the tape; therefore, every single shot in your tape has been tagged. This command helps you break all those shots on your videotape into individual "clips." You can make a master clip of the entire tape— or the portion you're interested in recording—and then use DV Scene Extraction to break each individual shot into subclips, automatically. This saves no space on your media drive, but it's a really fast way to break what you have into distinct clips.

Relink. It sometimes happens that the connection (link) between the master clip and the media file is broken. The clip appears offline, even though you know the media file is on the drive somewhere. In this case, you need to relink the clip to the media file.

Change Sample Rate. Digital audio—like that found on a CD or recorded by a DV camera—can be recorded at different sample rates, sort of like the audio equivalent of resolution. The higher the sample rate, the better the audio's quality. Common sample rates are 32 kHz, 44.1 kHz, and 48 kHz. You can edit material containing different sample rates and then, in the Bin menu, choose this command to determine one sample rate for the entire sequence. This is important when putting your sequence out to tape. Xpress projects are usually sampled at 48 kHz.

Launch In Native Application. Using After Effects, or Illustrator, you can create a company logo with an HTML link and embed it into the Timeline. This is called an *enhancement*. When you click on the enhancement, you can use this command to open the software (if you have it installed) that was used to create the enhancement.

Headings. We've already discussed this command in Chapter 3. It opens a dialog box that lists all the possible columns, by headings, that are available to you. You select the ones you want and deselect the ones you want hidden from view.

AutoSync(tm). This is especially handy when you're working on film projects. Film is recorded double-system, meaning the sound is recorded on a separate recorder and not by the film camera. You capture the picture, then the sound. The sound and picture are then placed in sync in the

Avid. Once synced, they can be locked together so sync breaks appear whenever sync is broken.

Group. This is an advanced feature, not found on Xpress DV. You can take clips that were shot with different cameras, and group them together into one clip. Once they are grouped, you can use Avid's MultiCamera editing features. Let's say you grouped four clips into one group. In Quad Split Mode, for instance, the Source Monitor shows all four clips. You can see all the choices and then cut into your sequence whichever one works best. It's a quick way to build a montage of different shots or to edit together various shots of the same action.

AutoSequence(tm). If the original videotape has no audio, as with a film-to-tape transfer, you can bring in the sound, sync it up, and then use this command to put the synced audio back onto that videotape.

Custom Sift. This command opens a dialog box in which you set various options and parameters for sifting through a bin to find clips you want to locate. You can sift by name, creation date, tape, duration, and so on.

Sort/Sort Again. We spent some time in Chapter 3 discussing this command. It enables you to choose a column in a bin and sort all the clips alphanumerically by that chosen column. After you have sorted, it will change to Sort Again.

Show Sifted. During sifting, this command displays only those items in a bin that met the sift criteria. All others are hidden from view.

Show Unsifted. This command restores the unsifted items for viewing.

Set Bin Display. This command presents a dialog box that lets you determine which items you want displayed in the bin. There are many choices. You're familiar with only a few. The choices are as follows:
- Master clips (you know all about these)
- Subclips (you know about these)
- Sequences (you know all about these)
- Sources (lists the tapes the material comes from)
- Effects (dissolves, wipes, etc.—we'll learn about these)
- Motion effects (freeze frames, slow motion—we'll learn about these)
- Rendered effects (we'll learn about these)

If you checked off all the choices, your bin would be packed with too much information, making it hard to find the sequences, clips, and subclips you need. When we learn about effects, titles, and motion effects and begin creating them, we'll often want to see them displayed in the bin.

Reverse Selection. Let's say you want to select all those clips that are close-ups. And let's say that of the 40 clips in the bin, 2 are wide shots and the other 38 are close-ups. Shift–click on the 2 that are wide shots and then on Reverse Selection—all 38 close-ups are selected. The two that are wide shots are deselected. You reversed your selection.

Select Offline Items. In the previous chapter, we learned about logging and capturing clips. Often when you're capturing, you're looking for clips that are offline—meaning they have no media files because they haven't been captured, just logged. It makes your life easier to be able to go to a bin, select this command, and have all the offline clips selected.

Select Media Relatives. This enables you to select a sequence or a clip and then have the Avid highlight all the objects related to it. Let's say you've finished the final sequence and you want to make sure you used all the shots available to you. Click on the sequence and then on Select Media Relatives; the Avid will highlight every clip that was used in the Sequence. For this to work, you need to be able to see two bins at once. If you're working with SuperBins, double click on the bin containing your sequence(s) and select a sequence, then single-click the bin containing your clips so you can see both bins at once. Now choose this command to see the media relatives.

Select Unreferenced Clips. This command works like the flip side of Select Media Relatives. Select a sequence and then choose this command. It shows you all the clips in the bin that have *not* been used in the sequence.

Loop Selected Clips. This is a great tool. Let's say you have two takes of an action or scene. Use Mark IN and OUT in the Source Monitor to select the part of each take you wish to compare, Now Shift–click the takes in the bin. Select Loop Selected Clips and the two takes will play, one at a time, in a loop, for comparison. You can do this with however many clips you want.

Align Columns/Align to Grid. When you are in Text View, this command puts the columns in nice neat rows. When you are in Frame View, this command changes to Align to Grid and aligns to a grid all your frames.

Fill Window. When you are in Frame View, this command distributes all the frames evenly inside the window.

Fill Sorted. You can't sort in Frame View, because there are no columns to sort; however, if you sort a bin in Brief or Text View, you can get into Frame View, select this command, and have the clips appear in Frame View according to how you sorted them in the other views.

Select Unrendered Titles. Titles often need to be rendered (created) by the computer before they play in real time. This shows you all the titles that have not been rendered.

CLIP MENU

In my opinion, the term "Clip menu" is a bit of a misnomer, as many of the commands here don't really have much to do with actual clips. I think these commands have a lot more to do with the Timeline. But here we go.

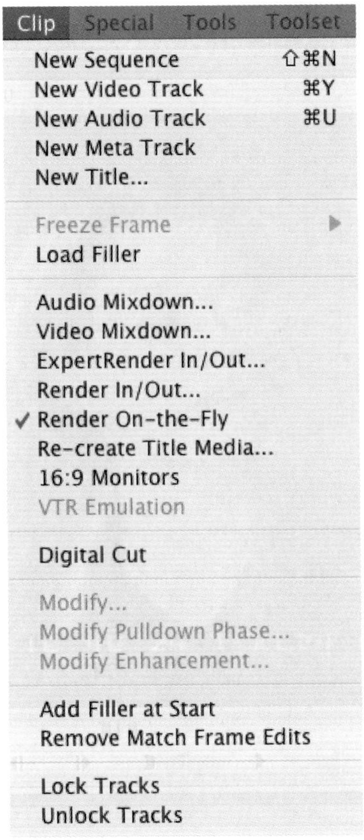

Clip	Special	Tools	Toolset

New Sequence ⇧⌘N
New Video Track ⌘Y
New Audio Track ⌘U
New Meta Track
New Title...

Freeze Frame ▶
Load Filler

Audio Mixdown...
Video Mixdown...
ExpertRender In/Out...
Render In/Out...
✓ Render On-the-Fly
Re-create Title Media...
16:9 Monitors
VTR Emulation

Digital Cut

Modify...
Modify Pulldown Phase...
Modify Enhancement...

Add Filler at Start
Remove Match Frame Edits

Lock Tracks
Unlock Tracks

Figure 7.6 Clip menu.

New Sequence. Whenever you want to create a new sequence, use this command.

New Video Track. This command creates a new video track on the Timeline. Later, when we create effects and titles, we'll want to put them on a new video track, such as V2, so picture images can be combined.

New Audio Track. The Avid can play between 8 and 24 tracks of audio simultaneously. If you add music, a narration track, and several sound effect tracks to your dialog tracks, you can easily need six or seven audio tracks. This command instantly creates a new track on the Timeline.

New Title. This command opens the Title Tool, which we'll use to create titles.

Freeze Frame. This command opens up a list of freeze frame lengths: 1 second, 5 seconds, 10 seconds, etc., and creates the freeze frame of your choice.

Load Filler. This opens up a pop-up Monitor that contains black filler. For filmmakers, it's like grabbing a roll of fill that you then splice onto your tracks to create a pause or to replace picture or audio. Let's say you want to put 30 frames (a second) of black between the end of one scene and the beginning of the next. Choose Load Filler. In the Pop-Up Monitor, mark an IN, go 29 frames, and mark an OUT. Then mark an IN on the Timeline where you want the fill to go. Select all your tracks and hit Splice. It acts just like any clip, except that this one has only black. (The Media Composer places this command in the Monitor menus. We'll examine these Monitor menus at the end of the chapter.)

Audio Mixdown. Use this command when you wish to mix your many tracks onto one (mono) or two tracks in order to send your sequence to the Web or some other application.

Video Mixdown. The same explanation and rationale given for audio mixdown applies here.

Expert Render In/Out. Effects often require the computer to create a combination of media. This creation of new media is called *rendering*. If the effect isn't too complicated, the Avid can often play it in real time, without having the computer create new media. This is nice because you can see if you like the effect and want to use it before you commit any media space on your drives to the effect. Sometimes the Avid can't play effects in real time, and they will have to be rendered for you to see them. With this command, the Avid will look at the effects you have on several tracks and decide which of them need to be rendered for all of them to play together. Instead of rendering them all, the Avid will "intelligently" render only those that need to be rendered.

Render In/Out or Render at Position. Eventually, you'll need to render all the effects if you want to send your work out into the world. If you have just one effect to render, you place the position indicator on that effect and choose Render at Position. If you have a number of effects that need to be rendered, you'll mark an IN before the first and an OUT after the last and then choose Render In/Out.

Render On-the-Fly. If you have combined several effects or if you have effects that are quite complex, the Avid might not be able to play them unless you render them; however, you can coax the Avid into showing you the effect before it's been rendered by turning on Render On-the-Fly. The effects won't play in real time, but with Render On-the-Fly selected you can see the effect by dragging the position indicator through the Timeline. It's a fudge, but often preferable to rendering the effect.

Re-create Title Media. Media Composer and Xpress Pro users often edit projects at a low resolution because it saves hard drive space and then recapture the final sequence at a higher resolution, for output to tape. Titles created at a lower resolution may not play. To get them to play at the new resolution, you may need to select Re-create Title Media. Now you have your titles in the higher resolution. Xpress DV users may take titles offline and then need to re-create them at a later time.

16:9 Monitors. This configures the Source Monitor and Record Monitor for the wide-screen aspect ratio. We'll discuss this at length in Chapters 15 and 16.

VTR Emulation. This is an advanced feature not found on the Xpress DV. If you have the right cable, you can have an external videotape editing system play your sequence. An external edit controller takes control of the Avid and plays the sequence as if it were just another source video in a videotape deck. In this way, you can have multiple source tapes, including the Avid sequence, edited together onto a master videotape.

Digital Cut. The Avid can be connected to sophisticated analog and digital video decks for recording the final, completed sequence onto tape. When you use the Digital Cut Tool, the Avid controls the videotape deck and records your sequence to tape using timecode.

Modify. This command allows you to change important data about a clip. For instance, you might mistakenly log a tape as having two audio tracks, when in fact there is only one useable audio track. You can select the clips you logged in the bin and then, using the Modify command, deselect one of the audio tracks. Now, when you go to capture the tapes, you won't be forced to capture two audio tracks.

Modify Pulldown Phase. When working with film that has been transferred to videotape, or with video cameras that record at 23.976 frames per second, you are working with frames that are pulled (or slowed) down. It sometimes happens that you need to modify the information about the way the pull-down occurred. We'll explore this in Chapters 14 and 19.

Modify Enhancement. Enhancements are things that can be imbedded into the Avid Timeline, such as HTML links. With this command you can change the size and shape of the enhancement and where it appears on the screen (not found on Xpress DV).

Add Filler at Start. This command adds a second of filler at the start of a new sequence. Handy.

Remove Match Frame Edits. We'll get to what are more often called *add edits* later in the book. With this command, you can mark an IN and then an OUT and remove add edits from your sequence.

Lock Tracks/Lock Bin. This command lets you lock one or more tracks. It's especially handy as you get to the end of your editing phase and don't want a lot of work dislodged inadvertently. A padlock symbol appears in the track selector box in the Timeline. When working in bins, this let's you lock bins so they can't be changed.

Unlock Tracks/Unlock Bin. This command unlocks the tracks or bin.

SPECIAL MENU

Xpress Pro, Xpress Pro HD, and Media Composer Avids have a Special menu (Figure 7.7).

Figure 7.7 Special menu.

Group Clip Mode. The Xpress Pro, like the media Composer, can group different clips together so they act as one master clip. In Quad Display, you can see the four clips—often four different camera angles—and with the touch of a button cut from one clip to the other on the fly. Group Clip Mode is one of the most advanced ways of editing grouped clips.

Read Audio Timecode. The Avid can read the longitudinal timecode recorded on an audio track and display that information in the auxiliary timecode column, which is one of the headings in Text View. You must be in Text View to select this command.

Device. This command directs the Avid to check to see what external devices are hooked up, such as the Avid Mojo or a deck attached to the FireWire port. Usually, you would do this if you wanted to send your sequence out to tape.

TOOLS MENU

All of your audio tools are found in the Tools menu, as well as many other handy items, like the Command Palette, which we discussed in Chapter 3. You'll also find tools that help you to keep track of all your media and control the way visual effects work.

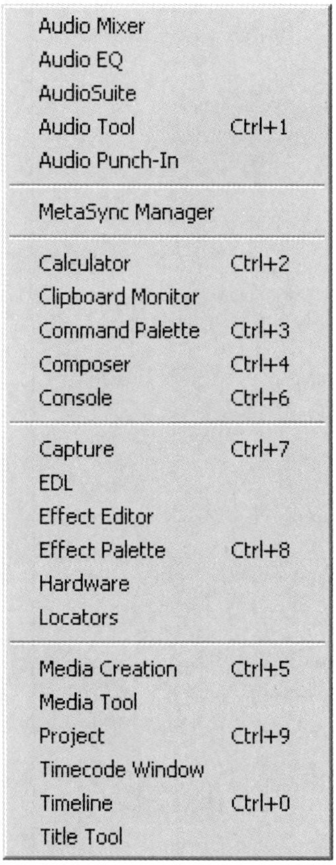

Audio Mixer	
Audio EQ	
AudioSuite	
Audio Tool	Ctrl+1
Audio Punch-In	
MetaSync Manager	
Calculator	Ctrl+2
Clipboard Monitor	
Command Palette	Ctrl+3
Composer	Ctrl+4
Console	Ctrl+6
Capture	Ctrl+7
EDL	
Effect Editor	
Effect Palette	Ctrl+8
Hardware	
Locators	
Media Creation	Ctrl+5
Media Tool	
Project	Ctrl+9
Timecode Window	
Timeline	Ctrl+0
Title Tool	

Figure 7.8   Tools menu.

Audio Mixer. This is an important tool. When it opens, you see what looks like a mixing board with volume and pan sliders. You can adjust volume and pan by dragging the sliders. You can make changes to individual clips, segments of the Timeline, or an entire track in the Timeline. We examine this in detail in Chapter 8.

Audio EQ. This opens a tool that enables you to adjust the equalization of individual audio clips in the Timeline. By changing the low, middle, and high frequencies, you can alter or improve your sound.

Automation Gain. This tool looks a lot like the Audio Mix tool, but it allows you to actually mix your tracks on the fly. As you play the sequence, you can change volume levels, and the ramps you create as you raise and lower the volume sliders are marked by key frames. When you look at the Timeline you'll see a visual representation of your level changes.

AudioSuite. This command opens a tool that gives you access to sophisticated audio tools such as pitch processing, time compression and expansion, and reversing of audio.

Audio Tool. This command brings up a tool that is like a digital VU meter. It measures the strength of the incoming or outgoing audio signals. Instead of depending on your ears to determine proper sound levels, use this meter's readings instead.

Audio Punch-In. This command opens a tool that allows you to record audio directly to the Timeline. It is used primarily to quickly add voice-over narration.

MetaSync Manager. Metadata is a new buzzword that refers to extra material embedded in a video or DVD, such as subtitles, close-captions, or links to the Internet. This command opens the tool that let's you place this metadata on the Avid's Timeline.

Calculator. This opens up a special calculator that helps you figure out different film and video durations. For instance, you could enter a duration in timecode numbers and then calculate the number of feet and frames it would equal in the 35-mm film format.

Clipboard Monitor. Several actions, such as Lift, Extract, and Paste, as well as clicking the Clipboard button, will send whatever has been marked in the Timeline to the Clipboard Monitor for temporary storage. This command opens the Clipboard Monitor. Once it's opened, you can splice or overwrite any or all of the Clipboard's contents into the Timeline.

Command Palette. All the commands available to you are contained in the Command Palette; there are over a hundred commands to choose from. You can map any of them to the keyboard to create a custom keyboard, or you can map them to the Source and Record row of command buttons. The palette looks like a file cabinet with tabs for categories of commands: Move, Play, Edit, Trim, FX, 3D, Mcam, Other, More. Click on the tab for the category you want, and you'll see all the command buttons.

Composer. This activates the Composer Monitor window.

Console. This opens the Console window, which gives you detailed information about your system, including your ID number and model. It provides information about bin objects and the sequence in the Timeline. It also provides a log of error messages, which you might read to an Avid technician who is trying to help you solve a problem over the phone.

Capture. This opens up a tool used to control the capturing process. When opened, it looks a lot like the working face of a video deck, with buttons for playing, fast-forwarding, and rewinding tapes.

EDL. This opens a tool that creates an Edit Decision List. Many projects that originated on high-end videotape are not finished on an Avid. The Avid is instead used to make all the editing decisions, then the original video-tapes are taken to an online video editing suite. The online editor assembles the show based on the EDL the Avid generates. If you find that the EDL Manager doesn't launch when you select this menu item, go to your applications folder and open it manually. We discuss this in Chapter 18.

Effect Editor. This tool opens the Effect Editor, which you use to adjust a visual effect's parameters. We'll examine it in detail in Chapter 11.

Effect Palette. This tool opens up a palette from which you can select all the various visual effects available to you.

Hardware. This tool gives you information about the computer hardware that makes up your Avid. This tool also shows you how much space is available on your various disk drives. Open it, and you'll see all your drives, with a bar graph next to each one that shows the amount of the drive that is filled and the amount that is still available.

Locators. Locators are like little colored labels that you can place on any track in the Timeline. They help you flag important points. You can even write yourself notes. This tool opens a window that shows you where all the locators are on your sequence and lets you view them in different ways.

Media Creation. This command opens a dialog box in which you tell the Avid how you want to handle all the media you bring into the Avid. To save drive space, you could set the resolution for the tapes you capture at a lower resolution and set your titles and imported files at the highest resolution. That way you could recapture only the shots used in your final sequence at the highest resolution and have your titles and effects already at that highest resolution.

Media Tool. This is a tool that looks and behaves just like a bin. It helps you find and manage all the project's media files.

Project. This command makes the Project window the active window.

Timecode Window. This opens a window that can display up to eight lines of timecode information. If you click on the window, a pop-up menu appears, giving you options, such as IN to OUT, sequence duration, and remaining time.

Timeline. If you inadvertently close the Timeline or find you don't have a Timeline, select this command and a Timeline will appear.

Title Tool. This opens the tool that we'll use to create titles. This command does the same thing as New Title in the Clip menu. They are identical.

TOOLSET MENU

The items on this menu change the look of the Avid. They open the tools you'll find most useful when performing common editing tasks such as capturing videotapes, color-correcting your shots, or adding visual effects. You could open

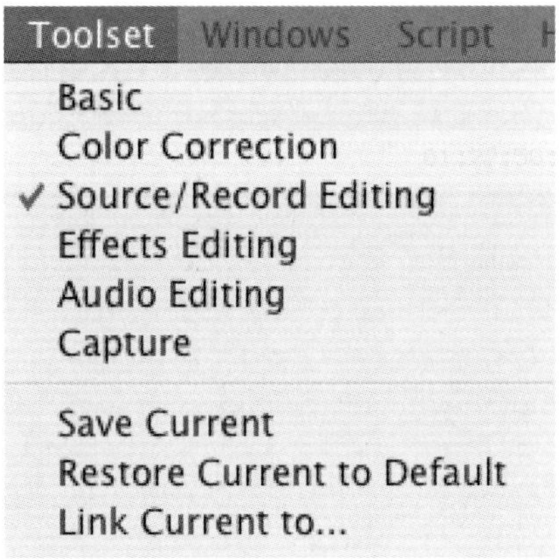

Figure 7.9 Toolset menu.

these different tools individually, but it's easier to do with one flick of the cursor. What's even better is that you can make changes to the way a particular Toolset works and save your changes with ease.

Basic. When you select Basic, the Source Monitor disappears, leaving just the Record Monitor. When you double-click on a clip to open it, it appears in a small window called a Pop-Up Monitor. I use Basic when I'm going to screen a fine cut for a couple of people. I'll drag on the corner of the Record Monitor to make it quite large and center it. Now my audience is looking at a single screen and not glancing anxiously at the empty Source Monitor.

Color Correction. This opens a series of tools that allow you to make very detailed adjustments to the color of a clip in your Timeline.

Source/Record Editing. This gives you a Source Monitor and a Record Monitor. It's the mode we have been using throughout this book.

Effects Editing. When you select this menu item, the Effect Palette Tool opens, showing you all of the visual effects available to you. The Effect Editor opens as well. The Effect Editor lets you change the way each individual effect works. You might add a border to an effect, change the transparency of an effect, or move the effect around within the Record Monitor. In fact, the Record Monitor changes as well. It no longer shows you the sequence. We'll spend a lot of time working in this mode in Chapter 11.

Audio Editing. This opens the Audio Mixer Tool to alter or improve the quality of your sound. Because you are working with clips in the Timeline, you don't need the Source Monitor, just the Timeline and the Record Monitor, so the Source Monitor disappears.

Capture. When you select this editing mode, the Capture Tool opens so you're ready to begin capturing tapes into the Avid.

Save Current. This lets you change the way the Toolset items are configured and save the changes. This command makes it easy to have it your way. For instance, when I'm in Source/Record mode, I like to have Brief View be the default view. So, I simply change the bin view from Frame to Brief and then select Save Current, and from then on that's the way Source/Record will work for me.

Restore Current to Default. Any changes you make to the default set up, using Save Current, get wiped away if you select this.

Link Current to. . . . In Chapter 3, we spent some time discussing Settings. We learned how to change the color of bins or the Timeline background. We changed the keyboard settings. We also learned to duplicate settings and to call the original setting "Default" and the new setting "Mine." With "Link Current to" you can have various settings, name them, and then connect those settings to particular Toolset modes.

WINDOWS MENU

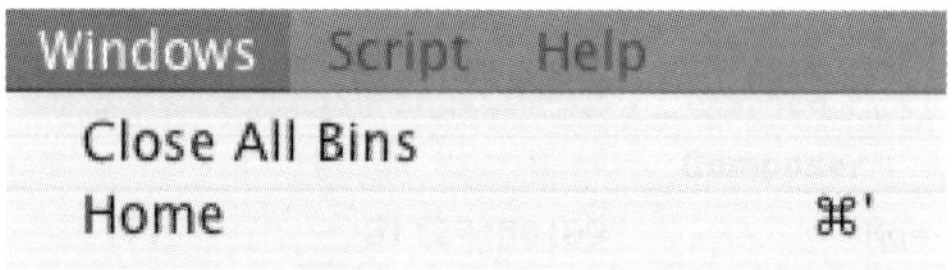

Figure 7.10   Windows menu.

Close All Bins. This closes all your bins. If you have a sequence loaded in the Record Monitor, it will disappear, as will your Timeline. I never use this command because I don't like what happens when I use it.

Home. This will return your active window, usually the Composer or Timeline window, to its proper placement on the computer monitor for video playback.

SCRIPT MENU

Script Integration is based on the style of editing commonly used on feature films. It is one of the Avid's most powerful features and requires an entire chapter to adequately explain it. We'll tackle all of its many features in Chapter 17.

HELP MENU

The Avid offers an online reference tool, called Help. When you select Shortcuts or Avid Xpress Pro Help, your Web browser launches and the Help site opens. If you're stuck and can't figure out how to do something, scroll though the entries until you find Avid's explanation. Read Me is an Acrobat text document, like a manual.

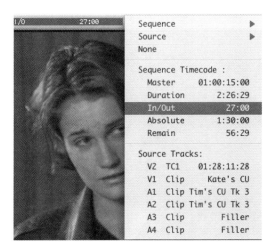

Figure 7.11 Help menu.

TRACKING AND MONITOR MENUS

Above the Source Monitor and Record Monitor is a bar that displays information about your project. It also contains pull-down menus.

Tracking Menu

The Tracking menu provides information about your clip or sequence in timecode, footage, or frames. There's a Tracking menu for the Source Monitor and one for the Record Monitor. The tracking information is updated continuously as you play either the source material or the sequence. When you drag and select one of the choices from the menu, that choice will be displayed in the tracking information display, above the monitor. Here I've selected I/O, which tells me the time, in seconds, between my IN and OUT marks—27 seconds. Let's look at some of the choices.

Figure 7.12 Record Tracking menu.

Sequence. Select this pull-down menu to choose how you want the information about your sequence listed—as timecode, footage, or frames. Here, I have selected timecode.

Source. Select this and you can choose the kind of information you would like to see in the Source Tracks.

None. No information will appear above the Record Monitor.

Master. This displays what is called the master timecode at the point where the position indicator is currently located. Let's say a sequence's starting timecode is set at 01;00;00;00. As you can see in Figure 7.12, we are stopped at a frame that is 15 seconds from the start of the sequence.

Duration. This displays the total duration of the sequence (or clip).

In/Out. This displays the amount of time between the IN and OUT marks.

Absolute. This number is the running time of the sequence, from the first frame to the position indicator.

Remain. This displays the time remaining from the position indicator to the end of the sequence.

Source Tracks. This lists all the tracks in your Timeline. You choose the type of information in the Source pull-down menu.

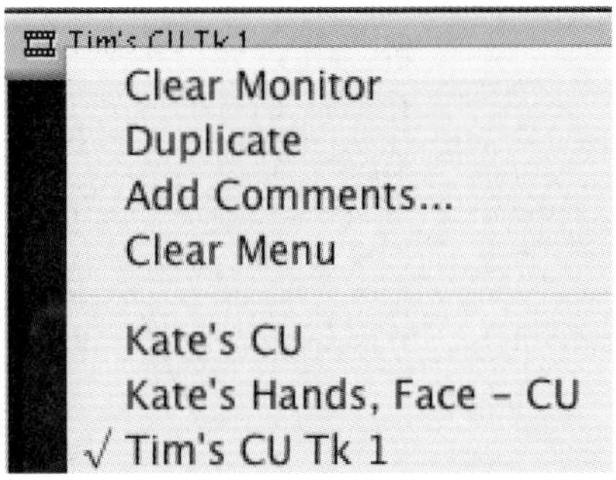

Figure 7.13 Source Monitor menu.

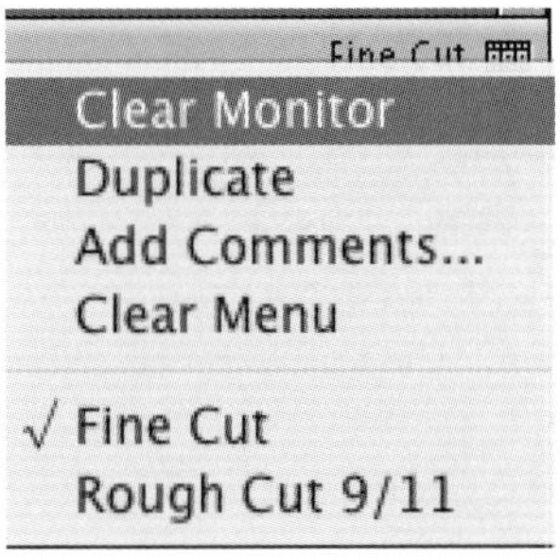

Figure 7.14 Record Monitor menu.

Monitor Menu

Both the Source Monitor and the Record Monitor have a Monitor menu. Just click on the name of the clip in the Source Monitor or the name of the sequence in the Record Monitor to open the Monitor menu.

> **Clear Monitor.** This clears the clips or sequences from the monitor. The monitor screen goes black, but all the clips or sequences are still loaded.
> **Duplicate.** This duplicates the clip or the sequence.
> **Add Comments.** You can add comments to a clip and they will appear in an EDL as well as in the Timeline if Comments is selected from the Timeline Fast menu.
> **Clear Menu.** This removes all but the current sequence or clip from the menu.
> **Clip/sequence list.** Below the Clear Menu item, you'll find a list of all the shots in the Source Monitor or all the sequences that have been loaded into the Record Monitor. The one with the checkmark is the one currently in the monitor.

Whew! We have spent considerable time and energy trying to digest the scores of commands located in the pull-down menus that are at the heart of Avid editing. We now have a much better sense of the Avid's rich working environment, and we've had a preview of the work we'll be doing from here on in. We also know where we can find the commands we'll need to do different sorts of tasks. You may never use some of these commands, while others will be in your repertory continually. Whenever there are keyboard equivalents listed in the menu, try learning them, as they will speed up your work considerably.

MAPPING MENU ITEMS TO KEYBOARD

You can place any command located on any menu onto any key on the keyboard or onto any of the command buttons. Let's try mapping a menu command to a keyboard key. Open your keyboard in the Settings window. You'll see most of the keys on the keyboard are already mapped with commands, but if you hold down the Shift key, you'll see there are many blank keys. We're going to place the New Title menu item, found in the Clip menu, on the Shift–T key. You'll notice that the T key already has a command on it—one that's not very useful. Yes, I could map to a blank key, but Shift–T for title is so easy to remember.

1. Open your keyboard in the Settings window—the one we created in Chapter 3.
2. Get the Command Palette from the Tools menu.

3. Select the 'Menu to Button' Reassignment box on the Command Palette—it doesn't matter which tab you select. Notice the mouse cursor now looks like a white menu.

4. On the real keyboard, hold down the Shift key.
5. Click the cursor on the computer monitor keyboard's T key so it turns a dark color.
6. Bring the cursor to the Clip menu and select New Title. You'll now see a large "T" on your Shift–T key on the Avid keyboard.
7. Close the Command Palette. Close the keyboard.

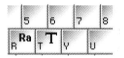

We won't need this until we get to Chapter 10, but then we'll find it very helpful. Remember, you can place any menu item on any button or keyboard key, but let's wait to map other menu commands until we're more familiar with the all the menu items.

8

Sound

THE IMPORTANCE OF SOUND

Many videomakers and filmmakers don't realize just how important sound is to the success of a project. "It's a visual medium" is the common wisdom handed down as gospel. Well, half-right is better than all wrong. I've organized a number of film festivals and served as a judge at others, and, while I have often been amazed by the stunning cinematography on display in student projects, just as often I've been dismayed by the poor quality of the sound. I think what separates a student project from a professional project is the lack of care that students give to their sound tracks.

On most films and videos, the only sound you care about during shooting is the sync sound—the dialog or words spoken by the subjects. A good sound recordist works really hard *not* to record the ambient sounds—the traffic, people in the background, footsteps, and so on. Yes, ambient sounds are vitally important, but you add them during editing.

If, for example, you record the hum of an air conditioner on your dialog track, it's very difficult to remove. But, if you turn the air conditioner off just before shooting you will have much clearer dialog. If the air conditioner's hum is important to the story, you can always record the hum separately and add it to your scene during editing. That way you can adjust the relative levels of the dialog and the air conditioner.

Most sounds are added to films and videos after the picture and dialog have been edited. This stage is often called *picture lock*. Once picture lock is reached, sound editors begin finding and creating the sound effects that were kept out during shooting. Often, sound editors must invent sounds. What does a dinosaur sound like? What sound does Darth Vader's laser sword make? Sound designers and sound editors such as Cecelia Hall (*Witness*, *Top Gun*, *Wayne's World*), and Gary Rydstrom (*Finding Nemo*, *Minority Report*) deserve as much credit for the success of the films they have worked on as the cinematographers who shot the films, because so much of the emotional impact comes from the sound track. Film is shot. Sound is built a layer at a time during editing.

Although the Avid is known for its ability to cut pictures, you'll soon realize that's only half the story. The Avid gives you tremendous control over your sound tracks. Take advantage of that capability. It'll make a huge difference in the success of your work.

TRACK MONITORS

The tiny speaker-shaped icons next to the track selector boxes show you that a track is being monitored. These are called *Track Monitors*. If you click on a Track Monitor, the icon inside it will disappear, indicating that you won't hear any sound from that track. To get the icon back, simply click in the Track Monitor and the icon reappears. Examine Figure 8.1.

Figure 8.1   Track Monitor icon for A1 is present, while A2 is turned off.

Monitoring Only One Track

Let's say you are monitoring eight tracks, and you hear a sound glitch but aren't sure which track it's on. You think the problem is on the narration track A1, but you aren't sure. One way to monitor just A1 is to deselect all the other Record Track Monitors; however, if there are eight of them, that's a pain. There is a faster way of monitoring one track (also known as *soloing* a track).

- Hold down the Command key (Mac) or Ctrl key (Windows) and click on that track's monitor. The indicator box turns *green* to show that this is the only track "on." All the other tracks are off (Figure 8.2).

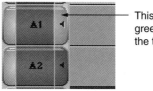

This will turn green and solo the track.

Figure 8.2

To return to monitoring all your tracks, simply click in the Track Monitor and it will no longer be soloed. You can solo more than one track by Command/Ctrl–clicking multiple Track Monitors.

The Hollow Speaker Icon

If you look at Figure 8.3, the speaker icons for tracks A1 and A2 are hollow. They are also gold, although it's a bit hard to pick that up from the black-and-white screen capture. The speaker icon for track A3 is neither hollow nor gold. The tracks with the hollow (and gold) speaker icon are special. Those are the tracks you are listening to when you play the sequence at speeds faster than normal (30 fps) or when you "scrub" your audio.

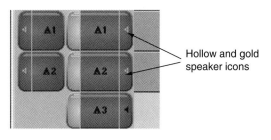

Hollow and gold speaker icons

Figure 8.3

AUDIO SCRUB

"Scrubbing" the audio is a technique used to concentrate on a particular piece of audio. You scrub it. There are two types of audio scrub: smooth audio scrub and digital audio scrub. Smooth audio scrub is quite simple:

- Hold down the K key (pause) while pressing the L key (forward). You hear what's on the hollow icon tracks in slow motion. It works backwards as well; use the J key.

Digital audio scrub involves sampling a frame of audio. Because it is sampled, the pitch and speed don't change.

1. Select the tracks you want to scrub.
2. Press the Caps Lock key or hold down the Shift key.
3. Step forward or backward by clicking the step-one-frame-forward or step-one-frame-backward button, or drag the position indicator forward or backward.

This is great for locating a specific sound that will become your cut point. Say you're searching in the Timeline for the first frame of a hammer striking a nail. Click on the Caps Lock button and press the step-one-frame-forward button (pretend it's five frames away). Step, step, step, step, step, *CRUNCH*. Ah, there it is.

Selecting the Tracks for Scrubbing

Now, let's say the hollow icons are on tracks A1 and A2, and the sound you want to scrub is on tracks A3 and A4. To move the hollow speaker icon to track A3, simply hold the Option (Alt) key and then click on the A3 speaker icon. A3 is now the track with the hollow icon. Now, Option (Alt)–click on A4. Remember: Option–click (or Alt–click) on the speaker icons you want to scrub.

ADDING AUDIO TRACKS

In the later stages of editing, you will want to add sound effects and music to your sequence. Those sounds require their own sound tracks; you don't want them messing up your sync dialog tracks. To create additional tracks:

- Go to the Clip menu and select New Audio Track, or
- Press Command–U (Mac) or Ctrl–U (Windows).

SCROLLING YOUR TRACKS

Whenever you have more tracks than can be viewed in the Timeline, a scroll bar appears on the right-hand side of the Timeline so you can scroll up and down to see different tracks. I often resize the tracks I'm not working with, making them smaller so I can see more tracks without having to scroll.

PATCHING AUDIO TRACKS

When you want to splice or overwrite a shot of video, it usually goes onto the V1 track. Your sync sound—the sounds that come with that video—usually goes onto A1, or, if you have stereo sync sound, onto A1 and A2. If you're bringing in music or sound effects, you don't want them to go onto A1 or A2 because they'll replace your sync sound. Music, sound effects, and narration are additional sound elements, and they need to go onto additional audio tracks.

Let's say you have a stereo music cue that you want to add to the scene. You want it to play underneath the dialog. You need to create two additional tracks, A3 and A4, and *patch* the audio onto A3 and A4. When you put a music clip into the Source Monitor, you'll see the source tracks A1 and A2 appear in the Timeline, parallel to record tracks A1 and A2.

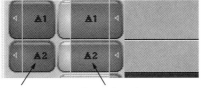

Source tracks   Record tracks

If you splice the music into A1 and A2, you throw your dialog out of sync. If you overwrite the music, you erase your dialog. Instead, you create two additional tracks, A3 and A4, and patch the tracks so your music will get spliced onto them.

To patch, click and hold the mouse on the first source track that you want to patch. In the example provided here, it's source track A2. Drag the mouse from A2 on the source side to A4 on the record side. You'll notice that as you hold down the mouse and drag, a white pointer arrow appears and points to A4; and when you release the mouse, the source track (A2) moves down to line up with your record track on A4 (Figures 8.4 and 8.5). Try it.

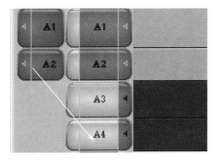

Figure 8.4

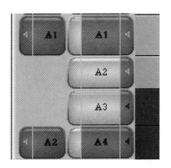

Figure 8.5

Do the same thing with A1. Move it to line up with A3. Now when you splice or overwrite, that's where your music will go—onto A3 and A4, not onto A1 and A2.

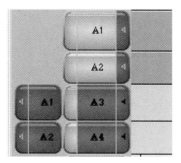

DELETING TRACKS

It sometimes happens that you need to get rid of one or more tracks. Perhaps you've created more tracks than you need, and the extra tracks just take up space on the computer screen. To delete a track, deselect all the other tracks and select just the one you want to delete. Press the Delete key on the keyboard. A dialog box will ask if you are sure you want to do that, and you click OK. If you make a mistake and inadvertently delete an important audio track, don't worry. Just press Command (Ctrl)–Z to undo the action. Deleting tracks works with video tracks just as well as with audio tracks.

CHANGING AUDIO LEVELS

When you digitize your audio, the sound levels aren't always perfect. Often you need to raise or lower the levels once you start editing. Changing levels becomes especially important when you begin to add audio tracks and mix a number of sounds together. For example, you wouldn't want your music to drown out the actors' voices or to have unintelligible narration because the sound-effect track is too loud. The Avid provides several tools to help you control the sound levels of your tracks so they work well together. Just imagine what it would sound like if you had 12 audio tracks and you couldn't change any of the levels.

Fixing Volume Output Levels

Before we change levels, let's start by making sure our Output settings are correct. The audio you get out of your speakers may be set too low. This can often happen on a Mac, where the Mac's volume control buttons on the keyboard can sometimes throw off the Avid's output settings, usually lowering them far more than you want. Here's how to set and check the output levels.

1. Go to the Project window and click on Settings.
2. Double-click on Audio Projects.
3. When the dialog box opens, click on the Output tab.

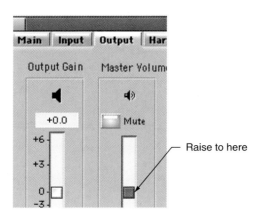

4. Raise the Master Volume slider to a point that is in line with the Output Gain slider (O).
5. Now close the dialog box.

Always check the Output setting before you make adjustments to your audio, and then make sure the volume on your speakers or headphones is always set at the same level. That way you're always starting from the same place.

Audio Mixer Tool

The first tool used to adjust volume is the Audio Mixer Tool (Figure 8.6). Open it by going to the Tools menu. It's the first selection.

The Audio Mixer Tool has two modes of operation. The first mode is called the Clip Gain Mode. You use it to raise or lower the volume of clips in the Timeline or change the pan of clips in the Timeline. The second mode, called Automation Gain Mode, lets you *record* volume and pan changes. The mode we'll use most often is the one you get when you open the Audio Mixer from the Tools menu—Clip Gain. It looks like a standard mixing board, with volume sliders for each track of audio. In Figure 8.6, you see we only have four tracks. If you are monitoring eight tracks, you have the option of looking at all eight by clicking on the Mix Panes button that shows four or eight tracks. To save screen space, you can keep it to four tracks and change the four you are viewing.

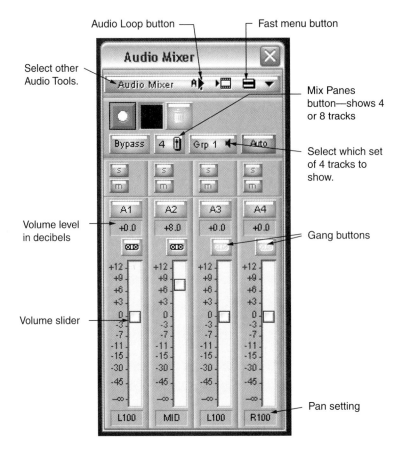

Figure 8.6   Audio Mixer Tool in Clip Gain Mode.

The Audio Mixer Tool can be used to change the volume of clips in the Source Monitor or clips that have been edited into the Timeline:

- To change the volume of a clip, place it in the Source Monitor and then raise or lower the slider.
- To change the volume of a clip in the Timeline, click on the Timeline (or the Record Monitor) and place the Position Indicator on the segment you want to change.

Now simply raise or lower the sliders to change your levels.

Usually, I don't change levels until I've edited the clips into a sequence. Most times the sound levels are good coming in, and the only reason I want to change them is to change the way they work with other tracks and within the sequence as a whole. Before I change a clip's volume, I want to see how it works with other clips. The one time I do change the levels of a clip in the Source Monitor is when I've brought in sound from a CD. (This is explained in Chapter 14.) Sometime those levels can be quite hot, and need adjusting before cutting them into the Timeline.

When adjusting clips in the Timeline, you'll notice that you are only affecting the level for the clip on which the position indicator sits. The entire track is not affected by the changes. This makes sense, when you stop to think about it, because often you want to raise one actor's level, while keeping another actor unchanged.

Mixing Tool with Audio Tool

I often have both the Audio Mixer Tool and the Audio Tool open at the same time so I can see the true audio levels as I make changes. Just get both of them from the Tools menu and place them together on the screen so they are easy to see. If you like the arrangement, go to the Toolset menu and select Save Current. They will then open together whenever you select Audio Editing from the Toolset menu.

Speed Tips

There are a couple of tricks that speed up the adjustment process. Let's say that A1 and A2 are stereo narration tracks, and you want to lower both of them at the same time. Click on the gang buttons for A1 and A2 (they'll turn a bright green). As you click on one slider, the other moves up and down with it. See Figure 8.7. Let's say you want to go back to 0 dB. Sure, you could drag the slider

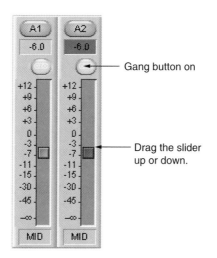

Figure 8.7

back to 0, but that's time consuming. Simply hold down the Option key (Mac) or the Alt key (Windows) and click on the slider button. The level will jump back to 0 dB.

Panning

The window at the bottom of each track is for *panning* the audio. Panning is a technique used whenever you have more than one channel of sound coming from more than one speaker. When you set the pan you are determining how much of the sound will come from the left speaker, how much from the middle (both speakers equally), and how much from the right speaker. To set the pan, click on the window and a horizontal slider will appear. Drag it left or right (Figure 8.8).

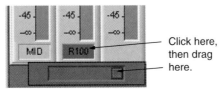

Figure 8.8

Option–click (Mac) or Alt–click (Windows) on the Pan button, and it will jump to MID, the center pan position.

Audio Clip Gain

As you use the Audio Mixer Tool to change levels on your clips in the Timeline, the Avid gives you a way to graphically see the decibel level at which you have set each clip. This Timeline view is called *Audio Clip Gain*, and you get it from the Timeline Fast menu. Audio Clip Gain also shows you which clips have been changed and which ones haven't.

Select the tracks in the Timeline you want to see and then go to the Timeline Fast menu and select Audio Clip Gain (Figure 8.9). Horizontal lines appear in the Timeline showing the clips that have been changed.

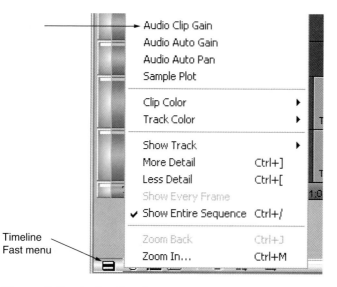

Figure 8.9 Audio Clip Gain.

If you enlarge the audio tracks, by selecting the track and pressing Command–L (Mac) or Ctrl–L (Windows) or by stretching the track with the mouse, decibel reference lines appear (Figure 8.10). Normally, you enlarge your tracks to this size only when you are making critical sound-level adjustments and you want to see the relationship between your setting and the 0-dB line.

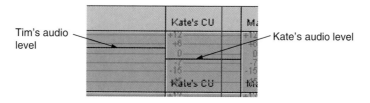

Figure 8.10 Audio Clip Gain.

Changing Volume and Panning on Multiple Clips

You will often want to change the pan or volume throughout the sequence, or a large portion of the sequence, rather than making changes to individual clips. Open the Audio Mixer Tool. To affect pan or volume levels for a segment of a track in your sequence:

1. Select the track.
2. Place an IN mark inside the first clip; place an OUT mark inside the last clip.

3. On the Audio Mixer Tool, click on the track button for that track (see Figure 8.11).
4. If you are changing more than one track, click the track button and gang button for each track to gang the tracks together.
5. Raise or lower the volume slider or the pan slider.
6. Go to the Audio Mixer Tool Fast menu and drag down to Set Level On Track—In/Out or Set Pan On Track—In/Out.

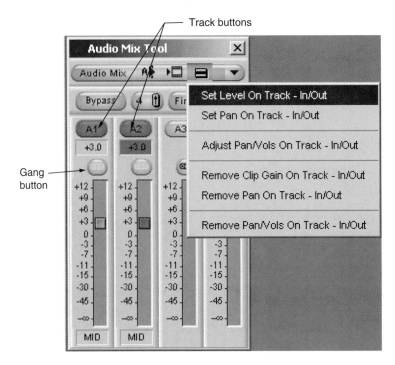

Figure 8.11

If you want to affect the entire track, rather than the area inside your marks, don't place any marks. Instead, do the following:

1. Select the track.
2. Remove any IN and OUT marks.
3. On the Audio Mixer Tool, click on the track button for that track (see Figure 8.11).
4. If you are changing more than one track, click the track button and gang button for each track to gang the tracks together.
5. Raise or lower the volume slider or the pan slider.
6. Go to the Audio Mixer Tool Fast menu and drag down to Set Level (or Pan) On Track—Global.

There are a few things to remember when using the Audio Mixer Tool. Because center pan is the standard for dialog and narration, the Avid allows you to set the pan before you bring the material in. In the Project window, select Settings. Audio is at the top of the list. Double-click it. Select "All Tracks Centered."

Although the Audio Mixer Tool is ideal for making changes to entire clips or large segments of your audio, Avid provides a second tool, called *Audio Auto Gain*, so you can really fine-tune your audio. With Audio Auto Gain, you can make many volume changes within a clip.

Automation Gain

Instead of using a slider to change the level of an entire clip, this tool/mode uses *key frames* to set and adjust levels within a clip. It is sometimes called *volume rubber-banding*. There are several ways you can use this feature: (1) You can set the key frames manually; (2) you can play the sequence and let the Avid place key frames as you move the sliders; or (3) you can attach a fader. The Avid supports several models. An external fader allows you to use your fingers to move multiple sliders, rather than having to use the mouse to make volume changes on the Avid interface's sliders.

We'll use the manual method first. From the Timeline Fast menu select Audio Auto Gain. Now select the tracks you want to work with. A thin gray line will appear across the selected tracks.

Placing Key Frames Manually

Place the blue Position Indicator in the Timeline where you want to make audio changes. Then hit the N key on the Xpress keyboard.

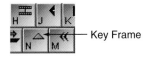

A key frame appears in the Timeline. Because both tracks, A3 and A4, are selected, key frames appear in both simultaneously. Move the blue position indicator in the Timeline further along the Timeline, and hit the Key Frame key again. Another key frame appears.

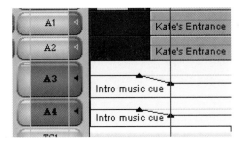

Figure 8.12 Key frames.

Using the mouse, move the pointer to the second key frame. Notice that the pointer changes into a hand. Now drag the key frame down, vertically, in the Timeline (Figure 8.12). You have created a volume ramp. Play the section in the Timeline and listen to the volume change.

Often, when working with stereo tracks, you want to create volume ramps on both tracks simultaneously. Simply select both tracks, and the key frames you place will appear in both tracks. All the actions you give to one track's key frames will affect those on the other track.

You may find that you have placed the key frame in the wrong place. You can easily move your key frames so they affect the sound at a precise point.

To move a key frame:

1. Hold the Option key (Mac) or Alt key (Windows).
2. Click the mouse on the key frame you want to move, and drag it to the new spot.

Now add two more key frames further down the clip in the Timeline, and drag the fourth key frame—this time up. Now, you have created an audio dip.

To delete a key frame:

Bring the mouse pointer over the key frame you want to remove, and when the cursor turns into a hand press the Delete key on the Keyboard.

Sometimes the Avid gets confused and thinks you are trying to delete an audio track, and you'll get a message asking you if you want to delete a track. Click No, and repeat the above steps. To remove multiple key frames, select IN and OUT points, and delete any key frame in the marked area.

Placing Key Frames Automatically

As mentioned, you can place the key frames automatically. This method imitates the way a mixer in a mixing studio works—you are making changes and recording those changes in real time. I don't use it that much because I'm not a professional mixer and I find it moves too fast for me, but you might like it.

From the Tools menu, get the Audio Mixer Tool. Click the Auto button so the sliders turn blue, the Record button is red, and the Trash icon is visible (Figure 8.13). By clicking the Auto button, you are changing the Audio Mixer Tool from the Clip Gain Mode to the Automation Gain Mode.

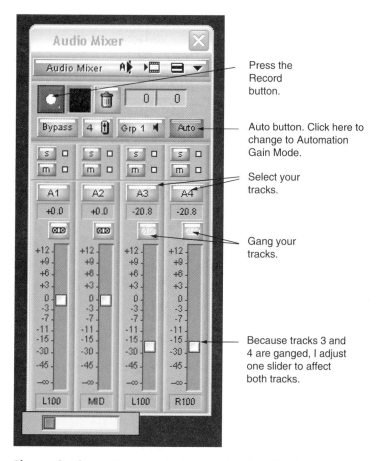

Figure 8.13   Audio Mixer in Automation Gain Mode.

This looks complicated, but it is not hard to use—just hard to use well. You can mix as much or as little as you like. If you're not happy with what you're doing, press the Trash icon to stop the recording. If, after you are through, you don't like what you've done, press Undo and it's all erased. Let's give it a try.

1. Place the position indicator at the beginning of your tracks or at the beginning of the section you'd like to change.
2. Place the Audio Mixer Tool in Automation Gain Mode by pressing the Auto button.
3. Select the tracks you want to mix by clicking on the track buttons (A3 and A4).
4. If you want to work on two tracks at once, such as stereo tracks, gang them.
5. Press the Record button.
6. As the position indicator plays through the Timeline, raise or lower the track's slider with your mouse.
7. Press the Record button to stop.

The "s" and "m" boxes let you solo and mute your tracks. If, after you have placed key frames in the Timeline, you deselect Auto Gain from the Timeline Fast menu, the key frames disappear but a single, small red key frame sits on the clip to show that key frames are in place.

Audio Auto Pan lets you change panning within a clip in the Timeline by placing key frames, just like Audio Auto Gain lets you change volume within a clip. You can place key frames either manually or on the fly using Automation Gain Mode. Just select it from the Timeline Fast menu. Again, I prefer doing it manually, dragging the Pan slider and setting key frames in the Timeline. With a long sound effect, such as a race car or jet plane, recording the Pan changes using Automation Audio Gain mode might work better.

EQUALIZATION

On most sound mixing boards there are dials that you can turn to boost or cut (decrease) various frequencies—low, midrange, high—to alter or improve the sound. Such alteration of frequencies is called *equalization*. For example, if a voice is too bass sounding, you can cut the low frequencies and boost the midrange frequencies.

The Avid has a tool that enables you to do the same thing. The EQ Tool is in the Tools menu. The EQ Tool affects clips in the Timeline. From the Tools menu, choose Audio EQ. A window appears.

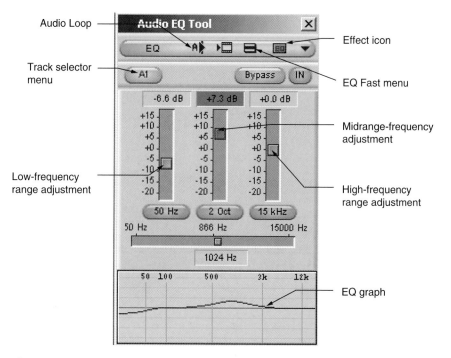

Figure 8.14

Setting the EQ

The sliders allow you to emphasize (boost) or de-emphasize (cut) the low, middle, and high frequencies. The horizontal slider allows you to change the shape and placement of the parametric curve. This adjustment allows you to locate the frequency that you most want to boost or cut. Watch the EQ graph to see the changes.

The Audio Loop button will play the sound in a continuous loop and allow you to hear the changes you make as you adjust the sliders. There is also an IN button, which gives you the opportunity to turn off the effect of the EQ so you can tell how your changes compare to the original sound. Are you making the sound better or worse? Click once and it turns gray, indicating that no equalization is taking place. Click again, and it turns yellow, indicating that the effect is on.

Steps in applying EQ:

1. Select the tracks you want to change.
2. If it's a single clip, place the position indicator on the clip.
3. Drag the sliders to select values.
4. Click the Audio Loop in order to hear the changes.

If it's a single clip, you're finished and you will see an EQ icon on the track.

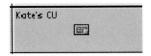

If it's more than one clip:

1. Identify a portion of the track with IN and OUT marks.
2. When you are satisfied, stop and then choose Set EQ In/Out from the EQ Fast menu.

To remove the EQ, you can use the Remove Effect button located on a Fast menu command palette. Click on the EQ effect in the Timeline and then press the Remove Effect button.

Remove Effect button

EQ Templates

Avid has a number of EQ templates that fix common audio problems. You can apply, but not change, any of these EQ templates.

1. Put the Position indicator on the audio clip in the Timeline that you want to change.
2. Choose the template from the EQ Fast menu (Figure 8.15). The EQ effect will be placed on the clip.

Figure 8.15

A good way to learn how to equalize your sound is to examine the graphs that these different templates produce. Look at the frequencies that are boosted and cut. Examine the point where the center of the parametric curve is located. These EQ templates cover most of the problems you'll encounter. Use them as a jumping-off point for fixing your sound. It's true you can't change them, but you can recreate them and then make adjustments to fit your own set of problems.

Saving Your EQ Effect

You can also save an EQ effect so you can use it later on in your project. You might spend ten minutes setting different EQ levels to fix a problem in Tim's dialog track. Once you have the effect set up the way you want, simply click and drag the *icon* (Figure 8.16) to whichever bin you would like it saved to. Try it. It's quite easy to do. Once it's in the bin, you can name it.

Now simply click and drag it from the bin to Tim's other clips in the Timeline, and they'll have the same EQ applied to them.

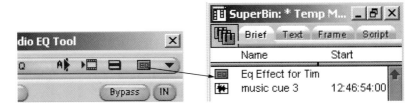

Figure 8.16   Drag the EQ icon to the bin.

WHEN TO USE THE DIFFERENT AUDIO TOOLS

Here's how I work with my audio tools. I use the Audio Mixer Tool to set the overall levels of my clips. I'll go into the Timeline, put the position indicator on Kate's CU, and then raise it or lower it with the slider. Then I'll do that with the next clip that needs adjustment. I might find that a whole section is too low. In that case, I'll mark an IN and then an OUT in the Timeline and using the Audio Mixer Tool menu I'll choose Set Levels On Tracks—In/Out (Figure 8.11).

Now, let's say I don't like the way something sounds—Kate's voice seems muffled, or there's too much sibilance, or there's a hum I don't like—then I'll use the EQ Tool. And the last tool I use, after I've set levels and EQ, is the Audio Auto Gain Tool. If I want an audio ramp because I have music or sound effects that I want to bring down or up, I'll go to the Timeline Fast menu and select Audio Auto Gain. When I see that gray line, I place key frames, using the N key on the keyboard, and then I raise or lower key frames to set a ramp up or down.

If I have a section of music that needs a lot of adjustment, I'll use the Automation Gain Tool, and while I'm listening and watching the picture I'll record my level changes and let the Avid set all those key frames automatically.

What's important to note is that the levels you set with the Audio Mixer Tool are memorized and kept. If you then add key frames, manually or automatically, those changes are added onto the settings you've already made.

Remember, do your gross adjustments first, using the Audio Mixer Tool, then work on the quality of the sound with the EQ tool, and then fine-tune the levels with the Audio Auto Gain.

WHAT LEVEL IS CORRECT?

When editing my sequence together, I will try to have normal conversation fall within the –30-dB to –14-dB range on the digital scale. Loud sounds will then have ample headroom, peaking at –4 for the loudest shout or bang, but I won't let any of my levels get higher than that. Place your average sounds at the reference level and let your loud sounds use the headroom, but never let anything get higher than –4.

WAVEFORMS

The audio *waveform* is a visual representation of your audio's signal strength, or amplitude. The Avid's Timeline has the ability to show you the waveform of your audio. This feature provides a handy way of finding specific sounds and "seeing" where to trim your sound.

Go to the Timeline Fast menu, deselect Audio Clip Gain and/or Audio Auto Gain, and select Sample Plot (Figure 8.17).

Figure 8.17

The Avid will draw the waveform. The speed with which the sample plot is drawn depends on your Timeline view and the number of tracks selected. Once the waveform is drawn, you can see where your sounds begin and end. This can be helpful when you're fine-tuning your audio. As you can see in Figure 8.18, the Timeline has been expanded so we can see music beats.

There are a couple of commands that help you to better see the waveforms:

- To make your tracks larger, use enlarge track—Command–L (Mac) or Ctrl–L (Windows).
- To make the waveform itself larger, use Command–Option–L (Mac) or Ctrl–Alt–L (Windows).

Figure 8.18

Waveforms are quite helpful whenever you're trying to edit complex sounds, such as music. For example, let's say you wanted to lengthen a music cue because it ends a bit too soon. You can easily do this by copying a section of the music into the Clipboard, opening the Clipboard Monitor, marking the section, and then cutting it into the Timeline at the end of the music. Now the music is extended. The waveform shows you where the beats are in the music. Use those beats to make your marks and edit points. Try it.

Using Trim Mode with Waveforms to Fix Audio

I often do my audio work using Trim Mode. Let's say you have a lot of narration that you have cut into your sequence and the narration track is a bit noisy. When the narrator speaks, you don't hear the hiss, but as soon as he or she stops talking you can hear the hiss or hum on the track.

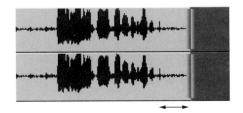

Figure 8.19   Use Dual-Roller Trim to get rid of this noise.

You want to clean the track up. The best way to do this is to enter Dual-Roller Trim Mode and cut the narration so the only segments left in the Timeline are those that contain the voice and not the "silent" bits, which are actually quite noisy.

OTHER AUDIO TECHNIQUES TO FIX PROBLEMS

When you're working on a cut in Trim Mode, you'll sometimes hear a glitch in the audio, but it's so close to the transition point that you aren't sure which side of the transition has the sound glitch. As you play the transition, the sound loops around. Try this. Press the Go to Mark IN key (Q on the keyboard). The loop will play on the outgoing clip, but not the incoming one.

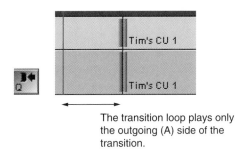

The transition loop plays only
the outgoing (A) side of the
transition.

The transition loop plays only the outgoing (A) side of the transition. To hear just the incoming, or B-side, side of the transition, press the Go to Mark OUT key (W on the keyboard). This technique allows you to locate spurious sound glitches. Once located, you can often get rid of them by using the Dual-Roller Trim to create a sound overlap. Here, the glitch is on the A-side. Create an overlap, and the glitch is gone.

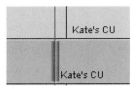

Replacing Bad Sound

If we continue with the example of the sound glitch on the outgoing clip, what do we do if the sound on the incoming clip isn't a good match and the Dual-Roller Trim makes the sound even worse? We can easily mark the area where the glitch is located and use Lift to get rid of it, but you can't have *nothing* on your soundtrack. You need to replace what was cut out with some sort of room tone, or ambient sound, in order to fill in the blank spot. Just go to the Source Monitor and put that clip there. Now play until you find "silence." You're not looking for silence, really, but ambience that matches. Simply mark an IN in the Source Monitor and overwrite that ambience into the Timeline, replacing what you lifted.

TIMELINE VIEWS

You can set up your tracks in the Timeline—the color of the tracks, the size of the tracks, whether or not you see Waveforms—and save those settings. All you have to do is fix the tracks just the way you want, then move your mouse all the way to the bottom of the Timeline (next to the Scale bar), and click and hold on Untitled. A pop-up menu comes up, and you can choose Save As. In the dialog box, type a name, such as Edit Mode, and click OK.

Now let's create more views. Set up your tracks to show the Sample Plot. Notice the Edit Mode name changes to look like it's italicized. Click on the Edit Mode name and choose Save As, and when the dialog box comes up, name it Sample Plot or Waveform.

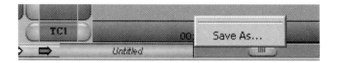

You can also make changes and then, instead of creating a new view, you can replace a view with a new one. Select the one you want to change, make changes, then update by holding down the Option key (Mac) or Alt key (Windows) and clicking on the Timeline name. You'll see Replace "Edit Mode." Select the view you want to replace from the list, and the replaced view will hold onto the changes.

SETTING UP YOUR TRACKS

With the Avid, it's easy to add tracks, but you should give some thought to how your tracks are laid out. In the Avid's Timeline, the tracks go one on top of each other, flowing left to right. If you have narration, it should go onto the topmost audio track—A1. Reserve the next two tracks for dialog. The sound effects come next. Finally, your music tracks go at the bottom of your Timeline. If you have no narration, the topmost tracks will contain your dialog.

Building Your Sound Tracks

1. Narration
2. Dialog
3. Sound effects
4. Music

PRO TOOLS®

The process of moving your audio to Pro Tools and Pro Tools LE is explained in Chapter 19.

TELL THE STORY FIRST

We've examined many of the important techniques and tools at your disposal, all of which will help you create clean, clear sound. Perhaps the most important advice I can give you is this: Wait to add sound effects and music until as late in the editing process as possible. Editors who are new to the Avid often create complex sound tracks much too early in the editing process, making even the simplest change an onerous task. Tell the story first, by cutting the picture and sync sound. Then build your other tracks, laying down the sound effects and music cues that will give tone and emotional content to your project.

SUGGESTED ASSIGNMENTS

1. Move the hollow speaker icon to different tracks.
2. Enlarge all your sound tracks.
3. Make individual tracks smaller.
4. Add two additional audio tracks.
5. Splice sound into these new tracks by patching.
6. Adjust the volume of your tracks using the Audio Mixer Tool.
7. Change the pan on three of your clips.
8. Select Audio Auto Gain from the Timeline Fast menu, and place several key frames on a clip. Create volume ramps.
9. Move the key frames in the Timeline.
10. From the Timeline Fast menu, leave Audio Auto Gain and go to Waveforms. Try cutting audio, using the waveforms as cutting guides.
11. Place an EQ template onto a clip in the Timeline.
12. Create an EQ effect for several clips in the Timeline and apply it using IN and OUT marks.
    (Remember, go to the EQ Fast menu and choose Set EQ In/Out.)
13. Save an EQ setting by placing it in a bin.
14. Create a Timeline view.

9

Advanced Editing

As we've noted on several occasions, the Avid is a complex editing system, loaded with features that give the editor tremendous flexibility. For the most part, we've stuck to the basics in order to limit the amount of material you must grapple with to get the job done. Now, we'll examine more advanced features, some of which are unique to nonlinear digital systems.

SEGMENT MODE EDITING

Segment Mode editing gets at the heart of nonlinear editing. It allows you to easily move clips around in the Timeline, changing the order of the shots in your sequence. The speed with which you can shift around whole segments of your project will astound you. Let's say that you realize that the first shot in your sequence should actually be the third shot. Enter Segment Mode, click on the shot in the Timeline, and drag it to the new position. Presto!

Segment Mode editing isn't really all that advanced a feature, but I have held off introducing it because it's much more useful to an editor working on a visual montage or working with documentary footage than it is to an editor cutting a narrative scene. When we were editing "Wanna Trade," you didn't have many opportunities to change the order of your shots, but now that you're working on a documentary or some other reality-based material, you'll find yourself wanting to move shots around.

There are two Segment Mode buttons, and they appear at the bottom of the Timeline on all Avid systems (Figure 9.1). The yellow arrow that appears to be

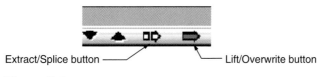

Extract/Splice button ⎯⎯⎯⎯⎯⎯⎯⎯   ⎯⎯⎯⎯ Lift/Overwrite button

Figure 9.1

179

missing its midsection is the Extract/Splice button, and the thick red arrow is the Lift/Overwrite button.

Before we go any further, notice the similarities and differences between the Splice and Overwrite keys and the two Segment Mode keys. When I was first learning the Avid, I often clicked the wrong one, and it took me a while to figure out what I'd done.

Splice and
Overwrite keys

Segment Mode keys

Timeline Setting

Before we begin, let's go to the Project window and click on Settings. Scroll down until you find Timeline. Double-click on it and click on the Edit tab. In the dialog box, check the Default Snap-To Edit box (Figure 9.2). This will make the process much easier to master.

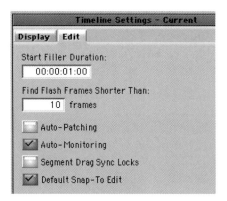

Figure 9.2

Extract/Splice Segment Mode Button

When you click on the Extract/Splice button, you'll enter Segment Mode.

Extract/Splice

To let you know you are in Segment Mode, the background color on the segment key at the bottom of the Timeline will darken. If you then click on a clip (segment) in the Timeline, the clip is highlighted. If the clip has picture and sync sound, you normally want to move both of them together. To select the sound clip, hold down the Shift key and click on the sound. Now both are selected, as shown here.

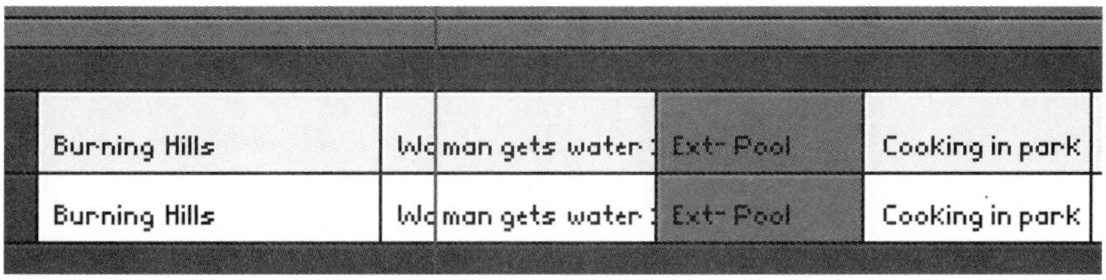

Burning Hills	Woman gets water	Ext-Pool	Cooking in park
Burning Hills	Woman gets water	Ext-Pool	Cooking in park

Figure 9.3

Let's say we want the shot called "Ext-Pool," which is the third shot in this sequence, to become the second shot (Figure 9.3). We want to move it so it comes after "Burning Hills." To move the clip, click on it and then drag it to the spot where you want it to go. As you drag, a white outline will appear around the clip to show you it is moving. When you drag your segment, it snaps to cut points or to the blue position indicator.

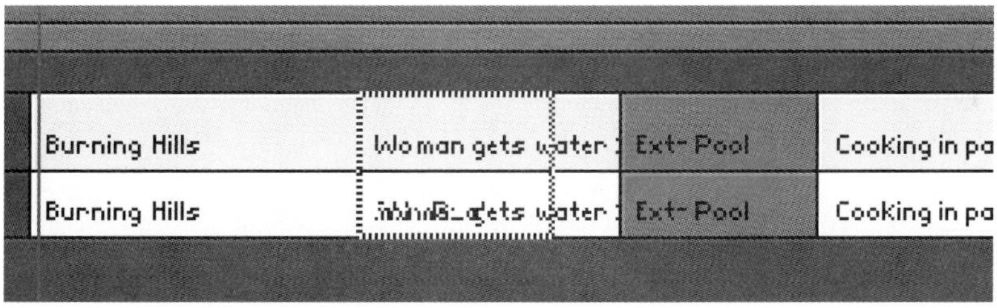

Burning Hills	Woman gets water	Ext-Pool	Cooking in pa
Burning Hills	Woman gets water	Ext-Pool	Cooking in pa

When you release the mouse, the clip moves to the new location.

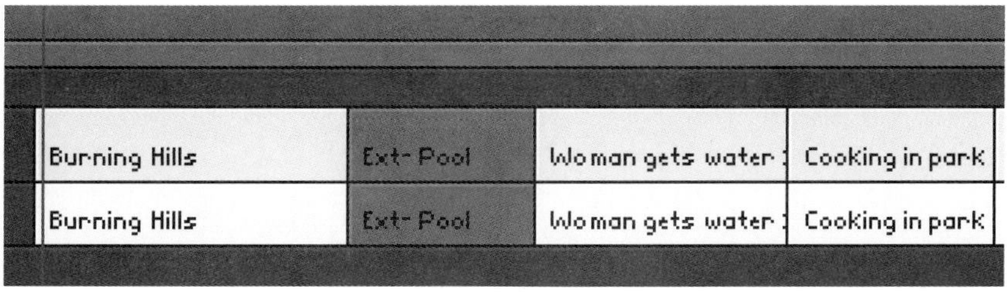

Burning Hills	Ext-Pool	Woman gets water	Cooking in park
Burning Hills	Ext-Pool	Woman gets water	Cooking in park

As you can see here, "Ext-Pool" is now the second shot in the sequence. What was the second shot becomes the third shot. Because you're moving segments, the length of the sequence remains the same, and everything stays in sync. You can drag shots in either direction.

To leave Segment Mode:

• Click on the highlighted segment button.

Lift/Overwrite Segment Mode Button

This button is a little less helpful, and you'll use it less often when moving shots around. When you click on the Lift/Overwrite button (red button) and drag your segment, it moves the segment you've chosen (fine) and overwrites the segment it lands on (not so fine). That's not usually what you want to do.

Look at the example provided (Figure 9.4). Here we selected "Ext-Pool" using the Lift/Overwrite button (red).

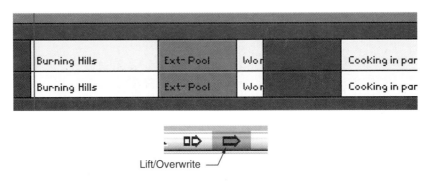

Figure 9.4

Examine what happens when we use Lift/Overwrite to drag "Ext-Pool" to the same spot as we did using the Extract/Splice segment button. The shot is lifted from its old position, leaving blank fill in its place, and is moved to its new position. But, instead of pushing "Woman Gets Water" to the third spot, it erases (overwrites) most of the clip.

Obviously, this is not what the Lift/Overwrite Segment Mode is used for. Its main function is to move blocks of sound quickly. Let's say we are working on a sequence involving a series of shots that are explained by voice-over narration. When you first cut in the narration, it doesn't flow as nicely as you might like. The narrator's sentences are too close together, so you decide to spread the narration out. Here's where the Lift/Overwrite Segment Mode button excels.

In the example in Figure 9.5, I want to move the narration on A1 toward the head of the visual on V1. I place the position indicator where I want the head of the narration to land.

Figure 9.5

Next I click the red segment button, click on the narration segment, and drag it to the position indicator.

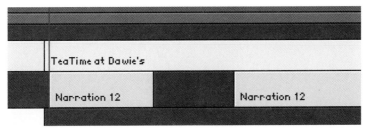

When I release the mouse, the block of narration is right where I want it, and nothing has been thrown out of sync (Figure 9.6).

Figure 9.6

Another handy trick involves the use of the Lift/Overwrite segment button with the Trim Frame keys. Press the red segment button, select the block of audio you want to move, and press the ≪ or < Trim Frame key to slide the segment of sound toward the head of the sequence or the > or ≫ Trim Frame key to slide the sound toward the tail. Try it. It is quite precise.

The Lift/Overwrite Segment Mode is also great for moving titles around. We'll try this in Chapter 10.

Moving Sound to Different Tracks

You'll also use the Lift/Overwrite segment button whenever you want to move a sound (or picture) clip that's on one track onto another track. In Figure 9.7, the sound for "TeaTime" is on A3, and I want it to go onto A2, just below the narration track. It's easy.

Figure 9.7

1. Click the Lift/Overwrite Segment button.
2. Click on the sound segment you want to move.
3. Drag it to the track where you want it to go.

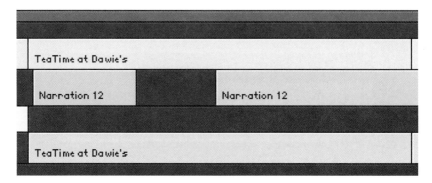

Again, a white outline will form around the box to show that it's moving and where it's moving to. The result, as shown in Figure 9.8, is what you expected. To keep the track from sliding horizontally and going out of sync, hold down the Control key (Mac) as you move the track vertically. Windows users hold down Shift+Ctrl keys as you drag.

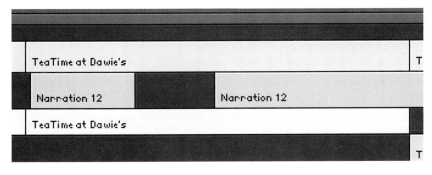

Figure 9.8

Lassoing to Get into Segment Mode

You've probably already done this by accident. As you know, you go into Trim Mode by lassoing a transition from left to right. If, instead of lassoing a transition, you lasso a segment, you'll go into Segment Mode.

Which Segment Mode will you enter when you lasso a segment? The button selected is the one you used last. If you want the other one, just click on it. Lassoing is a great way to select a number of clips at once. Lasso all of the clips you want.

You can move more than one segment at a time. For instance, you may want to take the fourth and fifth shots and move them to the beginning of your sequence. You could press a Segment Mode button, click on a segment, and then Shift–click to get all four segments selected (two picture and two sound), or you could lasso them all in one quick move. Although in the example here I'm only moving two shots, you can move 30 or 50 shots at once.

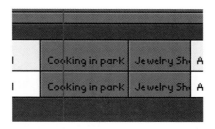

To sum up the Segment Mode buttons:

- Use Extract/Splice ![button] to move shots around in the Timeline.
- Use Lift/Overwrite ![button] to move blocks of sound in the Timeline.

TRIMMING IN TWO DIRECTIONS

Once you begin to add additional tracks to your sequence, using Trim Mode can get a little tricky. For example, say we have a clip on V1 of people voting in the first free election in South Africa. Your narration describes the action on A1, and your sync track is on A2. You're happy with the way the narration works with the picture and sync track. But let's say you need to trim the head of the clip because the sequence is running too long. I've placed red markers, called locators, on all three tracks to show what happens if you trim the voting clip without adjusting your narration track (Figure 9.9).

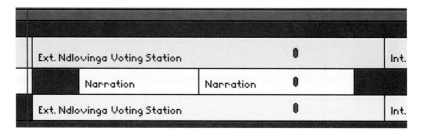

Figure 9.9 Before trimming.

In Figure 9.10 we have trimmed 30 frames off the head of the "Voting Station" picture and sync track. Tracks V1 and A2 have been shortened by 30 frames, while A1, containing the narration, has remained the same length. Everything is thrown off. You say, "We'll trim 30 frames off the narration and everything will be in sync." But we can't, because if we trim the head of the narration, we'll be cutting off the narrator's words! The solution is *trimming in two direc-*

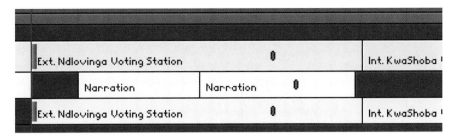

Figure 9.10   After trimming.

tions. The Avid realizes this is a common situation and allows you to trim in the black, or filler area, to keep tracks aligned. Watch.

By placing a single roller on the other side of the narration track, as shown in Figure 9.11a, where there is fill and no voice, and then trimming, the Avid takes 30 frames of black fill off the narration track while it takes 30 frames off the "Voting Station" clip. All the tracks are still aligned. As you can see, the arrows go in two different directions. We are trimming in two directions.

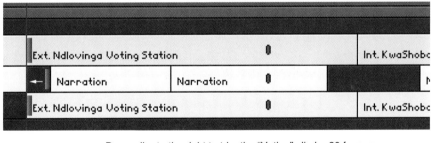

Drag roller to the right to trim the "Voting" clip by 30 frames.
Narration fill is shortened by 30 frames.

Figure 9.11a

We can use the Single-Roller Trim to *add* to the head of the "Voting Station" clip. This time we're dragging the rollers to the left to extend the clip by 30 frames. Again, we put the single roller on the black fill side of the narration (Figure 9.11b).

Ext. Ndlovinga Voting Station		Int. KwaShoba Vc
Narration	Narration	Narr
Ext. Ndlovinga Voting Station		Int. KwaShoba Vc

Drag roller to the left to extend the "Voting" clip by 30 frames. Narration fill is lengthened by 30 frames.

Figure 9.11b

It took me a while to get the hang of this trimming in two directions business. Just remember that once you have the clip you want to trim, in order for the other tracks to stay in alignment downstream of that trim, you have to add or subtract from every track or else you throw everything out of sync. Here's another example (Figure 9.12), showing many tracks having their black fill adjusted so the picture clip can be trimmed.

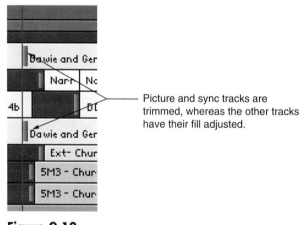

Picture and sync tracks are trimmed, whereas the other tracks have their fill adjusted.

Figure 9.12

Watch Point

The transition the Avid shows you in the Trim Mode window when you click on the Review Transition button is called the *watch point*. It's easy when there are only two tracks and everything is straight cut, because then there is only one transition to watch, but whenever you have transitions that aren't in a straight

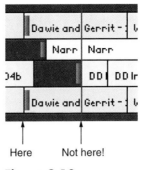

Here   Not here!

Figure 9.13

line the Avid can select only one of the transitions to show in the Trim Mode window. The last track selected for trimming is the one that becomes the watch point. This isn't necessarily the one you want to watch. Look at the location of the position indicator in the example in Figure 9.13. It's on the roller for a sound effect, but the whole reason you're making a trim is to adjust the picture and sync track. That's where you want the watch point to be.

To fix this situation, simply click the mouse on the roller at the transition you want. The position indicator jumps to that transition, and the watch point moves to the correct spot. Remember, the last transition you select is where the watch point will fall.

Practice this technique. See what happens when the watch point is wrong. Move the watch point so the transition you want to trim is shown in the Trim Mode display.

SLIPPING AND SLIDING

Slip and *Slide* are power-editing features that affect clips in the Timeline. They are unique versions of Trim Mode.

Slip

Slip is particularly handy. Say you have spliced a section of a master clip into the Timeline and after playing the sequence you see that the section of the clip you used just isn't right. Maybe you put your IN and OUT marks in the Source Monitor a bit too early. Without Slip, the only way to fix this would be to mark the clip in the Timeline and choose a new IN in the Source Monitor. Press Overwrite, and you've replaced the clip with a different section of the clip. If it still isn't right, try it again.

With Slip, you don't need to go back to the Source Monitor. You can change the clip in the Timeline. What you're doing is changing the IN and OUT at the same time. Think of Slip as working a bit like a conveyor belt. The whole belt is the master clip, and the portion of the belt you're seeing in the Timeline is the section you've spliced in.

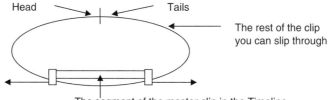

You can change the section that's in the Timeline with Slip. As you slip through the footage, the length of the clip in the Timeline remains the same. When you slip, you are adding frames to the head of the clip in the Timeline while trimming the tail by the same number of frames, or you can trim frames from the head of the shot while adding the same number of frames to the tail of the shot.

Dragging the rollers left reveals material that comes before what's in the Timeline—you're slipping toward the head. Dragging the rollers right reveals material that comes after what's in the Timeline—you're slipping toward the tail.

To get into Slip Mode:

- Lasso the clip from the right to the left. Or
- Get into Dual-Roller Trim Mode and right-click the clip segment. Choose Select Slip Trim from the pop-up menu.

Figure 9.14

Single-trim rollers will jump to the cut points. The Source and Record Monitors will change to four screens (Figure 9.14).

Kate's CU	Master Shot - Kate & Tim 2	Kate's CU
A	B	C
Kate's CU	Master Shot - Kate & Tim 2	Kate's CU

The two inner screens are the head and tail frames of the clip you are slipping—Master Shot (Clip B). The far-left screen is the tail frame of Clip A, and the far right is the head frame of Clip C. The frames of Clip B (Master Shot) will change as you slip it. The frames of Clip A and C will not change at all.

You can use the Trim Frame keys (≪, <, >, and ≫) to move the clip, or click on and drag either roller. The frames that appear in the two inner screens will change as you slip.

Getting out of Slip is just like leaving Trim Mode:

- Click on the timecode track. Or
- Press the Trim Mode button.

Slide

Slide is the inverse of Slip. It doesn't change any of the frames in the clip you're sliding (Clip B); instead, it moves Clip B along the Timeline. Here we are sliding Tim's CU (Figure 9.15). As you can see, the rollers jump to the other side of Tim's CU, and as you drag the rollers left or right, you move the clip to a different spot on the Timeline. Tim's CU doesn't change, but the shots on either side of it change. It's hard to imagine why you'd want to move a clip in this way. I mean, imagine sliding a clip along the Timeline, as we have in Figure 9.15. You'd lose all control of your shots.

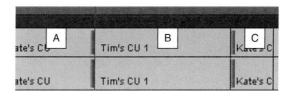

Figure 9.15

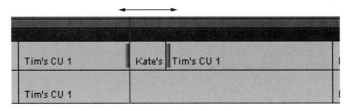

Figure 9.16

But, think about using Slide with a cutaway—now we're getting somewhere. Examine Figure 9.16. Here we have Tim's CU, in which Tim is telling Kate that the letters are now his and he can do whatever he wants with them. Let's say we want to see what Kate thinks of all this. We want to break up Tim's little speech with a cutaway of Kate, looking more than a bit disgruntled, so we overwrite just her picture somewhere over Tim's CU. But where should it go? Using Slide, we can move it along the Timeline until it's placed perfectly.

To enter Slide Mode:

- While holding down the Option key (Mac) or Shift+Alt keys (Windows), lasso the clip from right to left.
- Get into Dual-Roller Trim Mode and right-click the clip segment. Choose Select Slide Trim from the pop-up menu.

To get out of Slide:

- Click on the timecode track.
- Press the Trim Mode button.

J–K–L TRIMMING

This is one of the greatest editing innovations of all time. Some people call this trimming on the fly. You don't use the trim keys ≪ and ≫; instead, you trim as you play, using the J–K–L keys in Trim Mode, but first we need to make J–K–L Trim operational.

1. Go to the Project window and click on Settings.
2. Scroll down until you find the Trim setting.
3. Double-click on the Trim setting.
4. Click in the checkmark box to make J–K–L Trim active, and click OK.

Let's first try J–K–L trimming by working on the A-side or B-side of a transition, but not both.

1. Lasso a transition and then get into Single-Roller Trim.
2. Press the J or L keys. Your transitions will lengthen or shorten as you watch.
3. When you see the frame where you want to end the trim, press the K key or the spacebar.

When you first try this, things can get confusing, so slow things down by pressing and holding down the K key, and then J or L:

1. Hold the K key while pressing J or L to glide slowly backward or forward as you shorten or lengthen your clip.
2. When you reach the frame where you want to end the trim, release the K key.

Most people love this so much they're hooked forever.

Now try J–K–L trimming in Dual-Roller Trim Mode. You'll notice that only one side of the Trim Mode display will play in real time. The other side will catch up once you stop. Whichever side has the green line, just below the counters, is the one that plays in real time.

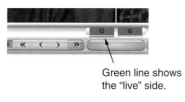

Green line shows
the "live" side.

Figure 9.17

Just move the mouse over the other window (don't click on it) to choose which side you want to see play. The green line shifts to the other side.

MATCH FRAME

Sometimes, when you're working in the Timeline, you want to see which clip a shot in the Timeline comes from, or you're wondering what comes before or after the section you spliced in. A quick way to open the entire clip is to hit Match Frame. Immediately, the entire clip will appear in the Source Monitor. Go to the Source/Record monitor's Fast menu to find the command.

Match Frame command

Place the position indicator on the clip in the Timeline and press the Match Frame button. (I usually place it at the head or tail of the clip.) Match Frame finds the source clip for whichever track is selected and opens it in the Source Monitor, with an IN mark showing you the exact frame you've marked with the position indicator. If you want to find the source clip for a clip of narration, make sure that's the track selected. If it's a picture, then make sure you select the video track.

REPLACE (NOT ON XPRESS DV)

Replace does what you'd expect—it replaces material in the sequence with other material of your choosing. Let's say you have placed a clip in the Source Monitor, marked an IN and an OUT, and spliced it into the Timeline. Looking at it, you think another take would work better. Without Replace, you would have to find the new take and overwrite it into the Timeline. Replace is different. Unlike overwrite, Replace doesn't need IN and OUT marks. It uses the location of the blue position indicators to do its work. I realize this is a new concept, so let's take a closer look at it.

Replace isn't on any key or Fast menu. You must go to the Tools menu and select Command Palette. When the Command Palette opens, click on the Edit tab. You decide where you want to put it. (I put mine on the Source/Record Fast menu, as shown in Figure 9.18.)

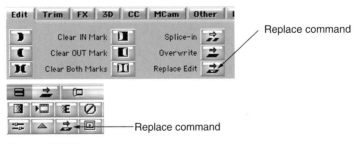

Replace command

Replace command

Figure 9.18

Let's say we have footage of two people swimming. What's shown in the picture in Figure 9.19 is taken from "Swim" Take 1. You cut this into the Timeline. When you review the sequence, you think Take 2 might be better, because when the woman lifts her head out of the water we see more of her face.

Figure 9.19

The most important action is the woman touching the wall and lifting her head, so I put the position indicator on that frame in the Timeline.

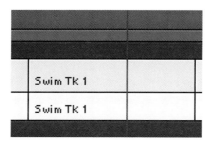

Then I go to the Source Monitor and get "Swim" Take 2. I play through the clip until I find the spot where she's lifting her head out of the water. I leave the position indicator there. Now, I hit the Replace command, located in the Source/Record Fast menu.

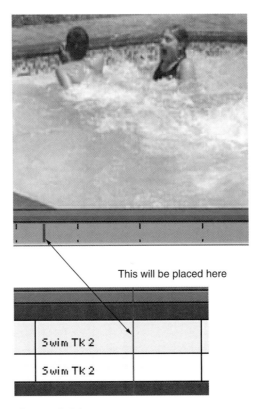

This will be placed here

Swim Tk 2

Swim Tk 2

Figure 9.20

I have now replaced "Swim" Take 1 with a clip of the same length taken from "Swim" Take 2, but the part of "Swim" Take 2 that is overwritten is based on the location of the position indicators. The woman's head will lift out of the water at the same point in the sequence as it did when Take 1 was there. In this case, we are matching the action while replacing.

What's special about Replace is it can replace sound and picture even if there is an overlap edit! It replaces sound based on the amount of sound used in the Timeline, even if there's more sound than picture (as might happen with an overlap) in the Timeline.

This command can also be useful if you want to try to replace a section of bad sync sound. Let's say there was a loud background noise during one take. The second take isn't as good visually, but it has cleaner sound. Just mark a word in the Timeline with the position indicator, then place the position indicator on the same word from the second take, which you've placed in the Source Monitor. Now hit Replace and you have better sound and hopefully pretty good sync.

SUGGESTED ASSIGNMENTS

1. Go into Segment Mode by clicking the Extract/Splice button. Now move a clip (Shift–click to get sound) toward the head of your sequence.
2. Undo. Leave Segment Mode.
3. Go into Segment Mode by clicking the Lift/Overwrite button. Move a clip to the head.
4. Undo. Leave Segment Mode.
5. Get into Segment Mode by clicking the Lift/Overwrite button. Move a clip of audio using Trim Frame keys. Undo.
6. Lasso three clips to get into Segment Mode.
7. Practice trimming in two directions.
8. Set the watch point to show the clip you want to watch in the Trim Mode display.
9. Get into Slip Mode and slip a clip.
10. Practice J–K–L trimming.
11. Select a video track and hit Match Frame.
12. Deselect the video tracks and select an audio track. Hit Match Frame.
13. Xpress Pro: Use Replace to change a clip in the Timeline, using the position indicators to replace the material in the Timeline with the material in the Source Monitor.

10

Titles

There are many different kinds of titles, and they serve different functions in a production. There's the main title of the show, and there are the opening and closing credits, identification titles (lower thirds), subtitles, and copyright information. When you think about it, you really can't finish a project without adding titles.

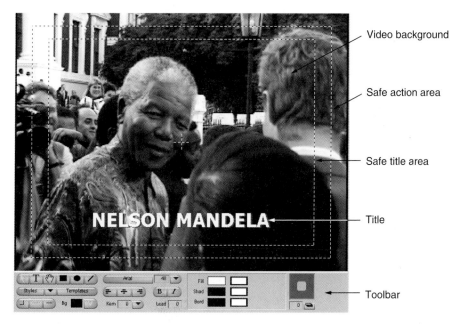

Figure 10.1 Title Tool.

Usually you add titles when you're nearing the end of the editing phase. If you're still making a lot of changes to your sequence and you cut titles in, they can easily get out of sync and drift away from the images they belong to—and it's a real pain to put everything back together. Trust me on this one. Wait to add titles as late in the editing process as possible. Because we're through editing "Wanna Trade" and possibly another short assignment, we can go back and add titles to them.

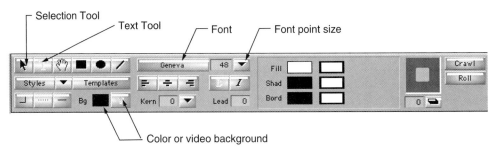

Figure 10.2

OPENING THE TITLE TOOL

If you're planning to add a title over a video image, normally you park the position indicator on that image in the Timeline and then open the Title Tool. That way, the background of your choice becomes the background that the Title Tool shows you. To open the Title Tool, go to the Clip menu and select New Title. The Title Tool will open, and you'll see the Title window. For those of you who practiced placing a menu item directly onto a keyboard key in Chapter 7, you'll remember that we placed the Title Tool menu command on Shift–T, so all you need to do is press Shift–T on your keyboard and the Title Tool will open.

CHOOSING A BACKGROUND

If you don't want a video image as the background for your title, click on the V toggle. The green V will turn black. Black is the default background color, but you can click and hold the cursor inside the Bg box and a color picker will appear. Move the cursor through the colors to select the one you want for your background. You can also use the eyedropper to pick a color.

Click and hold in box to open Color Picker.

CREATING YOUR FIRST TITLE

Creating titles is fairly straightforward. I'm going to create a title to go over a specific shot of Nelson Mandela greeting voters. I click on the V toggle so it turns green, and the video image appears in the Title Tool window. To type the letters, make sure the T (for Text Tool) is green. If not, click on the T to make it active. Now click on the image where you'd like the text to land. The cursor becomes an I-beam. As you type, the text will appear and flow to the next line. Don't worry—just type your text. You can delete letters, edit letters, type additional letters—basically all the functions provided by most word-processing programs.

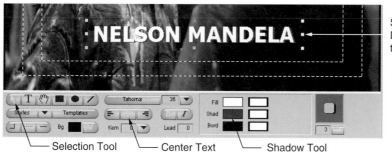

Selection handles: Drag this right or left to affect word wrap.

Selection Tool   Center Text   Shadow Tool

Figure 10.3

Selection Tool

On some systems, Geneva is the default font and 48 is the default font point size. You'll find that 48 is often too large. Once you're through typing, click on the Selection Tool (it's to the left of the Text Tool) so the arrow turns green. Now click on the title. A box with selection handles appears around the title. Change to another font simply by clicking on the font button and selecting a different font from the list. You can also select a different point size. Note that Bold is the default setting, so click on the letter B to make the text normal.

The selection handles also allow you to change the size of the box that the words fall into. If your words wrap around to a second line and you want them to all fall on one line, drag one of the right-hand selection handles—any of the three should work—all the way to the safe title line. Now drag a left-hand selection handle all the way to the safe title line. You'll see that your words have more room, so they fall onto one line. Click on Center text (not flush left or right), and your title will be perfectly centered. Now you can click anywhere inside the title and drag it to a different area of the frame. In Figure 10.3, I've dragged my title to the part of the frame often called the *lower third*, where most identification titles are placed.

Use the Text Tool to type the letters; use the Selection Tool to make changes to your title. I'm choosing Tahoma for my font and a point size of 36. This will allow the words "Nelson Mandela" to fit nicely on one line. *Kerning* allows you to change the spacing between letters. Select the text you want to kern, and pull down the Kerning menu or type a number into the box. Negative numbers tighten the spacing. Positive numbers loosen the spacing. *Leading* changes the spacing between lines of text.

Be aware of the safe title box—the dotted lines. Older television monitors can cut off the edges of your image, but by keeping your letters within the dotted lines you can make certain viewers see all your text.

SHADOWS

You can add a *drop shadow* or *depth shadow* to your titles. Shadowing can often make the letters stand out from a busy background. It's best to add shadows with the Selection Tool. Click on the title so the handles appear. Now go to the Shadow Tool. By clicking on the Shadow Tool and dragging in any direction inside the box, you will make a shadow appear. You can use the cursor to drag the shadow in any direction and increase or decrease the depth of shadow you'll add to your letters. The number will change in the Shadow Depth Selection box to indicate how much shadow you are creating. Here, I've set the direction so the shadow appears to the upper right of the letters and at a depth of 14. Really, 14 is a bit too much, but by exaggerating the effect you can see the difference better. By toggling the Drop and Depth Shadow buttons, you change from one type of shadow to the other (Figures 10.4 and 10.5).

Drag the shadow to set the direction and amount of shadow.

Toggle this button to go from drop shadow . . .

to depth shadow.

Figure 10.4

Drop shadow   Depth shadow

Figure 10.5   Drop shadow (left); depth shadow (right).

You can also click on the Shadow Depth Selection box, type a number, and press Enter or Return.

SAVING TITLES

Titles aren't saved automatically. You must save a title in a bin in order to use it. Go to the File menu and select Save Title as . . .

File	Edit	Bin	Clip	Tools	Toolset	Wir
New Title					Ctrl+N	
Open Bin...					Ctrl+O	
New Script...						
Close					Ctrl+W	
Save Title					Ctrl+S	
Save Title as...					Shift+Ctrl+S	

A dialog box will open, letting you select the bin that the title will be saved to, the hard-drive partition, and the resolution. After clicking OK, the title will be saved in the bin you selected. If you're through creating titles, go to the File menu and select Close. If you want to keep creating titles, choose New Title in the File menu.

CUTTING TITLES INTO YOUR SEQUENCE

You can't edit titles directly into the sequence from the Title Tool. Once you've saved your title and closed the Title Tool, you will find the title has been saved to your bin and conveniently placed in the Source Monitor.

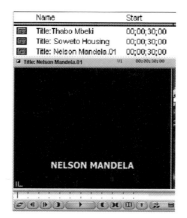

Figure 10.6 Title in bin and the Source Monitor.

With the title in the Source Monitor, you're ready to splice it into your sequence. But, wait—where will it go? Because this title is supposed to be superimposed over the video of Nelson Mandela, we need to open a second video track. Go to the Clip menu and choose New Video Track. V2 will appear in the Timeline. Now you must patch the source track to the V2 record track, as shown in Figure 10.7.

When you have made the patch, V2 will be highlighted and V1 will not be. Make sure the video monitor icon is on V2. Remember, the Avid will monitor all the video tracks at or below the track with the video monitor. If the icon stays on V1, it won't monitor any tracks above it.

Now you're ready to cut the title in using "three marks make an edit." There are a few things you should know before you make the edit.

Click here to move the Video Monitor icon to V2.

Figure 10.7

The Avid generates about two minutes of title material every time you create a title. Because that's far more than you'll ever need, don't mark your IN on the first frame in the Source Monitor. Instead, go in about 60 frames and then mark your IN. That way you can have fades and trim available. Mark an IN and an OUT and then look in the Source Monitor tracking menu to check the I/O of your marks. Three seconds is a good length for most short titles. Now go to the Timeline and mark the IN where you want to cut the title into the sequence. It's best to use *overwrite* instead of splice. As you can see, the title has been placed in the Timeline above the shot that it will be superimposed over.

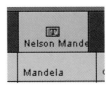

There's a tiny ball on the title icon, telling us that the title is *unrendered*. An unrendered effect is one in which the effect, in this case a title, has not been created inside the computer. The title, its color, shadow, point size, etc., have not been turned into one whole entity. When you render a title or an effect, you create a new thing—a media file on your media drive. Rendering titles takes up space on your media drive, so most people don't render titles or effects unless they have to.

RealTime Effects Button (Xpress Pro 4.+ Versions)

Xpress DV and Xpress Pro 4.+ users won't be able to see their titles in the default mode. Look at the Timeline tool bar (Figure 10.8) and you'll see that the RealTime Effect toggle button is blue (it looks like a ball). That's the default color.

RealTime Effects toggle button

Figure 10.8

Click on the RealTime Effects button (blue) and it will turn green. Now, your titles play in real time, even though they're not yet rendered. What's the big deal? We'll get deeper into this in the effects chapter, but for now the simple explanation is that you can't send your sequence out to tape if the RealTime Effects button is green.

RealTime Encoding (Xpress Pro 5.+)

With the newer versions of Xpress Pro there's no RealTime Effects toggle button. All titles play as soon as you cut them into the Timeline. There's no additional setting or button to push.

Adjusting Your Title's Length

If it turns out that the title is on screen a bit too long, use Dual-Roller Trim to trim the head or tail of the title. If it's not on long enough, use Dual-Roller Trim to extend the tail of the title.

Adding Fades to Your Title

The title I created looks fine, but after watching it I decide I don't like that it pops in and out on the screen. Let's add a half-second fade to the start and end of it.

1. Click the track selector to choose the track holding the title.
2. Place the position indicator so it's inside the title clip in the Timeline.

3. Click the Fade Effect button in the Fast menu between the Source Monitor and the Record Monitor.

Fade Effect button

A dialog box appears like the one in Figure 10.9. Type in the number of frames you want for your fade (15 frames) and click OK.

Figure 10.9

You won't see any indication in your Timeline that the fade effect is in place, but you'll see the results when you press play.

That's it. We've created a title with drop shadow, placed it in the lower third of the frame, saved it to a bin, cut it onto a new video track, and added a fade. There's a lot more you can do with the Title Tool, though.

COLORED TITLES

You can change the colors of the letters, the color of the shadow, or both. You can even create a blend so that, for example, a title starts out dark and becomes lighter as it progresses. (Because this book is in black and white, you're going to have to practice the techniques on your Avid in order to see the colors.)

Using the Title Tool, create a new title. Now let's try turning a white title into a title containing color. First select it with the Select Tool. Now click on the Fill window (Figure 10.10). Press and hold the mouse on the Fill window, and a Color Picker appears.

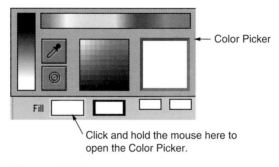

Figure 10.10

Drag through the colors and select the color you want, or click on the eyedropper and click inside the video frame to choose any color already inside the frame. In Figure 10.11, I've selected the color red to fill in the title letters.

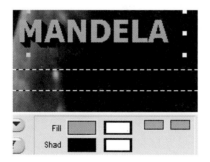

Figure 10.11

You can also select a color for the shadows. They don't have to be black. Select the title in the window, and then click and hold on the shadow window (Figure 10.12). The Color Picker appears, and you drag through the choices until you select the one you want. Here, I've selected a light red for the shadow. I've exaggerated the shadow by choosing a depth of 7 so the change is more pronounced (Figure 10.12). I have a white title with a red shadow.

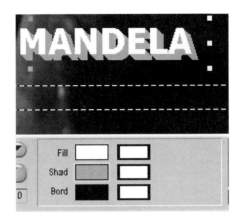

Figure 10.12

BLENDING A TITLE

Let's say the video background shifts from bright to dark so a white title won't show up in the bright areas and a dark title won't show up well in the dark areas. You can create a blend so the title changes from one color to another color. When I click on the Fill window (Figure 10.13), two small windows appear to its right. Click and hold on the left window and select a dark color. Click and hold on the right box and pick a lighter color. Your choices appear in the respective box, and

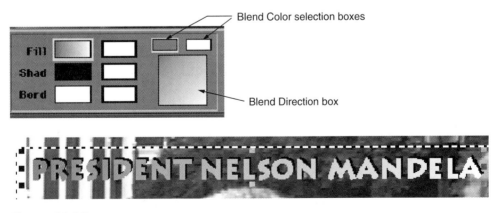

Figure 10.13

the mixture of the two appears in the Blend Direction box. You can change the direction of the blend by dragging the cursor inside this box. I've selected a dark gray in the left-hand box and white in the right-hand box.

Figure 10.13 shows the resulting title. Notice how the letters go from dark gray to white over the width of the title.

CREATING TITLE STYLE SHEETS

After doing a lot of work to set up the title just the way you like it, it would be nice not to have to reinvent the wheel the next time you create a similar title. Fortunately, the Title Tool has a Save As . . . feature that lets you create a *style sheet* so you can set the same title parameters to any new titles you create.

To create a style sheet:

1. Click on the title or object you want to save as a style sheet so it becomes a selection and the arrow lights up in the tool box.
2. Press the triangle next to Styles so the Save As . . . box appears.

3. Choose Save As . . . .
4. The Style Sheet dialog box appears.
5. Make sure that the parameters reflect your choices.
6. You'll see the name of the font style in a box. Type over this, substituting a name such as "Lower Thirds" or "Credits."
7. Click Done.

Once you have created a style, your style sheets appear in the Save As . . . window. To apply a style, simply type a new title, choose the Selection Tool, and then go to the Styles menu and select your choice. The same parameters will be applied to the new title.

SOFT SHADOWS

When you place shadows on the letters, they have a hard edge to them. Sometimes giving the shadow less definition improves its appearance. In the Title Tool, select a title that has shadowing and then go to the Object menu at the top of the computer screen. This menu and the Alignment menu appear only when the Title Tool is open. Select Soften Shadow—it's the last item at the bottom of the Object menu. As soon as you select it, a dialog box appears, like the one in Figure 10.14.

Type in an amount. The range is from 4 to 40. Try 5, and then press Apply. You'll see the amount of softening in the title's shadow. If you like what you see, press OK. If not, change the value and press Apply again until you're happy with the look.

Figure 10.14

GLOWING TITLES

Another look you can give your titles is to make them glow. The title will appear to be surrounded by a haze of color. To create a glow effect you will use the same tools we used to create Soft Shadow titles—only you'll use them a bit differently.

Open the Title Tool and type the text. Using the Selection Tool, position the text where you want. Make sure the title has no shadow value. If there is a number in the Shadow Depth Selection box, click on it and type 0 and press Return or Enter. Now go to the Shadow box and select a color. Try a light yellow or light red. I know it seems strange to pick a color for a shadow when there is no shadow, but have patience. Now, go to the Object menu and select Soften Shadow. Try typing in a value of 10. Press Apply to preview the look. Figure 10.15 shows the effect I got. It's difficult in a black and white screen capture to show off this feature, but I hope you can see that there is a softness coming around and through the letters.

DRAWING OBJECTS

The Title Tool has drawing tools with which you can create boxes, circles, lines, and arrows of various shapes and colors. The title in Figure 10.16 has white letters, a bit of drop shadow, and a red line below the letters to add emphasis. I created the line using the Rectangle Tool and just dragged the selection handles to make a long thin line.

Make sure there is "0" depth shadow and that you have selected a color in the Shadow box.

Figure 10.15

Figure 10.16

Rectangle, Circle, and Line Tools

Click here to select the shape of your corners.

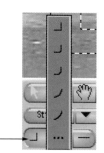

To give the red rectangle a more rounded look, I selected it, and then I went to the tool that changes the corners of all objects.

DELETE KEY

If you create a title or draw an object and you don't like it, just select it with the Selection Tool and press Delete. You can also use Undo.

TITLES WITH OBJECTS

To give you an example of some of the other things you can do with these tools, I've created a title that I want to superimpose over a shot showing swimmers in the ocean off Durban, South Africa (Figure 10.17). The white letters don't show up as well as I'd like, so I'm going to create a colored rectangle, which I'll place behind the title. First I'll select a color for the rectangle by clicking in the Fill and choosing an aqua blue color. Next I select the drawing tool that creates boxes (and rectangles). Because I want the rectangle to have rounded corners, I select the curved corner with the Corner Selection Tool.

When I drag the pointer across the title window, a blue rectangle with rounded corners appears.

Figure 10.17

Using the Selection Tool, I drag the rectangle on top of the title "Durban Water-front." The title is no longer visible. I know—that's not good. But I'm not finished. Now, I go up to the Object menu. I select Send To Back. This places the object that is in front—the blue rectangle—behind the title.

Object	Alignment	Help	
Bring To Front			Shift+Ctrl+L
Send To Back			Shift+Ctrl+K
Bring Forward			
Send Backward			

Figure 10.18

Now that's more like it. Our title is a lot more visible now that a blue rectangle surrounds it.

Figure 10.19

TRANSPARENCY

I'm not really happy with the title. I think the rectangle would look better if it were less opaque so some ocean showed through. To set the transparency of an object, select the transparency tool for the particular object you want to affect. The Transparency box is right next to the Fill box.

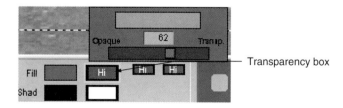

In this example, I've selected the Transparency box for the Fill, which affects the transparency of my blue rectangle. To make the blue box more transparent, I must first place it in the foreground. I choose Bring To Front from the Object menu. Then I click and hold on the Fill Transparency Tool. A slider appears, and as I drag it to the right the blue rectangle will become more transparent. It now has a Hi (high) degree of transparency. Now I need to send it to the back, using the Object Tool.

ALIGNMENT MENU

There's a second menu available once you've opened the Title Tool; it is called the Alignment menu. You'll see that it has many items that help you position selected objects inside the frame. Using the selection tool, practice using the various alignment choices available in the pull-down menu.

LINES AND ARROWS

There are tools for creating arrows and lines of various thickness. These work with the line-drawing tool and can be changed and manipulated just like the rectangle we created using the drawing tool. Select the line thickness or arrow shape, and then click on the Line Tool and then drag the cursor across the Title Tool to create a line or arrow.

OTHER BUTTONS

The Video Placement Tool is one tool I'd suggest you avoid using for now. It doesn't move objects within the frame; it moves the entire frame.

ROLLING TITLES

The many credits that appear at the end of films are usually handled by a lengthy rolling title. They're not that difficult to create. The one oddity is that the speed at which the title rolls is determined by the size of the clip in the Timeline. To make the crawl go faster, you trim the clip. To make it go slower, you extend its length (size) in the Timeline.

To create a rolling title:

1. Select a background, black or video, by clicking the V toggle in the Title tools (see "Choosing a Background" section earlier in this chapter).
2. From the Clip menu, choose New Title.
3. On the far right of the Title Tool, click the Roll button—it turns green.
4. Click on the Text Tool.
5. Choose your font and point size, and then click the centering text alignment box.
6. Type the text. As you type, the text might word wrap. Don't worry. Just keep typing. Press the return key at the end of each line of text.
7. Get the Selector tool and drag the handles to the left and right to make the text box wide enough to prevent word wrap.
8. If the text goes onto more than one page (screen), drag the scroll bar that appears on the right-hand side of the title window to scroll through the text.
9. Select Close from the File menu.
10. Save the title:
    • Select the target disk and bin.
    • Don't save with Fast Save.
11. Click OK.

The title is saved as a title in a bin.

Cutting in Rolling Titles

The rolling title will already be in the Source Monitor. Because it starts out black (empty), you won't see anything. (To see the titles, you've got to drag the Source Monitor position indicator to the middle of the position bar.)

Select the video track in the Timeline, patch the Source track, and now mark an IN in the Timeline where you want the rolling title to start. Next move the cursor along the Timeline and mark an OUT after your IN, calculating the number of seconds between your IN and your OUT. If the IN and OUT are 40 seconds apart, that will be the length of your rolling title. Now go to the Source Monitor and mark an IN at the very first frame of the title. You've got three marks. Now hit Overwrite.

You'll see the title is in the Timeline, with a small RT (for "rolling title"). Depending on your version of software, it might not play in real time. You may need to render it in order for it to play.

Rendering Your Titles

In Xpress Pro 4.+, you normally need to only render crawling and rolling titles. Regular titles play in real time.

Rendering a Rolling Title

1. Select the track containing the title.
2. Place the blue position indicator on the T icon in the Timeline.
3. Go to the Clip menu and choose Render at Position, or
4. Click the Render Effect button in the Fast menu between the Source Monitor and Record Monitor.

Render Effect button

5. When the dialog box appears, choose a target drive for the effect.
6. Click OK.

If you have a number of titles that need to be rendered, it's easier to render them all at the same time.

Rendering Multiple Titles

1. Click the track selector to choose the tracks holding titles you want to render.
2. Mark an IN before the first title and an OUT after the last title.
3. Go to the Clip menu and select Render In/Out.

Adjusting the Speed of the Rolling Titles

Once you see it play, you may decide it goes by too quickly (or too slowly). It will seem strange, but you use Trim Mode to change the speed of the rolling title.

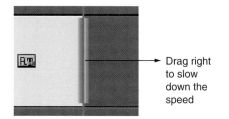

Drag right
to slow
down the
speed

Lasso the end of the title to get into Dual-Roller Trim. Now drag the roller toward the right (tail), and the rolling title slows down. Drag it toward the left (head), and the rolling title speeds up.

The rolling title will always start with the first line off-screen. It will then appear at the bottom of the screen and move upward. You can set IN and OUT marks in the Source Monitor to change the start and end points. For example, mark an IN and you can get the rolling title to begin with the first line already on screen.

CRAWLING TITLES

Avid calls a title that moves across the screen horizontally a *crawl*. The text runs along the frame from screen right to left. You create crawling titles the same way you create rolling titles, but you click on Crawl instead of Roll. You'll need to use the Selector Tool handles to keep the letters from word wrapping. For example, let's say you wanted the following title to crawl across the screen:

"Boston Red Sox win World Series! First time since 1918. Watch the News at Eleven for highlights."

To get this text to crawl as a single line, you'll need to drag the selector handle to the far right so the text doesn't word wrap, as this sentence does. To get the crawl to come true—folks around New England would say that took a miracle.

AVID MARQUEE

Xpress Pro 5.+ comes with a special titling software called Avid Marquee. It lets you create titles in three dimensions that can move around the screen like a five-star roller coaster. We're going to discuss more advanced titles at the end of the next chapter, after we have learned about Avid's visual effects, but I'm not going to get into Avid Marquee titles; it's so deep, it needs its own book.

SUGGESTED ASSIGNMENTS

1. Open the Title Tool and choose a font size.
2. Type a title.
3. Click on the Selector Tool and drag the right-hand selection handle to make the title fit on the line.
4. Move the title around inside the frame.
5. Add a drop shadow. Increase and decrease the depth and direction of the shadow.
6. Change to a depth shadow.
7. Save your title.
8. Close the Title Tool and cut the title into your Timeline. If you need to, create a V2 track.
9. Open the Title Tool. Create a colored title. Add a depth shadow. Now create a blend for that title.
10. Close the Title Tool and cut this title onto V2.
11. Open the Title Tool. Create a rolling title. Close the Title Tool, and cut this title into the Timeline.
12. Render the Title.
13. Change the speed of the rolling title.
14. Render the title.

11

Effects

I learned to make films before I ever worked in video, and I guess that's why it took me a while to take advantage of Avid's extensive effects. Effects are so expensive in film that you only use them when nothing else will work. It's different on an Avid. The effects are free, and you don't have to wait more than a few minutes—and usually much less—to see what they'll look like. Keep in mind that not every project benefits from a lot of effects. Scenes involving strong performances by talented actors are usually hurt by visual effects, because they steal the scene from the actors. Montage sequences that are music driven or contain stunning cinematography are great candidates for effects, because the right effect heightens the mood and visual impact of the sequence. Music videos, which are designed to be viewed many times, benefit from complex visual effects; otherwise, the video becomes stale after one or two viewings. Transitions before and after television commercials are often piled high with visual effects as a means of grabbing audience attention. The same can be said of the commercials themselves, which are often packed with stunning visual effects.

Some editors think of effects as crutches used to mask serious problems in the material. Others think they needlessly junk up a show. I think this is another area where the Avid comes in handy. Try it with, and try it without. You then can make your decision based on what the sequence looks like when you play it.

KINDS OF EFFECTS

There are two categories of effects. *Transition effects* are applied at the cut point, or transition point, in the Timeline. These effects change the way Shot A transitions to Shot B. A dissolve is an example of a transition effect. Instead of a straight cut, Shot A fades out while Shot B fades in, creating a melding of the two shots.

Segment effects are applied to the entire clip or segment in the Timeline. You might have a shot in the sequence where your actor is facing screen left to right, and by applying a *flop* the screen direction of the entire shot is changed so the actor is facing screen right to left. When you use a segment effect you are affecting a segment in the Timeline. Segment effects can work on one video track, like the flop, or on several video tracks. For instance, you might have an image on V2 interact with an image on V1. In a multilayered effect, V1 is always the background layer, and V2 (and V3 and V4) is layered on top of the background.

Many effects work as both transition effects and segment effects. They can be applied to either a transition or a segment. Applying effects to a transition or segment is really quite simple. Getting them to do what you want is a bit more complicated.

EFFECT PALETTE

Let's take a look at the Effect Palette. Go to the Tools menu and select Effect Palette. Or simply go to the Project window and click on the little tab that looks like one of those naval flags that's used to signal by semaphore. Once the Effect Palette opens, you'll see a box with two columns.

The left-hand column lists the categories of effects. When you click on a category, a list of the types of effects your system offers is displayed in the right-hand column. In Figure 11.1, I've clicked on the Image category, and my choices

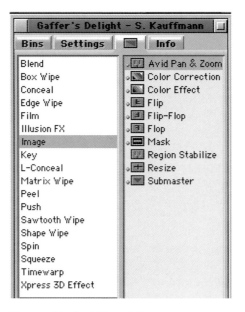

Figure 11.1 Effect Palette.

are listed in the right-hand column. Scroll through the category list, clicking on the different categories, and look at the many choices offered.

APPLYING AN EFFECT

It's easy to apply an effect. Just click on the icon for the effect you want, and drag it from the Effect Palette to the Timeline. Release it when you've reached the transition or segment of your choice.

Let's try a transition effect. Let's use a Squeeze effect. Click on the Squeeze category to see the choices. There are quite a few squeeze effects to choose from. Let's try a Centered Zoom.

Figure 11.2 is an outgoing shot of people climbing into a van, and Figure 11.3 is a dolly shot past a row of houses in Soweto, outside Johannesburg.

Figure 11.2

Figure 11.3

Now, I'm going to click on the Centered Zoom icon in the Effect Palette, drag it onto the transition point in the Timeline, and release it. There. I've got a centered zoom squeeze between the two shots.

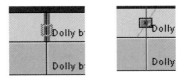

Drag the icon to the Timeline and release it.

Figure 11.4 gives you some idea of what the effect looks like. The house starts out small and then gets bigger and bigger as it squeezes out the shot of the people and the van.

Figure 11.4

Xpress Pro 4.+ RealTime Effects Button

Xpress Pro 5.+ users don't have to deal with RealTime Effects buttons, because all effects play as soon as you create them, but if you have a version before 5.0, you'll find you'll need to go to the Timeline tool bar and examine the RealTime Effects toggle button to see if it's green (it looks like a ball). If it's blue, you won't be able to play your effects. Click on the blue ball so it's green. Now your effects will play.

RealTime Effects toggle button ————

Applying More Effects

Let's try applying some different effects to other transitions. Click on the category called Shape Wipe. Click and drag the effect called Horizontal Bands to a transition in your Timeline. Admittedly, some of the effects are fairly goofy—transitional effects that only George Lucas could love.

Now let's try a segment effect. Scroll down the Effect Palette until you see the Image category in the left-hand column. Click on it. Now click on the effect called Flop. This effect changes the screen direction of a shot. Here is a shot showing South Africa's second black president, Thabo Mbeki, talking to South Africa's last white president, F. W. De Klerk. To change the clip's screen direction, I simply drag the Flop icon onto the clip itself, not onto the transition, and presto, the screen direction changes.

Figure 11.5   **Figure 11.6**

COLORED DOTS

When you look at an effect in the Effect Palette or at the effect icon in the Timeline, you'll see a colored dot. These dots tell you how complex the effect is and whether it will play in real time or will need to be rendered. We discussed rendering in Chapter 10. As you recall, an effect, such as a title, is a new creation. In order to see this new creation, the effect needs to be created by the computer so new media sits on your media drive, the way a master clip does; however, the Avid has the ability to play most effects in a sort of preview mode. These effects, which can be played in the Timeline even though they have not been rendered, are called *real-time effects*.

If you look at an effect in the Effect Palette, the effects with green dots to the left of their name are real-time effects—they will play in real time. You won't need to render them to see how they look. The effects with *no* dots are the complex effects. Once you place that effect in the Timeline, a blue dot will appear, and you must render the effect to see how it works.

THIRD-PARTY PLUG-IN EFFECTS

The latest Avid models come with effects created by Avid, as well as by other companies that specialize in visual effects. If you look at the Effect Palette in Figure 11.1, you'll see the category containing Illusion FX.

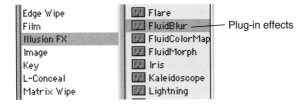

These are called *plug-in effects*. All the icons for plug-in effects look like electrical wall outlets. These are not real-time effects; they are quite complicated, and they take a long time to render. Let's skip them for now, until we have mastered the less complicated ones.

EFFECT EDITOR

So far we've looked at some fairly straightforward effects. As you can see, it's not all that difficult to apply an effect to either a transition or a segment in the Timeline. Now let's look at effects that can be changed in significant ways by the use of the Effect Editor.

Almost all effects have *parameters*, which are specific features that can be altered or adjusted. For example, you might have one shot on the screen, and then a second image appears inside a box that travels across the first image. There are a lot of parameters that you could manipulate to enhance this effect. You could, for instance, give the box a border. You could give the border a color. You could have the box get bigger as it moves across the screen. These are all parameters that you can control with the Effect Editor.

You can open the Effect Editor from the Tools menu, but I usually just click on the Effect Mode button located on the Timeline tool bar, the Source/Record Fast menu, and the keyboard.

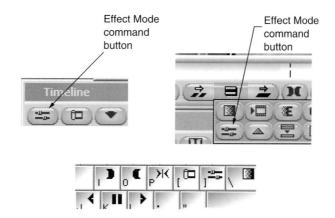

Apply an effect to the segment or transition in the Timeline and then make sure the track is selected:

1. Place the blue position indicator on the effect's icon in the Timeline.
2. Click the Effect Mode button.

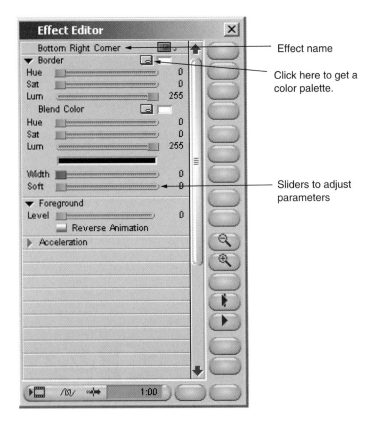

Effect name

Click here to get a color palette.

Sliders to adjust parameters

Figure 11.7 Effect Editor.

When the Effect Editor opens, you'll see that the Record Monitor changes appearance. It is now officially called the *Effect Preview Monitor,* and you're looking at just the clip containing the effect, not the entire sequence. Notice that two key frames are already set in the position bar (Figure 11.8).

Let's examine the Effect Editor. The one shown in Figure 11.9 is for a Peel effect called "Bottom Right Corner." At the top of the Effect Editor you'll see the name of the effect you are editing. Inside you'll see the parameters that can be changed. Triangle-shaped openers give you access to sliders, which control the amount or quantity of a particular parameter. Click on a triangle to show or hide the sliders.

Each effect will have different parameters because each effect behaves differently; however, the effects within a category usually have similar parameters. Figure 11.10 shows the Effect Editor at work. The Peel effect has been applied to a transition between a map of South Africa and a group of South Africans.

Figure 11.8 Effect Editor and Effect Preview Monitor.

Figure 11.9

Figure 11.10

Using the Effect Editor, I created a border, which makes the peel look like a page that's turning, and then I gave the border a cream color.

Here are some of the different parameters you'll encounter:

- *Border*. Changes the color of the border, or box, that surrounds an image. You can also change the border's width and transparency.
- *Foreground Level*. On blends and key effects, it represents the video's transparency. On transitional effects, this represents the proportion of incoming to outgoing frames.
- *Reverse*. This reverses the parameters you have set. All parameters are re-ordered last to first. Instead of a box starting out small and getting bigger, it will start big and shrink.
- *Acceleration*. This controls the start and end of a move so the move isn't too abrupt.
- *Scaling*. This changes the size of the box. You can manipulate the width and height of boxes. Most boxes have handles that you can drag to change the shape of the box. You can also click in the center of the box and drag it to a new position.

Effect Editing Tools

You'll notice that when you open the Effect Editor, the Record side of the Source/Record Monitor changes into the Effect Preview Monitor. The position bar offers a different set of command buttons, and it contains two key frames: one at the beginning and one at the end. You can add additional key frames with the Add Key Frame command. Key frames enable you to change a parameter's look over time. The number of key frames available on any given effect will depend on the version of Avid software you have.

Add key frames

The Effect Editor has toolbars containing helpful tools as well (Figure 11.11). One tool will render the effect and another allows you to type in a new length for a transitional effect. Just type a new value and press Return or Enter.

Another command lets you reduce the frame, so you can start an effect off-screen, and then enlarge the frame to return the screen to normal.

Let's work with a segment effect and use the Effect Editor and key frames to change the way a parameter works. We'll use the Superimpose segment effect and work with the Foreground Level parameter. The Superimpose effect is available in the Blend category of effects.

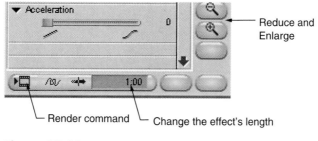

Reduce and Enlarge

Render command — Change the effect's length

Figure 11.11

For a superimposition to work, you need two images. First, I add a second video track, V2. I simply go to the Clip menu and select New Video Track. I then splice in the second clip onto track V2. Figures 11.12 and 11.13 show the two clips.

I next drag the Superimpose icon from the Effect Palette onto the V2 image.

Figure 11.12   The image on V1.   **Figure 11.13**   The image on V2.

Now I open the Effect Editor by placing the position indicator on the effect icon and pressing the Effect Editor command key.

Right now the effect gives me a superimposition of the image on V2 over the image on V1. The level is set at 50, meaning that the two images are blended evenly together (half and half, or 50%). If I click on the Play button, I'll see that the two images remain blended at this level throughout the length of the clip. That's not what I want. What I want to do is change the amount of superimposition over time.

First I click on the first key frame in the position bar to make it turn pink and to put the position indicator on top of it. Always do this whenever you're working with the Effect Editor to make sure you're starting at the beginning.

Now, I go to Effect Editor and drag the Level slider to the left, resulting in 0 opacity. When I do that, the foreground image, V2, will not be seen at all. I want this to be the case at the beginning of the effect.

Now I place a second key frame further along the position bar, as shown in Figure 11.14. To place a key frame, just drag the position indicator to a spot further along the position bar and then click on the Key Frame button. You can also use the N key on the keyboard, the same one you used to set audio key frames. Next click on the key frame to make sure it's pink. Now go to the Effect Editor and move the Level slider to 25.

Figure 11.14

Now I place a third key frame further along on the position bar, click on it to select it, and change the opacity to 75.

Now, the foreground image really starts to come through the background image.

Finally, I set the last key frame at the end and change the opacity to 100.

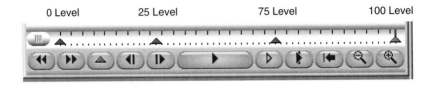

Now I've created my effect. The image begins with V1 totally filling the frame—Level is set at 0. Over time, the image on V2 slowly takes over, as increasing amounts of opacity are set at those key frames, until finally the opacity is set to 100 and only the V2 image appears on the screen.

Figure 11.15 Begin with just V1.

Figure 11.16 V2 is supered over V1.

Figure 11.17 V2 takes over the screen.

Manipulating Key Frames

- After you have created a key frame, you can move it by holding the Option key (Mac) or Alt key (Windows) and dragging it to a new position.
- You can change the parameter for any given key frame by clicking on it (it turns pink) and changing the parameters in the Effect Editor.
- You can delete a key frame by selecting it and hitting the Delete key.

Saving an Effect as a Template

After doing all the work involved in setting parameters for an effect, you can save those parameters so you can use them again on another transition or segment in the Timeline. Simply drag the icon in the Effect Editor window to a bin. Rename it in the bin. You have just created a template. To place the template you created on a different transition or a segment, simply click on it in the bin and drag it to the Timeline.

EFFECT QUICK REVIEW

Steps for adding effects:

- Load a sequence into the Timeline.
- Open Effect Palette from the Tools menu or from the Project window.
- Choose the effect and drag it into the Timeline.
- Adjust the effect's parameters with the Effect Editor (open it from the Tools menu, Timeline toolbar, Fast menu, or keyboard).

DELETING EFFECTS

It's easy to get rid of an effect you don't want anymore.

- Put the position indictor on the effect icon.
- Press the Remove Effect button.

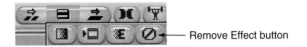

Remove Effect button

ADDING DISSOLVES

Dissolves are so common that there's a Dissolve key on the keyboard (the \ key), a Dissolve button on the Fast menu, and one on the Timeline toolbar. Just follow theses steps to get the dissolve you want.

Add Dissolve button

1. Put the blue position indicator on the transition.
2. Hit the Add Dissolve button.
3. A Quick Transition dialog box appears, giving you choices to control how the dissolve will look.
4. Choose the duration. A 30-frame dissolve is the default length.
5. Choose whether the dissolve is centered on the cut, starting on the cut, ending on the cut, or custom designed by you.
6. Choose the target disk.
7. Click Add to place the dissolve on the transition, or choose Add and Render to place it on the transition and have it rendered. I usually just click Add.

FREEZE FRAMES

There are two important effects that aren't found on the Effect Palette: freeze frames and motion effects. Freeze frames are given special status and are found in the Clip menu. Just follow these steps to create your first freeze. After you've done it once, you'll be able to do it in your sleep.

1.   In the Timeline, go to the tail of the shot you want to freeze and put the position indicator on the last frame. Remember, in the Timeline, Option–Command–click (Mac) or Ctrl–Alt–click (Windows) the position indicator to jump to the clip's tail frame.
2.   Select Match Frame (Fast menu item), and the clip will appear in the Source Monitor with the last frame marked by an IN.
3.   Go to the Clip menu and choose Freeze Frame.
4.   Select the length. Click OK. A new clip is created, labeled "Clip name" FF. It automatically opens in the Source Monitor.
5.   Mark an IN and an OUT in the Source Monitor.
6.   In the Timeline, go to the first frame of the next shot and mark an IN.
7.   Select all your tracks by clicking on the Record Track selectors.
8.   Splice in the freeze.

Remember, there will be no sound—just black fill.

RENDERING

If you use Avid's 3D Effects or third-party plug-in effects, they'll need to be rendered before they'll play in the Timeline. If you have a number of effects bunched together in the Timeline because you're creating a complex visual look and they need to be rendered to play, try selecting Expert Render from the Clip menu. The Avid will figure out the least number of effects that will need to be rendered to get the effects to play together. No matter how many real-time effects you use, at some point you'll need to render your effects to send your work out to tape. Rendering can take up a lot of time and some space on your hard drive, so render as late in the editing process as possible, and render only those effects you know are going in the final sequence.

Rendering Single Effects

1.   Place the blue position indicator on the effect's icon in the Timeline.
2.   Click the Render Effect button in the Fast menu, or choose Render from the Clip menu.
3.   When the dialog box appears, choose a target disk.
4.   Click OK.

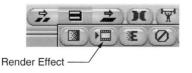

Render Effect

Rendering Multiple Effects

First, click the track selector boxes to choose the tracks holding the effects you want to render.

1. Mark an IN before the first effect and an OUT after the last effect.
2. Go to the Clip menu and select Render In/Out.
3. When the dialog box appears, choose a target disk.
4. Click OK.

Waiting for Effects to Render

If you have complex effects to render, the process can take a long time. I've often waited 5 minutes for an effect to render. Five minutes might not seem like a long time, but if you're really in a flow and coming up with a lot of ideas, it can be like watching water boil. One strategy is to wait until you've created a number of effects and then render them all at once, while you go do something else. Lunch is one possibility.

MOTION EFFECTS

This is a special effect that has its own button—this one is in the Source Monitor's toolbar. With this tool you can create slow and fast motion, reverse the motion, or create a strobe effect. You'll be working in the Source Monitor. You place the shot you want to change in the Source Monitor and mark the part you want to change, and then the Avid creates a new effect, which you cut into your Timeline. All the motion effects share the same dialog box (Figure 11.18).

Motion Effect command

Slow Motion/Fast Motion

1. Choose a clip in a bin that you want to apply a motion effect to, and double-click to open it.
2. In the Source Monitor, mark an IN and an OUT to show the section of the clip you want to use for the effect.
3. Press the Motion Effect command. A Motion Effect dialog box appears (Figure 11.18).

4. For Variable Speed effects, you'll see that 15 frames per second (fps) and 50% are the default settings. The resulting shot is twice as long, which is another way of saying it appears to be twice as slow as normal.
5. Choose another setting, such as 8 fps, to make it even slower.
6. When you click on Create and Render, the motion effect appears as a new clip in the Source Monitor.
7. Now you splice or overwrite it into your sequence.

Rendering choices pull-down menu

Figure 11.18

Rendering Two-Field Motion Effects

You have four choices when rendering your Motion Effect. This complication arises because each frame of interlaced video has two fields, and it's not easy to combine them when creating motion. Here are my suggestions, but try the other choices if you're not happy with how the effect looks.

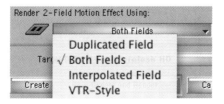

- I like Both Fields for most effects unless there's a lot of fast motion in the clip.
- Interpolated Fields will make fast motion look smoother, but it softens the image.
- Duplicated Fields is better if there's motion in the clip, but the soft look bothers me.
- I never use VTR-Style because it doesn't look as good as the other choices.

Reverse Motion

This is useful, for example, if you have a zoom that goes in and you want to make the zoom go out:

1. Select a clip in a bin that you want to apply a motion effect to, and double-click.
2. In the Source Monitor, mark an IN and an OUT on the section you want.
3. Press the Motion Effect button.
4. Put a minus sign (–) in front of the FPS or percent rate. Choose 30 fps if you want it to play at normal speed.
5. After clicking on Create and Render, cut the new clip into your sequence.

Strobe

1. Select a clip in a bin that you want to apply a motion effect to, and double-click.
2. In the Source Monitor, mark an IN and an OUT on the section you want.
3. Press the Motion Effect button on the Source Monitor toolbar.
4. Click on the Strobe Motion box and deselect the Variable Speed box.
5. Update Every 5 Frames is the default setting. This means every fifth frame is displayed, creating the strobe effect. Try five frames and then try another number.
6. After clicking on Create and Render, cut the new clip into your sequence.

COLOR CORRECTION

The latest versions of Avid come with a very powerful Color Correction Tool, which you'll access via the Toolset menu. Color Correction acts like an effect, but it's in the Toolset menu because it changes the appearance of the Avid screen rather dramatically (Figure 11.19). The tool is designed for professional colorists and experienced Avid editors. It's quite complex, but I hope I can help break its code so even a beginner can tap its power.

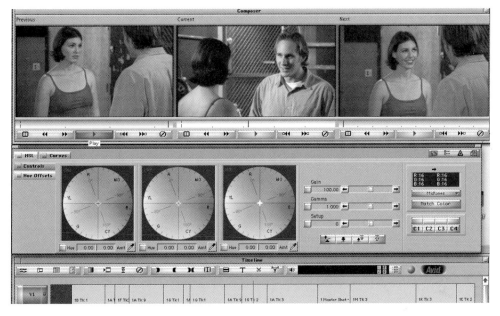

Figure 11.19 Color Correction Tool.

As soon as you select Color Correction in the Toolset menu you'll see three monitors showing you three segments (or clips) in the Timeline. Color correction is relative. Changing the color of one segment without seeing how it looks in comparison to the segment before (and after) would be a mistake, because shots in the same scene would not match.

The middle monitor shows the segment that the position indicator in the Timeline rests on. That's the segment whose colors you are changing. The left-hand monitor shows you the segment just before it, and the right-hand monitor shows you the segment just after it. Each monitor has a position indicator and commands so you can navigate the segment. The most interesting command is the first one—*Dual Split*. When you click that button the frame is split in two. The left half shows you your color correction and the other half remains unchanged.

Pull-Down Menus

If you look at the three monitors, from left to right, you'll see they are labeled Previous, Current, and Next. If you click and hold on the name, you'll see a pull-down menu that lets you change the segment that monitor displays (Figure 11.20).

Reference lets you lock a frame from a segment into one of the monitors (I use the left-hand one). With the left-hand monitor on Reference, I can hold a shot in that monitor and then move through the Timeline, looking at and fixing specific shots in the middle monitor; I always have this shot as a reference. Maybe I want to use flesh tones or a shirt color as a reference. When you choose Reference, whatever clip is in the center monitor becomes the Reference frame.

Figure 11.20

You can also use this pull-down menu to turn the monitor into waveforms and vectorscopes—tools that show luminance and chrominance levels, respectively. There are other ways of viewing luminance and chrominance information, as you can see from the menu in Figure 11.21. Quad Display lets you place multiple color reference tools in a single monitor so you can examine them all at once. It could take another whole book to explain the function of these color reference tools. Concentrate not on these tools but on making your shots look better—but, as you do that, watch the tools (I like YCbCr Histogram) to see how they change as you change the image.

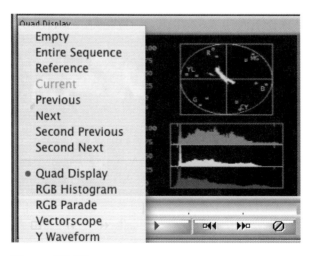

Figure 11.21

Your Tools—Groups

There are two primary groups: the HSL (hue, saturation, luminance) group and the Curves group. You choose one or the other by clicking on the tab.

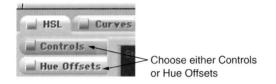

Choose either Controls
or Hue Offsets

The HSL group itself has two tabs: *Controls* and *Hue Offsets*. So, there are three different ways of attacking a color correction or exposure problem: Controls, Hue Offsets, and Curves.

- *Hue Offsets.* This is the group of tools you see as soon as you open Color Correction, and it looks the most daunting. In fact, this is easy to use and the one I use all the time to change the color of a shot. If the shot is too blue or too red, it's an easy fix with Hue Offsets.
- *Controls.* This is also much easier than it looks and the one I use to fix exposure problems. I also use it to increase or decrease the intensity (saturation) of the colors in a shot.
- *Curves.* This is perhaps the most difficult to master. It works a lot like Curves in Adobe Photoshop®, so if you're used to using Curves in Photoshop you might prefer Curves, though I believe the first two are easier for beginners to master.

If you adjust the image using one tool and then adjust the image using a second tool, the result will be a combination of *both* changes. If you're not satisfied with what you did in the second group, you can disable those changes by deselecting the Enable button (Figure 11.22). This doesn't affect any changes you made in the first group.

As soon you make your first change to the color of a shot, a Color Effect icon appears in the Timeline. Days later, if you aren't happy with the changes, just click on the Remove Effect command and the effect will disappear.

The HSL Group—Controls

Let's start with the HSL group and click on the Controls tab. It is very easy to use. Use it to make the following changes to your image:

- Drag the Hue slider or click on arrows to change the color.
- Drag the Saturation slider or click on arrows to raise or lower the amount of color.
- Drag the Brightness slider or click on arrows to raise or lower brightness.
- Drag the Contrast slider or click on arrows to change the contrast of the image.

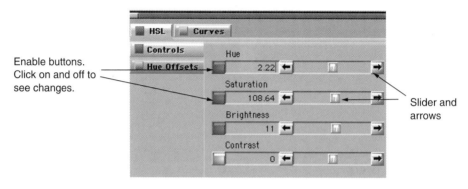

Figure 11.22

The HSL Group—Hue Offsets

This tool is the best for changing the color (hue) of a given image. The three wheels are for Shadows, Mid, and Highlights (Figure 11.23). If you want to add red (R), simply click on the center crosshair and drag it up toward the red area (11 o'clock). Play with all three to see the result.

Each wheel has its own Enable tab. Use the Enable buttons to toggle on and off the changes you've made. Compare with to without.

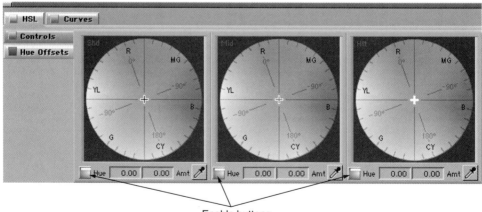

Figure 11.23

Returning to Default

If you don't like what you've done with any control, it's easy to return to the 0 or default setting. Simply Option–click (Mac) or Alt–click (Windows) the Enable buttons:

- Option–click (Mac) or Alt–click (Windows) the individual buttons to reset.
- Option–click (Mac) or Alt–click (Windows) the group button to reset everything—all the settings—in that group.

To get a better feel for what I'm accomplishing, I often go to the Toolset menu and switch to Source/Record Editing so I can play the sequence; then I return to Color Correction to continue the work of polishing each shot in the Timeline.

Saving Your Color Correction Settings

You will want to save a particular color effect to use on another segment or image. Just click and drag the Color Effect icon to a bin (Figure 11.24). I do this all the time for dialog scenes that are covered from several camera angles, such as in "Wanna Trade." Once I get a shot right, I'll apply the effect every time that shot appears again.

Color
Effect Icon

Figure 11.24

I'm not even going to get into Curves, leaving those controls to more experienced users. Clearly, the Color Correction Toolset offers vast capabilities. Like most of Avid's features, Color Correction gives you instant feedback. It either looks better or worse, and you can easily undo if things get out of control. The overview I've provided here should help you fix your problem shots and give your scenes a more consistent look.

A WORLD OF EFFECTS

We could write an entire book on effects; we've just touched the surface in this chapter. There's the whole subject of third-party plug-in effects and three-dimensional effects, which I've barely mentioned. The Avid Help menu has some additional information, as well as the CD-ROM that comes with the Avid software. But I believe you now have more than enough information to get started. Through practice and experimentation, I know you'll do fine.

12

Saving Your Work

IF IT'S A COMPUTER IT WILL CRASH

Not too long ago there were articles in newspapers, weekly magazines, and online news sites about the convergence of television and computers, with some prognosticators suggesting we would soon be watching television on our computer monitors. One scribe rebutted this suggestion by saying he didn't want to be watching the Super Bowl and have the system crash during a game-winning touchdown drive.

There is some truth to that observation. Computers do crash, they have bugs, and they are susceptible to viruses and other infestations. When you stop and think about it, those are problems we don't encounter on any of the other countless electronic products that surround us. My microwave doesn't crash, my television doesn't have bugs, and my digital camera hasn't caught a virus.

That said, the various Avids that I've been using for the past 9 years have been quite dependable. (Yes, the sound you hear is my knuckles striking wood.) They have only crashed about 40 times, and never have I lost more than about 10 minutes of work. Given how much I've used my Avid and the service it has rendered, I figure it's one of the most dependable things in my life! So, I'm a satisfied customer, and I don't hesitate to praise the Avid's dependability whenever I'm asked. Yet, as dependable as they are, the Avids will crash. And when they do, you'd better be ready.

BACKING UP

If there is a system crash, hard-drive glitch, or any number of horrors just waiting to befall you, *all* of your work can be lost—unless you back up your work. By that I mean placing the information about your bins and sequences on a CD, USB flash drive, or Zip disk. Here's how:

1. When you finish editing for the day, and after you save all your work, close the project and quit the application. You are returned to the desktop or Finder.
2. Double-click My Computer (Windows) or the Macintosh HD (Mac).
3. Windows users, go to Program Files\Avid\Avid Xpress (or Media Composer). Look for the folder called "Avid Projects." Mac users, go to the Users folder, then to Shared, and Xpress, where you'll find the Avid Projects folder.
4. Double-click the Avid Projects folder.

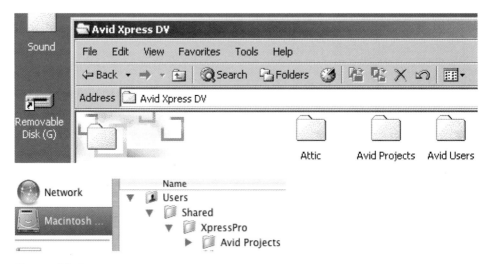

Figure 12.1 The Avid Projects folder on Windows and Mac.

5. Scroll through it until you find your project—the one you named.
6. Insert a CD-RW, flash drive, or a Zip disk into the computer's CPU slot for that type of storage device.

7. When the disk appears on the desktop, drag the project folder containing your project's name onto the storage device (see Figure 12.2). The computer will automatically begin to copy to that device.
8. If you have placed your project folder on a CD, you'll need to burn it before ejecting.

That wasn't so hard. Remember to do it daily.

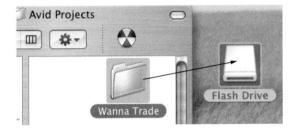

Figure 12.2 Backing up (Mac).

You should do this at the end of every editing session and then rename the latest version with the current date so you can easily find the one with the most recent changes.

All the project settings, sequences, and bins, including all your titles, effects, clips, subclips, and audio clip information—everything is copied to your backup disk. Open the most recent folder and you'll see that everything associated with the project has been backed up onto the back-up disk, as shown in Figure 12.3.

Figure 12.3 Contents of the "Wanna Trade" folder.

It's important to note that no media files—none of the digitized picture or sound—are copied to the back-up device. Only the information the Avid has created about the project is copied, but that's usually all you need.

AFTER THE CRASH

If there is a bad crash and your project is missing or badly corrupted or if someone removes your project from the CPU, you can reload all your files onto your Avid. All you have to do is insert your CD or flash drive into the CPU's drive and drag your project folder to the Avid Projects folder. Launch the Avid program and your project and all the clip information will be there. It will all be listed as "Media Offline," but you can easily recapture the clips. And, once you recapture the clips, all the sequences that you've edited using those clips will be just the way you left them, like magic. We'll learn to recapture your clips later in this chapter.

SAVING USER SETTINGS

You can back up your user settings the same way. All the user settings you made in the Settings area—how Trim Mode works, how the keyboard is configured, how auto save works, the color of your tracks in the Timeline—all of these are saved under your name in the Avid Users folder.

Copying User Settings

When you are on the desktop or Finder (the application is closed and the CPU's hard drive is open), repeat the steps you used to get to the Avid Projects folder and there you'll see the Avid Users folder. Double-click on the Avid Users folder and then drag your User Settings folder to a CD or flash drive as shown in Figure 12.4.

Figure 12.4 Locate your Avid User folder and drag it to the back-up disk.

If you become a freelance editor and work at different post-production houses, you can carry all your user settings—how the Avid looks, how the keyboard keys are mapped—with you on a flash drive or Zip disk. When you sit down at a new Avid editing station, insert your disk or connect your flash drive. In the Project window click on the Settings tab. Go to the User pull-down menu, as I have in Figure 12.5, and select Import User or User Profile. Navigate to the Zip disk or flash drive and select it.

Figure 12.5

THE ATTIC

If you recall the work we did with Settings, you'll remember that Bin Settings was one of the first settings we examined (see Figure 12.6). There you told the Avid how often and when you wanted your work saved to the *attic*. The attic, you'll recall, is like an attic in a house, where old items get stored. In this case, the old items are previous versions of your work. If there is a crash or if you lose a sequence or if something happens during an editing session, you can go to the attic and retrieve the bin containing your sequences. Whatever you're looking for, it's probably in the attic.

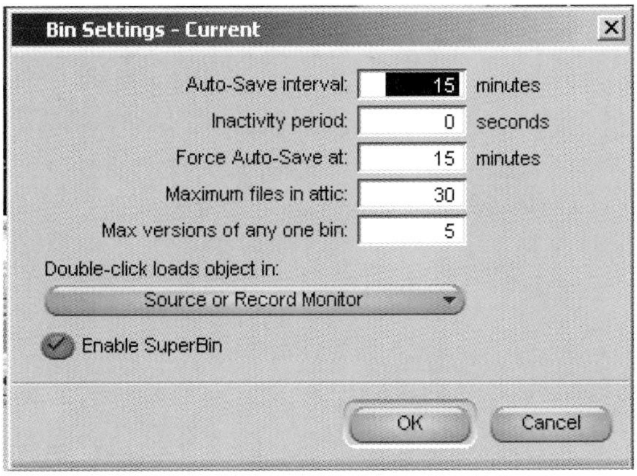

Figure 12.6

Double-click to open the Attic folder and then open your project folder (Figure 12.7). The Avid doesn't just save sequences; instead, it saves your bins.

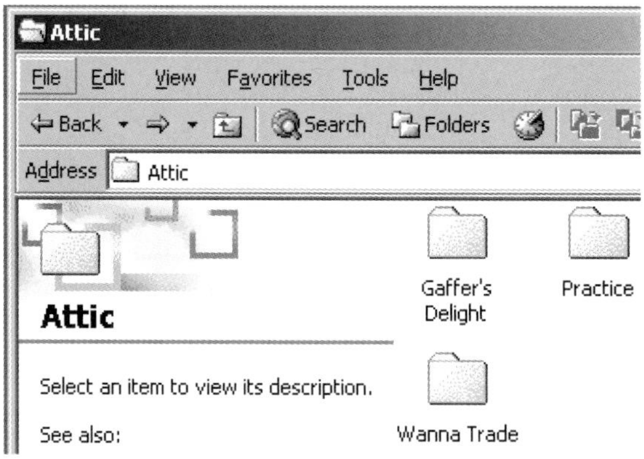

Figure 12.7 The Attic folder.

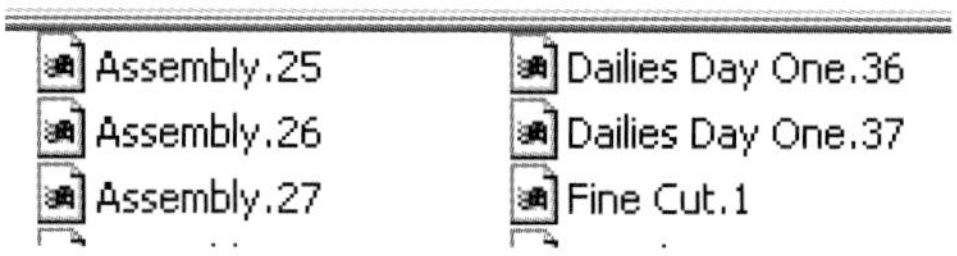

Figure 12.8 Bins that have been backed up.

Retrieving a File from the Attic

1. In the Project window, close all of your bins.
2. Minimize the Avid screen in Windows; on a Mac, hide the Avid screen by pressing Command–H.
3. Open the hard drive on the desktop.
4. Look for the Attic folder in the same place you found the Avid Projects and Avid User folders.

5. Open it.
6. Scroll through it until you find your project—the one you named. Open it.
7. Look for the bin you want. The smallest number (1.1) will be the oldest and the largest number will be the most recent version.
8. Ctrl–click (Windows) or Shift–click (Mac) the bin files you want.
9. Windows users, make a copy of the original bin in the Attic folder and paste it to the desktop. Mac users, Option–drag the files to the desktop.
10. Now open the Avid program from the task bar or dock.
11. When the Avid program opens, click on the Project window to make it active.
12. From the File menu, choose Open Bin. Navigate until you find the bin you just created on the desktop. Click Open.
13. Now create a new bin. Call it "Restore."
14. Select the sequence you want from the back-up bin, and then drag the sequence (Windows) or Option–drag (Mac) the duplicate sequence to the new bin, "Restore."

BATCH CAPTURE OFFLINE MEDIA

If your material goes offline (on purpose or by accident) or if you are going to capture material that you logged, the process of batch capturing is the same. Batch capture only works with material that has timecode—for example, DV 25, DVCPRO 50, or even DAT tapes.

Examine the accompanying bin in Frame View (Figure 12.9). The clip on the left is offline. The clip information is there, but the media file has either been erased or was never captured in the first place.

Figure 12.9

Before you capture anything, you must have the source tapes in front of you. You also need to connect your equipment so you can send your video and audio signals from the tape deck to the Avid. Take a look at Chapter 6 to review the steps you take to capture. Once you're set up:

1. In the bin, select all the video or audio clips that you wish to capture.
2. When all the offline clips are highlighted, go to the Toolset menu and select Capture.
3. Choose:
   - Your target bin
   - Your resolution
   - Tracks (V1, A1, A2, TC)
4. Go to the Bin menu and choose Batch Capture.
5. A dialog box will open. Make sure "Offline media only" is selected. Then click OK.

The Avid will then ask you for the first tape. You should have all the source tapes nearby and insert them as the Avid asks for them. Once the Avid begins to capture the offline clips, you can watch the process in action. Once a clip is captured, it is no longer highlighted, so over time, the list of highlighted clips gets smaller and smaller, until none is highlighted. You can abort the batching process at any time. To abort, click on the Trash icon on the Capture Tool.

BACKING UP MEDIA FILES

The Avid Unity MediaNetwork and Avid Unity LANshare are Avid's shared storage products. They allow multiple Avid machines to share the same media, but they also allow you to set them up to automatically back up any and all of your media files. For instance, if you had a system with 1.9 terabytes of capacity, you could use 1.2 terabytes for media and the other .7 terabyte as backup. These systems are typically used by television networks, larger stations, and big post-production companies.

For individuals not connected to networks and who own DVD burners, the decision to back up your media files depends a lot on the type of media in your project. If almost everything in your project was captured from tapes containing timecode, then there's little reason to back up your media files to DVD; however, if a lot of your project comes from imported graphics and animated files created by other applications or the audio has no timecode (like Nagra tapes or CDs), then you might want to consider backing up onto DVDs. Even those of you with just CD burners might consider backing up audio files onto CDs.

Backing Up Video

I don't normally back up my video files. I back up my project folder every day, and I have the source tapes with timecode stored safely away. I know that if anything goes wrong, I can batch capture from those tapes. If you have a lot of imported material that can't be batch captured and if you have a DVD burner, then it makes sense to back up your video *and* audio files together, rather than to separate them. To back up your files to a DVD, go to your media drive and open the OMFI MediaFiles folder. Select your project's video and audio files, drag them onto a DVD, and burn them.

```
▼  📁 OMFI MediaFiles
    ▶  📁 Creating
        📄 001120FBA01.3D51211C.738E70.aif  ◄──────── Audio file.
        📄 001120FBV01.3D51211C.738E80.omf  ◄──────── Video file.
```

Backing Up Audio

Because audio files are quite small compared to video files, you can back them up easily. If a lot of your audio comes from sound-effect CDs or music CDs, be aware that no timecode is associated with CDs so you can't batch capture, as you can with a DV tape. In Chapter 19, we'll learn about bringing in audio for film projects that was recorded using a Nagra 4.2 tape recorder. Because it's not a timecode machine, there's no way to recapture your Nagra tapes and have the material automatically go back into your edited sequences.

To back up your audio files, go to your media drive and open the OMFI MediaFiles folder. Select all of your project's audio files, drag them onto a CD or DVD, and burn them. Because the audio files are fairly small, you can easily fit them on one or two CDs or a single DVD. To figure out which are the audio files, they often have as a suffix "aif," whereas video files always have "omf" as a suffix. It makes it easier to find them if you organize them by date or size. They are the smallest files. If your audio goes offline, just drag it from the CD onto this OMFI MediaFiles folder, and everything will be back online.

Back up Daily

Once you've captured your media onto your drive, there's no point in backing up your media files to DVD or CD more than once—they don't change. But you should back up your Avid Projects folder at the end of every work day. That's the one that records your editing decisions—your creativity and hard work. You've been told that one of these days your beloved Avid is going to crash, so don't risk losing days or even weeks of work. Remember DID—Do It Daily.

SUGGESTED ASSIGNMENTS

1. Open the CPU's hard drive icon and examine the folders it contains.
2. Find the Avid Projects folder, the Avid Users folder, and the Attic folder.
3. Open the Avid Projects folder and back up your projects onto a CD or Flash drive.
4. Back up your user file to a CD or Flash drive.

13

Keeping in Sync

SYNC PROBLEMS

When I write about sync problems in this chapter, I have more in mind than just picture and audio tracks falling out of sync. To me, if a music cue is supposed to be heard as soon as a door opens and instead it comes in 2 seconds late—it's out of sync. If you spend a lot of time getting narration, music, or effects to land perfectly with a visual, and suddenly they don't—you're out of sync. If you have a lower-third title on V2 that says "Nelson Mandela" and when you play your sequence the title comes up over a shot of a building, your title is out of sync. You have sync problems.

Getting out of sync can be an editor's worst nightmare, especially if a client or producer is in the room. One second you're splicing shots, trimming transitions, building tracks, and working at a nice clip, and the next second you're lost. The sound is out of sync with the picture, the music comes in at the wrong moment, the titles land on the wrong shots—you don't know what's happened. And, as you try to solve the problem, the client is behind you, pacing back and forth, looking at the clock, and sighing meaningfully. It's not helping. If you haven't had this experience, you will, and if you have, I don't need to go any further because you've been there.

Prior to the use of digital editing equipment, editors working in film experienced these sorts of sync problems far more frequently than editors working on tape machines. Because film uses a "double system," meaning the sound is physically separated from the picture, it's easy for the sound and picture to become separated. With a tape editing machine, the picture and sound occupy the same tape, so sync problems are less frequent. Of course, film editors *want* the separation between picture and sound because it offers far greater flexibility and creative control.

The Avid provides the same flexibility that a traditional film editing machine provides, and with that flexibility come sync problems. In fact, because you can easily add multiple video and audio tracks to your sequences, the Avid actually increases the potential for sync problems. When you're working with three video tracks and six audio tracks, a sync problem results in a confusing mess in the Timeline. Fortunately, there are some tools that help you get back into sync quickly, and there are things you can do to avoid going out of sync in the first place.

THE SOURCE OF YOUR PROBLEMS

Before we talk about solutions, let's review the ways you can get out of sync. Know what can go wrong, and you'll be able to avoid the problem. Know what can go wrong, and you're in a better position to identify and fix the problem. How did you get out of sync? Here are the three actions most often responsible for sync problems. They are what the police would call the "usual suspects."

- Single-roller trimming (adding material to or subtracting it from one track but not the other)
- Splicing material to one track but not to the other
- Extracting material from one track but not from the other

Now that you know who they are, keep an eye on them. Stay alert whenever you're performing one of these three actions.

SYNC BREAK INDICATORS

If your audio and video were captured at the same time, the Avid will lock the two together. If you go out of sync, *sync break indicators* will appear in the Timeline to show you exactly how many frames out of sync you've fallen. Numbers appear in the Timeline on the video and its associated audio track, indicating precisely what went wrong and by how much.

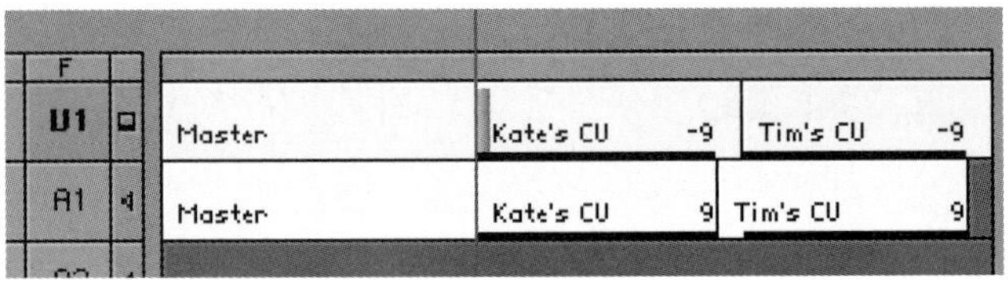

Figure 13.1

In the example shown in Figure 13.1, I made the mistake of entering Single-Roller Trim Mode on just one track. I inadvertently added nine frames to Kate's picture, but not to her sound. The sync break indicator shows the sync break as well as the number of frames by which the entire sequence has been thrown out of sync. It also tells me in which direction I need to go to get back into sync. To get back in sync, use Single-Roller Trim and add or subtract the number of frames indicated. Here, I need to either subtract nine frames (–9) from Kate's picture or add nine frames (+9) to Kate's sound.

MANY TRACKS MEAN MANY SYNC PROBLEMS

If you lose sync when cutting a sequence containing just a few tracks, you'll be able to restore sync without much trouble, but once you start adding tracks containing additional material into your sequence (such as narration, sound effects, titles, and music) sync problems can become more frequent and more confusing.

Figures 13.2 and 13.3 show a sequence containing material on two video tracks and three audio tracks. The main visual material consists of a dolly shot past rows of houses, with a title superimposed over the shot. Audio track A1 holds narration; A2 and A3 hold the sync audio.

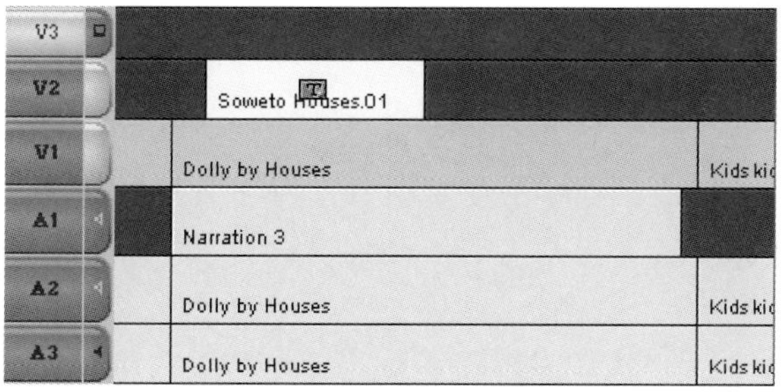

Figure 13.2   Before Single-Roller Trim.

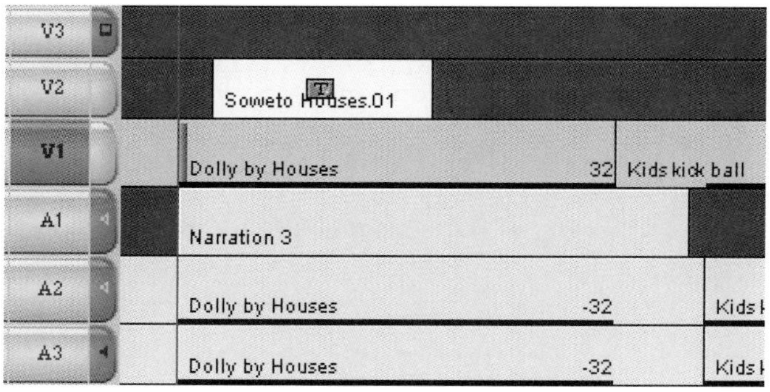

Figure 13.3   After trim, showing sync break.

Let's see what happens if I get out of sync. To get out of sync I place the Single-Roller Trim just on V1 and not on any other tracks, and trim (shorten) it by 32 frames. Immediately, sync break indicators appear.

Notice that the sync break indicators show that the dolly shot is out of sync by 32 frames. What you don't see is that the title on V2 and the narration on A1 are out of sync as well. If you are going to add or trim material from one track, you must add or trim material on *all* tracks; otherwise, you will get out of sync.

Why doesn't your Avid show that your title track (V2) and narration track (A1) are out of sync? Sync breaks only work with pictures and sounds that were captured together. The video and audio tracks containing material that you added later—the titles, narration, sound effects, and music—won't show sync breaks because they are independent of any video. There are several ways to solve this problem. I'll show you one of the quickest methods.

LOCATORS

Locators are handy tabs that you can place on any and all tracks in the Timeline to show you that you are in or out of sync. You can also use them to leave neat little messages in the Record Monitor.

Figure 13.4

If you click on the Add Locator command button, a locator will appear in the Timeline on whichever track is active. A pop-up window opens where you can write comments about the clip. As you may recall in Chapter 3, we opened the Command Palette and mapped the Add Locator button to the F5 key on the keyboard. Just select a track in the Timeline by clicking on its track selector button, and then press F5. A pop-up window opens in which you can also add comments.

For sync purposes, you want to place the locator on all the tracks so the locators line up in a straight vertical row. In Figure 13.5 you can see that I have placed locators on every track that contains a clip. You must place the locators on each track, one at a time. I deselected all the tracks except V2, and then I hit the Add Locator button. Then, without moving the position indicator, I deselected V2 and selected V1 and pressed the Add Locator button again, and so on until all the tracks had locators. (In the newest software versions, the pop-up window opens every time you add a locator and sort of gets in the way.)

Look what happens if any of my tracks gets thrown off (Figure 13.6). The sync break indicators tell me that the dolly shot and its sync tracks are out of sync, but now, because we added the locators, we can see that the title and narration are out of sync as well.

You don't need to put locators everywhere in the Timeline, but I would suggest you place a vertical row of them every 5 minutes or so in your project. That way, if you get out of sync, you don't have far to go before you have a checkpoint.

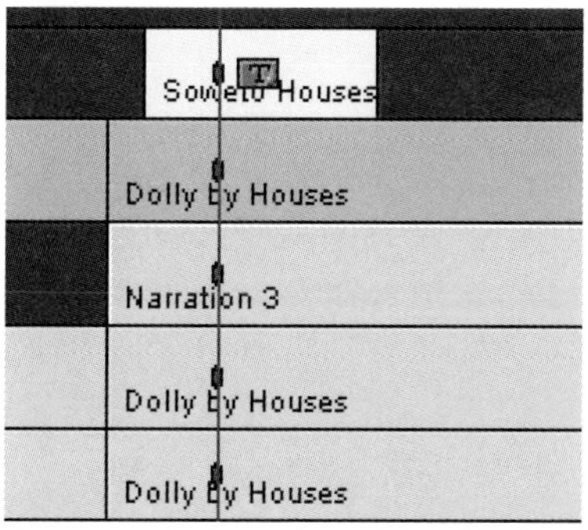

Figure 13.5   Tracks in sync.

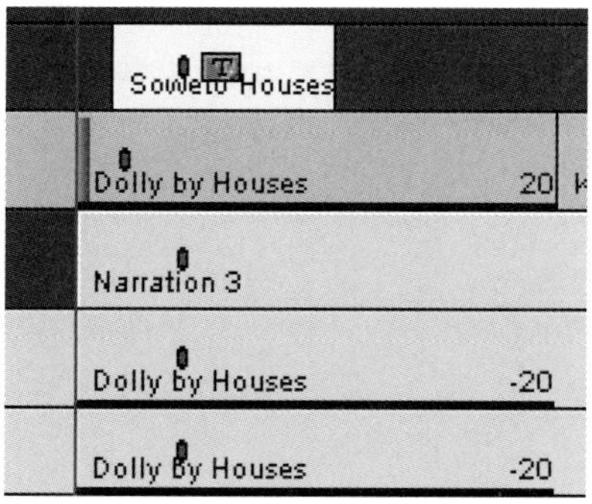

Figure 13.6   Tracks out of sync.

Deleting Locators

If you want to delete the locator (and its message), click on the locator in the position bar (the window under the monitor). If it doesn't appear in the monitor window, step-frame until it does, and then press the Delete key.

EDITING TRICKS TO STAY IN SYNC

In Chapter 9, we examined the topic "Trimming in Two Directions." Because this is a vital skill, let's take a moment to review it.

Trimming in Two Directions—A Review

If you want to add material (or trim material) in Single-Roller Trim Mode, you must trim all your tracks in order to keep their relationship the same. If you just trim V1 and A1 (picture and sync sound), all the music and narration will fall out of sync.

- Go into Single-Roller Trim Mode.
- Add rollers on the "fill" or black side (Shift-click on a transition to add a roller).
- Do this even if the rollers aren't all on the same side or going in the same direction.
- As you trim, Avid will add or take away black fill to keep all the tracks in sync.

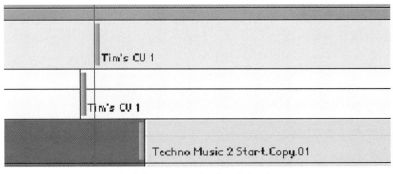

 Trims black leader to maintain relationships

Figure 13.7

In Figure 13.7, when we drag Tim's CU on track V1 and his overlapped audio on track A1 to the left, we are adding to it, or making the shot longer. That would normally throw the music out of sync. But, if we place a single roller on the fill side of the music on track A2, then as we drag left, the Avid *adds* black fill and sync is maintained. If we shortened Tim's shot by dragging right, the Avid would take away black fill to keep the music in sync. Remember, put the roller on the fill side of the music, not inside the music itself.

What happens if you want to trim a shot in a sequence containing many tracks, like the one in Figure 13.8? Let's say you're doing an hour show, and you have three video tracks and five or six tracks of audio. Let's say that the distance between where you want to trim and some of these other elements is too great to easily add rollers to them.

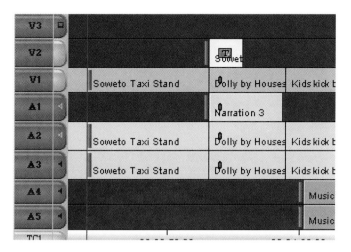

Figure 13.8

You can easily place single rollers on V2, V1, A1, A2, and A3. Tracks A4 and A5 are a slight pain to add rollers to, but not a huge deal. But you can't even see the material on track V3, and unless you expand the Timeline and add a roller to the clip on V3, it will go out of sync as soon as you trim. Also, don't forget that you have to move the Watch Point back to the shot you want to trim.

Add Edits in Black Fill

The solution is to lasso the transition that you want to trim, as I've done in Figure 13.9, and then hold the Option key (Mac) or the Alt key (Windows) while pressing the Add Edit key.

Add Edit key

When you press the Option key (Mac) or the Alt key (Windows) together with this key, the Add Edit is placed in the black fill. When you're in Trim Mode, rollers will automatically jump to all the add edits, just like in Figure 13.10.

Now, if you want to single-roller trim, just click on the A-side or B-side of the Trim Mode display, and the rollers will jump to that side.

Remember, the Option/Alt–Add Edit only puts the add edits in black, but this is good. I don't want an add edit in the middle of a shot. Now trim to your heart's content and know that the Avid will trim the fill to keep your tracks in sync.

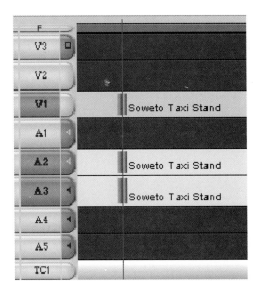

Figure 13.9

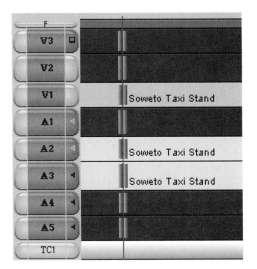

Figure 13.10

Deleting Add Edits

There's now a command for this task. Select the tracks containing the add edits you want to remove, then go to the Clip menu and select Remove Match Frame Edits, which is another name for add edits. If you want to remove some, but not all, don't use that menu item. Instead, get into Dual-Roller Trim Mode (so you have dual rollers on top of these edit lines in the Timeline), and hit the Delete key.

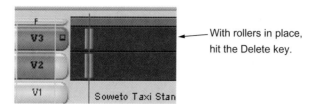

With rollers in place, hit the Delete key.

Sync Locks

The Avid knows how important it is to maintain sync, especially when you're getting toward the end of editing and the tracks are filling up with titles, visual effects, sound effects, and music. So, it gives you a tool in the Timeline that enables you to lock your tracks together; it's aptly named *sync locks*.

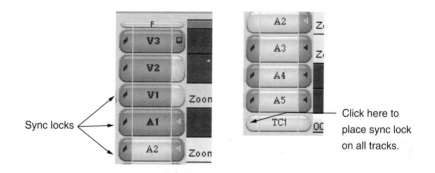

Sync locks

Click here to place sync lock on all tracks.

In the track selector area, there is a small box just to the left of the tracks. By clicking in the small box, you can place a sync lock on your track. You can lock two, three, or all of your tracks together. Click in the empty box in the TC1, or timecode track, and you'll place locks in all the boxes.

Sync locks are supposed to work only in Trim Mode, but you'll find that they also work with Lift and Extract. Their main function is to prevent you from going out of sync when in Single-Roller Trim Mode. In Single-Roller Trim Mode, the Avid will maintain the proper relationship with all your other tracks.

Figure 13.11 shows an example. I've placed single rollers on the A-side of this transition, on tracks V1, A2, and A3, but I forgot to place trim rollers on the narration on A1 and the music cue on A4 and A5. What happens if I trim this shot? I'll throw the narration and music cue off, because I haven't trimmed in two directions. Right? Wrong. Because the sync locks are "on," the Avid will keep the A1, A4, and A5 tracks locked together with V1, A2, and A3. It will automatically adjust the fill to keep all the tracks in sync.

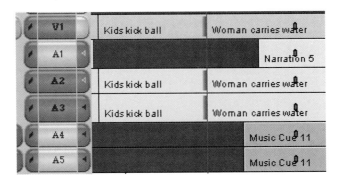

Figure 13.11

Don't believe me? Examine Figure 13.12. Although the "Kids kick ball" shot has been shortened, the music and narration are still in sync. The Avid shortened the black fill on A1, A4, and A5 in order to keep the narration and music cue where they belong. Even though I didn't "trim in two directions," the Avid's sync locks did it for me.

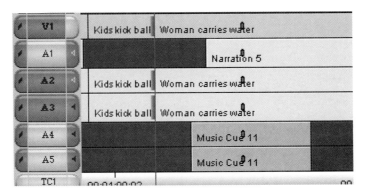

Figure 13.12 Even though there are no rollers on A1, A4, and A5, they will stay in sync because the sync locks are on.

"Hey," you might say, "if this works so well, why did you spend so much time teaching us about trimming in two directions, and Watch Points, and placing add edits in fill?" My answer is twofold. First, you need to know about all those other things to fully understand the value of sync locks, but mainly because sync locks don't always work. Another way to put it is that they work *too* well.

With sync locks, if the other tracks inline (vertically) with the tracks you are cutting are empty, the Avid adds or subtracts fill to keep your tracks in sync—and everyone is happy. But, if the other tracks have material inline with the tracks you are cutting, the Avid cuts material from those tracks as well. This is a problem. Suddenly your narration and your music have disappeared. You're in sync, all right, but you've lost your narrator! Or a chunk of your music is missing!

Look at Figure 13.13. I've got sync locks on all tracks, and I'm going to extend the tail of the shot—the A-side.

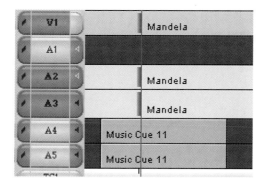

Figure 13.13

Watch what happens with the sync locks turned on. Examine Figure 13.14.

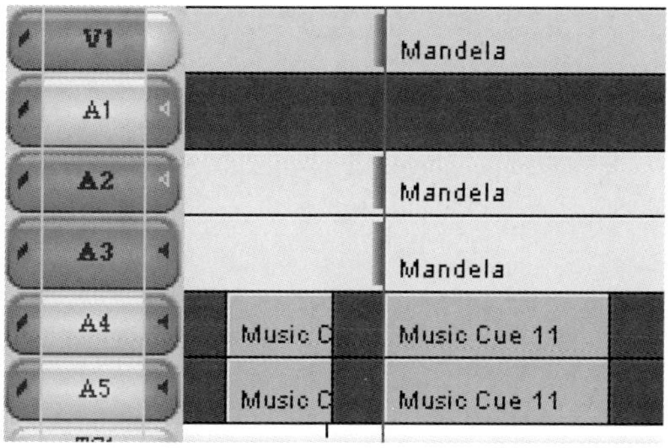

Figure 13.14

Whoa! My music cue has been cut in two and a chunk of black fill (silence) has been added. I certainly didn't want *that*. Why did it happen? Because even though A4 and A5 weren't selected for trimming, they are sync locked to the other tracks. With the sync locks on, I used Trim Mode to extend the tail of my shot. The Avid did whatever it took to keep my tracks in sync, even if that meant adding fill in the middle of my music cue.

Figure 13.15 shows another example. I've got single rollers on the B-side video and sync audio tracks but not on the narration. I want to extend the head of the "Girls watch bus" shot by ten frames.

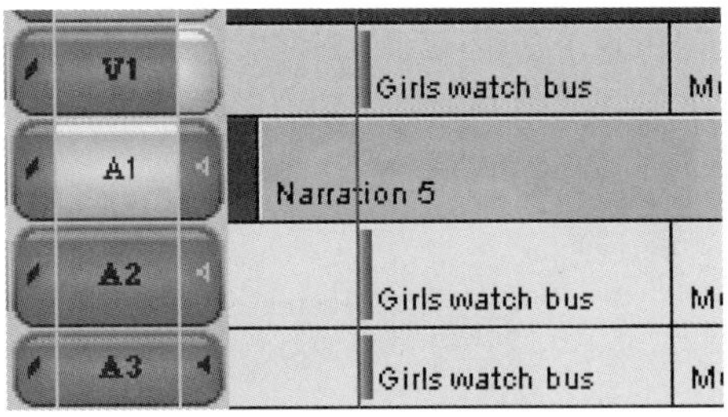

V1	Girls watch bus	M
A1	Narration 5	
A2	Girls watch bus	M
A3	Girls watch bus	M

Figure 13.15

V1	Girls watch bus	M
A1	Narra	Narration 5	
A2	Girls watch bus	M
A3	Girls watch bus	M

Drag rollers to the left to extend.

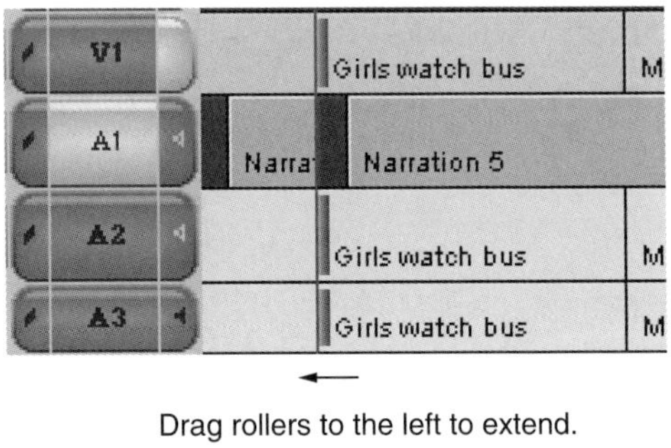

Figure 13.16

Look what happens in Figure 13.16 when I drag the rollers to the left to extend the shot. Yikes! The Avid has added black fill in the middle of the narration. That's not going to sound very good.

So, as you can see, sync locks work some of the time, but not all of the time. If the other tracks inline (vertically) with the tracks you are editing are empty, sync locks can be fast and foolproof. But if the other tracks have material inline with the tracks you are cutting or trimming, the Avid will blindly remove important material in its quest to keep you in sync.

That's when all the work we've done before we were introduced to sync locks starts to pay off. Take the situation in Figure 13.17. To extend the "Girls watch bus" shot, we don't use sync locks. Instead, we'll trim in two directions by placing a roller in the fill side of A1—the narration. Now when we drag left to extend the shot and its sync tracks, the narration will stay in sync.

Figure 13.17

LOCKING TRACKS

You can also "lock" your tracks to prevent accidental changes. Locking is different from sync locking. When you lock a track, no further editing can take place on that track. You can lock picture and/or audio tracks. Let's say you have several sync dialog tracks and a narration track that are all in perfect sync with the video track, and you need to work on your music and sound effects tracks. You can lock the picture, narration, and dialog tracks. Now you don't have to worry about messing up those tracks while you work on your music and sound effects tracks.

To lock tracks:

1. Select the tracks you want to lock and deselect the others.
2. From the Clip menu choose Lock Tracks. A padlock icon appears in the track lock indicator space.

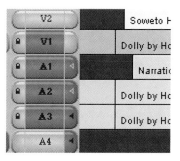

Because you're beginning to take advantage of all the Avid has to offer, you're in danger of going out of sync. You're adding video tracks for titles and effects. You're adding tracks to hold music and narration. Once you go beyond cutting just a few tracks, sync problems can really cause you heartache. We've spent a lot of time on the subject of sync, because losing it can be so painful. My best advice is to keep it as simple as you can for as long as you can. Don't add titles, music, and sound effects until you've reached a fine cut. Tell the story first. Otherwise, you'll spend your time repairing sync, rather than editing.

SUGGESTED ASSIGNMENTS

1. Place a single roller (Trim Mode) on one track and not the other. Drag left and look at the sync break. Leave Trim Mode. Now go back into Trim Mode and fix the sync break.
2. Place a row of locators on your tracks.
3. Leave yourself a message, using the locator message function.
4. Delete the locator.
5. Enter Trim Mode and Option/Alt–Add Edit.
6. Use Single-Roller Trim Mode to add or remove material on all your tracks.
7. Delete the add edits.
8. Place sync locks on your tracks. Try extracting material. Try single-roller trimming.
9. Place locks on one or more tracks. Try editing the locked tracks.

14

Importing and Exporting

For those of you who have imported and exported various files before, this chapter may seem a bit simplistic. Accept my apologies. It's just that I'm not worried about you—you simply need to be shown how to use Avid's import and export tools and off you'll go. This chapter is aimed at those of you who have never imported or exported files before and who think the whole business sounds incredibly difficult. I've streamlined and simplified the process as much as possible so you'll be able to master it, if you give it a try.

TYPES OF FILES

Because the Avid deals with digital information, just about any digital information can be brought in or sent out of the Avid. Here are several examples:

- You could import a music track from a CD.
- Using Adobe Photoshop®, you could create an opening title that combines text with a special effect. You could save that title as a graphic file, import it into one of your bins, and then cut it into your sequence.
- You could create an image or sequence of images in the Avid, export it as a file to a program like After Effects®, make changes to create a special look, and then reimport it into a bin and cut it into your sequence.
- You could take an audio clip that has sound problems and export it as an audio file. You could then bring it to a digital audio workstation (DAW) for audio sweetening and reimport it back into the Avid.

You can import and export many kinds of graphic files, picture files, animation files, and audio files.

IMPORTING

In order to import, there must first be a file to import. It can be located on the Avid hard drive or on a Zip disk, flash drive, or CD that you've inserted into your CPU. To import, simply select Import from the File menu. If Import is dimmed on the menu, it's because a bin has not been selected. Click anywhere in the bin that you want to import the file to. After you select Import, an Import dialog box opens. I've included the boxes for Windows and Mac Avids (Figure 14.1 and Figure 14.2).

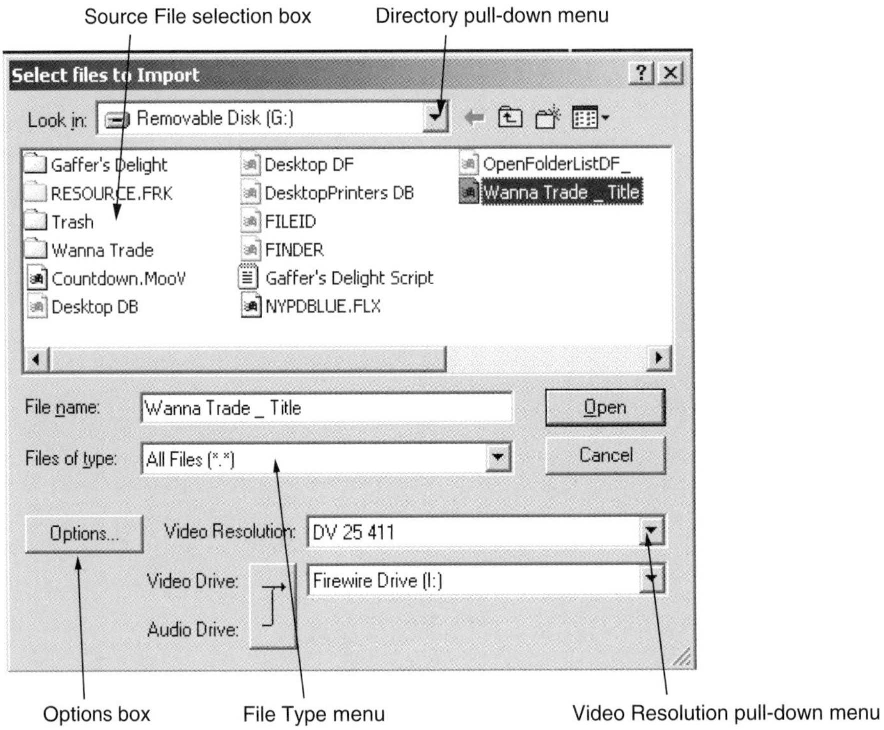

Figure 14.1 Windows Import dialog box.

As you can see, although they appear to be quite different, the Mac and Windows Import windows offer the same choices.

IMPORTING A PICTURE FILE

Perhaps the most confusing aspect of importing is the various options you need to set for each kind of file. I'm going to walk you through the Import of a picture file, saved as a .tif file. I place the title on a flash drive and carry it from my

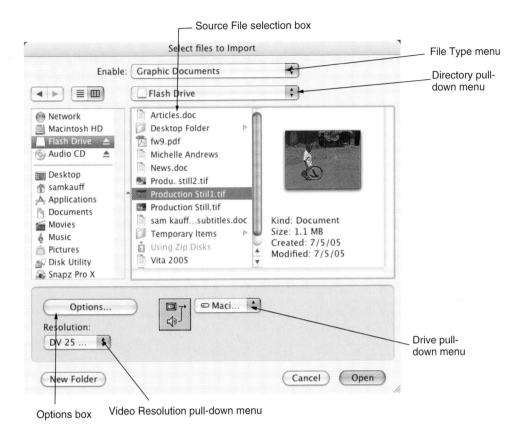

Figure 14.2 Mac Import dialog box.

graphics computer to the Avid. I insert the flash drive into a USB port on my computer and then, using the Import dialog box's directory pop-up menu, I'll search the computer's hierarchical file system and find it.

Let's trace the steps I'll take to do this Import, and then we'll examine the choices I made and why. Examine Figure 14.1 (Windows) or Figure 14.2 (Mac) as you follow my steps:

1. First I select a bin by clicking on it. In this case I've created a new bin called "Imported Files."
2. I choose Import from the File menu.
3. From the Files of Type (Windows) or Enable (Mac), I select the sort of document I'm looking for: Graphic, Audio, etc. Because my title is a .tif file, I choose Graphic Files (Windows) or Graphic Documents (Mac). If, for some reason, the Import box won't recognize your file type or you're not sure what type of file it is, change back to All Files (Windows) or Any Documents (Mac), as I've done in Figure 14.1.

4. Using the Directory pull-down menu, I navigate through the desktop or hard drive. I double-click on disks and folders in the list to open them, and I scroll through them to locate the file I want. Once I find it in the Source File selection box, I simply click on it so it's highlighted.
5. I click on Options, and a box opens. See Figure 14.3.
6. Media Composer users, choose 601, non-square. XpressDV users, choose Maintain, non-square.
7. Choose Non-interlaced in the File Field Order box.
8. In the Color Levels, choose RGB.
9. In the Alpha, select Ignore.
10. In the Single Frame Import box, I choose 10 seconds as my duration. If I want it to be longer or shorter, I change the number.
11. I click OK. The Options box closes.

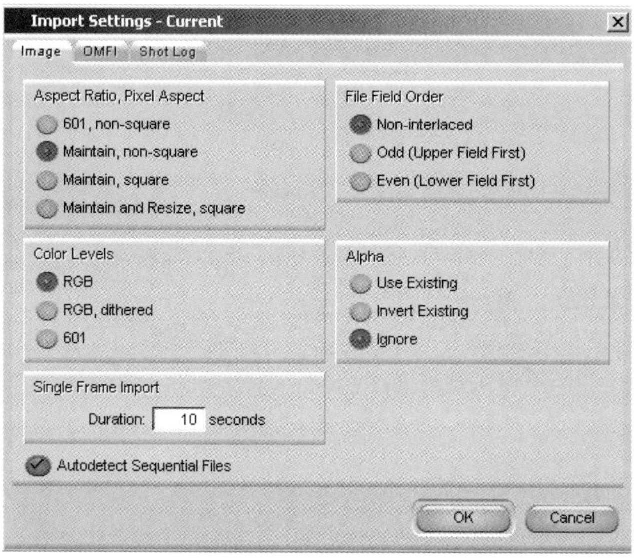

Figure 14.3 Graphic options dialog box.

12. Back in the Select files to Import window, I choose a Video Drive to store the media.
13. Because it's a graphic, I select a resolution in the Video Resolution box that matches the resolution of my sequence.
14. When I'm finished, I click Open.

I look in my bin. There it is, saved as a master clip that is 10 seconds long. Now that I've walked you through an import, let's examine the rationale behind the choices and settings we made.

Please keep in mind that your computer won't crash or blow a fuse if you choose the wrong setting. If it looks bad, try the next choice. Who knows, you might like the way an import looks with the wrong setting better than the right one.

COMPUTERS VERSUS TELEVISION

Most of the problems associated with importing files into the Avid stem from the fact that you are creating many of your files on a computer, and while the Avid is a computer it doesn't behave like one. It behaves like a digital television set. A computer and the Avid deal with images differently. The main differences involve aspect ratio, pixel shape, and color. The standard-definition Avid uses the digital video standard known as ITU-R 601, where each horizontal line contains 720 pixels and each vertical line contains 486 pixels.

Aspect Ratio

Aspect ratio refers to the dimensions of a rectangle. In our case, the rectangle is a picture image, film or video frame, or screen size. You determine a rectangle's aspect ratio by dividing its width by its height. (A square has an aspect ratio of 1:1, because the width is the same as the height.) Look at any standard television screen. It's not a square; it's a rectangle. The frame is wider than it is high. On a standard analog television set, the aspect ratio is 4:3. Filmmakers are more familiar with the number 1.33:1, which comes from dividing 4 by 3.

The new standard for high-definition television (HDTV) presents an even wider frame, with an aspect ratio of 16:9.

In the computer domain, the image is usually described in terms of pixels: the number and shape of the pixels that make up the image. Graphic artists often work on a computer creating images that have a frame of 648 (width) by 486 (height) *square* pixels. Divide 648 by 486 and you get an aspect ratio of 4:3, or 1.33:1.

The Avid's frame in pixel terms is slightly different because it comes from Avid's video capture board. It is 720 (width) by 486 (height), *non-square* pixels. When you do the math, you see that instead of an aspect ratio of 1.33:1, you get an aspect ratio of 1.48:1 (720 divided by 486). This never made sense to me. Why would a video capture board give you an image that didn't match the 4:3

standard for all analog television screens? The answer lies in the pixel shape the Avid creates. It's not shaped like a square. It's tall and thin.

Square pixel   Avid's non-square pixel

If Avid's pixels were square, like the ones a computer generates, the aspect ratio would be wrong, but because the pixels are non-square and thinner, 720 of them take up the same space as 648 square ones. So, Avid's 720 × 486 non-square pixels provide the same aspect ratio as a computer's 648 × 486 square pixels, namely 4:3.

DV Aspect Ratio and Pixels

Although the DV frame has the same aspect ratio, 4:3, as standard NTSC video, it has six fewer horizontal lines. Instead of 486 vertical lines, it has 480. Its native size is 720 × 480, not 720 × 486.

Color

At this level, you don't need to know that much about the different ways the Avid and a computer monitor handle color. Just remember that computer color is referred to as RGB color, whereas the Avid's color conforms to the ITU-R 601 digital video standard in standard definition (SD) and the ITU-R 709 color space in high definition (HD).

IMPORT OPTIONS

Now, armed with this information, let's look again at the Options choices in Figure 14.3. The Avid is asking for information about your file so it can properly translate it into the Avid's format. The first box you'll see is Aspect Ratio, Pixel Aspect. There are four choices: (1) 601, non-square; (2) Maintain, non-square; (3) Maintain, square; and (4) Maintain and Resize, square.

601, non-square takes graphics with the correct aspect ratio, no matter what the pixel shape, and makes them fit the Avid's 601, non-square standard. So, if the title you created in Photoshop has the right aspect ratio for the Avid but has square pixels, select this option and it will import nicely.

Maintain, non-square is often the correct choice for DV users who are bringing in files that are correct for digital television (720 × 486). It cuts off the top four lines and the bottom two lines to conform to the NTSC DV standard of 480 horizontal lines.

Maintain, square keeps the graphic just the way you designed it, with no change in size. For instance, you might not want a logo to fill the Avid's frame but stay in the corner of the frame. This setting will do that. It will keep your image size and shape just the way it was created.

Maintain and Resize, square forces the graphic to fit the Avid's frame no matter what. Often, the Avid places a black border around your image to make it fit. Use this option if the file is the wrong size and shape but you want it to fill the frame anyway. This is a good choice now with HD going to SD and SD going to HD.

File Field Order

The choices here are Non-Interlaced, Odd (Upper Field First), and Even (Lower Field First). In Chapter 1, we learned that a video frame is made up of two fields—one containing all the odd lines and the other containing all the even lines. The Avid cares about the ordering of the lines in the digital file. So, whenever you are working with graphics that originated as video or have video attributes, you need to set the field order. On an NTSC project, Avid wants Even (Lower Field First). If you're working on a PAL project, then the Avid wants Odd (Upper Field First).

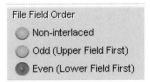

If the file you are importing doesn't deal with fields (for example, a TIFF or PICT file), then Non-interlaced is the correct choice. I chose Non-interlaced when I imported the photograph because it is a TIFF file, not a video file.

Color Levels

Color Levels deals with the color issue. If the file you are importing was created on a computer, then it probably has RGB color levels. If it came from a videotape or video camera, select 601. The photo I imported was created with a digital camera, not a video camera, so RGB is the correct setting. If the picture image you're importing has a fine gradient and you see some ugly banding when you import it and cut it into your sequence, try importing it again using RGB, dithered.

Alpha

If the image you are importing has an opaque layer and a transparent layer, then you need to tell the Avid how the image was created. The transparent layer is called the *alpha channel*. Most animation and graphic applications set up the alpha channel so black is the transparent layer and white is the opaque layer. This is the opposite of what the Avid wants, so if that's how your application works you want to select Invert Existing. If you have the layers set up so white represents the transparent layer, then select Use Existing. The photograph I'm importing doesn't have a transparency layer, so it isn't an issue and I choose Ignore. But you can create files using graphic programs such as Photoshop that will superimpose over a background shot. Keep the layers separate; don't "flatten" the image. If you have a transparent layer, select Invert Existing.

Single Frame

I imported the still photograph as a *single frame*. Once I import it, the Avid is going to turn that single frame into a master clip. In the Options box, I tell the Avid how long I want that master clip to last. The default is 10 seconds. That's plenty for a single image.

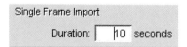

IMPORTING AUDIO FROM A CD

This is a great way to bring in sound effects from a sound-effects library, temp music for editing, or music cues from your composer. The process goes much faster if you have already picked out the tracks you want to import:

1. Place a CD into the computer's CD drive.
2. In the Avid application, select a bin and choose Import from the File menu.
3. Select Audio Documents in the Enable/Show menu (Mac) or Audio Files in the File of Type menu (Windows).
4. In the Directory pull-down window, navigate through the folders on your computer to locate the CD.
5. Choose the track you want.
6. Click Open.

Audio CDs are sampled at 44.1 kHz. If you're editing at 48 kHz, you will get a message telling you that the sample rate of the track you're importing doesn't match your project and asking if you want the sample rate converted to 48 kHz. Click "Yes." The file will be converted to 48 kHz. The import will take several minutes, and when the track comes into your bin as a clip it will be too loud to use.

Double-click the clip's icon to put it into the Source Monitor. Go to the Tools menu, open the Audio Mix or Audio Mixer Tool (XpressPro 5.+), click on the Gang button for tracks 1 and 2, and then lower the volume to around –11 dB. Adjust from there.

IMPORTING COLOR BARS

Let's import something else. Normally, when you send a sequence to videotape (which we'll do in Chapter 18), you put SMPTE bars at the head of the tape so a video engineer can use them as a reference in order to properly set up the playback monitor and tape recorder. Let's import the SMPTE bars that come bundled with the Avid software. This file is already loaded on your computer. It's actually a PICT file, but it has digital video attributes, so you treat it as video.

1. When you are in your project, click on a bin.
2. From the File menu, select Import. The Import window opens.
3. Select Graphic as the file type.

such as Pro Tools, After Effects, Photoshop, Maya™, and countless others. If you don't have much experience with these applications, ask for help from the graphic artists, sound engineers, and animators living in your area who work with the software application on a daily basis. Ask them to walk you through the settings and options required for a successful export for each specific application.

Preparing to Export

There are several things you should do to make sure your export goes smoothly:

- If you are exporting a sequence or the audio tracks from a sequence, you should duplicate the sequence before initiating an export. Create a new bin for the duplicate and export it. If anything goes wrong, you have an original to return to.
- If you're exporting a frame, there's no need to duplicate anything.
- Make sure you render any and all effects that exist on the tracks you are exporting.
- If you are exporting more than V1, make sure the video track monitor is on the highest level.
- Make sure the material you want to export is selected.
  - If it's a frame, mark the frame by placing an IN mark.
  - If it's one or more tracks, click on the track selector panel to select the ones you want and deselect the ones you don't.
  - If you want to export a section of a sequence, place IN and OUT marks in the Timeline.

EXPORTING A PRODUCTION STILL

Exporting a frame from a sequence to create a production still is an important task, especially as many budgets don't include money for a still photographer. Instead, we'll get our production stills right off the Timeline. Fortunately, Avid provides a template to make this a breeze.

Put a sequence in the Timeline, and place an IN mark on the frame you'd like to export. If possible, choose a frame that has as little movement as possible. Now go to the File menu and choose Export. The Export As . . . box will appear, as shown in Figures 14.5 and 14.6.

1. Go to the Export As . . . window and select either Windows Image or Macintosh Image (depending on the machine you're on).
2. Type a name for the file.
3. Choose a destination (Desktop, flash drive).
4. Click Save.

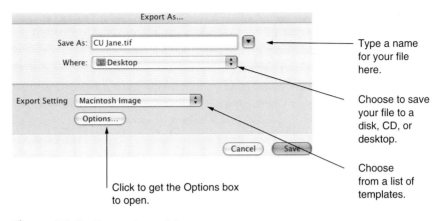

Type a name for your file here.

Choose to save your file to a disk, CD, or desktop.

Choose from a list of templates.

Click to get the Options box to open.

Figure 14.5 Export As . . . Mac.

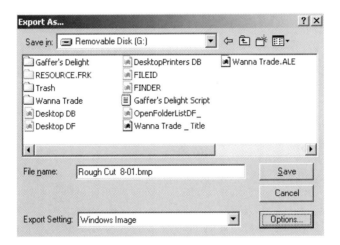

Figure 14.6 Export As . . . Windows.

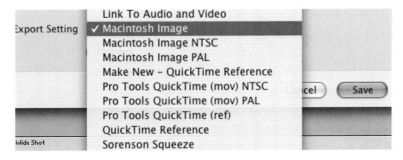

Figure 14.7 Export Setting templates.

It's that easy. But, now, let's look at the settings the Avid template chose for us to see if we need to make any changes. Repeat the steps above, but don't press Save in Step 4. Instead click on the Options button.

The Export Settings window opens, like the one shown in Figure 14.8. As you can see, there are a number of settings to choose from, and for the purposes of creating a production still these are the ones that usually work best. But let's go through them to see why they were chosen.

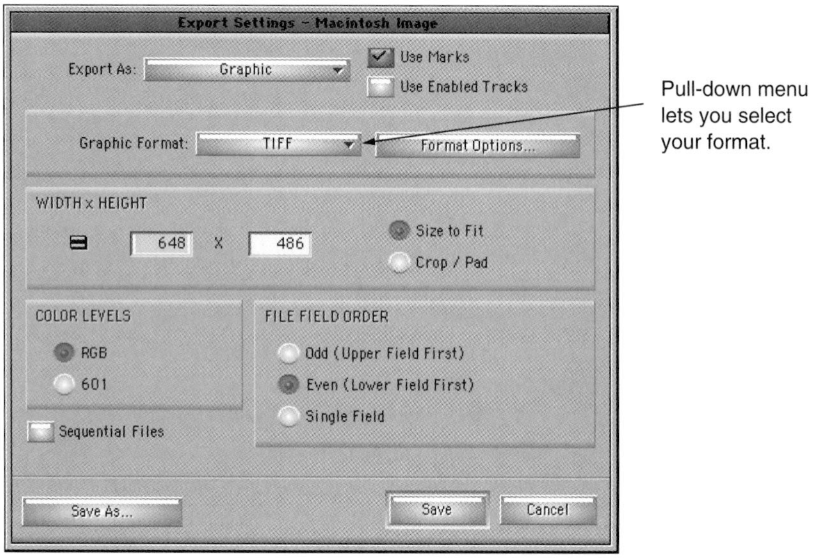

Figure 14.8 Export Settings for a single frame.

1. In the Export Settings menu, Graphic is chosen because we asked for the Macintosh Image or Windows Image and Avid knows it's a graphic file.
2. Because we are exporting a specific frame, Use Marks is selected. Remember, we placed an IN mark in the Timeline on the frame we wanted to export.
3. In the Graphic Format window, we want TIFF.
4. In the Width × Height Fast menu, 648 × 486 (4:3 square pixel) is chosen. If your project is 16:9, you would instead choose 864 × 486, as shown in Figure 14.9.
5. Choose Size to Fit. Select Crop/Pad only when exporting a frame for use in a DVD project.
6. Choose RGB. This is a graphics file.
7. Choose Even (Lower Field First).
8. Press Save.

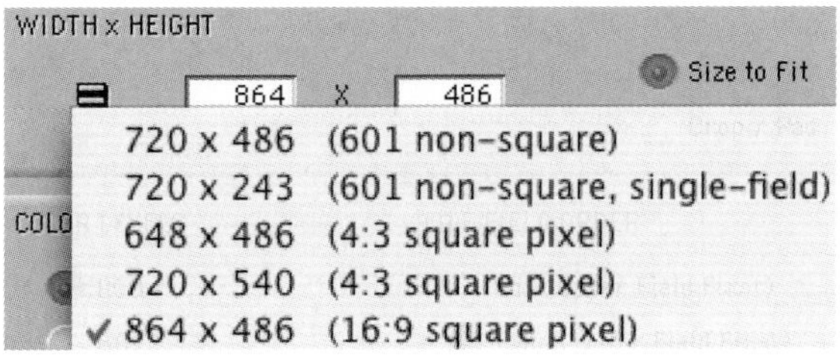

Figure 14.9

If you always work in the 16:9 format, you might want to create a new setting for exporting 864 × 486 images. If so, then select Save As. A dialog box will open, and you would type a name such as "16:9 Macintosh [or Windows] Image." You'll find all your settings saved as a template under that name in the Export Settings window.

EXPORTING MOTION VIDEO

When you need to export motion video, QuickTime is usually your first choice. There are two kinds of QuickTime movies: QuickTime Reference and QuickTime. A QuickTime Reference movie is like a shell. The guts of the QuickTime—the media—are on your hard drive. When you export a QuickTime Reference you are using the audio and video files already on your drive to fill in the shell. The QuickTime Reference only plays if it is on the same drive as the media files.

A QuickTime movie is the real deal. You can send it anywhere and it will play because it's not a shell—it contains all the media. QuickTime Reference movies take up little additional drive space—they are small files. They just take seconds to export. QuickTime movies take up a lot of drive space—they are large files. They can take hours to export.

When do you use one and not the other? If you have software applications, like After Effects or DVD Studio Pro® already on your computer, you can save time and space by creating a QuickTime Reference movie, because all the media files are right there. If, however, you are sending a 90-second sequence to a 3D animator in Toronto, you'll send her a QuickTime movie.

Exporting a QuickTime Reference Movie

Let's export a QuickTime Reference movie first. Put your sequence in the Timeline. If you don't want the entire sequence, place IN and OUT marks. Make sure all your tracks are selected.

Here are the steps we will take to export a sequence.

1. Choose Export from the File menu.
2. In the Save As ... window, choose QuickTime Reference from the Export Setting pull-down menu (Figure 14.7).
3. Press Save.

That was easy. Let's click on Options, to see what settings were chosen for us, in case we want to make changes. A window like the one in Figure 14.10 opens.

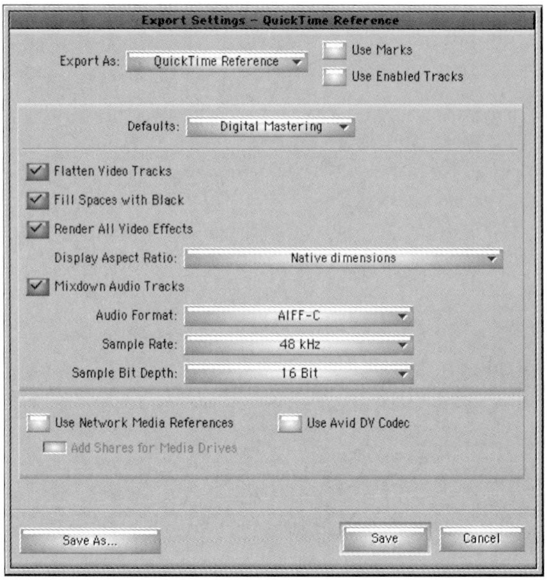

Figure 14.10

Export As: QuickTime Reference is selected because that's the template we chose. The reason why the Use Marks and Use Enabled Tracks boxes are not checked is because we want the *entire* sequence exported. If we wanted only the material on tracks V1 and A1, we would deselect the other tracks in the Timeline and check "Use Enabled Tracks." If we were exporting some of the sequence, but not all, we'd place marks and then check "Use Marks."

The other settings are fairly self-explanatory. Flatten Video Tracks means that V3, V2, and V1 will be combined into one track. Your audio tracks will be mixed onto one track. AIFF-C, 48 kHz, and 16 Bit are simply our Audio Project Settings.

Exporting a QuickTime Movie

Put your sequence in the Timeline. If you don't want the entire sequence, place IN and OUT marks. Make sure all your tracks are selected.

1. Choose Export from the File menu.
2. In the Export As . . . window, choose "Fast-Export QuickTime" from the Export Setting pull-down menu.
3. Click the Options button.
4. You will see your choices in the box, like the one in Figure 14.11.

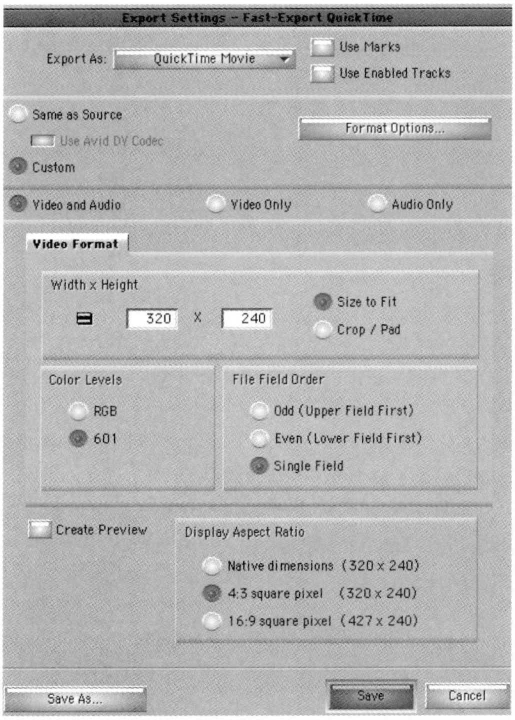

Figure 14.11

The settings shown in Figure 14.11 create a file suited for distribution on the Web. Notice in Figure 14.11 that the Custom setting button is selected and that the Width × Height pull-down menu is at 320 × 240. This will create a small file that is quite compressed. If we click on the Format Options . . . button (Figure 14.11), we see in the Movie Settings window that this export is set up as Sorenson Video 3 (Figure 14.12). Sorenson is a well-known codec (compression/decompression) used to make small files for the Web.

Notice in Figure 14.12 that the quality is "Least" and the frame rate is 15. This might be perfect for Web distribution. You can choose different compression settings by clicking on the Settings . . . button and exploring the various pull-down menus in the Compression Settings window (Figure 14.13).

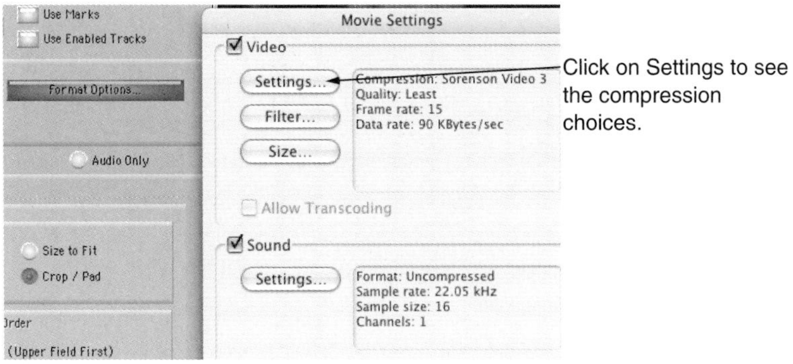

Figure 14.12

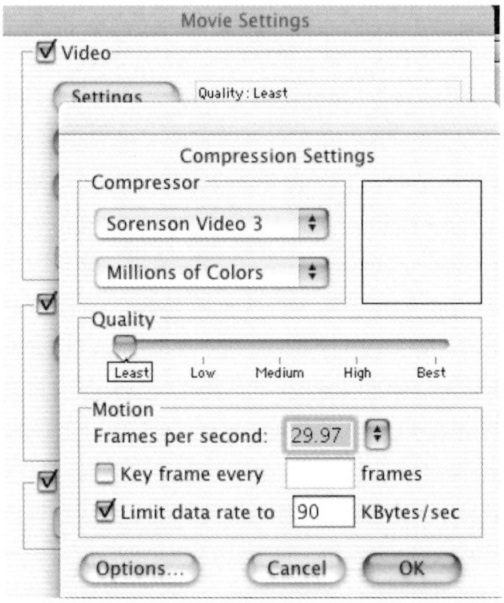

Figure 14.13

If we want the highest quality export (say we were going to give the Quick-Time movie to a 3D animator who is using Maya), then we need to click on the Same as Source button in the main Export Settings dialog box. Once we do that, we will be exporting full height and width and at whatever resolution we used to capture our tapes (probably DV 25).

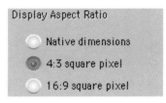

If the 3D animator wants just video, click on Video Only. If our project was captured in DV 25, and we're going to a system that has the Avid DV codec, we'll select the Use Avid DV Codec box. If we're going to a system that doesn't have the Avid DV codec, we'll deselect it. If we don't know, we'll ask the 3D animator.

Finally, in the Display Aspect Ratio window you would choose Native dimensions, 4:3 square pixel, or 16:9 square pixel. If you'll be bringing the sequence back to your Avid after the 3D animator works her magic, you'll probably want Native; otherwise, always use 4:3. If you have an anamorphic project, which we'll examine in the next chapter, select the 16:9 aspect ratio.

There. We have chosen settings for either a high-quality movie suitable for export to another program or a lesser-quality movie that is more suitable for the Web.

1. Now click Save. When you are returned to the Export As . . . window, name the file (the name of the sequence will be the default name).
2. Choose a destination (desktop, external hard drive, DVD-R).
3. Click Save.

EXPORTING AUDIO TO A PRO TOOLS® WORK STATION

Although the Avid is capable of fairly sophisticated audio manipulation, it is not as sophisticated as Pro Tools. Pro Tools is an Avid product and is the industry leader in audio mixing and sound manipulation. Avid sells Xpress Pro and Xpress Pro HD software bundled with Pro Tools LE (a light version of Pro Tools) in a package called Avid Xpress Studio. A more expensive package comes with Mbox, a two-channel USB audio peripheral device. An even more expensive version, called Avid Xpress Studio Complete, includes Mojo DNA and a mixing board called Digi 002.

Going to Pro Tools

In the first example here, we'll assume you have Xpress Pro and Pro Tools bundled on your computer. If you have Pro Tools LE it must come with an option called "DV Toolkit for Pro Tools LE." Another possibility is that you have your Avid Project folder and all your media on a portable drive that you can bring to the Pro Tools station. If that is the case, this is quite easy.

Both Pro Tools and Pro Tools LE with the DV Toolkit for Pro Tools LE option have what's called a Digi Translator 02. This translator lets you bring both your audio and video into Pro Tools so you can mix your sounds while watching your video. You're not just bringing in audio files.

First, make a duplicate of your final sequence. Create a new bin, label it Pro Tools Sequence, and place the duplicate in the bin. Place the sequence in the Record Monitor. Now follow these steps.

1. Make sure all your audio and video effects are rendered and all your tracks are selected.
2. Make sure all your audio has been converted to 48 kHz (or whatever sample rate you're using).
3. Select the sequence in the bin.
4. Choose Export from the File menu.
5. In the Export As . . . window, choose Avid Pro Tools LE (002) from the Export Setting pull-down menu.
6. Click the Options button to see your choices. (If a Pro Tools setting is not available in step 5, click on Options and choose AAF in the Export As . . . pull-down menu.)

7. Examine Figure 14.14 to make sure your settings look like this.
8. Click Save.
9. When you return to the Export As . . . window, save the file inside your OMFI MediaFiles folder on your drive (or the external FireWire drive).
10. Click Save.

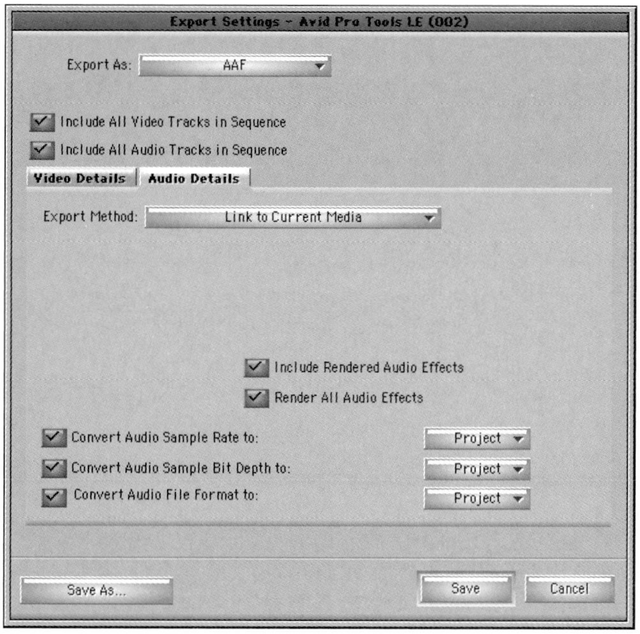

Figure 14.14

You will now have an AAF file inside your OMFI MediaFiles folder.

When you launch Pro Tools, you don't open a new session. That's because an Avid AAF sequence is the same thing as a Pro Tools session. Instead, select New Session, navigate until you find the AAF file inside the OMFI MediaFiles folder, and open it. That AAF sequence is your Pro Tools session.

Going to Pro Tools LE

If you have Pro Tools LE without the DV Toolkit for Pro Tools LE, then the settings are different:

1. Choose Export from the File menu.
2. In the Export As . . . window, choose Avid Pro Tools LE (002) from the Export Setting pull-down menu.
3. Click the Options button to see your choices.

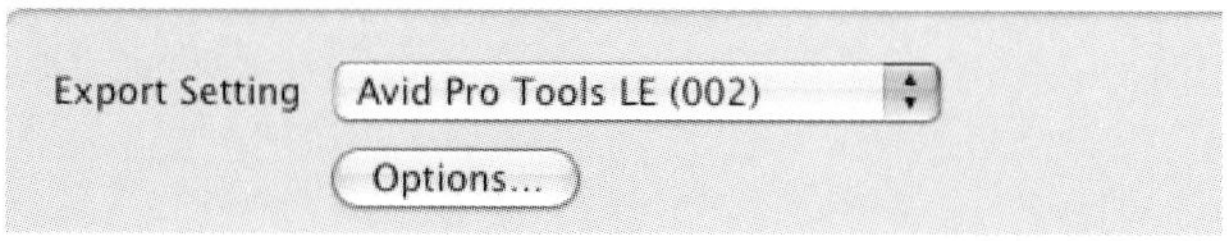

4. When the Export Settings window opens, you are going to choose the settings that I've provided in Figure 14.15.
5. In the Export As . . . pull-down menu, choose OMF 1.0.
6. Deselect Include All Video Tracks in Sequence.
7. Now click Save.
8. In the Export As . . . window, go to Save As . . . to change the name from "Sequence name.aaf" to "Sequence name.omf."
9. Save the file inside your OMFI MediaFiles folder.
10. Click Save.

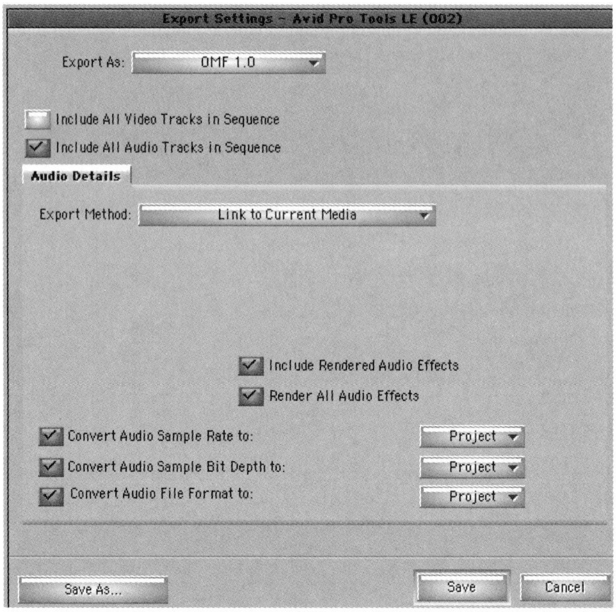

Figure 14.15

You will now have an OMF file inside your OMFI MediaFiles folder. When you launch Pro Tools, select New Session from the menu and navigate until you find the OMF file inside the OMFI MediaFiles folder.

If you think you may go to an outside vendor (such as a professional mixer with a Pro Tools station), talk to the vendor because the steps may be a bit different. This outline will give you a great place to start the conversation. You can then make whatever changes to this list of steps that the vendor suggests.

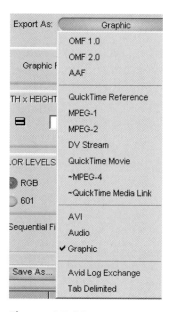

Figure 14.16 File types.

EXPORTING OTHER FILE TYPES

If you look at the Export As: menu (Figure 14.16), you'll see that you can choose from a number of file types. In Chapter 19, we'll learn about Avid Log Exchange and Tab Delimited.

MPEG-2 is used by DVD authoring software. AVI was Microsoft's first attempt at competing with Apple's QuickTime. We've discussed exporting TIFF graphic files. There are scores of other supported file types. It all depends on the application you're exporting the material to.

Exporting is more complicated than importing because you could be exporting to hundreds of applications but you are only importing to one application—your Avid. Just as I did with importing, I've tried to make exporting as simple as possible. Needless to say, I haven't covered all the hundreds of choices or options.

To become expert at exporting, you need to learn about the applications you're exporting to, such as After Effects, Photoshop, and Pro Tools. The more applications you master, the more valuable you are to your client or employer. Or, if you're editing your own projects, you will need to hire fewer outside vendors or freelance people.

SUGGESTED ASSIGNMENTS

1. Import Color Bars from the Avid Test Patterns folder.
2. Import a file created in Photoshop. If you don't have a file, borrow one from a friend. Ask him or her to save it as a TIFF file.
3. Cut it into a sequence.
4. Export a frame from a sequence.
5. Export a sequence as a QuickTime movie and play it on another computer.

15

Digital Filmmaking at 24p

Perhaps three people in a hundred think standard-definition video looks better than film. That explains why, for many years, companies have been making software that purported to give video a "film" look. By and large, these have been a complete waste of both time and money because the results never even came close, but that didn't stop people from dreaming. For many decades, independent filmmakers dreamed of using inexpensive video cameras to shoot their projects, and through careful lighting and inventive post-production techniques they hoped to create a look indistinguishable from film. The dream was to then enter festivals and win top prizes. Sundance would call and a distributor would offer a distribution deal. That meant transferring their inexpensive video to 35-mm film. It's an involved process, but in the dream it worked, and soon their low-budget project would be shown in theaters all over the world.

Just a pipe dream—until now. Thanks to the 24p technology that Panasonic unveiled in 2003, that dream is becoming a reality—filmmakers are now transferring their video projects to film and getting theatrical prints.

Even if a theatrical release isn't in your immediate plans, creating a video that looks like film is within your reach. So, what happened to transform the ugly duckling into a swan? The answer is simple—24p.

This chapter explains how to edit videotapes that were captured with standard-definition cameras shooting at 24p. The cameras are the Canon XL2, the Panasonic DVX100, and the Panasonic SDX900. We'll discuss high-definition (HD) and high-definition video (HDV) cameras in the next chapter.

Many people are choosing to shoot their projects with one of these three standard-definition cameras instead of using an HDV camera because HDV looks a lot like video, with the added problem of having *too much* detail. (*Note:* Avid Xpress DV does not offer 24p capabilities at this time.)

In this chapter we will not only explain how to achieve the image quality of film using 24p video cameras, but we'll also explain how to get the widescreen look.

Figure 15.1 Panasonic's DVX100A 24p camera. (Courtesy of Panasonic.)

This chapter examines all aspects of standard-definition 16:9 filmmaking, including native 16:9, anamorphic 16:9, and transferring Super 16-mm film to 16:9 video.

INTERLACED VERSUS PROGRESSIVE

In standard-definition video there are 525 horizontal lines of picture information in each frame (although only 486 contain visible picture information), but each frame doesn't hold that information as one complete image. Instead, each frame is made up of two *fields*. The first field holds half the image's picture elements— all the odd lines: 1, 3, 5, 7, and so on to 525. The second field holds all the even lines: 2, 4, 6, and so on to 524. The electron gun in the television monitor scans the lines from left to right, top to bottom. It scans the odd lines first—the first field—and then all the even ones—the second field.

When the two fields are displayed to make one frame, they are *interlaced* together, which is why standard-definition video is called an interlaced medium. The reason for this goes back to the early days of television and we've been stuck with the system ever since.

Film is a *progressive* medium. Each frame holds all of the image's picture information—there are no separate fields. By doing away with fields and the whole interlacing business, you suddenly get a look on video that's much closer to film.

The second factor that contributes to the film look is film's frame rate. Motion picture film runs at 24 frames per second (fps). Video, on the other hand, runs at 30 fps. Studies have been done that indicate that people find 24 fps to be more pleasing to the eye than other frame rates, and people associate that rate with storytelling. To summarize:

- The video look = interlaced images at 30 fps.
- The film look = progressive images at 24 fps.

What Panasonic came up with was a video camera that ran at 24 fps and captured images progressively. Combine 24 fps with progressive frames, and your videotape has a richer look. The image looks less intense—it lacks that exaggerated sharpness associated with video. Canon has licensed Panasonic's 24p technology and incorporated it in their XL2 camera, so the Canon XL2, Panasonic DVX100, and SDX900 all handle the 24p issue the same way.

24P IS REALLY 23.976

To be accurate, standard definition video doesn't run at 30 fps. Before the advent of color, it did, but the rate had to be slowed down when color was introduced many decades ago, in order to get the color information to fit in. So video runs at 29.97 fps. It turns out that the difference between 30 and 29.97 is 0.1%. Well, in order to get motion picture film to transfer properly to videotape running at 29.976 fps, they had to slow down film's frame per second rate by the same amount—0.1%—during the film-to-tape transfer. The film is slowed down from 24 to 23.976 fps.

The Panasonic and Canon cameras we are discussing don't actually record at 24 fps, even though they're called 24p cameras. In reality, they are running at 23.976—the same frame rate as film when it is transferred to videotape.

CAMERA MODES

When shooting with cameras that incorporate Panasonic's 24p technology, you have four ways to capture images:

- Progressive Off or 30i (sometimes called 60i)
- 24p
- 24p Advanced
- 30p

These are settings you select using the camera's Scene Files and/or the camera's menu settings. In Figure 15.2, I have selected the 24p Advanced setting on the Panasonic DVX100A.

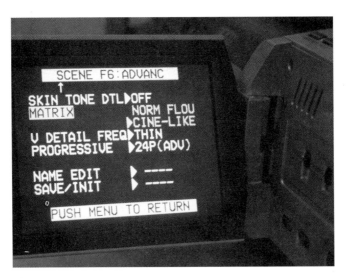

Figure 15.2   A menu inside a 24p camera.

Here is an explanation for each camera setting and when you would use them.

Progressive Off or 30i

This choice gives you standard video mode—what you get with any NTSC video camera. It's called 30i, which stands for 30 fps, interlaced. (It's sometimes called 60i, for 60 fields per second, interlaced). Don't choose this if you want a film look; if you want your video to look like video, though, then this is it. When you want to capture your 30i tapes using your Avid, you'll click on New Project, name the project, and select 30i NTSC in the format window (Figure 15.3).

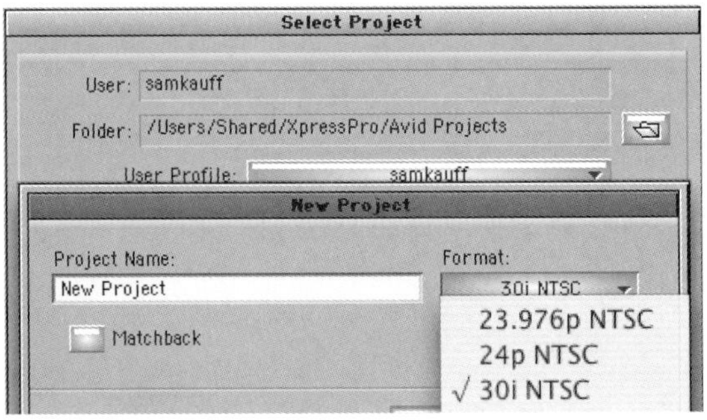

Figure 15.3   Choose this format for standard video.

24p Normal

When you shoot in the 24p mode, the camera places the images on tape in such a way that they can most easily be played back at the standard television rate of 29.97 fps. The latest Avid versions give you a choice: You can shoot 24p Normal and edit at 30i NTSC (see Figure 15.3) and become interlaced, or you can edit at 23.976 NTSC and stay in the progressive mode. If you're not sure where your show will end up or how it will be used, then 24p Normal is a good choice because it gives you flexibility.

Recently I was in Uganda, and I shot a film called *Living with Slim: Kids Talk About HIV/AIDS* using a Panasonic DVX100 in the 24p mode. I edited it at 30i NTSC. It looks very rich; the colors are gorgeous, and many people think I shot it on film. When it has been shown at festivals, alongside other videos, it really stands out. The colors are more vivid, but there is none of that crisp video look to it. People are constantly asking me how I shot it. I mastered it on DVCAM and have made Beta SP copies, which is what a lot of festivals still prefer. It has been shown in huge auditoriums, including the 650-seat theater at the Museum of Fine Arts in Boston. If you plan to distribute on tape or for a local television station, shoot 24p Normal and choose 30i NTSC in the Format pull-down menu when setting up your Avid project. From then on, capture and edit as you would any video project—but with the advantage of film-like video. If you might be using stock footage (interlaced) in your project, choose 24p and edit at 30i.

If you decide after shooting that you're going to concentrate on DVD distribution and no interlaced material will be part of your Timeline, then you would select 23.976 NTSC when editing.

24p Advanced

When the videographer selects 24p Advanced on the camera, as I have in Figure 15.2, the camera puts the images onto tape in a way that will allow the Avid to keep the images progressive—you are leaving the interlaced world. It is best to shoot the entire project in this mode and not switch between 24p and 24p Advanced; however, Xpress Pro v. 5.1 allows you to shoot a project using both 24p and 24p Advanced, in case you mistakenly selected 24p and not 24p Advanced. When editing tapes shot with the 24p Advanced on the Avid, you must select the correct format. In the Select Project window, after clicking New Project, name the project and select 23.976p NTSC in the format window, as shown in Figure 15.4. Do *not* choose 24p NTSC—that's for motion picture film projects. You want 23.976p NTSC.

Now when you capture your tapes, the Avid will keep the footage in the progressive mode.

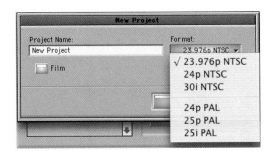

Figure 15.4 Choose this format for 24p Advanced tapes.

DELAY THE AUDIO

When shooting in either 24p mode, you will find that, once the footage is captured in the Avid, the audio is one frame ahead of the video, making it slightly
out of sync. This is true with the Canon XL2 and the Panasonic DVX100 and
SDX900. Knowing this, Avid has incorporated a Delay audio pop-up menu in
the Capture Tool that lets you delay the audio by one frame during capture.
Select 1 frame.

HOW PROGRESSIVE WORKS—PULLDOWN

Figure 15.5 shows you how advanced pulldown works with standard videotape.
Remember, NTSC video records 30 frames every second, but the camera captures
24 progressive frames every second, so we're trying to get 24 frames to go onto
tape that's recording at 30 frames per second. (OK, we know it's really 23.976
and 29.97, but to make this easier we'll stick with whole numbers.) How can 24
go into 30?

Advanced Pulldown

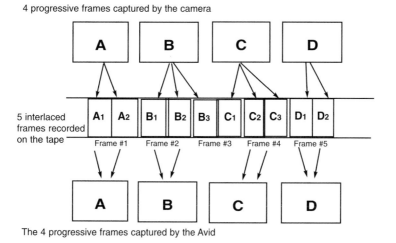

4 progressive frames captured by the camera

5 interlaced frames recorded on the tape

Frame #1 Frame #2 Frame #3 Frame #4 Frame #5

The 4 progressive frames captured by the Avid

Figure 15.5

Let's start with a shot that is just four frames long to see how this works. We'll label the four progressive frames A, B, C, and D. We are going to use the fact that there are two interlaced video fields in every video frame to get the math to work.

The first progressive frame, A, is placed on the two fields of the first frame of video. The second progressive frame, B, is placed across three fields—two fields on video frame 2 and the first field of video frame 3. It's actually held for a tiny bit longer to get it to go across three fields. The C frame is also placed on three fields, and the D frame is placed on two fields. So you have two fields, three fields, three fields, and two fields, written as 2:3:3:2. You now have four progressive frames placed onto five interlaced video frames. No matter how long your shot is, the same 2:3:3:2 process happens.

During the capture process, the Avid extracts the original four progressive frames from the tape—A, B, C, and D. Can you see from the illustration which video frame the Avid ignores? That's right—it ignores video frame 3. Some people notice a sort of stutter, which results from this pulldown process. In truth, the stutter is far more pronounced in the camera's viewfinder than it is once the tapes have been captured. When properly shot and edited, the stutter looks just like any film that has been transferred to tape. In fact, it's part of what gives film its distinctive look.

SETTINGS

In the Settings window, when you're in a 23.976p NTSC project on the Avid, you'll see a Film and 24p setting. If you double-click to open it, you'll see the window in Figure 15.6.

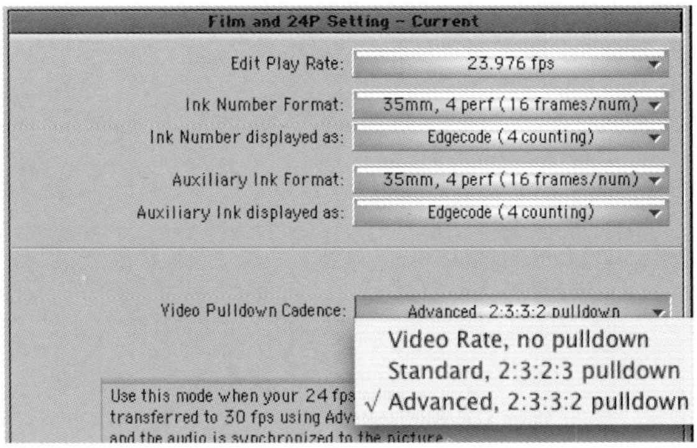

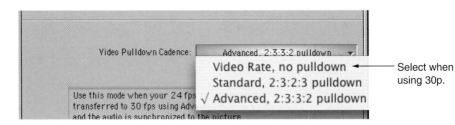

Figure 15.6

Ignore the Ink format choices; just make sure you have selected the Edit Play Rate of 23.976, and a Video Pulldown Cadence of Advanced, 2:3:3:2 pulldown. The Avid will capture at the proper 2:3:3:2 even without you setting it here. I just want you to know this setting window exists and how it should be set up, so you don't panic. Also, at the bottom of this dialog box (not shown), there's a checkbox for selecting Pulldown Phase of timecode. Leave the box unchecked.

30p

For those of you paying attention, you'll notice that I haven't explained the Panasonic or Canon 30p mode. The only time you'll ever want to use this setting is if you want to create a slow-motion effect. If you shoot at 30 fps and then bring that footage into your 24-fps project, you'll slow that footage down by 25%. It's not a lot of slow motion (slow-motion film cameras often shoot from 60 to 200 frames per second), but it's enough. Remember, slow motion suppresses shakiness. Shooting at 30p will make a hand-held shot look as smooth as a Steadicam. Obviously, you can't shoot dialog at this speed. In fact, the Avid will ignore your audio during capture. On the Avid, go to the Film and 24p settings (Figure 15.7) and select Video Rate, no pulldown.

Figure 15.7

ADVANTAGES OF 24p OVER 30i

There are three reasons to shoot and edit in the 24p mode:

- You can make a progressive DVD.
- You can easily transfer your project to PAL.
- You can transfer your project to film for a theatrical release.

Progressive DVD

DVDs are becoming the format of choice for festivals and independent distribution. Having a progressive DVD is a real advantage because the project looks better—more of the film look is preserved, plus you won't have interlacing artifacts, which look like hash marks on the edge of things that move. We will examine the steps you will take to create a DVD in Chapter 18.

Transferring to PAL

It is much easier to convert a 24-fps project to 25 fps than to go from 29.97 to 25. There is actually a 4.1% increase in speed, but it's not really noticeable. In fact, every feature film shown on European television is handled this way, and no one even notices the increase in speed.

35-mm Theatrical Release Print

Theatrical distribution means 35-mm film prints and that's expensive, but if a distributor is putting up the money, well, no worries, mate. We'll examine this process in detail in Chapter 18. If you do intend to make a film print, you should shoot your project in the 16:9 format. Perhaps it's time to examine the whole 16:9 process.

STANDARD DEFINITION 16:9

As you will see in the next chapter, HD presents many challenges, and for now there isn't a huge demand for your HD tapes. When you think of all the people you know who could play your HD tape, it's a pretty short list. You don't have to shoot HD to get a 16:9 aspect ratio. There are many standard-definition cameras that have a true 16:9 chipset and thus offer the same aspect ratio as HD. Two of the cameras we discussed earlier in this chapter, the Panasonic SDX900 and Canon XL2, are native 16:9 cameras and can also shoot at 24p (really 23.976). Thus far, we've examined what you can achieve using the 23.976 frame rate and scanning the image progressively. Add a 16:9 aspect ratio, and you're getting the film look you want without the hassles associated with HD.

Let's compare the frame size of standard television to the wide-screen 16:9 version. As you can see in Figure 15.8, I've placed a 4:3 standard television frame inside a 16:9 television.

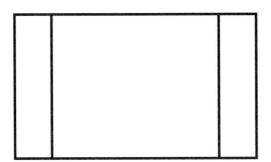

Figure 15.8 4:3 inside a 16:9 screen.

Obviously, the 16:9 is designed to be more like the movie theater experience, which, when you think about it, is more like the way our eyes perceive the world.

16:9 WITH 4:3 CAMERAS

You don't even need a native 16:9 camera to achieve a wide-screen look. Many 4:3 cameras offer a 16:9 setting among their extensive menu options; however, I don't recommend this as a viable choice for acquiring 16:9 images, especially if you're considering a film blow-up. These cameras use a 4:3 digital capture area, and they manipulate the pixels to fill a 16:9 frame. There just aren't enough pixels or picture information to do this successfully, but there is a way to use a 4:3 camera to get 16:9 images. You place an *anamorphic converter* (Figure 15.9) on the front of your DV camera and then use an NLE editor, such as the Avid, to give you 16:9 wide-screen video. This process is called *anamorphic photography*.

Figure 15.9　16:9 anamorphic attachment. (Courtesy of Century Optics.)

ANAMORPHIC PHOTOGRAPHY

We've all been to an amusement park and stood before those funny mirrors. One makes you look tall and thin and another one makes you look short and wide. These mirrors use the same principle that gave rise to CinemaScope movies in the 1950s. Scope pictures, with their 2.35:1 aspect ratio, are still in vogue today. Early on, cinematographers placed anamorphic converters in front of their lenses to achieve the wide-screen effect, but today companies such as Panavision manufacture a wide range of anamorphic lenses for use on 35-mm and 70-mm cameras and theater projectors.

The anamorphic converter, or lens, compresses the image in one plane and not the other. The converter compresses or squeezes the image horizontally, while keeping the vertical image fixed. Look at a film shot with an anamorphic lens. The people and objects look like they've been placed in a vise and squeezed together (Figure 15.10). Now project that same film with a projector outfitted

Figure 15.10　Image anamorphically squeezed.

with an anamorphic lens, and the image is stretched horizontally. The people and objects are restored to their normal proportions, but you also have a much wider screen image—the amusement park mirror without the distortion (Figure 15.11).

Figure 15.11   Image stretched during projection.

Anamorphic DV

If you place an anamorphic converter on a DV camera, you get the same result as with a 35-mm Scope movie. Play that tape on a standard NTSC monitor and everything looks squeezed; however, when you display your videotape on one of today's 16:9 monitors, electronics in the monitor stretch the image to fill the 16:9 wide screen, as you can see in Figure 15.12.

Figure 15.12   A wide-screen television monitor.

Panasonic makes a 16:9 converter for its DVX100A. As we discussed earlier, this camera provides stunning images in its 24p Normal and 24p Advanced modes. Combined with a 16:9 anamorphic converter, it gives you a moderately priced DV camera that can compete nicely with HDV cameras. The Canon XL2 is native 16:9 so you don't need an anamorphic converter.

SUPER 16-mm FILM

Super 16-mm (Super-16) offers another way to achieve 16:9 and one that can be transferred to standard or HD formats. Super-16 film is really just 16-mm film. Instead of manufacturing it with perforations (or sprocket holes) on both sides of the film, the manufacturer makes a single-perforated version. With a row of perforations removed, there is more usable negative because the area taken up by the perforations is replaced by exposable film. Super-16 has an aspect ratio of 1.66:1, which is very close to 16:9. Aaton and Arriflex make several state-of-the-art Super-16 cameras.

Figure 15.13   A telecine suite at Finish Editorial in Boston.

Anamorphic Film-to-Tape Transfer

Instead of using an anamorphic converter on the lens of a 16-mm camera, you can get a superior picture by anamorphically squeezing the image during the film-to-tape transfer. When the Super-16 film is scanned during telecine, the image can be squeezed and stored that way on any standard-definition tape such as Beta SP, DigiBeta, DVCAM, or mini-DV. When you display the tape on a standard 4:3 monitor, the actors will look squeezed—tall and thin. However, if you use a wide-screen television, electronics in the monitor stretch the image to fill the 16:9 frame. This is often called *anamorphic video.*

Obviously, not all film-to-tape transfer machines have anamorphic capability. You need a flying-spot scanner, or equivalent. Using Super-16 film, with its wide image area, and then transferring the film anamorphically gives spectacular results. When played on a wide-screen television, the picture quality rivals 35 mm. (You could also transfer it to high-definition tape, such as Panasonic's DVCPRO100, and edit it on an Avid Xpress Pro HD, as described in the next chapter.)

16:9 EDITING

You may shoot your own footage using an SDTV video camera with a true 16:9 chip or a DV camera using an anamorphic converter on the lens. Or you may shoot with a Super-16 camera and then transfer your film anamorphically. Either way, the end result is squeezed people and objects. All Avid software, including Xpress DV, Xpress Pro, and Xpress Pro HD, can easily change the shape of the Source Monitor and Record Monitor so you can edit in the 16:9 aspect ratio. To the Avid it's all just pixels to be manipulated.

To get the Avid to change the aspect ratio of the monitors, simply go to the Source/Record Monitor and click on it to make it active. Then go to the Clip menu and select 16:9 monitors. It's that simple. As you can see in Figure 15.14, the Avid changes the shape of the Source Monitor and Record Monitor to accommodate the 16:9 images. You may have to resize the Timeline and various bins to get everything to fit nicely on your computer screen.

Figure 15.14

YOUR FINISHED PROJECT

Once you're through editing the 16:9 project, you can output it to any tape format. The tape will contain the squeezed material, but a wide-screen television or video projector will easily stretch the footage. In fact, today's video projectors can make this video material look as if it were shot in high definition by displaying it in a wide-screen format. With DVD a popular choice for distribution, you can also burn your project to DVD, select 16:9 as your aspect ratio, and maintain the wide-screen look.

MULTIPLE FORMATS

Although having a wide-screen version is great, you will also want the option of playing your project on any standard television, not just the wide-screen ones. The Avid has tools to create a 4:3 version and a 4:3 letterbox version as well. You can record those out to tape or DVD and therefore have several options for showing your work. Creating a letterbox version is amazingly simple, and, depending on your software, can be done in a matter of minutes. With letterboxing, you get to keep the wide-screen composition, but in order to do so you have to put black bands above and below the picture information.

4:3 Letterbox Version—Xpress Pro, Xpress Pro HD 5.+, and Media Composer

1. Click anywhere on the Source/Record Monitor to make it active.
2. Create a V2 track. Make sure nothing else is on it. (If there is, create a V3 track.)
3. Click the Monitor track box so the icon moves up to V2.
4. Go to the Effect Palette, click on the Reformat category of effects, and drag the 16:9 Letterbox icon to the V2 track (see Figure 15.15).

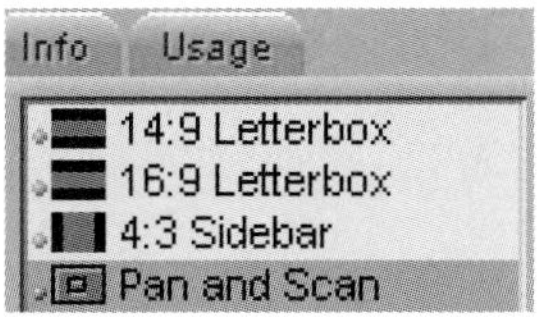

Figure 15.15

You will now see your sequence with normal 4:3 proportions but with the wide-screen composition maintained, thanks to the letterboxing. Look at Figure 15.16.

Figure 15.16

4:3 Letterbox Version—Xpress DV and Xpress Pro 4.+

The Xpress DV and earlier versions of Xpress Pro don't have the Reformat category of effects, but even if they did I've encountered a problem with the way they handle certain effects. They won't allow you to place an effect, such as Mask or Resize, onto an empty video track. You can't place an effect on V2, so the effect is a layer above your clips in the Timeline. However, I've discovered a workaround. Examine Figure 15.17. If you place anything at the head of V2 (or V3), such as a title, you can then drag an effect, such as Resize, onto V2. Once you've done that, the effect can work on all the clips in the Timeline. Without this ability, you have to drag the Resize icon onto each and every clip. In Figure 15.17, you can see that by placing a title in V2 I was able to drag the Resize effect onto the entire V2 track.

With a title in place, I dragged the Resize Effect onto V2. ——

F						
V2	Main T.	Filler				⊞
V1		1B Tk 1	1A Tk 8	1F Tk3	1A Tk 9	
A1		1B Tk 1	1A Tk 8	1F Tk3	1A Tk 9	

Figure 15.17

Follow these steps to create a letterbox version:

1. Click anywhere on the Source/Record Monitor to make it active.
2. In the Clip menu, select 16:9 again so you're back in 4:3 mode. Everything will appear squeezed.
3. Create a title and splice it so it's on V2, before the clips in your sequence, as shown in Figure 15.17.
4. Go to the Effect Palette, then Image, and then drag the Resize icon to the V2 track.
5. You will have one solid effect covering the entire track.
6. After placing the blue position indicator on the Resize effect icon in the Timeline, open the Effect Editor.
7. Set the Scaling sliders to Wid 100 (normal) and Hgt 75.

Figure 15.18

That's all there is to it. You now have reformatted your entire sequence to 4:3.

Creating a 4:3 Pan and Scan Version for Standard Television

Most video distributors of feature films believe that viewers won't accept letterboxing of any stripe, so they crop all feature films, cutting off the edges and showing you what occurs in the center of the frame or panning to the left or right if the composition warrants it. Networks and cable companies do the same whenever they show feature films on television, but for true film lovers this seems like a bad compromise. You're not seeing the film's original composition—you're not seeing the sets, or the art direction, or some of the action because large sections of the frame are being cropped out. Fortunately, more and more DVDs are offering a wide-screen version that, when played on a wide-screen television, shows you the entire wide-screen picture.

But, for now, you will still need a 4:3 version of your project, and, like Hollywood, you will need to crop your own project to conform to the 4:3 aspect ratio of standard television. We'll first capture the center of the wide-screen composition, dropping off the sides of each shot in the sequence. Then we'll recompose the image, panning left or right to make each shot compositionally more effective. The simplest method uses a feature available on Avid's newer models called Pan and Scan.

Pan and Scan Effect: The Media Composer and the newer Xpress Pro versions have a Reformat category of effects that allows you to reformat to different aspect ratios as well as Pan and Scan. When you are through editing, leave your Source/Record Monitor in the 16:9 mode. Now follow these steps:

1. Create a video track that is above your titles and clips (V2, V3, or higher).
2. Go to the Effect Palette, and click on Reformat.

Figure 15.19

3. Drag the Pan and Scan effect icon to the top-most video track—the one that is empty.
4. After placing the blue position indicator on the effect icon in the Timeline, open the Effect Editor.

5. Click on the Aspect Ratio triangle, so it opens. In the Source pop-up menu, select 16:9 Anamorphic. In the Target pop-up menu, select 1.33 (4:3).

Now you'll see a wire frame inside the Effect Preview Monitor. Usually the Pan and Scan chooses the middle of the wide-screen frame as its default selection. If that works as a starting point for all your shots, go to the Actions triangle and click on Establish Origin. If that doesn't work as a starting point for most of your shots, move the wire frame with your cursor to select a more appropriate composition and then click on Establish Origin.

Under the Actions triangle, you'll see Subdivide Effect. If all your shots in your sequence require the same amount of panning, then you could leave the Pan and Scan effect just as it is. But, of course, just about every shot will have different panning requirements. That's where Subdivide Effect comes in. It breaks the Pan and Scan effect into sections that match the length of each clip in your Timeline.

Now you need to go to each clip that needs recomposing, open the Effect Editor, and, using key frames, either drag the wire frame or use the H Pos slider in the Position triangle to set the panning.

If at any time you want to get back to your starting point, click on Reset Origin in the Action section and you'll return to your original, or base, composition.

4:3 on Xpress DV and Earlier Xpress Pro Versions

Let's look at a work-around for those systems that don't have Pan and Scan. What we're going to do is use the Resize effect, just as we did with the letterbox version.

Using the Resize Effect

1. Click anywhere on the Source/Record Monitor to make it active.
2. In the Clip menu, select 16:9 again so you're back in 4:3 mode. Everything will appear squeezed.
3. Go to the Effect Palette, then Image, and then drag the Resize icon to the first clip.
4. After placing the blue position indicator on the Resize effect icon in the Timeline, open the Effect Editor.
5. Set the Scaling sliders to Wid 133 and Hgt 100.

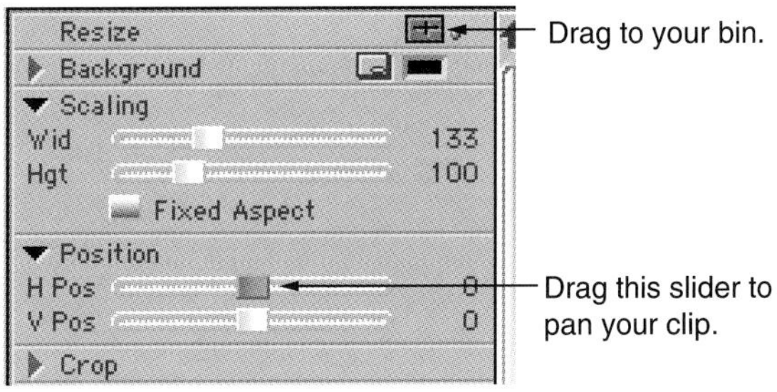

Figure 15.20

You'll see that your first clip now has a perfectly proportioned 4:3 image. That part was easy. Now, create a template for this effect by dragging the effect icon from the Effect Editor to a bin. Name it "Resize 4×3."

6. Place this template on all the shots in your sequence. Now you have resized all your shots, and all your composition shows the middle of each shot, with the sides dropped out. But it might look better if some shots were panned left or right.
7. Re-open the Effect Editor.
8. Open the Position triangle.
9. Set the opening key frame by clicking on the opening key frame and then moving the H Pos slider to pan either left or right.
10. Copy that H Pos setting and paste it onto the end key frame.

This will maintain the same composition—the pan—throughout the shot. You can use multiple key frames to pan during the shot. Set an opening composition on the first key frame and then add key frames and change the H Pos slider at every key frame. You can even make several templates and use them for a variety of similar clips requiring the same composition.

GO WIDE

There are now three ways to create and edit a 16:9 project in standard definition:

- DV standard-definition camera with anamorphic attachment.
- 16:9 standard-definition camera.
- Super 16-mm film with an anamorphic film-to-tape transfer.

In the next chapter, we'll explore the many versions of high definition. The one thing that all high-definition formats have in common is the 16:9 aspect ratio.

A DREAM COME TRUE?

Now we have created, in standard definition, the total film look—using 24p and the 16:9 aspect ratio. I'm not claiming that a project shot on DV tape can achieve the same quality as 16-mm or 35-mm film, but given the price differential it's now an option. But remember that a lot of what distinguishes 16-mm or 35-mm film isn't just the recording medium—it's the quality of the script, the actors, the lighting, and the sound. Often, films look better than videos because of the care the filmmakers put into what happens in front of the camera, not what's inside it. Put the same care into your 24p project as you would into an expensive 16-mm project, and it will be much harder to distinguish between the two.

SUGGESTED ASSIGNMENTS

1. Open the "Gaffer's Delight" project and place several clips in the Source Monitor.
2. Go to the Clip menu and select 16:9.
3. Edit several clips together and then letterbox your sequence.
4. Create a 4:3 Pan and Scan version.

16

HD and HDV

I'm sure you've noticed how often various high-tech gurus, self-appointed or real, have importantly declared: "This is the year of high definition (HD)." And, when nothing comes of it, they come back the next year stating with even more conviction, "No, this really *is* the year!" While waiting patiently for their prognostications to come true, we have gone about our business of creating powerful, effective, and useful videos in standard definition (SD).

If you're like me, you've probably hesitated to dip your toes into the murky HD waters for several reasons: The equipment seems prohibitively expensive, the data rates are enormous, and there exists a dizzying array of competing standards. But, the main reason is this: You haven't been able to figure out what to do with an HD tape if you had one. It's hard to find film festivals that want them, and you don't know of any movie theater, museum, or public screening facility that will play them. So, if no one wants the darn things, why shoot HD?

You're right, but you're wrong. I'm going to have to finally agree with the techies. The year of HD has finally arrived; it's time to grapple with the whole HD mess. What made me change my mind? Three things: First, HD isn't just 16:9 video with a lot more detail. HD now offers many different looks—a film look, a video look, and something in between. Second, your Avid software can now edit HD over FireWire. And, third, it is a lot easier to convert HD to SD, but I'm getting ahead of myself.

IT'S THE QUALITY

People have been shooting television shows and commercials on 16-mm and 35-mm film for many years, even though none of us has a film projector at home. *The Sopranos*, *Lost*, *24 Hours*—you name the prime-time drama and it's been shot on film. Though it starts out as film, most people watch the shows on standard-definition television. So why do television producers go to all the trouble and expense of shooting on film? Because of the quality of the image. The look of film carries over no matter what format it ends up on. The same argument applies to HD. Shoot HD and finish in HD, or convert the signal to standard definition for a better-looking SDTV image.

Unfortunately, HD has always been too expensive on the shooting end and too expensive and complicated on the editing end to convince us to take the plunge, but now Avid's Xpress Pro HD software (Mac or Windows) can handle HD without forcing us to buy expensive RAID drives or fancy break-out boxes. We can now shoot HD, capture over FireWire, edit HD, and output to HD or output to standard-definition NTSC tapes.

With the post-production end sorted out (we'll sort it out in this chapter), we can finally start looking at the various HD and HDV flavors.

HD PRIMER

High definition used to mean a 16:9 aspect ratio with a *lot* more detail in the image, but now HD has evolved to the point where producers can choose from a number of HD flavors, depending on the look they want. In the beginning, there were just two players in the HD world—Sony and Panasonic—and they came at the problem with two different approaches. Panasonic developed an HD system called 720p and Sony developed 1080i. ABC and Fox chose Panasonic's approach, while NBC and CBS picked Sony's.

There are now many HD flavors within these two approaches. Most HD systems use a progressive scan, and one uses an interlaced scan. Also, there are many frame rates to choose from, depending on the look you're after. If you want your dramatic project to have a film look, you choose a progressive HD format with a frame rate of 23.976. If you want your sports programming to look like video, you choose an interlaced HD format running at 29.97. If you want your reality TV show to look in between, you choose a progressive HD format running at 29.97. The choice is yours.

In the HD world, things are described a bit differently than in the standard-definition world. First, HD formats are described by how many horizontal lines they contain; thus, we have systems with 720 horizontal lines or 1080 horizontal lines. HD formats are also described by the way in which those horizontal lines are scanned, whether progressive or interlaced. A lowercase "p" or "i" is added to the number of lines, as in 720p or 1080i, for identification purposes. Finally, the frames-per-second rate is often used to help differentiate between similar HD formats.

Let's begin our examination of HD by reviewing what we know about standard definition but using HD terminology. We'll use DV (mini-DV and DVCAM) for purposes of comparison, building on everything we've learned in the previous chapters.

DV

- Aspect ratio: 4:3
- Interlaced scanning
- Pixel aspect ratio: 720 × 480
- Frames-per-second rate: 29.97
- 210,000 pixels per frame

Using HD nomenclature, our DV format would be called 480i/29.97, meaning there are 480 visible horizontal lines, with interlace scanning, running at 29.97 frames per second. Now, let's look at the same variables in the HD world.

720p

- Aspect ratio: 16:9
- Progressive scanning
- Pixel aspect ratio: 1280 × 720
- Frames-per-second rates: 23.976, 24, 29.97, 30, and 60
- 921,600 pixels per frame

This is Panasonic's format, and the one JVC adopted. Because 720p is a progressive format, it looks very pleasing to the eye and has a filmic look to it. Because its datastream is smaller than the other types of HD, this is the choice for many independent filmmakers. Xpress Pro HD software can capture and output this format through a FireWire connection. We'll examine 720p in greater detail later in this chapter.

1080i

- Aspect ratio: 16:9
- Interlaced scanning
- Pixel aspect ratio: 1920 × 1080
- Frames-per-second rates: 29.97 frames (59.94i) and 30 (60i)
- 1,555,200 pixels per frame

This is Sony's baby—and a big one it is. This is the format producers choose when they want HD to look like video—or reality TV. Network sports want an interlaced HD look, and they achieve it with 1080i. It produces a huge datastream, seven times greater than DV—well beyond the capacity of a FireWire-based system such as Xpress Pro HD. You need a high-end Avid like the Media Composer Adrenaline HD to capture 1080i. For several years, these were the two choices, but Sony recently developed a third choice to compete more directly with motion picture film.

1080p

- Aspect ratio: 16:9
- Progressive scanning
- Pixel aspect ratio: 1920 × 1080
- Frames per second rates: 23.976, 24, 25p, 29.97, 30, 59.94i, 60i
- 2,073,600 pixels per frame

This is the latest HD flavor and the largest. Again, Sony is its parent. This HD has 2,073,600 pixels per frame, about ten times more pixels than a standard-definition frame. Storage needs are immense. This is the HD flavor that comes closest to 35-mm film in terms of look and picture quality. Every year more and more features and prime-time television dramas are shot on this HD format because it offers progressive scanning, like film, and offers film's 24 frames-per-second rate. You'd need Avid's more powerful units to work with this format.

HDV

This is an HD-light format that generated a lot of buzz when it first came out in 2003 with JVC's GY-HD10. It's a sort of fudged high-definition format that uses MPEG-2 encoding, just like DVD's encoding. JVC's camera, the GY-HD100 (Figure 16.1), is a 720p version, while Sony's FX1 and Z1 are 1080i versions. These are real HD signals that get crammed, by way of a great deal of compression, onto a mini-DV tape. What makes HDV difficult to capture and edit is the complicated encoding system.

Figure 16.1 JVC's HDV camera. (Courtesy of JVC.)

For comparison, let's look at any standard DV camera. The camera compresses the signal using a 5:1 compression ratio as it records it to DV tape. When we capture the DV tape into our Avid, the Avid deals with what it's given—

already compressed frames. But in HDV, some of the frames contain all the picture information—we'll call them the "Big Frames"—while others carry only the information that has changed from the previous Big Frame (this explanation is somewhat simplified and uses my own terminology).

The first frame is a Big Frame, but the next 13 frames are "shells." They hold only what has changed. The next frame—the 15th frame in the group—is also a Big Frame and is related to the previous 13 shells. Fifteen frames make a Group of Pictures (GOP) that relate to each other. The 16th frame is part of the next group and starts the process over again. If the subject you are shooting is static, the 13 in-between frames don't have much new information and so are fairly empty. But, if the shot is a quick pan or a subject with lots of motion, those in-between frames get really taxed.

Not all HDV cameras use a 15-frame GOP (some use a 6-frame GOP), but you get the idea. Sometimes the images don't look great if there is a lot of motion. That's why people doing documentaries with a lot of run-and-gun tend to stick with a standard-definition camera like the Panasonic DVX100A.

This GOP system is tough on desktop and laptop editing machines, such as Xpress Pro HD, because when you hit Play the Avid has to fill in the shells with all that material. You need the fastest processors with as much RAM as you can get.

At first, the target audience for HDV was wealthy folks with HD televisions in their living rooms who wanted to take home movies of their kids in HD. But, when independent filmmakers got a hold of them, they started exploring the possibilities. And, once that happened, NLE companies responded. With the advent of Panasonic's HVX200—a DV-priced 720p HD camcorder, excitement for HDV has dropped a bit.

ALL THOSE PESKY HD FRAMES-PER-SECOND RATES

As you've noted, some of the HD formats offer several different frame rates. Camera manufacturers want to make one camera that can be used for a variety of tasks—so they can sell more of them. That is why the more expensive progressive cameras can shoot at 23.976p for a film look or 29.97p for a video look. 24p (not 23.976) is only used when shooting for a theatrical film release—one that is going to a film print. 25p is chosen when shooting for PAL countries.

The more expensive interlaced cameras shoot 59.94i (same as 29.97 frames per second) or 50i (same as PAL's 25 frames per second). The really expensive cameras can shoot progressive and interlaced at all the above frame rates. Don't be confused by all the frame rates; Avid can handle them all—it just depends on the look you want and whether you're shooting for an NTSC or PAL country. Another bit of confusion comes when various manufacturers use 23.98 or 23.97, when what they really mean is 23.976. Or they say 24, when they really mean

23.976. Let's face it, the year of HD would have come a lot sooner if these mooks—I mean techies—were just a little bit more plain talking.

CAMERAS—EXPENSIVE TO UNBELIEVABLY EXPENSIVE

In the HDV world, Sony and JVC both have cameras in the $3000 to $6000 range: Sony in a 1080i version and JVC in a 720p version. The camera often serves as the deck for capture into your NLE over a FireWire. The tape is the same DV tape used in standard-definition DV cameras.

Figure 16.2 Panasonic's HVX200 camera. (Photograph courtesy of Panasonic.)

The eagerly awaited Panasonic's HVX200 ($6000) (Figure 16.2) is a true HD camera in that it doesn't use GOP; instead, each frame stands alone. It can't record HD to tape but instead places the sound and picture on a memory card—a P2 flash card—rather than videotape. It works like the flash card in a digital camera. When you want to capture what you've shot, simply remove the card from the camera, put it in a card reader attached to you computer, and download the files to your Avid's storage device. The P2 cards are quite expensive, $3000 and more, depending on the capacity. This camera records both 1080i and 720p HD, and you can also use it as a standard-definition camera—one that shoots at 23.976 in the 16:9 format, just like the Canon XL2. It records standard-definition signals onto tape.

The next level up, in terms of cost and quality, is the Panasonic HDC27F camcorder, called the VariCam (Figure 16.3). This is a 720p HD camera. It commonly rents for as much as $950 per day, so it's not something the average student or independent can budget for. In fact, an Arriflex 535B film camera, often used to shoot commercials and features, rents for $250 less per day.

Figure 16.3 Panasonic's 720p VariCam. (Photograph courtesy of Panasonic.)

The VariCam is often used just like a 35-mm motion picture camera. The standard frames-per-second rate is 23.976, but it can shoot at rates from 4 to 60 frames per second. If you edit your project at 23.976, and bring in material shot at 60 frames per second, you have slow motion. If you bring in material at 4 frames per second, you get sped-up motion (clouds going by quickly). The HDX400 camcorder is a less expensive alternative. Both cameras record onto DVCPRO HD tape, also called DVCPRO100.

The Panasonic 1200A deck is the one most commonly used to capture DVCPRO HD tapes shot by these cameras. Despite a $21,000 price tag, you still need to purchase a FireWire option that costs another $3200 to bring the tapes into your Avid Xpress Pro HD. These decks rent for $500 per day—so much for affordable HD! I've included information about the VariCam camera and Panasonic deck because you might be hired to edit a project shot on this increasingly popular system.

The highest HD quality comes from 1080i and 1080p HD cameras. These are eye-poppingly expensive and can't be directly captured by an Xpress Pro HD. Cameras are in the $100,000 price range. Sony's HDW F950 camera has been used on several feature films, including the most recent *Star Wars* trilogy. Cost to rent is $1200 per day or $3600 per week. Sony has its own line of decks and tape systems. The tapes are called HDCAM and HDCAM SR (Superior Resolution).

HDCAM SR is for storing the largest datastreams. Two premiere motion picture camera companies, Panavision and Arriflex, have introduced HD cameras that produce more resolution than any tape formats can currently handle.

Often the huge signals produced by these cameras bypass videotape altogether and are stored on large drives that can be transferred directly to motion picture film. In fact, we will see a day when there will be no more videotape of any kind. All picture and sound will be captured onto memory cards or drives.

EDITING HD

Fortunately for us, Avid is the most trusted name in HD. Ask the producers of just about any prime-time television show, from *CSI* to *American Idol*. They all cut on Avid systems.

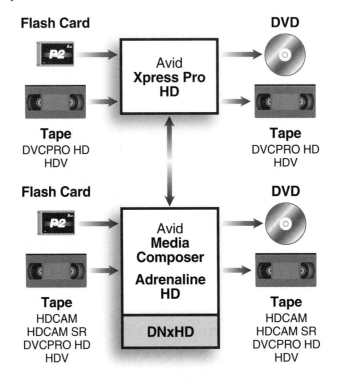

Xpress Pro HD Workflow

Figure 16.4 Xpress Pro's HD workflow.

Avid Xpress Pro HD can capture and output a wide range of HD and HDV tapes. That means you can capture tapes shot with Panasonic's VariCam, JVC's GY-HD100, or Sony's Z1, using just a FireWire drive. You can also bring in HD files from a P2 flash card, like the one in Panasonic's HVX200 camera.

You can edit the large Sony HDCAM formats on Xpress Pro HD, but you would need to capture the material on a higher end Avid, such as a Media Composer Adrenaline HD, and then bring the drive to your Xpress Pro HD. Avid has developed an efficient HD codec, called DNxHD, which enables Avid to capture the largest HD datastreams and to compress them into several different levels of compression—all gorgeous. The Media Composer Adrenaline HD could compress the signals, and then you could bring the compressed files to your Xpress Pro HD for editing. You can transfer these files over a network, from an external drive, or even a DVD, then simply select the correct HD format, as shown in Figure 16.5.

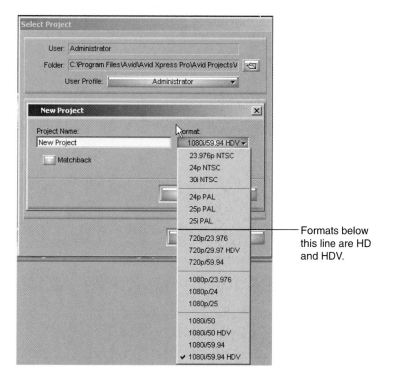

Figure 16.5 HD and HDV format choices.

Capturing HD Tapes

Xpress Pro HD can capture natively over FireWire all of Panasonic's DVCPRO HD flavors, including 1080i/59.94, 1080i/50, 720p/60 and 720p/24. Capturing from Panasonic's 1200A DVCPRO HD deck with a FireWire option isn't any different from capturing from a standard DV deck. You'll need to configure the deck, just like we did in Chapter 6. First, connect the 6-pin FireWire cable from the deck to your computer. When you launch a new project, select 1080i/59.94, 720p/60 or 720p/24 from the Format pull-down menu. In Settings, configure the camera or Panasonic deck, just as we did in Chapter 6.

If you're using Mojo and have a DVCPRO HD camera or deck running via a FireWire cable, go to the Special Menu (see below) and select Device. Choose the IEEE 1394 card, not Mojo.

Panasonic's DVCPRO HD format is compatible with DVCPRO and DVCPRO 50 cameras and decks. In fact the tape can be used in any DVCPRO, DVCPRO 50, and DVCPRO HD cameras or decks. So it's a format a lot of television stations and independent producers who work with television stations are comfortable with.

Capturing HDV Tapes

As we learned earlier, HDV comes in two flavors, Sony's 1080i and JVC's 720p. They both record an HD signal onto DV tape. Chances are you'll use the camera to play the tapes while you capture them onto the Avid, although HDV decks are available for sale or rent. When you've connected the FireWire cable that comes with the camera to your computer, launch the Xpress Pro HD software, and in the New Project dialog box you'll choose either 720p/29.97 HDV or 1080i/59.94 HDV from the Format pull-down menu (Figure 16.5). For example, if you're using the JVC HDV camera, you'll choose 720p/29.97 HDV. If you're using one of Sony's HDV cameras, select 1080i/59.94 HDV. In Settings, configure the HDV camera or HDV deck, just as we did in Chapter 6. There's also a 1080i/50 HDV choice for those shooting with PAL HDV cameras.

Using Mojo to Monitor Your HD or HDV Video

If you can afford it, buy an HD monitor. If funds are short and if you have a Mojo DNA, you may be able to play your HD project on a standard-definition monitor using Mojo. After capturing from the deck to your computer over the FireWire cable, go to Source/Record mode, and disconnect the FireWire cable from the deck and run it to the Mojo unit. Now run the S-Video cable from the Mojo's S-Video output to the television monitor. The easiest configuration is to have a second FireWire card on a separate bus on your CPU. Plug the Mojo into the first card and the deck into the second card, and you can capture and view at the same time. The chances of this working are best if it's a 29.97 frames per second project.

16:9 Source/Record Monitors

To get the Avid to change the aspect ratio of the monitors, simply go to the Source/Record Monitor and click on it to make it active. Then go to the Clip menu and select 16:9 Monitors. Or right-click on the Record Monitor (Mac users, Shift+Ctrl) as shown in Figure 16.6.

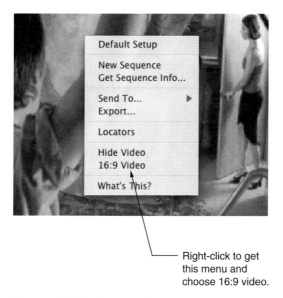

Right-click to get this menu and choose 16:9 video.

Figure 16.6 Opening the 16:9 Monitor view.

Playback Performance

Playback performance can be enhanced by clicking on the Video Quality icon near the Timeline Fast menu (Figure 16.7) and right-clicking it to see your choices (Mac users, Shift+Ctrl and click). The choices depend on whether you have a DV device, like a deck, or Mojo connected, or nothing connected. You'll get better performance the lower the quality you choose.

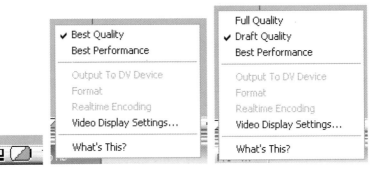

Figure 16.7 Video Quality icon (left) and your choices, depending on your DV device.

Output to an HD Deck

The workflow for sending your HD or HDV project to tape is the same whether you're cutting on HD or DV. We will examine the steps involved in sending your project to tape in Chapter 18.

MAKING A 35-mm THEATRICAL RELEASE PRINT

If you use the Panasonic VariCam, which is 720p and can be shot at 23.976, you can get a 35-mm print made for theatrical release. Just follow the instructions provided in Chapter 18 on pages 376–378. Because there is more picture information, the results will look even better than a standard-definition 23.976 project.

DOWNCONVERTING TO GET THE STANDARD-DEFINITION VERSION

For those of you who edit HD or HDV at the native resolution, you now have your HD or HDV tape, but there still aren't many places to send that HD or HDV tape. So, it's important to be able to *downcovert* the high-definition signal to standard-definition tape. When you do, it will still be in the 16:9 aspect ratio. Most HDV cameras and decks will do the downconversion for you. After recording your sequence back to the camera, run a FireWire cable from the camera to a DV deck and hit play. The Xpress Pro HD can also downconvert your HD and HDVmaterial. Simply select the sequence in the bin, go to the Bin menu, and select Consolidate/Transcode (Figure 16.8).

1. When the Consolidate/Transcode window opens (Figure 16.9), click on the Transcode hot button.
2. Choose a target drive.

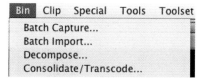

Figure 16.8

3. Choose a Target Video Resolution and Target drive(s).
4. If any audio files need to be converted, check the boxes.
5. Click Transcode.

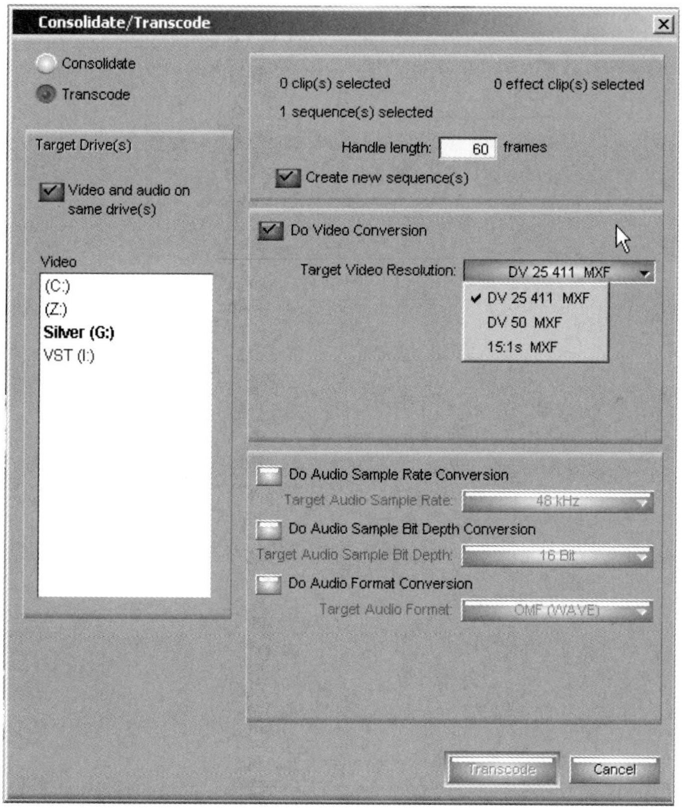

Figure 16.9

Now you'll find a new sequence in your bin that is at the video resolution you selected. It will be anamorphic 16:9, but we learned in Chapter 15 how to make 4:3 versions—either letterbox or full-frame 4:3 centered.

HAVE AN HD YEAR

With Avid's ability to capture HD and HDV natively over FireWire and its ability to transcode to DV 25 or even DV 50, we have the ability to create both high-definition projects and standard-definition projects. Finally, the roadblocks that prevented us from shooting HD are removed.

As editors, it's important for us to stay ahead of the technical curves that come our way so we can give advice to the producers and directors who approach us seeking information about which formats to shoot for different projects. With the emergence of HD and HDV this is truer than ever before. In fact, because there are so many formats to choose from and post-production issues are becoming increasingly complicated, I believe editors will be among the first crew members hired on future projects. So, this is the year we must continue to educate ourselves about HD and HDV issues. Use the information in this chapter as the foundation of your HD knowledge base and build up from here.

As HD formats gain wider acceptance, more and more people will choose to shoot their projects on HD or HDV. In a few years we'll forget we ever shot in standard definition, and what seems complicated now will soon become standard operating procedure. Don't be afraid to tell a client that they're better off shooting in standard definition if you believe that's the case. Don't do HD for the sake of doing it, but if it's right you're ready to show the way.

17

Script Integration

Script Integration is found on Media Composers and all the Xpress family. I believe it is the most dynamic and exciting feature on any NLE system in the world. Yet, despite its strong points, Script Integration is perhaps the least used of all Avid's features. Why? First, you have to have a script. For many films and videos, from experimental to *verite*, there's no script so there's no script to integrate. Even those filmmakers who do work from a script often think Script Integration is just too much work. You can't just open a bin and start editing. You must import the script, drag all your clips to it, and mark individual lines of dialog or action. At first glance, it seems like a waste of good editing time; however, the time spent on the front end is more than made up on the back end. Once you get the hang of it, you'll wonder how you ever got along without it.

HOLLYWOOD-STYLE EDITING

Script Integration is based on the style of editing commonly used for feature films. During production, information about the way each scene was shot gets written onto the script by the script supervisor. The script supervisor draws lines through the script, indicating the amount of the scene each camera angle covers. At the end of production, the editor receives a copy of this "lined script." With the lined script in hand, the editor knows what footage is available for each line of action and dialog. The script supervisor also makes detailed notes about how many times each camera set-up was repeated and which are the preferred takes.

An Avid with Script Integration follows this lined script system but adds its own powerful digital editing tools. You import the script right into the Avid. You select the portion of the script that is covered by a particular clip with your cursor and then drag the clip to that section of the script. Each camera set-up is represented by a *slate*, showing a frame from that clip (Figure 17.1). Different takes are indicated by tabs at the bottom of the slates. Once all the clips are linked

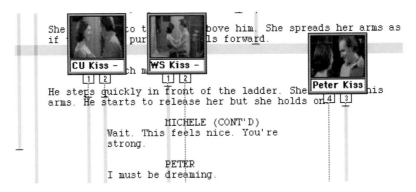

Figure 17.1 A script with attached clips and slates.

to the appropriate sections of the script, you can click on a line of dialog and have the takes play automatically so you can compare them. When you're ready to start editing a scene, you can quickly go through the script, double-click on the preferred takes, and create a rough cut in a matter of minutes. The Avid can handle documentary scripts as easily as narrative scripts, and the set-up and procedures are the same.

AN EXAMPLE

The screen captures in this chapter are from a scene entitled "Gaffer's Delight," which I made with the help of students and staff at Boston University. A copy of the project files, media files, and the script can be found on the DVD that comes with the book. A copy of the lined script is provided at the end of this chapter. The scene was covered with a master shot, showing both actors, and then shot again from many different angles to cover the actors as they move around the set. Each camera set-up was repeated several times, as Take 1, Take 2, and so on. Follow the DVD instructions at the end of this book to mount the project and media files onto your Avid. I'll explain how to bring in the script shortly.

USING TWO MONITORS

This is one editing mode where having two computer monitors can be helpful. One monitor holds all the bins, including the script, and a second monitor holds the Source/Record Monitor and the Timeline. You can do it with one monitor, because the script can be resized and moved around the screen, but it's a lot easier with two. Setting up a second monitor is pretty easy. Read your computer guide to find out how to hook up a second monitor and to set the second monitor's screen resolution. You want *dual display* rather than *mirroring*. In dual-display mode, the second monitor extends the real estate of the Avid so you can drag the

Script window to the second monitor. Video mirroring simply shows the same Avid screen on both monitors. You might have to go to your local computer store to get the right cable to run from you computer to a second monitor. I did.

NAMING CLIPS

Before you even digitize your material, you should give some thought to how you name your clips. Long clip names, such as "Over-the-Shoulder on Peter" or "Close-Up on Hands," are easy to read in your bin when you're in Text View Mode but don't work as well with the slates, which are the heart of Script Integration. Try using clip names such as "1D Tk 1" to indicate the scene, camera set-up, and take, because such names will fit more easily on the script page. If your clip names are too long, the Avid will shorten them, but in doing so the Avid might hide important information. For the purposes of the book, I have used clip names that describe the action to make it easier for the reader to follow. On the DVD, for those of you who will actually edit the scene, I have used the shorter scene and take numbers, such as "1D Tk 1."

GETTING THE SCRIPT

I use Final Draft®, the popular scriptwriting software, as do many of my students. Because Avid and Final Draft have collaborated on Script Integration, it's easy to bring a Final Draft script into the Avid. If you don't have scriptwriting software, you can save a Word document as a Rich Text Format document and that will work.

1. Open your script in Final Draft and, once it's open, choose Save As from the File menu.
2. In the dialog box, go to the Format box and choose Avid Script Based Editing and click on Save (Figure 17.2).

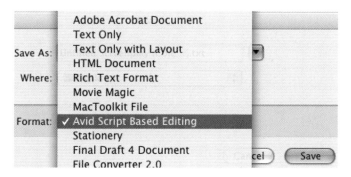

Figure 17.2

Save it to your desktop and launch your Avid system. If you're going to be bringing it to a different computer, save it on a flash drive or Zip disk. Just in case your version of Final Draft isn't compatible with the latest Avid software, go to the Format box and save your script as Rich Text Format—which will work as well.

Once you've launched your Avid software, open the project and follow these simple steps:

1. Click on the Project window to make it the active window.
2. Select New Script from the File menu.
3. Search through the directory dialog box that appears and find the script file.
4. Select the file and click the Open button.

Your script will appear in the Bin monitor, looking much like this (Figure 17.3):

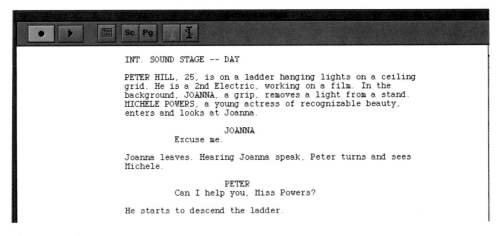

Figure 17.3 The script, as it appears in the Avid.

The Avid will also create a special script bin, bearing the same name as the script file you're bringing in. When you close the script, it will go inside the script bin, as shown in Figure 17.4.

Figure 17.4

GETTING STARTED

Your script should look like it did in your screenplay software. You can make changes to the script once it's in the Avid. You can delete lines of dialog or action (the Delete key won't work—use the Cut command to remove text instead), and you can move segments or scenes around, but you can't change individual words. In fact, you can't even select a word. The smallest segment of the script you can work with is an individual line. You'll see this makes sense once you start working with it. It's editing software, not scriptwriting software. The way you select lines or sections of your script is pretty standard. You either lasso the lines using the mouse or click on one line and keep pressing the Shift key to include more lines. You'll find lassoing text the best way to go.

LINKING CLIPS TO THE SCRIPT

Bringing clips from your bin to the script and linking them to specific lines is actually quite simple:

1. Open the script by double-clicking on it in the script bin.
2. Open the bin containing your clips (Figure 17.5).
3. Select the part of the script you want the first clip to cover by lassoing the script lines with the mouse. That portion of the script becomes highlighted.
4. Go to your clips bin, select the first clip, and drag its icon from the bin to the script.

A *slate*, or frame from that clip, will appear above the text (see Figure 17.5). The slate will show a frame from that shot, include the name of the clip, and have a box (or boxes) at the bottom to show different takes. Once you've placed the first clip onto the script, you'll want to drag additional takes to that slate.

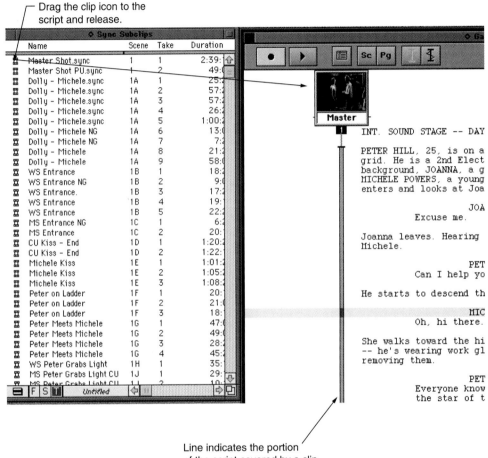

Figure 17.5

ADDING TAKES

The process of adding takes to a slate is similar to placing the first clip onto the script. Whichever take you brought over first establishes the slate. The next take goes on top of that slate and adds a second little box at the bottom. There's no difference, really, between the first take (the one you dragged onto the script first) and the second take. But, first, you must create a column for the takes so take numbers appear in the little boxes below the Slate.

Takes don't show up in Brief View, so you need to switch to Text View.

1. Go to the Headings column in the Bin menu and select it.
2. In the list of headings, find the Take heading and click on it to select it.
3. Click OK.
4. In the bin, scroll to the right and find the Take column heading, click on the word Take so the entire column is highlighted, and then drag the column all the way to the left, just next to the Name column.

Now, enter the take information by clicking in the column (Figure 17.6).

Figure 17.6

To add takes to a slate:

1. Lasso the portion of the script that the second take covers.
2. In your shots bin, click and drag the clip that represents the second take, and drag it onto the slate already in the script.

Now you can see that the slate has two boxes hanging from it, one for each take (Figure 17.7). Let's call them *take tabs*. Clicking on either take tab will select that take. The frame in the slate will change depending on which take is selected.

Figure 17.7   Take tabs.

There's a faster way to create slates and add takes to that slate. Say you have a shot with five takes. Simply lasso the portion of the script the shot covers, lasso or Shift–click all five takes in the bin, and drag them all to the script at once. In Figure 17.8, you can see that I have dragged several clips, some with multiple takes, onto the script.

Remember that the key to this process is lassoing portions of the script that are covered by that particular clip. Once the portion is highlighted, when you drag the clip the Avid will place the vertical lines appropriately. The end result will look like a professionally lined shooting script.

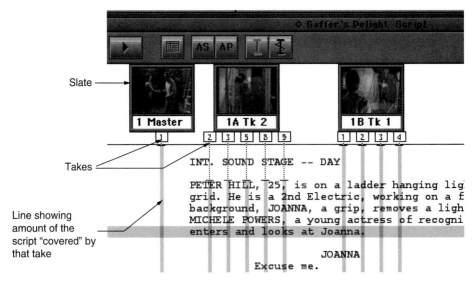

Figure 17.8

CHANGING THE SLATE

You can make the same changes to a slate as you would to a frame in Frame view in the bin. To change the size of the slate, choose Enlarge or Reduce from the Edit menu. To change the representative frame that appears in the slate:

1. Select the take you want to change. Click on the take tab or take line.
2. Press the step-one-frame or step-ten-frame key, stepping either forward or backward.

Don't use J–K–L keys, because that won't work. Click on the take tab and then press and hold the step-one-frame-forward key (the 2 key on the keyboard) to go forward. Press the step-one-frame-back key (the 1 key on the keyboard) to step backward.

REVIEW

In "Gaffer's Delight," I have a complicated dolly shot (1A). Because there is a lot of actor and camera movement, we shot it nine times, resulting in nine takes, although only five of the nine were worth capturing. First I highlight the portion of the script that the first good take covers. Then I click on that take and drag it to the script. A slate appears with a box and a line running through the script all the way to the last line covered by that dolly shot. If the other four takes ended about the same place, I would Shift–click on them in the bin and drag all four of them onto the slate that's there.

Individual takes often end at a different point in the script. Takes 2 and 3 might get cut early because there's a bump in the dolly shot or an actor flubs a line. Only the completed takes end at the same point. If I have shorter takes that are worth looking at, I'll treat each take individually. I lasso the portion of the script that Take 2 covers and then drag it to the slate. Then I lasso the area Take 3 covers and drag it to the slate. Another way to handle this is to adjust the take lines.

ADJUSTING TAKE LINES

The vertical lines showing how much of the script a single take covers are called *take lines*. Where the line begins and ends is denoted by a short horizontal dash, called a beginning or ending mark. Let's say that you highlighted too much of the script, and the vertical line the Avid draws goes beyond where the shot actually ends or the take starts later than indicated. It's easy to correct where these lines start and end (Figure 17.9).

1. Go to the End Mark (or Start Mark) and hold down the Command key (Mac) or the Ctrl key (Windows). The icon changes shape.
2. Drag the mark to the correct line in the script and release.

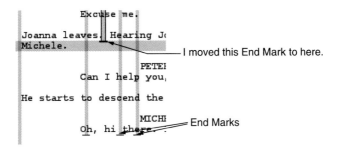

Figure 17.9

SELECTING MULTIPLE TAKES

It's helpful to be able to select more than one slate or take at a time. To select a single slate or take, just click on the take tab. Shift–click to add additional slates or takes. Another way to select multiple takes and slates is to lasso the portion of the script covered by the takes you wish to select.

MOVING SLATES

You might find that a slate ends up obscuring a line of dialog from view and you want to move it to another place on the script page. Just click on the slate with your mouse and drag it to the left or right or up and down; however, if you want to move the slate vertically and at the same time change the position of the take lines, hold down the Command key (Mac) or Ctrl key (Windows) as you move the slate.

DELETING TAKES AND SLATES

You may make a mistake and put the wrong take on a slate or put the wrong clip in the script. To delete a slate or take, click on it and press the Delete key. The resulting dialog box looks intimidating (Figure 17.10). Just press OK. The takes in the bin will still be there, but the slate (here made up of two takes) will be removed from the script.

Figure 17.10

LOADING AND PLAYING TAKES

We still have more work to do before the script is truly integrated and we can take advantage of all Script Integration has to offer. Before we take the next step, let's play around a little to get some satisfaction for all our work. If you double-click on a take tab, the clip will load in the Source Monitor. If you want to select all the takes for a shot, just lasso the take lines and they all will be selected. Now double-click on any take, and they'll all move to the Source Monitor.

You can play takes in two different ways. You can use the Play keys or J–K–L keys once the clips are loaded into the Source Monitor, just as you would any other clips. A better way is to lasso the take lines or Shift–click the take tabs, and then press the Play key at the top of the script window (Figure 17.11) or you can use the spacebar.

Figure 17.11

Either method will play the clips you selected one after another, in a continuous loop. Now you can get a sense of the power of Script Integration. You don't have to waste time messing with the Source Monitor menu or using Play keys. One button will load the takes in the Source Monitor *and* play them. If you want to stop at any point, hit the spacebar.

THE TAB KEY

In earlier versions of Xpress software, I recommended the use of the Tab key as a helpful tool in the Script Integration toolbox; however, recent upgrades have resulted in an annoying bug, which Avid has yet to fix. I have brought this to the company's attention and have been promised it will be fixed by the time this edition is published, so I will explain how the Tab key *should* work. Before trying this, save all your work. If your system freezes when following these instructions, the bug hasn't been fixed. Media Composer versions don't have this bug.

The Tab key on the keyboard can be very useful when used with this special Play Key. After selecting the takes you want to look at, press this special Play Key (Figure 7.11) and they will load in the Source Monitor and begin to play in order. If you want to see the next take, without waiting for the current one to finish, press the Tab key. The Tab key gives you control over what you watch. Often you don't want to see the rest of the take. You want to jump ahead to the next one, and the Tab key gives you that ability. This works with slates as well as takes. If you lasso a section of your script, including one or more slates, all the takes for every shot will load and play. Let's practice.

1. Select one or more takes by:
   * Lassoing a portion of the script covered by several takes, or
   * Shift–clicking on several take tabs.
   You will see that the tabs are dark (selected).
2. Press the Play Key at the top of the Script window.
3. Press the Tab key to jump to the next take.

PLACING SCRIPT MARKS

To harness the power of Script Integration, we need to take one more step. We need to place *script marks*. These marks, when placed in the script, will allow you to look at all the material covering any portion of the script you want—and only that portion. It's time consuming at first, to place all these marks, but once you get the hang of it, it's not so bad.

When you place a script mark, a double-sided arrow appears on a take line. When you double-click on this arrow, the take loads in the Source Monitor on that precise line. You don't have to look at what comes before it.

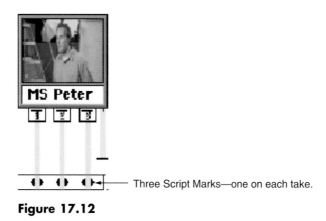

 —— Three Script Marks—one on each take.

Figure 17.12

In order to place script marks, you'll need the command that places script marks in the script. Go to the Tools menu and open the Command Palette.

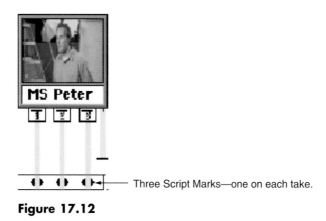

—— Add Script Mark

Figure 17.13

Go to the Other tab, and you'll see Add Script Mark. With the Button to Button Reassignment box selected, click and drag the Add Script Mark button to any one of your Source Monitor buttons, as I have in Figure 17.14.

Source Monitor with the Add
Script Mark button

Figure 17.14

Now, go to the script and find the take you want to mark first. Let's say you want to place a script mark on Take 3, where Peter says, "Everyone knows who you are." Double-click anywhere on that take line. Take 3 will be selected, it will load in the Source Monitor, and that line will be highlighted.

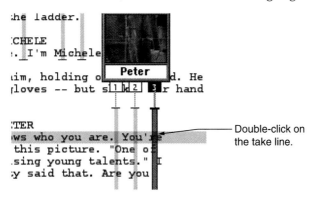

Double-click on
the take line.

Figure 17.15

Right now, the entire take will load from the beginning of the clip. You must play the clip in the Source Monitor as you normally would, using J–K–L keys (not the spacebar). When you get to the part of the clip where Peter is about to say the line, press the K key to stop. Now, using the cursor, single-click on the take line where it intersects with that line of dialog, as shown in Figure 17.15. Now press the Add Script Mark button. A double-sided arrow will appear at that spot in the script. Now, that point in the script is linked to that point in the clip (Figure 17.16).

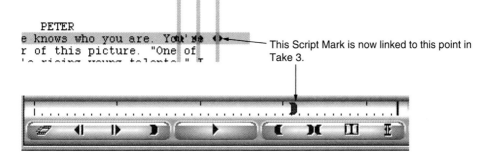

This Script Mark is now linked to this point in
Take 3.

Figure 17.16

Let's add script marks to the other takes of this line of dialog.

1. Double-click on the take line for Take 2. Take 2 will load in the Source Monitor.
2. Play through the clip until the actor reaches the line and then shuttle back until just before he speaks.
3. Single-click on the take line where it intersects with that line of dialog, as shown in Figure 17.15.
4. Press the Add Script Mark button.

Repeat these steps until all the takes of this line of dialog have script marks as in Figure 17.17.

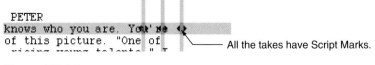

Figure 17.17

PLAYING MARKED TAKES

Let's see how this works. With your mouse, lasso Peter's line of dialog so you are lassoing all the take lines and script marks.

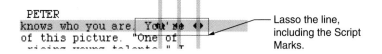

Now press the Play Key on top of the Script window or the spacebar. All four takes will load into the Source Monitor and start playing, not from the beginning of the clip but starting just before the line. They will keep playing in a continuous loop, first Take 1, then Take 2, and so on. If there is a script mark below the one you've lassoed, the take will end there and jump to the next take. If there is no script mark below the one you lassoed, use the Tab key (if it's working) to jump to the next take.

You will notice that if the takes are longish and have a lot of material after the line you've marked, you'll want to keep placing marks at other points on these takes. (This way you don't need to use the Tab key to jump to the next take.) I like to place a script mark whenever an actor starts a new segment of dialog.

In Figure 17.18, I have placed additional marks on Peter's next line of dialog. When I lasso the first row of script marks and press the Play key above the Script window, Take 1 loads and starts where I want it to and loads the next take as soon as Michele finishes the line, "No. I came here looking for you."

```
                PETER
    Everyone knows who you are. You're ◀▶◀▶ ◀───── First Script
    the star of this picture. "One of                Marks
    America's rising young talents." I
    think Variety said that. Are you
    lost?

                MICHELE
    No. I came here looking for you.

                PETER
    Me?                           ◀▶ ◀▶ ◀▶◀ ───── Additional Script
                                                   Marks are placed here.
```

Figure 17.18

Another great thing about having lots of script marks is that any time you want to play a line of dialog or go to a place in any scene in the script you can just click on the script mark and hit the spacebar. That scene loads and plays right where you clicked. And by lassoing a number of takes, you can concentrate on just one section of dialog and have all the takes of that line play in a loop. You can see and hear the differences and decide which one works best.

A FASTER WAY TO PLACE SCRIPT MARKS

In the previous section, I described how to manually place script marks. There's a faster way, although it is trickier to master. You will play a take and click on the take line at the point where you want to insert a script mark—and it will appear right where you clicked.

1. Select the first take you would like to mark by clicking on the take tab.
2. Go to the top of the Script window and press the Record button (pink).

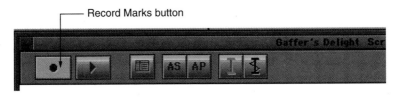

Record Marks button

Figure 17.19

The first take's vertical line will turn green, and the clip will load into the Source Monitor. It will start to play.

3. As soon as the dialog or action appears in the Source Monitor, position the mouse and click on the take line in the Script window where you want the script mark placed. A script mark will appear (be patient, it may take a second to appear).

4. Move down the take line with your mouse, and as the take continues to play in the Source Monitor keep clicking on the take line to place additional script marks.

5. Click on the keyboard's spacebar to stop the process.

6. Now select the next take tab and repeat the process.

You may find that the script marks don't appear as soon as you click on the line. Don't worry, they will appear soon. Just keep clicking on the green take line.

This method is obviously faster, but it's tricky because, unless you know the script well, you don't click the take line in time. If you're a bit late, the mark falls a few beats after the line of dialog begins. That's a problem, because the whole point of marking the script is to take you to the lines you want to review—not halfway into the next line.

Fortunately there are several remedies for this. You can click the Record button again and then click on the misplaced script mark at the correct moment. You'll replace that mark with a new one and correct the sync point in the clip. If the script mark is way off, you can simply delete it. Just click on it and press the Delete key. A dialog box appears. Click OK. Now press the Record button and place a new script mark.

THE FASTEST WAY

Perhaps the fastest way of all is to get an assistant editor and have him or her do all of this work for you. Really, in some ways, Script Integration was designed for feature-length projects—particularly the ones employing several assistants. On the other hand, because most people have never taken the time to learn Script Integration, this might be a good way for you to get your foot in the door and land that first job on a feature. You master this, and you'll have skills few others possess.

MOVING MARKED TAKES

You may find that the script mark is linked properly but has landed in the wrong place on the script. That's an easy fix. Just press the Command (Ctrl) key. The cursor changes. Click on the script mark, and drag it up or down on the take line.

LOOKING AT YOUR COVERAGE

Not only does this system work for takes involving a specific slate (or camera set-up) but it is also designed to show you all the choices for a specific portion of your script. Take the time to place script marks on all the takes for all the slates covering a section of your script. Now, lasso *all* the script marks for a specific line of dialog, including all the coverage. As you can see in Figure 17.20, I have lassoed the wide shot of Peter and the medium shot of Peter. Now, when I press the spacebar, I'll see Peter saying his line in the wide shot, and as soon as that is finished I'll see, in quick succession, Take 1, Take 2, and Take 3 from the medium shot.

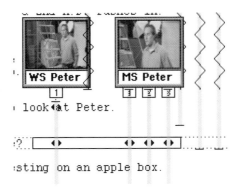

Figure 17.20

PAGE AND SCENE NUMBERS

Although your script has scene and page numbers, they aren't recognized by the Avid. You'll need to add new ones. The steps for adding scene and page numbers are the same.

1. Go to the first line of the new page or new scene and click it.
2. Click either the Add Scene (AS) or Add Page (AP) button on the Script Window, and a dialog box appears.

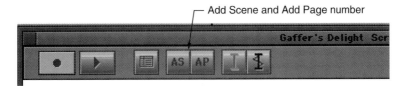

Figure 17.21

3. Type the page/scene number and click OK.

The nice thing about adding page and scene numbers is that you can now use the Goto Scene or Goto Page commands in the Script menu (see Figure 17.23) to jump to the scene or page you want. Without page and scene numbers, a 120-page script would be difficult to work with. To change the number, repeat the process. The dialog box will now say Change Scene or Page Number. To delete page and scene numbers, select the line containing the number and press Delete.

FIND SCRIPT

The Find Script button is another handy command button that helps you stay in control of your script. Place this command key on one of your rows of buttons in your Source Monitor or a Fast menu. You need to go to the Command Palette to find it. It's in the Other tab.

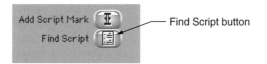

Say you have a clip loaded in the Source Monitor, and you're not sure which part of the script it comes from. Just click on the Find Script button and the Avid will scroll to the place in the script where the clip is linked and will highlight that section.

OFF-SCREEN DIALOG

When shooting a scene involving two actors, more often than not the director will shoot it several times from different camera angles. In the simplest form of coverage, there is a master shot of both actors and then individual close-ups of the two actors. When the close-ups are shot, one actor is on-camera (on-screen) and the other actor is standing off-screen but saying his or her dialog so the on-screen actor has someone to act with. When the script supervisor "lines the script" during shooting, jagged lines are drawn on the script to indicate off-screen dialog. You can easily add these jagged lines to the script in the Avid.

1. Lasso the portion of the script where you want to place off-screen marks. Make sure you lasso only those take lines that represent off-screen dialog (Figure 17.22).

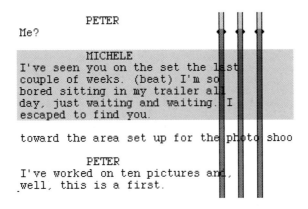

Figure 17.22

2. Click on the Off-Screen button.

Your script will now have a series of jagged lines, showing which lines of dialog were spoken off-screen.

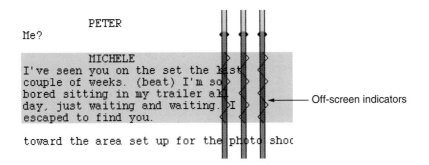

ONLY ONE TAKE LINE

Sometimes, when you have a lot of takes for a particular shot, all those take lines can overwhelm the script and make it hard to look at. To show only one take line, go to the Script menu and select Show All Takes. Only one take line will appear on the page and all the rest will disappear; however, if you then select a slate by clicking on it, all of that slate's take lines will appear. If you select Show All Takes from the Script menu, you'll reverse the action and all the take lines will appear once more.

COLOR LINES

Last, but not least, you can place one of six colors on your take lines to indicate a preferred take or a problem or whatever you want to highlight. Just go to the Script menu (Figure 17.23), and select Color; a choice of six colors will appear. Select one.

Now follow these steps:

1. Lasso the portion of the take line (or the entire take) that you want to color.
2. Click on the Color button on top of the Script window.

Lassoing the colored section and clicking the Color button again will remove the color.

Figure 17.23 The Script menu.

IDENTIFYING THE PREFERRED TAKE

The ability to mark the preferred take with a color is all part of the organizing process that takes place before the editor even walks in the door. Often on a feature, the director will indicate which take is the preferred one during the screening of the dailies. Using the notes supplied to the editorial department, an assistant links all the takes to the script and then highlights the preferred takes in red. With all that done, the editor can sit down and put together a rough cut of the scene in a matter of minutes.

With the preferred takes color-coded, the editor need only go through the script and click on the script mark for the take marked in red. The preferred take will load into the Source Monitor, with an IN mark already in place. The editor then plays to the spot where she wants to end the shot and places an OUT and then hits Splice or Overwrite. She clicks on the next color-coded take and splices that into the Timeline, repeating the process until each color-coded take has been placed in the Timeline.

Yes, it'll be a bit rough, but by using Single-Roller Trim she can clean up each transition, and in a matter of minutes the entire scene has been put together. Now the real editing can begin. Maybe a preferred take doesn't work as well as hoped, once it's been cut into the sequence. It's easy to replace it. Try another take. Often it's better to whittle away all the choices, put together a rough cut, and work from there, rather than going over all the choices a hundred times until everything looks like a blur and you're lost in the land of indecision.

OTHER MENU ITEMS

There are a few other Script menu items that you may find useful; they let you fine-tune the appearance of the script or make it easier for you to navigate through it:

- *Left Margin.* You can drag the box located in the lower right-hand corner of the script to resize the right-hand margin, but not the left-hand margin. Left Margin lets you make this adjustment.
- *Interpolate Position.* With this command you can click in a take line within a script, and the image in the Source Monitor updates to the approximate position in the take where you have clicked. If you deselect this option, the Source monitor does not interpolate when you click in a take line.
- *Hold Slates Onscreen.* With this command selected, when you scroll through the script the slate will stay in view until you scroll past the point covered by that slate, at which point it will disappear. This lets you see the slate for as long as possible as you scroll through the script.

A SELECT FEW

You are now one of only a handful of people who know how to use Script Integration. I think we can all agree, Script Integration doesn't make sense for every project, but for those script-based projects involving lots of camera coverage with multiple takes, it is worth the effort. And, if you have an assistant to do the grunt work, think how quickly you can really get to the heart of the scene. If you're the person hired to do the grunt work, maybe Script Integration doesn't seem so special. But, hey, at least you've got a job.

1.   INT. SOUND STAGE -- DAY

PETER HILL, 25, is on a ladder hanging lights on a ceiling
grid. He is a 2nd Electric working on a film. In the
background, JOANNA removes a light from a stand. MICHELE
POWERS, a young actress of recognizable beauty, enters and
looks at Joanna.

                    JOANNA
              Excuse me.

Joanna leaves. Hearing Joanna speak, Peter turns and sees
Michele.

                    PETER
              Can I help you, Miss Powers?

He starts to descend the ladder.

                    MICHELE
              Oh, hi there. I'm Michele Powers.

She walks toward the him, holding out her hand. He hesitates
-- he's wearing work gloves -- but shakes her hand after
removing them.

                    PETER
              Everyone knows who you are. You're
              the star of this picture. "One of
              America's rising young talents." I
              think Variety said that. Are you
              lost?

                    MICHELE
              No. I came here looking for you.

                    PETER
              Me?

                    MICHELE
              I've seen you on the set the last
              couple of weeks. (beat) I get so
              bored sitting in my trailer all
              day, just waiting and waiting. So I
              escaped to find you.

She walks toward the area set up for the photo shoot.

                    PETER
              I've worked on ten pictures and,
              well, this is a first.

                    MICHELE
              What are you doing?

2.

1   1M

Peter walks up and stands near her.

                    PETER
              Talking to a movie star.

Michele smiles.

                    PETER (CONT'D)
              I'm pre-rigging lights for
              tomorrow. The fashion model scene.

                    MICHELE
              Right.   1K

She walks to the ladder and starts to climb up.

                    PETER
              Whoa! Not so fast.

He chases after her and reaches the foot of the ladder.
                                      1E
                    MICHELE
              It's fun up here.

                    PETER
              You fall and get hurt, I'm
              unemployed.

She descends to two steps above him. She spreads her arms as
if to fly and purposely falls forward.

                    MICHELE
              Catch me!   1D   1L
He steps quickly in front of the ladder. She lands in his
arms. He starts to release her but she holds on.

                    MICHELE (CONT'D)
              Wait. This feels nice. You're
              strong.

                    PETER
              I must be dreaming.

                    MICHELE
              Will you kiss me?

Peter looks into her eyes and is encouraged by the warmth he
sees. He kisses her gently, softly. Finally, she breaks off.

                    MICHELE
              Oh my God! Can you kiss!

3.

1   1D   1E   1K   1L

Peter releases her. She holds her chest to catch her breath.

                        MICHELE (CONT'D)
          None of my leads _ever_ kissed like
          that.

                        PETER
          Come on? What about Brad, or Matt,
          or Ben?

                        MICHELE
          They were good, -- but you!

She moves back to him and settles into his arms.

                        MICHELE (CONT'D)
          Could we try that one more time?

Suddenly there's a commotion. ELAINE, a 2nd A.D. rushes in.
Peter and Michele separate quickly.

                        ELAINE
          There you are. You were due in
          wardrobe twenty minutes ago.
          Please, we've got to hurry.

                1H   1J

Michele starts to leave, but turns to look at Peter.

                        MICHELE
          Um. (beat) What's your name?

Peter laughs. He grabs a nearby 2K resting on an apple box.

                        PETER
          Maybe that's for me to know and you
          to find out. (beat) If that's um,
          what you want to do.

He begins to climb the ladder with the heavy 2K. There is a
gleam in Michele's eye as she turns to go.

                        FADE TO BLACK

18

Finishing

I think successful video and filmmakers are product oriented. Let's face it, a lot of people start films and videos, but only the truly dedicated finish them. It's easy to give up, to run out of steam, to take a never-ending break from a project. Making a film or video is a lot of hard work, and often you do it for little reward. I think the reason some people finish their projects while others abandon theirs is that they love having a product. They can't stop until they hold something in their hands, whether it's a videotape, film, or DVD.

"Here," they say, "is my project. Come look at it."

They're the ones I admire. They finished. It's an accomplishment worthy of our praise. Let's be like them. Let's learn how to finish a project on the Avid.

PATHS TO THE FINISH LINE

Here are five paths that lead to a finished project:

1. You can output your sequence to videotape.
2. You can create an Edit Decision List (EDL) and take your tapes to a tape facility for an online editing session.
3. If your project originated on film, you can create a Cut List so a negative cutter can conform your camera negative to the Avid sequence, and from that you can make a 16-mm or 35-mm print.
4. You can create a DVD.
5. You can make a 35-mm theatrical film print from your 23.976 video project.

Chapter 19 is devoted to path number 3. It takes you through all the steps involved in getting a print of your film. In this chapter, we're going to concentrate on outputting your sequence to tape, creating an EDL, sending your project to a DVD, and getting a 35-mm print from your 23.976 video project.

EXAMINING YOUR MEDIA DRIVES

It often happens that, just when you're almost ready to output your project to tape or to a DVD, there's no more space left on your media drives. Most drives behave best when they are only 90% full and get sluggish as they reach full capacity. So let's check our drive space.

You can easily see how much room you have on your media drives by choosing the Hardware Tool in the Tools menu. In Figure 18.1, you can see that the Media Drive (F:) is empty and the FireWire Drive (I:) has lots of available space.

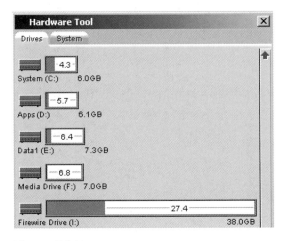

Figure 18.1

But look at Figure 18.2. Here, the Media Drive that is being used for storing a feature-length documentary is nearly full, and we've got a few more graphics and titles to add.

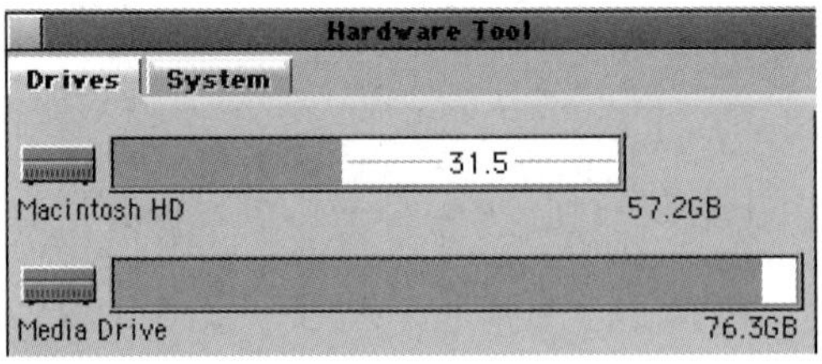

Figure 18.2

One simple way to take back some much-needed storage space is to get rid of your unreferenced precomputes. Unreferenced precomputes are the mohair sweaters of the digital editing world—they take up space and you never use them.

Deleting Unreferenced Precomputes

A *precompute* is the new media the computer creates when you render an effect or a title. If, while editing your sequence, you change or delete some of your titles or effects, those old precomputes don't get deleted. They remain on the media drive, taking up valuable space. These hidden hard-drive hogs are called *unreferenced precomputes*. It's frightening how many of them you'll find and amazing how satisfying it is to blow them away.

Why, when you delete unwanted effects, does the Avid hold onto the pre-computes? One reason is so you can use Undo to change your mind. If your Avid didn't hang on to the precompute, it couldn't perform the Undo. You also may want to remove the effects from sequence 5, but keep them for sequences 1 through 4. Because the Avid doesn't know what you want, it holds onto all of the unreferenced precomputes. I understand all that; however, I do think Avid should rewrite the software so you can determine a length of time (in days or weeks) after which unreferenced precomputes are automatically removed from your system. You shouldn't have to keep tracking them down, like some Vin Diesel wannabe.

You'll use the Media Tool for this mission. Go to the bin that holds all your sequences and Shift–click all the ones you still use.

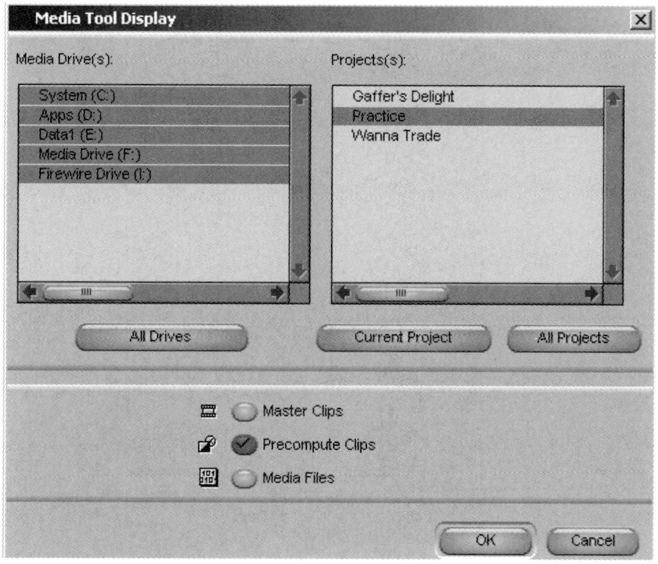

Figure 18.3 Media Tool.

1. In the Tools menu, open the Media Tool.
2. In the Media Tool Display, click on All Drives and Current Project.
3. Select Precompute Clips. Deselect the other choices. Click OK.

4. Now, go back to the bin that contains your sequences. Make sure the sequences you care about are highlighted. If not, Shift–click to select them. Go to the Bin Fast menu and choose Select Media Relatives.

Fast menu

Bins

Reverse Selection
Select Offline Items
Select Media Relatives
Select Unreferenced Clips

Align to Grid   Ctrl+T
Fill Window
Fill Sorted
Select Unrendered Titles

5. Go to the Media Tool window and click on the title bar to activate the window. All the precomputes associated with the selected sequences are highlighted. They're the ones you want to keep.
6. Go to the Media Tool's Fast menu and choose Reverse Selection. Now all the unreferenced precomputes are revealed.
7. Press the Delete key. In the Delete Media dialog box that appears, make sure only the precomputes are selected (Figure 18.4).

Delete Media

Selected captured clip(s)

V Delete video file(s)

A1 Delete audio file(s)

A2 Delete audio file(s)

A3 Delete audio file(s)

A4 Delete audio file(s)

A5 Delete audio file(s)

A6 Delete audio file(s)

A7 Delete audio file(s)

A8 Delete audio file(s)

Selected 557 precomputed file(s)

☑ V Delete 192 video file(s)

A Delete 365 audio file(s)

OK   Cancel

Figure 18.4

There are hundreds of unreferenced precomputes in this project. I deselect the audio files because they take up no space, so why delete them? The video precomputes are a different story. Click OK, and they're gone. Now you've got some space to work with.

CAN YOU SKIP AHEAD?

If you captured your material at the same resolution as you plan to send it out, you can skip the next few sections and go straight to the "Checking Your Audio" section. For example, if you captured at DV 25 or DV 50, and all the material in your Timeline is at DV 25 or DV 50, there is no need to recapture at a different resolution, as outlined in the next section. Pass Go (skip to "Checking Your Audio"), and collect $200 (be thankful you don't have to digest the next few pages).

RECAPTURING YOUR SEQUENCE

These next few steps are for Xpress Pro, Xpress Pro HD, and Media Composer users who are using their Avids for more complicated projects and need to recapture their entire final sequence. Here are several reasons why you might want to do this:

1. You edited the project using an offline resolution, such as 15:1s, and now you want to recapture at DV 25, 2:1, or 1:1.
2. You shot on film and captured tapes with timecode and keycode burned into the image. You want to recapture the final sequence using tapes that don't have those numbers burned in (see Chapter 19).

Both reasons will necessitate more drive space. The first reason will require a *lot* more drive space. True, you won't be recapturing all the tapes, just the clips in the final sequence, but even so you're going to recapture at a much higher resolution. If your sequence is over 15 minutes long, you may need to purchase an additional drive.

Keep in mind that you will not be recapturing your audio. That stays just as is. You are only recapturing picture. All your sound tracks will be untouched.

Preparing to Recapture Your Sequence

There are several steps you need to take before you start to recapture:

1. Make sure you have all your source videotapes with you.
2. Create a new bin and call it "Online."
3. Duplicate your final sequence (select it and hit Command–D or Ctrl–D) in its original bin and drag the duplicate copy to the new Online bin.
4. Name the duplicate sequence "Online Sequence."

5. Delete all the audio tracks in the duplicate. To do this, place the Online Sequence in the Record Monitor so the tracks appear in the Timeline. Select the audio tracks and deselect the video tracks. Hit the Delete key.

6. Close all your bins except the newly created Online bin.

The Recapturing Process

In order to recapture your sequence, you'll need to hook up your videotape deck. See Chapter 6 for suggestions on how to do this. Remember to open the Video Tool and set it to DV 25, 1:1, component, composite, or S-video—depending on your source tapes. Now we're going to get gruesome.

Decompose

One of the nicest features on the Xpress Pro, Xpress Pro HD, and Media Composer comes with the most grisly name—Decompose. When you *decompose* your final sequence, it breaks the sequence into all the many clips that are part of that sequence. Once the sequence is broken down this way, you can organize the clips any way you wish, select them in the bin, and batch capture. Without Decompose, the Avid controls the recapture process, and there's no way to change or stop it. With Decompose, you can recapture some clips today, then quit and do the rest tomorrow.

Let's begin:

1. Select the sequence in the Online bin (it should be the only one there).
2. Choose Decompose from the Clip menu.
3. Deselect the choice Offline media only.
4. Select a Handle Length. The default (60 frames) will work fine.
5. Click OK.

Clips with the suffix "new" will appear in the bin. These are all the clips that make up the final sequence, but they are all off-line, waiting to be selected and recaptured. When you recapture, each clip will have an extra 60 frames on either end—the "handle." This gives you flexibility in case you want to tweak a shot a few frames either way.

6. Get the Capture Tool from the Tools menu.
7. Select the finishing Resolution—DV 25, 1:1, or DV 50.
8. In the Video pull-down menu, select Composite, SVideo, Component, or DV.

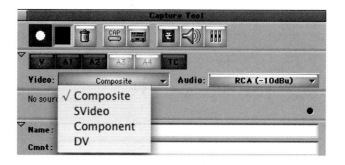

9. Choose the target drive (your Media Drive).
10. In the Online bin, select the "new" clips. You can select them all, you can select as many clips as you have time to capture, or you can first organize them by tape (use Text View Mode to see which tape the clips came from).
11. Select Batch Capture from the Bin menu.
12. The Avid will ask you for the first tape, by name. Feed it the tape and click OK. When all the clips from tape 001 are captured, it will ask for the next tape, or, if all the clips you selected have been captured, you'll get a message saying "Batch Capture Complete."
13. Continue until all the clips have been captured.

TIMECODE BREAKS

It will sometimes happen during the batch capture process that, when the Avid is searching for the next clip to capture, you'll suddenly get an error message saying the Avid can't execute the preroll. Don't panic. The Avid is trying to get to the timecode for the next clip, but it bumps up against a break in the time-code. Abort the batch capture and fast forward until you find the timecode the Avid was searching for. You are crossing over the timecode break. Select the remaining clips and select Batch Capture. Now the Avid will find the timecode and continue batch capturing.

REPLACING YOUR AUDIO TRACKS

When the recapturing process is complete, you'll see that you need to restore the audio tracks that you deleted earlier.

1. To get your sound tracks, open the bin that contains the final sequence—the one at the lower resolution.
2. Click and drag the sequence icon to the Source Monitor (not the Record Monitor).
3. In the Source Monitor, go to the very first frame of the offline sequence. Mark an IN. Go to the very last frame and mark an OUT.
4. Now, make your Timeline active and go to the very first frame of the Online Sequence. Mark an IN.
5. Now you're ready to splice the sound tracks into your Online Timeline. To do this you will need to create new audio tracks—as many as there are source tracks (Command–U or Ctrl–U).
6. In the Timeline, select the audio tracks and deselect your video tracks. Now hit the Splice button. All your audio should splice into the Timeline.

RECREATING TITLE MEDIA

If you recaptured at a higher resolution, you may need to recreate your titles because they were created at a lower resolution:

1. Select all your titles by selecting the video tracks and marking an IN and an OUT in the Online Timeline.
2. Go to the Clip menu and choose Recreate Title Media. Your titles will be recreated at your new resolution.

CHECKING YOUR AUDIO

Before you output the final sequence to tape, examine your sound one last time. Get a pair of isolating headphones that prevents you from hearing anything other than what's coming through the earpieces. Are your dialog tracks centered? They should be. Open the Audio Mixer Tool and fix any dialog or narration that is panned left or right. Open the Audio Tool and set the Input/Output toggle to O so you're monitoring the sound levels you are sending out. Check your levels one last time.

OUTPUTTING TO TAPE

Now your sequence is just as you wished. It looks and sounds perfect. You're itching to get it onto tape, but first there are a few things you need to do to get ready. You should import SMPTE color bars and cut them into the beginning of your sequence. Chapter 14 walks you through the process. Make sure you import the file at the correct resolution and that you bring in at least 60 seconds. Cut them into your sequence. If you sync-lock all your tracks before you splice in the bars, everything will stay in sync.

Now cut in a reference head tone at 1000 Hz to go with the SMPTE bars. To create this tone:

1. Get the Audio Tool from the Tools menu.
2. Click and hold on the PH box in the Audio Tool. A menu will open. Select the last option in the menu, Create Tone Media (Figure 18.5).

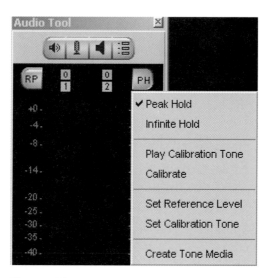

Figure 18.5

3. In the dialog box, set the reference tone to a desired decibel and choose the length of tone in seconds. A tone of −14 dB is the default setting, which works nicely. You need a length to match your SMPTE bars—60 seconds.
4. Click OK.
5. The 1000-Hz tone appears in your bin as a clip. Overwrite it into your sequence so it lines up with the bars. Now you have bars and tone.
6. Put in 15 seconds of black (fill) on all your tracks between the bars and tone and the first frame of your show.

Now get the Audio Mixer Tool. With the Audio Tool still open, play the bars and tone and check to see that the 1000-Hz tone lands at −14 dB. If it doesn't fall precisely on that line, use the slider on the Audio Mixer Tool to adjust the volume level until it does.

Connecting and Powering Up a DV Device

Save everything and then quit out of your Avid software. Now make sure the 4 × 6-pin FireWire cable from the deck or camera's DV In/Out is connected to the computer's FireWire port. Turn on power to the deck or camera. Xpress Pro and Xpress HD users working with Mojo, as well as Media Composer editors: If you're using FireWire you don't need to move anything (the same cable works both ways), so go to the next section. However, if you're using the component cables with Mojo or another of Avid's DNA break-out boxes, you'll need to reconfigure things.

You were sending video signals out from the tape deck to the Mojo's input connectors; now you need to connect the cables so they run from the Mojo's output connectors to the deck. You'll also need to connect the audio cables so they go from the Mojo's Audio Out to the videotape deck's Audio In. If your Avid facility has some sort of patching panel, you may not need to touch any cables at all. Just select the right buttons. Once you're connected and the deck is powered, launch your Avid software.

Manual Recording or Crash Recording to Tape

If you are cutting a DV 25 project, the simplest method of recording to tape is called *manual recording*. You don't need to be a video engineer to get it to work. You simply set your video deck or camera to record and then play your sequence. If you do a manual recording, you will first need to render all your titles and effects.

The only problem you may encounter with this method occurs at the end of your sequence, especially with DV projects (but we can fix the problem). When you manually record to tape, the last shot holds onscreen or else it doesn't completely fade out. There's a menu command to add filler at the start, but not at the end. There's a trick to fix this problem, though.

Go to the end of your sequence and add a clip that is 15 seconds in length. Now place an IN at the start of this clip and then mark an OUT near the end, but leave 10 frames at the end. Lift this marked section out of the sequence. Now you have nearly 15 seconds of black between the last shot of your sequence and the 10-frame clip at the very end. Now place a fade-out on your last real clip (Figure 18.6). Your fade will be perfect, and you'll have 15 seconds to press the stop button on your camera or record deck when manual record is over. (If you use the Digital Cut Tool, this work-around is not necessary.)

Figure 18.6

Now, with your Online Sequence in the Timeline and the cables hooked up and patching connected, you are ready to manually record to your DV deck or camera.

Manual Record to a DV Deck or Camera

1. Render all your effects and titles. Select all your tracks and then Mark an IN at the beginning of your sequence and an OUT at the end. Now select Render In to Out from the Clip menu. *Xpress Pro 5.1.x users*—In the Timeline bottom toolbar, click on the Video Quality button and choose Full Quality. In the Output Mode drop-down menu, choose DV 25. *Xpress DV and Xpress Pro 4.x users*—Click on the Toggle RealTime Effect button so it turns blue.
2. Put a new DV tape in the deck.
3. Place the Position Indicator at the start of your sequence.
4. On the DV deck, set the Remote/Local switch on the video deck to Local.
5. On the DV camera, place the Camera/VTR switch to VTR.
6. On the DV deck, press the Record (or Play/Record) button, then count 10 seconds and play your sequence on the Avid.
7. On the VTR controls panel of the DV camera, press the Record (or DV Record) button and then play your sequence on the Avid.
8. When the sequence is over, press Stop. (If you have added a shot at the end to create 15 seconds of black, make sure you stop the deck before you reach this extraneous shot.)

There. You're finished. Congratulations.

DIGITAL CUT

The Digital Cut Tool on Xpress DV and Xpress Pro 4.x is a bit different from the one on Xpress Pro 5.1.x. The newer versions take advantage of today's more powerful computers and Avid's Mojo DNA. No matter which version you're using, the Digital Cut Tool gives you frame-accurate recording using timecode. The Avid acts as the edit controller for the video deck. This is the preferred method for projects that will be aired by a television station. It's a bit more complicated than crash recording.

To use the Digital Cut Tool, you must use a master videotape that has been *striped*. A striped tape is one that has a prerecorded control track and timecode on the entire tape. With timecode already on the master tape, the Avid can control the tape deck. The advantage to this method, compared to a manual recording, is that you can predetermine the finished tape's timecode. You can also make changes to the master tape without rerecording the entire sequence. You can go back later on and do an insert edit.

You can ask for a prestriped tape from a tape facility. Obviously, it costs more than a blank tape. Or, you can set your deck's timecode and blacken a tape yourself. Not all decks can do this. My Sony DSR-11 doesn't have this capability. A friend with a Sony DSR-25 deck does it for me. When you order your striped tape, instruct the tape facility to stripe the tape so the timecode they lay down starts at 00:58:30:00. Make sure to tell whoever stripes your tape whether your sequence contains semicolons for drop-frame timecode or colons for non-drop-frame timecode.

Changing the Sequence Timecode

Depending on your Avid, the default starting timecode of your sequence can be anywhere from 00:30:00:00 to 01:00:00:00. Most television stations want the show's first frame to start at 01:00:00:00 timecode. But, if your sequence starts at 01:00:00:00 and you add 60 seconds of bars and tone before the beginning of your show and 15 seconds of black fill before the first frame, as you should, then the show's first frame will be 1:01:15:00. You need to change the default starting timecode.

With your final sequence loaded in the Record Monitor, click on the Record Monitor to make it active. Go to the File menu and select Get Sequence Information. In the box that opens, type 00:58:45:00 in the Starting TC window, as I have in Figure 18.7.

Type colons if your show's timecode is non-drop-frame and semicolons if it is drop-frame. When you click OK, your sequence will now have new timecode that conforms to industry standard.

The Digital Cut Tool

Go to the Clip menu and select Digital Cut. The Digital Cut Tool (Figure 18.8) looks a bit like the face of a videotape recorder.

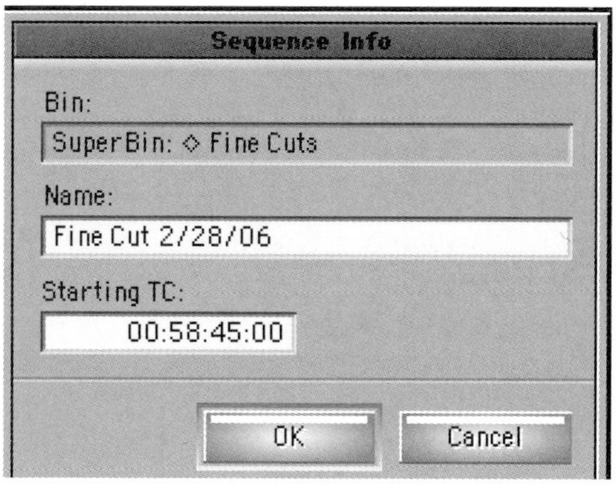

Figure 18.7

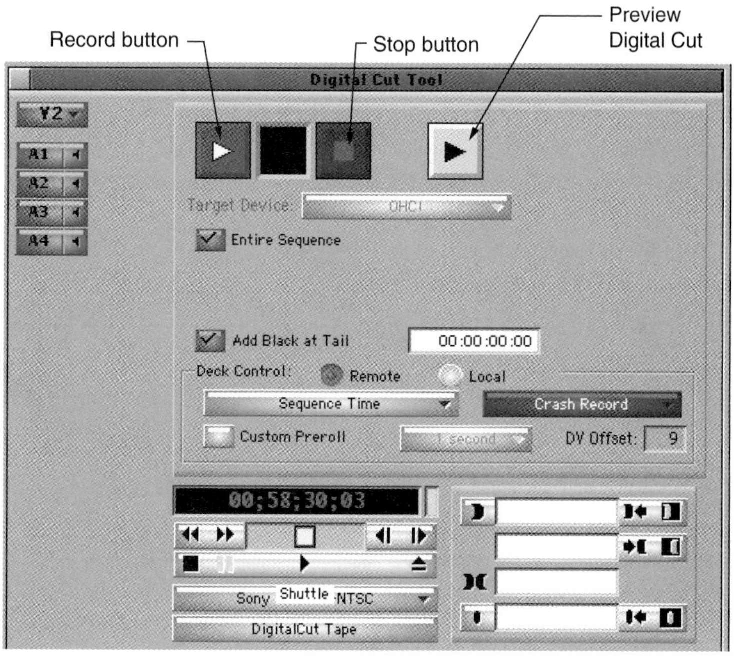

Figure 18.8 Digital Cut Tool.

Xpress DV and Xpress Pro 4.x

To perform a digital cut:

1. After connecting the cables from the Avid to your timecode deck, place the deck's Remote/Local switch on Remote or Wireless.
2. Load your online sequence into the Record Monitor.

3. Click on the Toggle RealTime Effect button so it turns blue.
4. Select all your tracks. Mark an IN at the beginning of your sequence and an OUT at the end. Go to the Clip menu and select Render In to Out.
5. Choose Digital Cut from the Clip menu. The Digital Cut Tool opens.
6. Make sure all the tracks you wish to record are selected.
7. Check the Entire Sequence box.
8. Select Add Black at Tail and then type a number, such as 00:00:10:00, for 10 seconds of black.
9. Select Sequence Time in the menu window.
10. Choose a deck from the Deck Selection pop-up menu.
11. Press the Record button.

The Avid cues up the tape and begins recording your sequence to tape. If you need to stop at any time, press the Stop button.

The Digital Cut Tool Xpress Pro and Pro HD Version 5.1.x

One of the changes in the new version of Xpress Pro and Xpress Pro HD deals with RealTime Effects. You don't need to render your effects to do a digital cut. I find these choices can be a bit overwhelming, so if you're worried, just render your titles and effects beforehand.

1. Connect a deck either through Mojo or your 1394 FireWire port.
2. Launch your Avid software.
3. Click the DNA/1394 toggle button on the Timeline row of buttons.
   - Select Mojo if it is connected and if you are outputting standard-definition (SD) analog formats or a mixture of SD analog and DV25.
   - Select 1394 if you want to output DV25, DV50, or DVCPRO HD. You will send these formats through your 1394 FireWire port to a suitable deck.

Click here to choose Mojo or FireWire connection.

4. In the Timeline bottom toolbar, click on the Video Quality button and choose the highest video quality: Full Quality (Mojo) or Best Quality. If you are cutting an HD project, choose Best Quality.

5. Open the Digital Cut Tool from the Clip menu.
6. In the Output Mode pull-down menu (see Figure 18.9) choose:
   - RT DNA if you have Mojo connected and you don't want to render your SD effects. This is for analog SD projects, such as Beta SP projects.
   - RT DV25 if you have DV25 material and you don't want to render your effects.
   - RT DV50 if you have DV25 and DV50 material and you don't want to render your effects. Everything will encode as DV50.
   - DV25 if you're outputting through your 1394 FireWire port, all your media are DV25, and all effects are rendered.
   - DV50 if you're outputting through your 1394 FireWire port and your entire project is DV50. All effects are rendered.
   - DVCPRO HD if all your media are DVCPRO HD and everything has been rendered. You must output DVCPRO HD through your 1394 FireWire port.

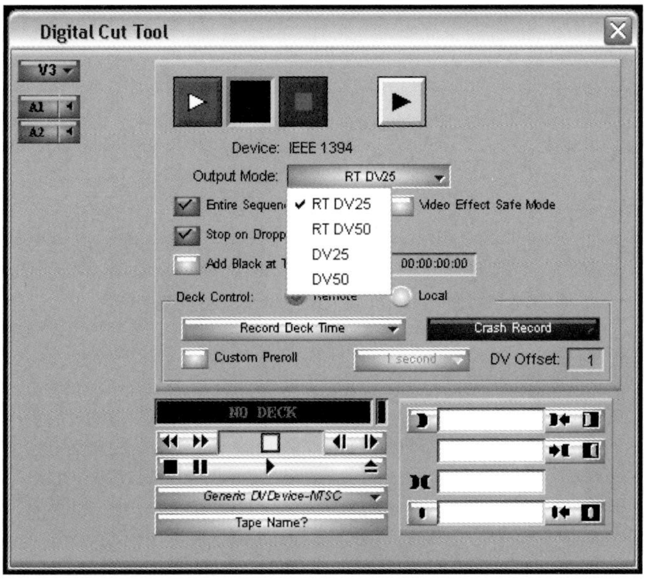

Figure 18.9

If you're putting out to tape a 720p HD project that you edited at 23.976 using the Digital Cut Tool, the Avid will reintroduce the 2:3 pulldown to create a 29.97 frame rate (59.94), which is expected/required by the 720p HD tape format.

EDIT DECISION LIST (EDL)

For awhile, it looked as though companies such as Avid were going to make obsolete the process of generating an Edit Decision List for conforming your project back to videotape. With cheap FireWire drives, most filmmakers began to capture at full resolution and saw no reason to ever go back to the original tapes. Just finish on an Avid, and all the effects you've generated can be recreated perfectly. Or, if you edited at another resolution, you could recapture your sequence on your own Avid, as we described earlier in this chapter, without the hassles or the expense of an online tape-to-tape session.

Well, the coming of high definition, especially the bigger HD formats such as 1080i and 1080p, has brought the online tape session back in vogue. Many projects will shoot on those big HD formats, but because they require such massive amounts of storage, and a more expensive Avid, many users will capture their HD tapes on a Media Composer Adrenaline HD, using DNxHD compression to make the files manageable. They can then use an Xpress Pro HD to edit the project, and then, when they are through editing, get the Xpress Pro HD to spit out a list of editing decisions that they bring to an *online* facility. The online editor will take the HD tapes and the EDL and create a high-resolution HD version based on the decisions made on the Xpress Pro HD. In fact, several feature films have been edited this way.

Xpress users should pay particular attention to the EDL process. In many ways, the Xpress is the perfect offline machine, set up to deliver an EDL. For an amazingly low price, you can edit any HD project, shot on any HD format.

In theory generating an EDL and handing it to a tape facility are simple. With your EDL and the source tapes, the online facility can finish your program using a sophisticated videotape system and edit controller, such as those manufactured by CMX, Grass Valley Group, Ampex, and Sony.

What Exactly Is an EDL?

Basically an EDL is a list of all your editing decisions. It lists all your shots in the final sequence, according to their start and end timecode. The EDL also figures out where on a master tape, or record tape, those shots will be recorded. The EDL doesn't use the paradigm of clips in a sequence. It replaces your clips in the Timeline with source tape timecode numbers and record tape timecode numbers.

The EDL is made up of lines showing all of your editing decisions. Every line is made up of at least four sets of timecode numbers. The first pair of timecode numbers gives the IN and OUT timecode for the first clip you spliced into your final sequence. The second pair of numbers shows where that clip will be placed on the master, or record tape.

Examine the EDL in Figure 18.10. The first shot in the sequence is 10 seconds long. In the EDL, it is event 001. We see that its starting timecode is 01:06:45:01

and its ending timecode is 01:06:55:01, for a total of 10 seconds. That's the source tape. On the record tape (the master tape), this clip would be recorded at 01:00:00:00 and run until 01:00:10:00, for a total of 10 seconds. The second shot is 2 seconds and six frames long. You can tell by the timecode of the source tape where that shot would end in the master tape.

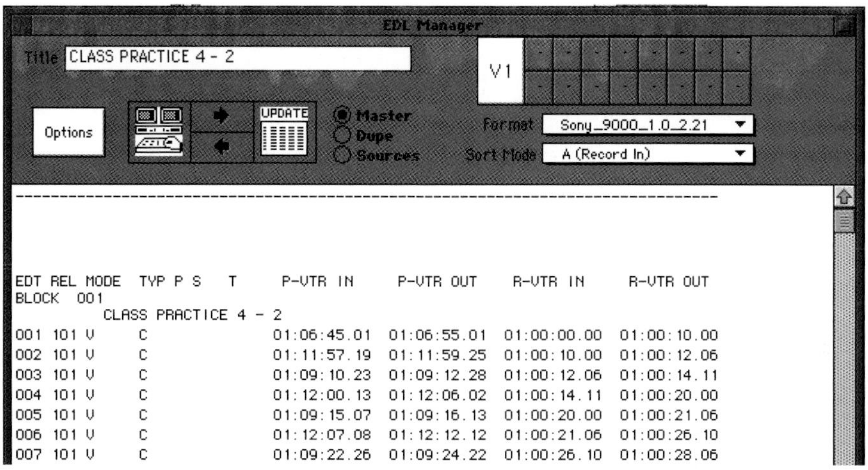

Figure 18.10 EDL Manager window.

Talk to Your Online Facility

This is the first step, after getting prices from a variety of suppliers. Once you've selected a post-production facility to do your work, you need to have a long, detailed conversation about your job and their requirements. For example, your Avid will print out and put onto a disk all your editing decisions in a form that can be read by many different edit controllers. Your first step is to ask the online facility what tape edit controller they will be using. The Avid will support many different edit controller formats, but because so many of them are incompatible you must provide the right one. An EDL formatted for a Sony 9500 won't do your tape house much good if they have a CMX machine.

All the steps listed here should be used as a guide to make your conversation with the online editor at your tape house more productive. There's no way for me to know what settings are correct for their equipment, but I want you to be able to find the options and select the settings your tape facility asks for.

Getting Started

First, make a new bin, call it EDL Sequence, and then duplicate your final sequence and place the duplicate inside this EDL Sequence bin. Now, place this sequence in the Record Monitor. Now, go to the Tools menu and select EDL. After a few seconds the EDL Manager (a separate piece of software) will launch. If nothing happens, search for the EDL manager application and launch it manually by double-clicking on its icon.

Once the program is running, you will see the EDL Manager menu items at the top of your computer screen. Go to the Windows menu (Figure 18.11) and select EDL Mgr Ctrl+1 (or Command+1).

Figure 18.11

The EDL Manager will open, but nothing will be in the window. Click on the arrow (Figure 18.12) between the two icons and the EDL of your sequence will appear, like the one shown in Figure 18.13.

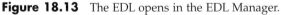

Click here.

Figure 18.12

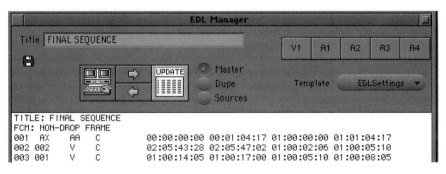

Figure 18.13 The EDL opens in the EDL Manager.

You'll need to make changes to the default set-up to configure it to your online facility's system:

1. Go to the Windows menu (in the menu bar at the top of your computer screen), and choose Options. The Options window opens like the one in Figure 18.14.
2. Select the options asked for by your online facility.
3. In the Format window, select the format they require, such as Sony_9000 or GVG_7.0_7.0.
4. In the Sort Mode menu, select the sort mode they ask for.
5. The Apply button will flash if you have made changes. Press Apply in order to apply your changes.

The Options window will close and you are returned to the EDL Manager. The changes you made will be reflected in the way the EDL numbers are displayed.

I'll admit the Options window looks complicated. These choices determine the order your source tapes will be used, the way visual effects will be handled, and the kind of information that will be included on the EDL.

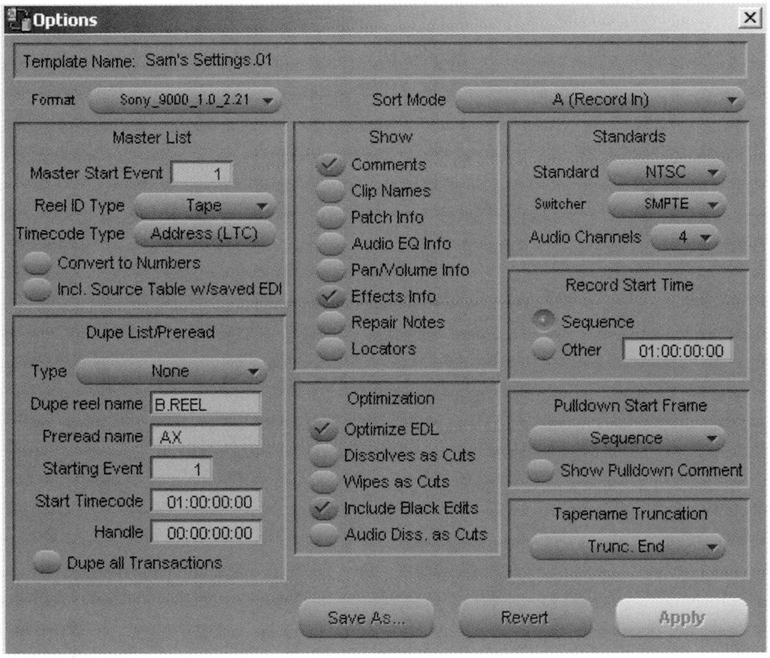

Figure 18.14 Options window.

If you are asked by the Online editor to deselect the audio tracks or the video tracks, click on the EDL Manager and click on the tracks. A menu will allow you to change the tracks or deselect them (as indicated by a horizontal line). Press the Update box to apply this change.

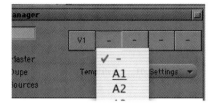

Saving the EDL to a Disk

The steps involved in saving your EDL can be the most complicated part of the EDL process. The problem most people face when bringing a project to an online editing facility is that most of these online editing controllers are quite old. Many were built at the dawn of PCs (circa 1985) and won't accept a Zip disk. Some require a diskette you probably have never even seen before, such as an RT11 diskette, or can barely remember, such as a double-density disk. Your Avid computer might not even recognize them if you were to insert one into your floppy drive (if you have a floppy drive). You really must work closely with the online facility you've chosen. Often they will send you a couple of disks already properly formatted for use in your Avid. The File menu has RT11 commands you may be asked to use. Perhaps the easiest way to send the EDL is via the Internet.

EDL and Audio

Often the EDL is for your video tracks only. Your audio will already have been mixed by a professional mixer on Pro Tools®. You'll then bring the mixed audio to the online session and have the online editor lay the final mixed tracks to the online tape. Sometimes the EDL is all about the audio. In Hollywood, the sound editor often asks the film editor to provide an EDL of the audio tracks so she or he can go back to various reels and tapes that were used to digitize the sound into the Avid.

Visual Effects

If there aren't too many visual effects, it is not that difficult for the online tape facility to reproduce your sequence based on an EDL. But, if your sequence is made up of many multilayered effects that took a lot of time to render, chances are the online facility will be hard pressed to recreate them accurately. And you might find that the whole process costs a lot of money. Most offline editors work closely with the online facility during the editing stage so there aren't any expensive surprises when they go into the online session.

OUTPUT TO DVD

If you have a DVD-R burner attached to your Avid computer and DVD authoring software, you can burn your sequence onto a DVD. Most people use iDVD or DVD Studio Pro® on a Mac or Avid DVD on a PC. Not surprisingly, the Windows and Mac applications handle this task differently. Whichever system you're on, remember that the process can be slow—sometimes many hours. It can also be frustrating. I suggest you start by burning a very short sequence—no longer than a minute—to work the kinks out. Oh, and you should have more than one DVD-R available. We're going to make a QuickTime Reference Movie and store it with the media and project folder on our FireWire drive.

DVD on Mac

1. Create a new folder (call it DVD Folder) and place it on your FireWire drive—the same drive that holds your media and project folder.
2. Launch Avid.
3. Load the sequence to be burned. Make sure all effects have been rendered and all tracks have been selected.
4. Click on the sequence in the bin so it's highlighted.
5. From the File menu, choose Send To DVD. When the Send To DVD dialog box opens (Figure 18.15), in Destination, click Set and search for the drive that contains the DVD folder you created in step 1.

Figure 18.15

6. Click on Auto Launch and choose iDVD or DVD Studio Pro.
7. Click on Options (Figure 18.15).
8. The Option window opens (Figure 18.16). If you shot in the 16:9 format, choose 864 × 480 or 16:9 in the Display Aspect Ratio pull-down menu.
9. Make sure the audio information is correct—most likely AIFF-C, 48 kHz, and 16 Bit. If you have a DV25 project, choose Use Avid DV Codec.
10. Deselect both Use Marks and Use Enabled tracks (so you'll send the entire sequence to DVD).
11. Your settings should look like those in Figure 18.16.
12. Click Save. When you're returned to the Send to QuickTime Reference window, click OK.

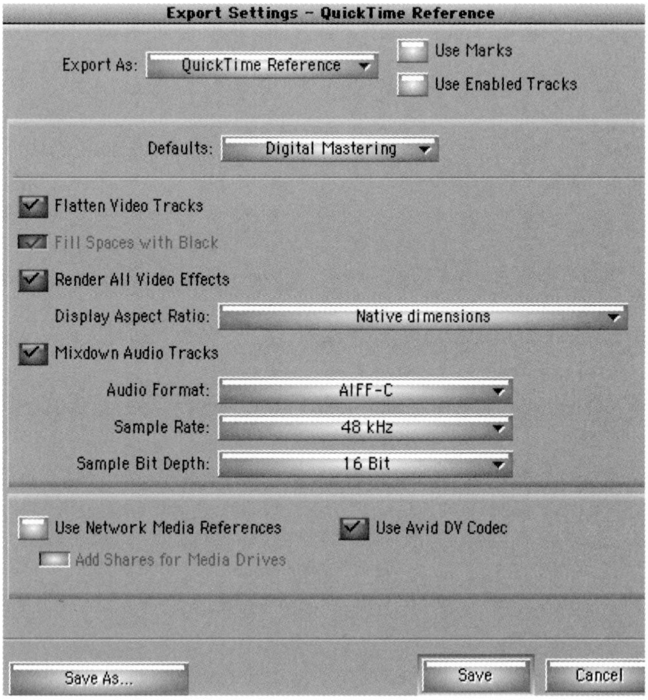

Figure 18.16

You'll find your QuickTime Reference Movie in the DVD folder, as well as an audio .aif file. At this point, you'll launch your DVD software and create a new project. Usually, you will find the files and either open them or drag them onto the DVD authoring software's project window.

DVD on Windows

1. Create a new folder (call it DVD Folder) and place it on your FireWire drive—the same drive that holds your media and project folder.
2. Launch Avid.
3. Load the sequence to be burned. Make sure all effects have been rendered and all tracks have been selected.
4. Click on the sequence in the bin so it's highlighted.
5. Go to the File menu and choose Send To . . . . In the Send To dialog box, go to the Send To pull-down menu and select Sorenson Squeeze.
6. Deselect both Use Marks and Use Enabled tracks (so you will send out the entire sequence).
7. Choose 4:3 (most likely) or 16:9 (if your footage was shot in this aspect ratio).
8. Click Browse to select a destination on your hard drive to store the files before they get burned onto the DVD.
9. Click OK. A QuickTime Reference Movie and audio file is created.
10. The Sorenson Squeeze® application will launch. Drag the QuickTime Reference Movie to the window to start the MPEG-2 encoding.

Making a Progressive DVD

In Chapter 16, we discussed the advantages of shooting your standard-definition projects using 24p cameras. Chief among those advantages is the ability to create a progressive DVD. You'll use a compression tool like Sorenson Squeeze 4 or ProCoder® 2 to create the MPEG-2 compression from your QuickTime Reference Movie. And then you'll use DVD Studio Pro (Mac) or Avid DVD (PC) as your authoring software when making the progressive DVD. Michael Phillips does a nice job of explaining this process on his www.24p.com website. I lean heavily on his article entitled "24p NTSC DVD Creation Using Sorenson Squeeze" for the information below.

With your QuickTime reference file on your drive, launch Sorenson Squeeze (often included with your Avid software). Here are the choices you're looking for—or similar ones, depending on your software:

1. Stream Type—Select Elementary.
2. Video Output—Select MPEG-2 Video. Click on the Options button and in the dialog box select Progressive as your Field Encoding. In Pixel Aspect Ratio, select 4:3; choose 16:9 if you have an anamorphic project and want it to play correctly on a wide-screen television. It will look squeezed on a 4:3 television.
3. Format—Choose NTSC and 29.97 even if you have a 23.976 or 24p project.

4.   Your frame size is 720 × 480.
5.   For I Frame Rate, select 6 frames.

You'll also have a choice of how much compression you'd like—anywhere from 6 to 9 megabits (6 is more compression and less quality; 9 is less compression, the highest quality). If your project is less than an hour in length, you could choose a constant bit rate of 8 megabits (9 will choke older DVD players) and everything will fit nicely onto one DVD. If your project is an hour or longer, use a variable bit rate to make sure it all fits on one DVD.

Once you click OK, you need to go to the Filter Settings on the main menu bar. Although it's counterintuitive, in the Deinterlace pull-down menu select None. That's because you already took care of this when you chose Progressive in step 2. When you have encoded the files, you can launch your DVD authoring application.

MAKING A 35-mm THEATRICAL RELEASE PRINT

If you shot your standard-definition (or high-definition) project at 23.976 and edited it at 23.976p, you can easily make a 35-mm print (I said easily, not cheaply). In the past, people have paid huge sums to have electronic beam recorders scan the video image, but the process here, which was used for the theatrically released film *Incident at Loch Ness*, involves simply exporting a TIFF image of every frame in your Timeline. If your film is 10 minutes in length, you will have 14,400 sequential images (10 minutes × 60 seconds × 24 frames per second = 14,400). You would hand these TIFF images to your lab for printing, one image at a time, onto 35-mm film. Pretty slick.

1.   Create a folder on an external FireWire drive connected to your computer and call it "tiff output".
2.   Name your final sequence "16 × 9 Film Transfer," and place it in the Timeline.
3.   Select V1 and deselect the other tracks.
4.   Go to the File menu and select Export.
5.   Click on the Export Options button.
6.   Select Use Enabled Tracks.
7.   In the Graphic Format pull-down menu, select TIFF.
8.   Choose 864 × 486 and all the other choices shown in Figure 18.17.
9.   Make sure you check the Sequential Files box.

You can click the Save As . . . button and name it RGB Sequential TIFF, and then click Save. When the Export As window opens (Figure 18.18), choose as your destination the "tiff output" folder you created in step 1.

Click the Save button in the Export As . . . window.

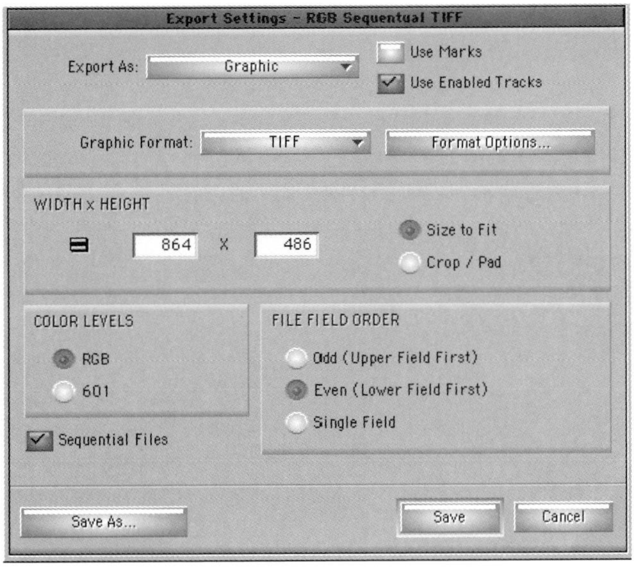

Figure 18.17

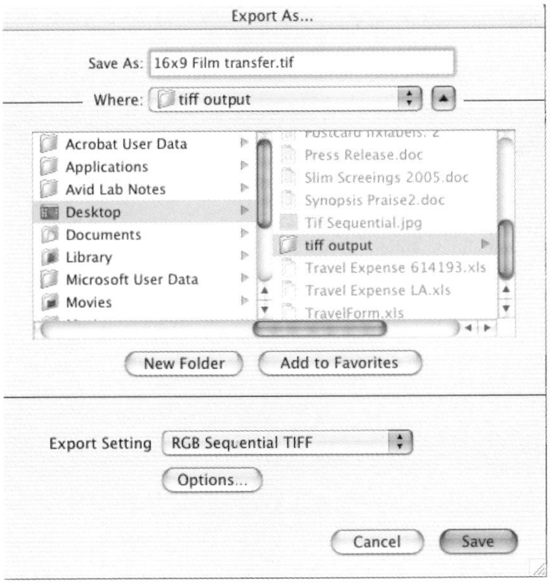

Figure 18.18

The Avid will send out 24 TIFF files for every second in your timeline. When the export is complete, you'll find that your folder contains 14,400 uncompressed TIFF pictures—one for every single frame in your 10-minute film. Your lab can now make a 35-mm silent answer print from those images.

Obviously, not every lab can handle this. Find one that has done it before and ask a lab representative to walk you through the lab's role and what they will need from you (besides a big check). All 35-mm films are divided up into reels of about 18 to 20 minutes each, so if your film is 90 minutes long you will divide your Timeline into five sections. You want to make the break between scenes, not in the middle of a scene. Create a different folder—Tiff Output Reel 1, Tiff Output Reel 2, and so forth—for each 20-minute sequential export you'll place on the external FireWire drive. You should add SMPTE leader (as explained in Chapter 19) with an audio "pop" on the sound tracks at the 2-frame. Do this at the head of each section so your sound can be placed in sync with the picture.

SOUND

Once you have a print you're happy with, you can make a married print—one with picture *and* sound. Inside the Avid, your sound and picture were actually traveling at 23.976 fps. When you make a 35-mm print, the picture travels through the projector at 24 fps, or 0.1 percent faster than it ran inside the Avid. So you'll need to have a mixing facility not only create the Dolby®-encoded sound track but also speed up your audio by 0.1 percent—the same amount the picture was changed. They'll also break the sound into sound reels that match the picture reels.

DONE

Well, that was: (1) easy; (2) fun; (3) interesting; (4) frustrating; (5) !x(#&#*!. Hey, we finished, didn't we? And that's an achievement worthy of praise.

19

Shooting on Film, Finishing on Film

This chapter is designed to help those Xpress Pro or Media Composer users who want to cut film projects on their Avids that will result in either 16-mm or 35-mm projection prints. Xpress Pro users will need Avid's FilmScribe™ software, which comes bundled on their Xpress installation DVDs.

WHY FILM?

The main problem with video as a medium of distribution is that there are just so many video formats and standards in use around the world. There are many high-definition formats, and things are even more confusing in the standard-definition world, where one is faced with SECAM, PAL, and NTSC standards, depending on world geography and former colonial ties. And each standard has at least ten different tape formats. And none of them plays on any other format's tape machines. What a mess.

The great thing about a film print is that there is only one standard and only a couple of formats. A 16-mm or 35-mm print can be shown at festivals and theaters anywhere in the world, from Afghanistan to Zimbabwe, from Sydney to Cannes. And it can be transferred to any standard or high-definition format—now or in the future. However, making that film print can be a challenge.

FILM AND THE AVID

There are several ways to transfer film directly onto an Avid drive, but unless you have a lot of money and one of the most expensive Avids you'll first transfer the film to videotape. Once your film is on tape, you can capture it, using the Capture Tool, just as you would any other videotape.

THE FILM-TO-TAPE TRANSFER

After you have shot your footage, you take the exposed film to a laboratory for processing. When the film has been processed, it has an image, either negative or positive. You then take your processed film to a telecine facility (many labs have them) for a film-to-tape transfer. The film's individual frames are projected or scanned onto videotape. A variety of telecine systems are in use today, ranging from film projectors beaming the film's image onto a video camera to highly sophisticated machines using a flying-spot scanner, capable of incredible image manipulations. Many flying-spot systems cost over $500,000. The film is transported on rollers that never touch the image surface, so your film won't get scratched or damaged. A flying-spot scanner can also transpose a negative image to a positive one. So, if you shoot negative film, as most people do, you don't have to make a positive print of your film to get it transferred.

FINISHING ON FILM OR FINISHING ON TAPE

Television commercials, rock videos, and many episodic television dramas are shot on film, but the finished product is a videotape. If the end result of your film project is a videotape, then once the film is transferred you no longer need the film. And, to be honest, you don't need to know much about the film-to-tape process. However, if you plan to make a projection print of your film, which is currently the case for most feature films and some student film projects, then you need to pay a lot of attention to the film-to-tape transfer. Why? Because after cutting your project on the Avid, you will then ask a negative cutter to go back to the original film and conform that film to match your Avid sequence. Think about it. The negative cutter must be able to locate hundreds of strips of film and splice those strips together in the right order and at the right length, based on an edited sequence that was captured not from that film but from a video copy of that film! Needless to say, the process is far from straightforward. You can help the negative cutter do the job correctly and save yourself a lot of money if you know how the process works.

HIRE A NEGATIVE CUTTER FIRST

Usually filmmakers finish editing their film and then go in search of a negative cutter. That's not a good idea when cutting your film on an Avid. The negative cutter can help you even before you send your exposed film to the lab. By the end of this chapter, you and your negative cutter will speak the same language. In fact, you'll probably know more about the overall process than most negative cutters do. Still, I urge you to contact a negative cutter even before you send your film for processing.

THE $64,000 QUESTION

The key question when editing a film project on the Avid is this: Which frame of film was placed on which frame of video during the film-to-tape transfer? Everything depends on that. The Avid can tell you which frame of video you edited. That's easy. The difficult part is figuring out which film frame that video frame represents. What's the big deal, you ask? Film runs at 24 frames per second (fps), and video doesn't. And that, as they say, is a problem.

THE 2:3 STANDARD PULLDOWN

Film intended for projection in a theater is shot at 24 fps. Videotape travels at different speeds, depending on the country you live in and the tape standard that country has adopted. In the United States, we use the NTSC standard, and NTSC tapes travel at approximately 30 fps. Transferring film onto tape in a NTSC country is a bit tricky, as you can imagine. How do you transfer 24 frames of film onto 30 frames of video? And how do you do it in a way that will allow a negative cutter to go back to the film and cut the correct frame?

Fortunately, it's not that difficult to get 24 frames to fit nicely onto 30 frames. Each frame of videotape is made up of two fields. (Each field contains half the frame's total lines, which are scanned horizontally; odd lines are scanned first, then even lines, to give the total image.) During the transfer process, the telecine machine places four frames of film onto five frames of video, using the two fields to make the math work. We examined this pulldown process in Chapter 15 when dealing with the 23.976 frame rate found on the Canon XL2 and the Panasonic DVX100 and SDX900 cameras. It's the same process, only in reverse. Let's examine Figure 19.1.

The first film frame, called the A-frame, goes onto the first two fields of the videotape. The second frame of film, called the B-frame, goes onto three fields. The third film frame, the C-frame, goes onto two fields, and the fourth film frame, the D-frame, goes onto three fields. Two fields then three fields, two fields then three fields, and on and on like that. In this case we have a 2:3:2:3 pulldown.

As you can see in Figure 19.1, four film frames are transferred onto five video frames. If you do this six times (6×4 film frames = 24, or one second, and 6×5 video frames = 30, or one second), you have a second of film and a second of video.

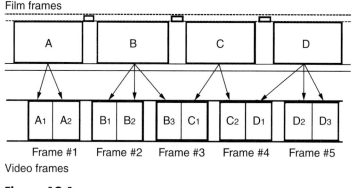

Figure 19.1

Look closely at this diagram. Notice that each frame of film (A, B, C, D) is transferred differently. The A-frame is the only one that is transferred onto a single frame of video, all by itself. The C film frame is like the A film frame in that it covers just two fields, but the C film frame is transferred onto two different video frames. B and D are transferred onto three fields, but the way each goes onto those three fields is different. If you transfer 10,000 frames, each frame is A, B, C, or D. The way the four film frames are placed on the video is called the frame "pullin," and it is critical to the process of identifying which video frame holds which film frame.

IT'S REALLY 29.97

As we noted in Chapters 15 and 16, another complication arises from the fact that NTSC video doesn't actually run at 30 fps. It used to, but with the development of color television, many decades ago, the frame rate of NTSC videotape changed to 29.97 fps. It turns out that the difference between 30 and 29.97 is .1%. So, what film-to-tape transfer facilities do is actually slow the film down by .1% when doing the film-to-tape transfer. The film is slowed down from 24 fps to 23.976 fps. The difference between 23.976 fps and 24 fps is .1%. I know I'm repeating myself, but, yes, the film's running speed is "pulled down" by .1% during transfer.

KEYCODE AND TIMECODE

Knowing that we can accurately transfer from film to tape doesn't entirely solve the problem of identifying which frame of videotape contains which frame of film. In the beginning of this textbook, we discussed the timecode system that video uses to identify each and every frame. Using a system based on clock time, every video frame has its own unique number. Film has a corresponding system using *key numbers,* which look something like this: KL74 0246 8805, where the two letters indicate the film's manufacturer and the film type, the first six digits identify the film roll, and the last four digits provide the footage count on that roll. Strictly speaking, *keycode* is a machine-readable bar code version of the key numbers, but most people just say keycode when referring to the numbers as well as the bar code version. Keycode isn't placed on every frame of film. In 16 mm, for instance, the key numbers are placed every 20 frames. (There are 40 frames in a foot of 16-mm film, so every half foot.) But, even though there isn't keycode on every frame, it's easy to identify each frame by counting the frames in between the keycode. Computers are good at this sort of counting, and during the transfer from film to tape, not only is the keycode read by a *keycode reader* but the frames in between the keycode are also counted and given numbers. Those numbers are the frame *offsets.*

Pretend you're the negative cutter. Examine the strip of film and try to find the frame that is six frames past the frame containing the key number KL74 0246 9612.

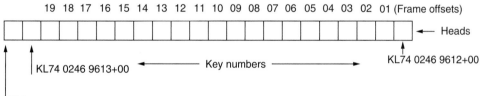

Because the film has keycode and the videotape has timecode, during the film-to-tape transfer you place the keycode information onto the videotape, together with the tape's timecode information, but there's one more crucial piece of information needed—the frame pullin. Remember that the 2:3 pulldown process places four frames of film (A, B, C, or D) onto five frames of video. Each frame of video must contain this pullin information. Each video frame must say, "I've got an A frame," or "I've got part of a B frame," or "I've got the other part of the B frame," in order for the negative cutter to know which frame of film that videotape frame holds.

During the film-to-tape transfer, a machine locks together each frame's keycode information, timecode information, and frame pullin information. Because this information is critical, it is burned onto the videotape so all the information is visible whenever the tape is played. As you can see in Figure 19.2, the timecode information is displayed on the left and the key number, with frame offset (count) and pullin, is displayed on the right. This frame of video contains the film frame that is six frames past the frame containing the key number KL74 0246 9612. It is a C pullin.

Figure 19.2 A video frame displaying the timecode, key number, frame offset, and pullin.

IDENTIFYING THE FIRST FRAME WITH A PUNCH

As I said before, it's critical for the negative cutter to know which video frame holds which film frame. The pullin (A, B, C, D) helps us know which film frame landed on which video frame, but for this to work we need a place to start, so everyone knows which is the first frame.

After processing the film, your lab should punch a hole in the frame containing the first visible key number at the head of each camera roll—the "dot frame" or 00 frame. The telecine facility then lines up that punched frame so it is an A-frame pullin. All the timecode and keycode numbers, all the frame offsets, and all the pullin letters have that punch as a common reference point. Many labs only punch the first 00 frame in a *lab flat* (two or more camera rolls spliced together), which may contain three camera rolls. This can be a big problem. Be explicit in your work order and then don't accept this sort of shoddy work.

As the film is transferred, the keycode numbers are sent to a box that burns them onto the videotape. Part of the process involves a controller, such as a Time

Logic Controller, which keeps the timecode locked together with the keycode coming from the keycode reader.

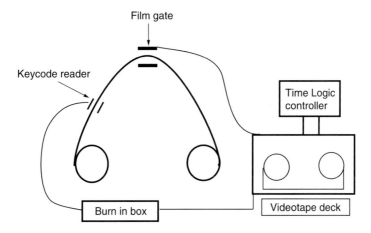

Figure 19.3 The telecine process.

TYPES OF TIMECODE

Speaking of timecode, there are actually two kinds of timecode: non-drop-frame and drop-frame. As you know, videotape used to run at 30 fps, but when color was introduced the rate was changed to 29.97. Because of that slight difference, whenever non-drop-frame timecode is used, a show's running time and its time-code time can be off by several seconds. To solve this problem, drop-frame time-code was introduced. No frames are actually dropped, but some frame numbers are dropped to make up for the difference between 30 and 29.97. Video engineers prefer drop-frame because an hour show equals an hour of timecode, whereas one hour of NDF timecode equals 00:59:56:12 in real time. The film industry uses non-drop-frame because *all* those frame numbers are critical and none can be dropped. If you're working on a film project, always specify non-drop-frame when given a choice.

How do you tell the difference? The Avid can tell, almost as soon as you feed a tape into the deck during capturing. Non-drop-frame will display colons (01:23:54:21), whereas drop-frame will display semicolons (01;23;54;21).

WORK ORDER TO YOUR LAB

As mentioned earlier, you should speak with your negative cutter before taking any film to the lab to be processed and transferred to tape. The negative cutter can offer suggestions as to how he or she wants the camera rolls prepared. The main points you would stress in your work order to the lab and transfer facility are as follows.

Lab

1. Develop all rolls Normal.
2. Prep negative for video transfer.
3. Punch the head of *each* camera roll at the first visible key number/dot frame (the 00 frame).
4. Send prepped negative to your transfer facility for a film-to-tape transfer.

Transfer Facility

1. Perform a 2:3 pulldown starting with the A frame at the head punch of each camera roll and at the starting hour of timecode.
2. Use non-drop-frame timecode.
3. Transfer the camera negative to the enclosed DVCAM (Beta SP) tapes with timecode and keycode burn-in on one tape and simultaneously transfer to the second tape so both tapes have identical timecode but the second tape is clean, with no burn-in.
4. On the first tape, place the burn-in at the bottom of the frame, within the safe title area.
5. Provide a log file on a disk (or CD).

When you've finished editing, the negative cutter will want you to provide a tape of the final sequence with the timecode and key numbers visible on the screen. That way the negative cutter can play the tape and check the numbers at each cut point. However, you will also want a clean video copy.

A CLEAN VIDEO COPY

Because you will want a clean video copy, one with no burn-in information in the frame, as well as a film print, the work order (above) asks the transfer facility to make a simultaneous DVCAM copy of the film-to-tape transfer. This copy is made at the same time the film is transferred to the master tape, and it contains the same timecode as the master tape. Because it is clean (contains no burn-in information), you can recapture your final sequence using these clean tapes, rather than the ones with the burn-in. With this method, you can have beautiful tapes to give to festivals, actors, agents, etc. We went over the process of recapturing your sequence in Chapter 18. You'll do this after making a video copy of the final sequence containing all the burn-in numbers.

My students save money by purchasing the DVCAM tape stock themselves and sending it to the transfer facility, rather than having the transfer house gouge them for the tape stock. Let's say you shot eight 400-foot rolls, and need two 60-minute tapes. Instead of sending two tapes, send four and include instructions to the transfer facility, as I did in step 3 above, asking that a copy be made containing the same timecode but without the burn-in.

TELECINE LOG FILE

You should ask the transfer facility to make a *telecine log file*. This is a file containing all the timecode, keycode, and pullin information pertaining to your film-to-tape transfer. It contains all the information you, the Avid, and your negative cutter will need to conform the film to the Avid version. It eliminates the need for logging each take on each camera roll. A FLEx file is perhaps the most common type, and it is created whenever the transfer facility has used a Time Logic machine during the transfer. If an Aaton system was used, the file will be an ATN file, and if an Evertz was used the file will be an FTL. Some transfer facilities charge a lot of money for the telecine log file. One New York transfer facility was asking over $100 for each one, and there's one for each tape. Others charge you no more than the cost of a CD.

Once you insert the CD or disk into your computer, you need to convert these log types to the Avid log format. Avid gives you a utility, already installed in your computer, to do this. To find the utility, go to your programs or applications and look for a folder called ALE. Inside is the Avid Log Exchange (ALE) utility. Just double-click to open it.

Figure 19.4

I've only imported FLEx files, so it's the file most often discussed in this chapter. You don't even have to know what kind of file you have. Just set the ALE utility to Automatic (Figure 19.5) and it will figure it out for you.

Steps for importing a FLEx file:

1. Insert the disk containing the FLEx file into the CPU's drive.
2. Open the disk and drag the file onto the desktop.
3. Look for the ALE folder on the CPU's hard drive, either in the Applications folder or Avid Utilities folder.
4. Open (double-click) the ALE utility. There are two columns—one for input and one for output.
5. Select INPUT: Automatic; OUTPUT: ALE.

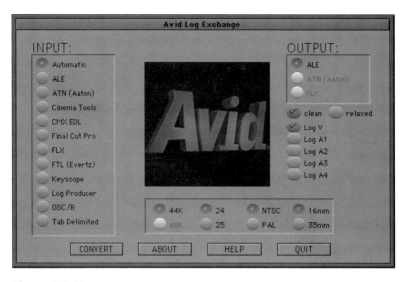

Figure 19.5

6. Unless you had the transfer facility sync up your audio, deselect the Log Audio tracks, keeping only Log V for Video.
7. Choose your frame rate (24), video standard (NTSC), and film format (16mm or 35mm).
8. Click CONVERT.
9. The Select File to Convert dialog box appears. Navigate until you find your log file on the desktop of your computer. Click on it.
10. Click on OPEN. Your file will be converted to ALE.
11. Quit the ALE utility.

SETTING UP YOUR FILM PROJECT

The Xpress Pro and Media Composers give you a choice of formats when starting a new project. All three are shown in Figure 19.6.

Figure 19.6 Select 24p NTSC if captured on a Media Composer.

The 30i option is the standard video option. We examined 23.976 at length in Chapter 16. The 24p setting is for film projects. This format emulates the way the famed Avid Film Composer has worked since 1992. When the film is transferred to tape, it is slowed down to 23.976. When captured by the Avid, the frames are stamped as 24 fps, and they run at 24 fps inside the Avid. The Xpress Pro cannot capture and stamp these frames—you need a Media Composer to do it—but an Xpress Pro can edit the project, once captured on a Media Composer. Simply select 24p NTSC when setting up the project and then choose the film type, either 16 mm or 35 mm.

This choice is really for advanced users working on bigger budget feature films and is beyond the purview of this book. You'll probably have a post-production supervisor who will walk you through all the steps. I'm going to concentrate on those of you who will be editing your film project as a *matchback* project. This is the choice for those of you who will be making a film print only if one of the world's most prestigious festivals request a film print. The advantage to this matchback is it's easy to put out a video copy *and* a film print.

Matchback

This is the choice I recommend, unless you know you'll get the money to make a film print. This choice gives you the opportunity to create a video, enter your project into festivals, and later, if a distributor or big-name festival wants a print, gives you that option. After naming the project, go to the Format menu and select 30i NTSC (Figure 19.7). Once you do that, the Matchback box appears. Check on the box and then select either 16 mm or 35 mm in the Film Type pull-down menu.

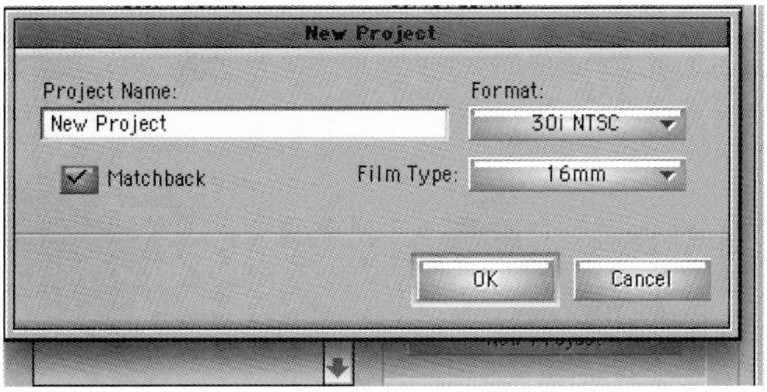

Figure 19.7

Importing Your Telecine Log File

Now that you've set up your project, you will want to import the log file you converted with the Avid Log Exchange utility. To import the log file:

1. Create a new bin and name it (Dailies Day 1 or Camera Roll 1, for example).
2. Click on the bin to make it active.
3. Choose Import from the File menu.
4. In the Import window, select File of Type (Windows) or Enable (Mac), and choose Shot Log Documents.
5. Scroll through the directory until you find your file (Name-ALE). It's on the desktop.
6. Click Open.

Depending on the transfer facility, in the bin you will either see just a single master clip of the entire camera roll (if you have a really lazy facility) or all the scenes and takes (a good facility), with the Start and End timecode.

To see the key numbers, you'll need to get into Text View, then go to the Bin menu, choose Headings, and select Camroll, KN Start, KN End, KN Duration, Pullin, Scene, and Take. A faster way to select these headings is to go to the window next to the bin's Fast menu and click on "Untitled." A menu appears. Select Film.

Click here to get the pop-up list.

This will select the headings you need.

Now select all the takes in the Bin, go to the Bin menu, and choose Batch Capture. I suggest you always create a new bin for each camera roll and import the log file for that camera roll into that bin.

SOUND AND THE AVID

Those who cut a film on a Media Composer or on an Xpress Pro using files captured on a Media Composer will set up their projects using the 24p setting. That way they can bring in their audio without changing the audio's speed or sample rate. But those of us using the matchback setting (30i) will have to adjust the speed of the sound.

When you record your field tapes on either a Nagra or a DAT recorder, you set those machines to work with a film camera running at 24 fps. To do this, you use a Nagra set at 60 Hz or a DAT set to record at 30 fps, non-drop-frame.

Remember that your film was slowed down in the telecine from 24 to 23.976 fps. It was slowed down by .1%. For your field tapes to sync up with the film, they will need to be slowed down as well. During post-production, they must be played back at a speed that is .1% slower than normal in order to be in sync with the picture that's already inside the Avid.

For a hefty fee, your transfer facility will do this for you. They will play the field audio tapes, slow them down, and then lay your audio in sync with the picture on your videotape. That way, when the videotapes are delivered to you, you can capture picture and sound together. You no longer have to deal with all the issues of slowing down the sound or syncing up the rushes. Needless to say, it's quite expensive.

FIELD RECORDING WITH A TIMECODE DAT

If you recorded your field tapes on a sophisticated DAT machine, such as an HHB or Fostex, you can record your sound in the field using a sampling rate of 48.048 K. Then, when you rerecord it at a sample rate of 48, you will automatically slow the audio by .1%. If your DAT can't record at this faster sample rate, then you'll need to slow the DAT when you capture it. No matter what your sample rate, you want the DAT set up to run at 30-frames, non-drop-frame. That's important—always 30 NDF.

NAGRA 4.2

You can save a lot of money doing the syncing of the field tapes yourself. Many students and low-budget filmmakers use analog Nagras to record sound for their films because they're reliable, inexpensive (relatively speaking), and provide great sound. Always have your Nagra set to run at 60 Hz (NTSC). It will be set up that way, so you don't need to do anything, but don't let anyone talk you into a different set-up.

Once the sound has been recorded in the field you can slow your Nagra down by .1% and transfer the sound into the Avid by using a device that slows the Nagra down from 60 Hz to 59.94 Hz (.1%). I bought one of these devices from Equipment Emporium in Mission Hills, CA (www.equipmentemporium.com). They call it a TX-8 59.94 Crystal. It's a snap to use. Just plug it into the Pilot Socket where the "Crystal cap" goes. For those of you using the Xpress Pro to edit your film projects, this is a fairly inexpensive solution. You can use your Mojo DNA to bring in the audio from the Nagra. Just run the audio cables from the Nagra to the Mojo and from there into the Xpress Pro.

If you don't have Mojo, you'll need a deck capable of acting as a transcoder—one that can convert an analog signal to DV. Most of the medium-priced models can do this. Plug your Nagra into this DV deck, with the Crystal device hooked up to the Nagra. Now use the deck as a transcoder to convert the analog signal to a DV signal. You slow the Nagra down with this 59.94 Crystal device as you record your tapes into the Xpress.

SLOWING DOWN THE DAT DURING DIGITIZING

If you haven't slowed down your audio using one of the methods described above, then you must slow it down as you play it into the Avid. One method is to use the pitch adjustment on the DAT recorder to set the pitch to −.1% when digitizing into the Avid. A better method is to send a video signal (at 29.97) to the DAT recorder and have the DAT recorder use this video reference to determine its clock or speed. Because the DAT was recorded at 30 fps, this slows the tape by the requisite .1%.

ONE BIN PER AUDIO TAPE

I usually set up a separate bin for each audio tape and capture the clips into that bin. I usually don't digitize the audio as individual takes but as larger master clips containing six to eight takes each. Once the audio is in the bin, I'm ready to sync up the sound takes to the picture takes.

SYNCING RUSHES

Syncing picture and sound is a time-consuming endeavor. Usually, you have a lot of takes on a camera roll and each one has to be synced by hand. Of course, the process is the same if you are on a KEM or Steenbeck. Usually film projects hire assistant editors to do the syncing. If you have 50 rolls of film, and you've had your fill of syncing after just three rolls, you might think about finding an assistant editor.

The Avid has an AutoSync feature, which we'll use to sync our footage. It's a bit misnamed, as there's nothing automatic about it. There's a small bug in the Xpress Pro that makes this more difficult than it should be.

1. Create a new bin and call it "Synced Takes." Now create a second new bin and call it "Sync Subclips."
2. Open the bin with the picture clips (Dailies—Day 1).
3. Open the first clip to be synced: Scene 1 Take 1.
4. In the Source Monitor, find the first frame where the clapstick closes. If there was sound, it would "crunch" here. Mark this frame with an IN. Go to the end of the take and mark an OUT.
5. Make a subclip of this by holding the Option key (Mac) or Alt key (Windows), clicking on the picture in the Monitor, and dragging the picture to the Sync Subclips bin (you should see the subclip symbol).

6. Press the Caps Lock key so you can use "digital scrub" to hear the sound.
7. Locate the audio clip for the first scene: Scene 1 Take 1. Open it.
8. In the Source Window, find the first full frame of "crunch." Use the step-one-frame button to locate it precisely. Mark an IN.
9. Go to the end of the take and mark an OUT.
10. Make a subclip of this audio by holding the Option key (Mac) or Alt key (Windows) and dragging the audio to the Sync Subclips bin (you should see the subclip symbol).
11. Now you have two subclips in the bin. There should be an IN mark at the head of each subclip, but the bug I mentioned drops the IN. So, double-click on the picture subclip and as soon as it opens mark an IN at the very head. Close it. Now open the audio subclip and mark an IN at the very head. Close it.
12. Back in the bin, Shift–click so that both these subclips are selected. Go to the Bin menu and choose AutoSync.
13. A dialog window appears. Select the Inpoints box and click OK.
14. A third subclip is formed—combining sound and picture locked in sync. Drag that to the Synced Takes bin.
15. Hit Command/Ctrl–S to save what you have done.
16. Play it in the Source Monitor to check sync.
17. If there is a problem with the sync, delete it and the subclips you used to make it, and try it again.
18. Now sync up the next take in the same way.

To make identifying the audio "crunch" easier, you can use waveforms. We're accustomed to looking at the Timeline and seeing what is in the Record Monitor, but you can have the Timeline show what's in the Source Monitor instead. Just click on the Source/Record toggle command (Figure 19.8). It looks like two computer screens. Now select Sample Plot from the Timeline fast menu, and you can easily see where the clapsticks meet. To return the Timeline view to Record, click on the toggle command button again.

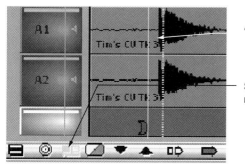

"Crunch" from clapsticks

Source/Record Toggle in source mode

Figure 19.8

DUPE DETECTION

When you are editing your sequence, you may inadvertently use the same shot twice or part of a shot twice. That second use of the same material is called a *dupe*. It's done all the time with video projects, but film is different. There is only one negative, and the negative cutter can't use the negative twice. So, if you use even a frame more than once, you'll have to pay big bucks to duplicate that single frame. Avids with FilmScribe have a feature, found in the Timeline Fast menu, that when turned on will warn you if you use any material more than once.

Don't forget, also, that the negative cutter needs at least half of a frame to make a cement splice, so you have to make sure you leave that "extra" frame. First, go to the Settings window and double-click on the Timeline setting. Click the Edit tab, and in the Dupe Detection Handles pull-down menu select 0.5 frames.

To turn on Dupe Detection, go to the Timeline Fast menu and select it.

If you use a frame more than once, you'll now see a colored bar in the Timeline on the video segments that are dupes. The first color you'll see is red. If there are more instances of dupes, other colors will appear.

EFFECTS

Fades and dissolves are the only effects that I recommend you add to your sequence. You can do wonderful things with the Effect Palette, but each effect you add to your sequence will cost you hundreds, if not thousands, of dollars to recreate on film. Fades and dissolves can be created when you make a 16-mm or 35-mm print. A single fade or dissolve only adds about $5 to your laboratory bill. All the other effects available on the Avid will cost you serious, eyepopping, wallet-breaking money.

When placing fades and dissolves in your Timeline, choose them by seconds and parts of seconds, and then translate them into video frames. For example, choose a 30-frame fade-in if you want a 1-second fade to go into your film. Choose a 45-frame fade-in if you want the fade to last a second and a half. Of course, you can have another sequence and you can have as many effects as you want, but the sequence the negative cutter sees must be devoid of expensive effects.

ADD EDITS

Once you've finished cutting your film on the Avid, go through and delete any Add Edits that might appear on your video track. You don't want them to throw off your Cut List. See page 262 for instructions on deleting Add Edits.

SMPTE LEADER AND BEEP

You need a SMPTE leader at the head of your film, and the negative cutter wants to see one at the head of your Avid sequence. The easiest way to accomplish this is to digitize a SMPTE leader (ask your lab to splice one onto the negative before the transfer so it's on your videotape) and then cut it into your Timeline. Take out any bars and tone you might have added to your sequence. The Picture Start frame on the SMPTE leader must be the very first frame in your sequence. The 8, 7, 6, 5, 4, 3 will follow until the single frame of 2 appears. After the 2 frame, there is a precise amount of black: 47 film frames on the leader or 59 video frames in the Avid. The very next is the first frame of your picture—whether it is a shot, a title, or a fade-in of a shot. Once the SMPTE leader has been cut into your Timeline, splice in a single frame of 1000-Hz tone (the beep) into your audio tracks in sync with the number 2 on the SMPTE leader.

The Picture Start frame becomes the 0 point of your footage on the Avid, and if you have cut the SMPTE leader in correctly the first frame of your show (59 frames after the 2) would be listed in the Cut List as starting at 4 feet and 32 frames (4 + 32). Look at the Cut List in Figure 19.11. When you preview the Cut List, check this. If your first shot doesn't start at 4 + 32, recut the SMPTE Leader until it does.

OPENING THE CUT LISTS TOOL

Once you have a final sequence, it's not that difficult to get a Cut List. After loading your sequence into the Record Monitor, open the Cut List Tool. Media Composer users will find the tool in the Output menu. Xpress Pro users need to open the FilmScribe utility. Windows users, go to Start→Programs→Avid→ FilmScribe. Mac users will find it in the Applications folder. Generally, you will find the FilmScribe utility in the same place you found the EDL Manager and Avid Log Exchange utility.

The FilmScribe utility is a very sophisticated piece of software. It has all the capabilities you'd find on an $80,000 Film Composer. I've tried to make it easier for you by providing suggested settings for the many different options.

Media Composer users:

1. Load your sequence into the Record Monitor.
2. In the Output menu, select Cut List.
3. Click on Get Sequence from the Cut List Tool, or Open from the File menu.
4. Navigate through the directory window until you get to Avid Projects, then your project, and finally the bin containing your sequence.

Xpress Pro users:

1. Launch the FilmScribe utility.
2. Go to the File menu at the top your screen and select Open.
3. Navigate through the directory window until you get to Avid Projects, then your project, and finally the bin containing your sequence.
4. Click on the name of the bin containing the sequence you want. Then click Open.
5. In the dialog box that appears, double-click on the sequence you want.

The Cut List Tool will open, similar to the one shown in Figure 19.9.

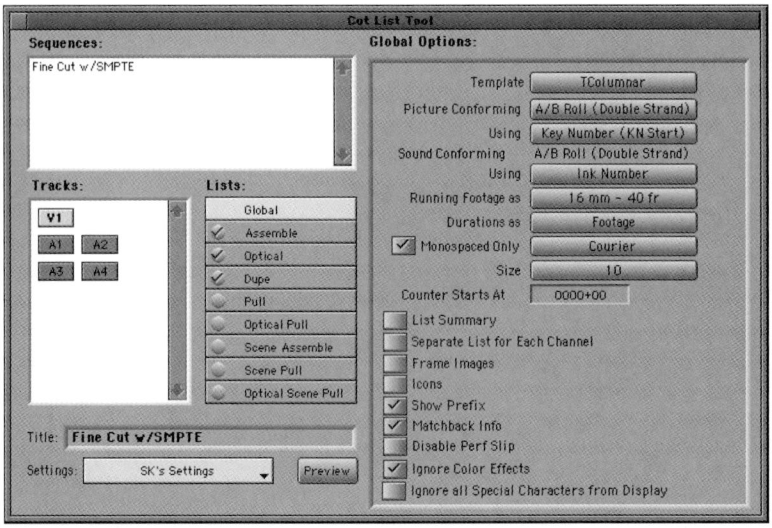

Figure 19.9 Cut List Tool with Global Options.

Select the video tracks you want to include so they are highlighted. Usually, select just V1, unless you have multilayered effects and the money to pay for them.

The right-hand side of the Cut List Tool shows the Global Options. This is where you tell the Avid what kind of project you've been editing and how you want the lists to appear. I've set this one up for a standard 16-mm project. Follow my settings and you'll be fine. If you shot 35-mm film, you'll want to indicate that in the Running Footage as menu; find out from your negative cutter whether she will be conforming using single or double strand.

The Avid generates eight different lists. The most important list is the Assemble list. Click on the button to select it, and then click on the Assemble box so the Assemble List Options window opens (Figure 19.10).

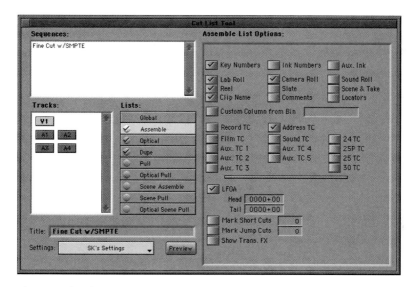

Figure 19.10 Assemble List Options.

Again, I have made choices that will work well for almost all your projects. The other lists you may need to check are the Optical list and Dupe list. A true optical effect, like a freeze frame, would require that the negative cutter pull the shot from the negative camera roll and have it sent to an optical house. If you have a true optical, then the negative cutter would need this list as well as the Pull list. If you have any opticals, understand that they will take time to prepare and cost serious money.

The Dupe list shows you where you have used any footage or frames more than once. If you have used Avid's Dupe Detection feature, you shouldn't have any dupes, but just in case check this one off. Get the dupe list and make sure there are no dupes. If you have dupes, find out where they are and use some other footage or be prepared to pay for optical printing.

All the lists have an options window where you can determine how you want the list to look. Fortunately, the Avid takes the options you used when setting up the Assemble list as the default set-up for all the other lists, so you don't have to check off any more boxes, unless your negative cutter asks you to make changes. I have saved all these settings under my name in the Settings window.

Now click the box that says Preview. Several dialog boxes may appear, saying that the sequence has no edgecode track or the SMPTE leader has no key numbers. Just click OK until your list appears, like the one in Figure 19.11. Now go to the File menu and choose Save As. Save your lists to your desktop or CD.

When you're connected to a printer, open the Cut List file using any popular word-processing program. The resulting columns of numbers and text are easier to read when you set your page orientation to horizontal, rather than the standard vertical page set-up. You may have to fiddle with the columns, using the Tab key to line things up. When they look good, print them.

Cut List

Footage	Duration	First/Last Key	Address TC	Cam Roll	Sc/Tk	Clip Name
1. 0+00 4+31	4+32	NO EDGE NUMBERS				ACADEMY LEADER
2. 04+32 20+06	16+15	Opt 1-0000+00 Opt 1-0050+06				OPTICAL #1
3. 20+07 25+23	5+17	KL 74 0246-8770&19 KL 74 0246-8781&15	01:04:54:29 01:05:03:29	1		2B/1CU HANDS
4. 25+24 28+38	3+15	KL 74 0246-8795&18 KL 74 0246-8802&12	01:05:15:23 01:05:21:11	1		2B/1CU HANDS

Matchback shortened the tail of the clip by 1 frame.

Figure 19.11

The negative cutter will also need a video copy of your finished project in which the timecode and keycode burn-in is clearly visible. Some want a VHS copy; others want Beta SP. You can also export the sequence as a QuickTime Movie, but make sure your negative cutter would prefer this. Armed with Cut Lists, the video copy of your film, and the negative camera rolls, the negative cutter can now conform and A/B roll your film.

"MATCHBACK SHORTENED THE TAIL OF THE CLIP BY 1 FRAME"

Look at the Cut List in Figure 19.11, and you'll see a message: "Matchback shortened the tail of the clip by 1 frame." This is because we are using Matchback and not a 24p Media Composer. When you make a cut to your sequence that cut point corresponds to a video frame, and that video won't always conform to a film frame. (Look at a C frame for an example of this.) Because you can't split a film frame in half, the Avid will adjust the length of a clip by shortening or lengthening it by one film frame to get things to work out. You can be out of sync by a frame, but that will be made up, or corrected, at the next cut point.

MIX AND OPTICAL SOUND TRACK

After you've locked your picture and done your sound work, you can do a sound mix on the Avid. Check your levels by playing your tracks with the Audio Tool open, set to Output. Use isolating headphones as you watch your levels. When you're happy with everything, you can send your final mixed tracks to DAT. The DAT becomes your mixed master. Now you're ready to make the optical sound track, either a 16-mm mono track or a 35-mm stereo track. Xpress Pro users can record their final sound tracks to DVCAM at the 48K sample rate and either dub that to DAT or see if the sound facility that will make the optical track can handle the DVCAM format.

Most people suggest that you not speed up the sound yourself; let the sound facility do it when they make your optical track. Remember, you slowed the sound down by .1% to match the telecine process, which slowed the film down. Rather than speeding it up yourself to match the 24 fps film print, let the sound facility do that for you. If you're using a DAT deck, transfer your sound to DAT set at 30 non-drop-frame with the pitch shift off.

Send the DAT or DVCAM tape to the sound facility with instructions indicating that "the DAT tape is referenced to video" or that it is "recorded at 59.94." They will speed it up .1% so it will sync up with your film print. Remember to ask for a B-wind optical track.

CHECKING SYNC

If you are nervous about sync—and who wouldn't be—try the following. Have the lab make a silent answer print from the A/B rolls. Then have the sound facility make a magnetic film track (mixed mag) from your DAT before you have an optical track made. Make sure they have correctly sped up the audio that's on the magnetic track. Once you have the sped-up magnetic track and the silent answer print, get on a Steenbeck and check out the sync by lining up the number

2 on the print to the beep on the magnetic film track. Obviously, it should all be in sync. If it isn't, you can at least figure out why before you have an optical track and a married print made.

IT WORKS

For the past few years, I've taught a class called Film Production III. Under-graduate students in the class use Avids with matchback software to cut their senior thesis films. Several of the films produced in that class have been made into 16-mm prints. The steps I've outlined here are the same steps my students used. In fact, we worked together, often by trial and error, to come up with them. One recent student didn't plan to make a 16-mm print of his project, but he went through all these steps just in case. Then, when his film was nominated for a Student Academy Award, he needed a print fast. Needless to say, he was quite happy that he'd gone through all this trouble, because he was able to get a 16-mm print in time for the final judging.

NEXT STOP CANNES

Is it simple? Not exactly. But, then, what in life that's worth doing ever is? Don't be afraid to ask for guidance from your negative cutter, film lab, transfer facility, and sound studio. Remember, you're paying them, not the other way around. Keep at it, and soon you'll have a print that you can show anywhere in the world.
  Bonne chance.

20

Present and Future

WHERE DO YOU GO FROM HERE?

If you want to make videos and films, then go make videos and films. You now know enough about the Avid to edit your own projects, and what you don't know you can figure out. However, if you want to be an Avid editor, this book is a beginning, not an end. I'll be the first to admit that this book doesn't cover every Avid command or examine all of Avid's capabilities. Far from it. I've tried to give you all the information you need to efficiently edit your projects, but there is certainly more to learn. There are several excellent books on the market that I urge you to read. *The Avid Handbook*, by Steve Bayes, covers in great detail many areas that I have treated lightly. It is for advanced users, but you're fast becoming one. *The Avid Digital Editing Room Handbook*, by Tony Solomons, is particularly helpful for those of you hoping to edit feature films on an Avid. Although it's not a book on nonlinear editing, I highly recommend *The Filmmaker's Handbook*, by Steven Ascher and Edward Pincus. This book covers nearly every aspect of video and film production and will answer just about any question you might have about moviemaking.

Three books about the art of editing are definitely worth reading: *The Techniques of Film Editing*, by Karel Reisz and Gavin Millar; *On Film Editing*, by Edward Dmytryk; and *In the Blink of an Eye*, by Walter Murch. The first two were published decades ago but are valuable for their insights and the historical perspective they provide. Walter Murch's book is the most recent and contains some interesting observations about the pitfalls of digital editing.

Last, but not least, I recommend the various user manuals that Avid supplies when it sells a system. Much of my understanding of Avid's products comes from these manuals, which are often clearly written. The problem with all manuals is that everything is treated as if it is of equal importance to you, when clearly some things deserve more attention than others. You also need to buy an

Avid system to get the Avid manuals, which is one reason I wrote this book. This book might seem expensive, but you didn't have to shell out thousands of dollars to get it.

INFORMATION ON THE INTERNET

Like all modern companies, Avid has a well-maintained Web site (www. avid.com). You'll find lots of hype as well as information about new products and upgrades. There are a number of user groups on the Internet that discuss digital products like the Avid. One of the most helpful ones I've encountered is called the Avid-L. The vast majority of Avid-L subscribers are professional Avid editors, living and working all over the world. Most of the postings are by editors seeking specific help for problems they are having on real projects, and the answers come from experienced editors who've encountered similar problems and are offering suggestions, workarounds, and quick fixes. You can learn a lot just by following the postings over time. Despite the fact that Avid is now the host site for the group, these editors owe no allegiance to Avid and are just as likely to blast the company for its missteps as to praise it for its achievements. To subscribe to the Avid-L, go to Avid's website and click on Community, or go to www.avid.com/community/ and scroll down until you find the Avid-L. You'll find other user groups listed there as well.

Creative Cow has an Avid forum that many people new to Avid have found helpful; go to www.creativecow.net. *DV* magazine has many articles that relate to the Avid and digital editing in general, and it has a useful website as well; visit www.dv.com. Another website devoted to digital video editing is www. digitalvideoediting.com, which often has interesting columns and product reviews. There is a wealth of information about HD and 24p issues at www. 24p.com, hosted by Avid guru Michael Phillips.

GETTING A JOB AS AN AVID EDITOR

If you want to be an Avid editor, I suggest that you find an entry-level position or internship at an editing facility that uses Avids and works on the sorts of projects you're interested in. I know it's wrong to generalize about people, but it's been my experience that editors are the most down-to-earth and helpful people in the film and television industry, and many enjoy sharing their knowledge. Once you get a foot in the door, seek out a mentor and ask her or him to teach you what she or he knows in exchange for loyal and dependable assistance. Ask if you can get on a machine after hours and try your hand at cutting the day's work. Employee turnover at some post houses can be amazingly fast, and you may find yourself moving up the ladder quickly. You need to demonstrate four things: your reliability, your proficiency with the equipment, your ability to please clients, and your creativity. You'll find that the order of importance varies from company to company.

OTHER AVID PRODUCTS

Avid now offers a full range of products on both Macintosh and Windows platforms. We've concentrated on the Xpress family. The next product up from the Xpress is the Media Composer Adrenaline HD. It's like a turnkey version of Xpress Pro HD, but with more HD and 24p film capabilities. Part of Avid's huge advantage in the feature film world rests on the film capabilities offered by the Media Composer. From the Media Composer you can move up to the Symphony Nitris, which offers all the Media Composer capabilities plus more real-time HD and SD options. You can start in HD, stay in HD, and/or deliver in any SD format—4:3, 16:9, PAL, or NTSC.

The mother ship in this post-production stream is the Avid DS Nitris, which allows multistream, 10-bit, uncompressed HD editing. You can even take HD datastreams that are too large for HD tape formats and bring them in as 2K/4K files.

The Avid Storage group offers a variety of storage devices, many of which work with its shared storage software. Avid Unity LANshare works well with ten or more Xpress stations, while the Avid Unity MediaNetwork lets groups of Media Composer, Symphony, and Avid DS Nitris stations share storage and editing capabilities. You could capture your HD project on an Avid DS Nitris, cut it on a Media Composer, and finish on the Symphony Nitris—all by sending files over a cable. Most of the shows you watch on television are edited on Avids that are connected by the Avid Unity MediaNetwork.

Avid offers advanced video game design and three-dimensional animation through its SOFTIMAGEIXS line. This line is also used for graphics- and effects-centric television commercials, station promos, bumpers, and music videos.

Avid has pretty much captured the broadcast journalism arena with its sophisticated storage, network, and HD capabilities. The Avid Newscutter uses the script as the heart of its interface.

And, last but not least, Avid's Digidesign subsidiary offers Pro Tools® and Pro Tools® LE. Avid is starting to leverage its many audio advantages, compared to its competitors, by bundling Pro Tools software and hardware with Xpress Pro software in its various Xpress Studio packages. It's also making the integration between the Avid and Pro Tools more seamless.

AVID'S FUTURE

Avid was once the Goliath of NLE systems, with lots of Davids on the prowl. Now the tables have turned a bit. Although there are other systems out there, for the most part the NLE scene is divided into two camps—Avid and Apple's Final Cut®. It's hard to say which camp has the David and which one the Goliath. Today, Apple is a corporate behemoth that looks and acts more like Microsoft than an upstart computer company. It's not the computer for the rest of us—it's too expensive to qualify for that. If Boston University hadn't purchased my Mac Powerbook, I'd own a PC. Recently, I spent 7 months in Uganda, helping start a video production program at Makerere University in Kampala. There are no Apples in Africa—folks there have more important things to do with their money. Thanks to Avid and some cheap PCs, I was able to set up an editing suite with five workstations running Xpress Pro.

Many Mac users ask why Avid is slow to qualify the latest software on Macs, assuming it's Avid's fault. In fact, Apple wants to squeeze Avid a bit and is slow to provide access to Apple's code. Adobe Premiere® used to be a cross-platform NLE, but Apple made it hard for them to stay Mac based, so now Adobe Premiere runs only on PCs.

What happened to the companies that bought licenses to make Mac clones? In the mid-1990s, Power Computing made better Macs than Apple did and charged less for them. Lots of people lost their jobs when Steve Jobs returned to Apple and pulled the plug on the Mac clone vendors, forever putting the kibosh on low-priced Macs.

So who's the Goliath? I bring this up because some Final Cut® users seem to believe Apple Computer is like a Jedi knight, while everyone else is skulking along with the Dark Side. There are no good guys and bad guys, just big, publicly traded corporations. The competition between Avid and Final Cut® has brought prices down and features up. Hopefully, people will choose their system based on their editing needs and goals.

For my students and me that means Avid. Boston University attracts students from countries all over the world—many of which have no Apple computers. Avid has a global presence that Final Cut® lacks.

I want to train students on the industry-leading software. Feature films, commercials, music videos, primetime television shows—that's where Avids are used. At today's tuition rates, I'd be doing my students a disservice by training them on Final Cut®. And I think Avid finally gets it. The decisions it makes, the prices it sets, and the attention it gives to you, the customer, show a better understanding of the needs of the editor than ever before.

But, what's important isn't the software we use; it's the projects we produce. Let's keep pushing ourselves to make projects that matter. We live in a world that needs more compassion, greater understanding, and better communication from all of us.

Index

DVD-ROM Instructions

This DVD-ROM contains all the video and audio clips for two projects entitled "Wanna Trade" and "Gaffer's Delight." In order to fit both projects onto one DVD, I created "Wanna Trade" in the standard-definition DV25 format. All Avid systems can easily work in DV25. The second project, "Gaffer's Delight," is more challenging. The action is covered by many different camera angles and each angle has multiple takes. In all, there are 36 clips. The clips are in the 16:9 widescreen format. Due to space considerations, I had to create it in a compressed version of DV25; it was captured at 15:1s. This is a format that Xpress DV can't access. To accommodate Xpress DV users so they can practice the 16:9 techniques discussed in the book, I captured several clips from the "Gaffer's Delight" scene in uncompressed DV25. These practice clips for Xpress DV users are contained in the folders labeled Xpress DV 16 × 9 Media and Xpress DV 16 × 9 Practice (Figure 1).

> ▶ 📁 Gaffer's Delight
> ▶ 📁 Gaffer's Delight Media
>   📄 Gaffer's Delight Script.TXT
> ▶ 📁 Wanna Trade Media
> ▶ 📁 Wanna Trade Scene
> ▶ 📁 Xpress DV 16x9 Media
> ▶ 📁 Xpress DV 16x9 Practice

Figure 1   Contents of the DVD-ROM.

The contents of the DVD-ROM will mount on Macintosh and PC platforms and should work with Media Composer 9.0 and higher, Xpress Pro HD 5.0 and higher, Xpress Pro 4.0 and higher, and Xpress DV 3.0 and higher. All the audio is sampled at 48K. Instructions provided here explain how to mount the projects onto your Avid. Depending on your platform and software version, find the correct mounting instructions and follow them carefully. Whenever possible, you should download the latest version of your software from www.avid.com.

INSTRUCTIONS FOR MOUNTIÞG "WANNA TRADE" ONTO A MACINTOSH COMPUTEᴿ.

Insert the DVD-ROM iᵣ ⁻ᵤₑ DVD-ROM drawer. If your DVD player starts, quit the DVD player. ᴿᵤble-click on the DVD-ROM's icon. When the DVD-ROM opens, you'll ⁻ₑ six folders and a script. One folder is labeled Wanna Trade Scene and anᵒᵗʰᵉr is labeled Wanna Trade Media.

1. Open your Macintosh computer's (internal) hard drive. Find the folder called Avid Projects (Users → Shared → Xpress Pro/Xpress DV/Media Composer → Avid Projects). Now, drag the Wanna Trade Scene folder from the DVD-ROM to the Avid Projects folder and release it. It should copy in seconds.

2. Click on this newly copied Wanna Trade Scene folder and press Command–I to open Get Information. In the Ownership and Permissions, make sure you can Read and Write all the files. If you must change the permission from Read to Read and Write, click on "Apply to enclosed items." Now go back to your Desktop.

3. All your drives should be visible on the desktop. Find the folder called OMFI MediaFiles on the hard drive most likely to contain your media. If you don't find one, create a new folder called OMFI MediaFiles and place it on the highest level of your hard drive. The spelling "OMFI MediaFiles" must be exact.

4. Go to the DVD-ROM and double-click on the Wanna Trade Media folder. There you'll find an OMFI MediaFiles folder. Double-click to open it. You'll see audio and video media files. Select all the media files by pressing Command–A. They will all be highlighted. Now drag them to the hard drive's OMFI MediaFiles folder and release. It will take several minutes for these files to copy onto the hard drive.

5. Now, close the hard drive folder; then close the DVD-ROM folder. Eject the DVD-ROM. Launch your Avid software and open the Wanna Trade Scene.

INSTRUCTIONS FOR MOUNTING "WANNA TRADE" ONTO A PC COMPUTER

Insert the DVD-ROM in the DVD-ROM drawer. If your DVD player starts, exit the DVD player. Double-click on the DVD-ROM's icon. When the DVD-ROM opens, you'll see four folders and a script. One folder is labeled Wanna Trade and another is labeled Wanna Trade Media.

1. Double-click on My Computer. Double-click on the computer's media drive. Locate the OMFI MediaFiles folder. Double-click on My Computer again.

2. If you don't find the folder, create a new folder called OMFI MediaFiles and place it on the highest level of your hard drive. The spelling "OMFI MediaFiles" must be exact. Double-click on My Computer again.

3. Click on the purple (or top) bar and drag it so you can see both screens.

4. Double-click on the DVD-ROM's Wanna Trade Media folder to open it. There you'll find a folder labeled OMFI MediaFiles. Open it. Select all the media files (Ctrl-A) in the folder and drag them to the OMFI Media-Files folder on the media drive. It will take several minutes for the media files to copy onto the media drive.

5. Now, click on your computer's internal drive—the C: drive. Double-click on Program Files.

6. Double-click on the Avid folder to open it. Then double-click on the Avid Xpress Pro/Xpress DV/Media Composer folder. Now, double-click on the Avid Projects folder.

7. Go to the DVD-ROM folder and drag the Wanna Trade Scene folder from the DVD-ROM to the Avid Projects folder and release. It should copy in seconds.

8. Looking at the Avid Projects folder, you will see the Wanna Trade Scene folder. Right-click on the folder and the Properties menu will open.

9. Click on the Read Only radio button so the check mark is removed (empty). Click Apply. Another dialog box appears. There are two radio buttons. Make sure the Apply Changes to This Folder, Subfolders, and Files radio button is checked. If it isn't, click on it. Now click OK. Click OK again.

10. Close all the folders, including the DVD-ROM folders, external drive folders, and C: drive folders. Now eject the DVD-ROM.

INSTRUCTIONS FOR MOUNTING "GAFFER'S DELIGHT" (NOT AVAILABLE FOR XPRESS DV)

Follow the instructions provided above for mounting "Wanna Trade" onto your Avid. Wherever the instructions mention the Wanna Trade Scene folder substitute the Gaffer's Delight Scene folder, and wherever you see the Wanna Trade Media folder, substitute the Gaffer's Delight Media folder.

INSTRUCTIONS FOR MOUNTING XPRESS DV 16 × 9 PRACTICE FOR XPRESS DV USERS

Follow the instructions provided above for mounting "Wanna Trade" onto your Avid. Wherever the instructions mention the Wanna Trade Scene folder substitute the Xpress DV 16 × 9 Practice folder, and wherever you see the Wanna Trade Media folder, substitute the Xpress DV 16 × 9 Media folder.

LIMITED WARRANTY AND DISCLAIMER OF LIABILITY